Broadband

Broadband

*Should We Regulate
High-Speed
Internet Access?*

Robert W. Crandall
James H. Alleman
Editors

AEI-BROOKINGS JOINT CENTER
FOR REGULATORY STUDIES
Washington, D.C.

Broadband may be ordered from:
Brookings Institution Press
1775 Massachusetts Avenue, N.W.
Washington, D.C. 20036
Tel.: 1-800-275-1447 or (202) 797-6258
Fax: (202) 797-6004
www.brookings.edu

Library of Congress Cataloging-in-Publication data

Broadband: should we regulate high-speed internet access?/Robert W. Crandall and James H. Alleman, editors.
   p. cm.
Papers from two conferences: one held by AEI-Brookings Joint Center for Regulatory Studies, Oct. 4–5, 2001 and the other by Columbia University Center for Tele-Information in New York.
ISBN 0-8157-1592-7 (cloth : alk. paper) —
ISBN 0-8157-1591-9 (pbk. : alk. paper)
   1. Telecommunication policy—United States. 2. Internet—Government policy—United States. 3. Internet users—United States. 4. Broadband communication systems—United States. 1. Crandall, Robert W. II. Alleman, James H. III. AEI-Brookings Joint Center for Regulatory Studies.

HE7781 .B747 2002
384.3'3—dc21   2002012472

9 8 7 6 5 4 3 2 1

The paper used in this publication meets minimum requirements of the American National Standard for Information Sciences—Permanence of Paper for Printed Library Materials: ANSI Z39.48-1992.

Typeset in Adobe Garamond

Composition by Circle Graphics
Columbia, Maryland

Printed by R. R. Donnelley and Sons
Harrisonburg, Virginia

Foreword

Economists are now beginning to recognize that the "new economy" could have a pronounced effect on economic growth. There is still great debate about how large this effect will be and what form it will take. At the center of the new economy is the Internet. One of the critical policy issues facing the country is how to regulate the Internet, particularly the delivery of high-speed, or "broadband," services. In this volume, experts examine the economic potential of broadband and evaluate different approaches to its regulation.

Broadband could be a key driver in the economy for both consumers and businesses. It is likely to provide new ways for consumers to acquire information, enjoy audio and video entertainment, monitor remote locations, receive medical care, and engage in business transactions. In addition, broadband could provide businesses with new opportunities to reduce their costs and to reach consumers with products and services. These benefits are likely to be very large as broadband spreads over the nation's households. Some research suggests potential economic benefits of hundreds of billions of dollars annually.

There is no guarantee, however, that the full potential of broadband services will be realized. The success of this new service depends on whether the firms that must make huge investments to develop networks have the opportunities to earn returns commensurate with the risks they face. Firms making such investments operate in the highly regulated communications sector. Telephone and cable companies have been subject to regulation by federal, state, and even local authorities for decades. The regulation of broadband poses challenges for countries around the world. A central policy question is whether different providers of broadband services should be regulated differently, as is currently the case in the United States, where broadband services are provided by phone companies, cable companies, and satellite services under very different regulatory regimes. The degree and type of regulation that communications companies face in the delivery of new broadband services could play an important role in determining whether they can earn adequate returns on the investments required to deliver these services.

This collection of essays provides a state-of-the-art analysis of the economics of broadband. It is the result of a conference held by the AEI-Brookings Joint Center for Regulatory Studies on October 4–5, 2001, and also includes two essays presented at a later conference at Columbia University. The scholars who participated in these conferences reflected diverse points of view. Some saw broadband as a relatively unimportant phenomenon, while others thought it would be quite significant. Some believed that the form of regulation was not critical to the rate of diffusion of broadband, while others thought that regulation could have a substantial impact on the rate of diffusion.

The volume editors wish to thank Daniel Puskin for research assistance, Diane Hammond for editing the manuscript, Gloria Paniagua for verifying its factual accuracy, Inge Lockwood for proofreading the pages, Robert Swanson for providing an index, and Donald Tench IV for conference planning and logistical assistance.

This volume is one in a series commissioned by the AEI-Brookings Joint Center for Regulatory Studies to contribute to the continuing debate over regulatory reform. The series addresses several fundamental issues in regulation, including the design of effective reforms, the impact of proposed reforms on the public, and the political and institutional forces that affect reform. We hope that this series will help illuminate many of the complex issues involved in designing and implementing regulation and regulatory reforms at all levels of government.

The views expressed here are those of the authors and should not be attributed to the trustees, officers, or staff members of the American Enterprise Institute or the Brookings Institution.

ROBERT W. HAHN

ROBERT E. LITAN

AEI-Brookings Joint Center for Regulatory Studies

Contents

Broadband

JAMES H. ALLEMAN
ROBERT W. CRANDALL

1 Introduction

The 1990s was the decade of the Internet and the stock market bubble, two phenomena that were likely related. After the bubble burst and the stock market settled down to more normal levels, economists began to measure the real effects of the information technology revolution on the economy—and were often pleasantly surprised. Productivity growth accelerated in the late 1990s, fed in large part by investments in information technology and the growth of the Internet. Some fear, however, that public policy may be impeding the development of the Internet into a high-speed communications network capable of delivering full video images, complicated games, and comprehensive audio entertainment. In the absence of a wide diffusion of high-speed Internet connections, the demand for information technology equipment and new Internet service applications has remained stagnant.

On October 4 and 5, 2001, the AEI-Brookings Joint Center for Regulatory Studies convened a conference of telecommunications scholars to address the public policy issues that arose over the dispersion of broadband telecommunications services to residential and small business customers. Subsequently, the Columbia Institute for Tele-Information (CITI) held a similar conference in New York, which included many of the same scholars. This volume includes papers from both conferences.

The Issues

Any discussion of telecommunications policy in the current era of market liberalization engenders enormous controversy. Public policy on broadband technology is among the most controversial, in large part because of the differences among regulatory regimes faced by various carriers. Cable television companies, incumbent local telephone companies, and new entrants into telecommunications services compete to provide households and small businesses with not only high-speed Internet connections but also satellite services. Cable television companies are now largely deregulated and therefore face neither retail price regulation of their cable modem services nor requirements to make their facilities available to competitors. (As part of the merger agreement, AOL Time Warner must offer its cable customers alternative Internet service providers.) The incumbent local exchange carriers, on the other hand, face both retail price regulation and a requirement, imposed by the 1996 Telecommunications Act, that they unbundle their network facilities and lease them to rivals. Finally, new entrants are largely unregulated, but many rely upon the incumbent telephone companies for the loop (the "last mile") to connect their customers to their high-speed Internet services.

The primary focus of the two conferences was on such asymmetric regulation. In addition, many papers addressed the issue of subsidies for the diffusion of broadband technology, the availability of technologies for its diffusion, likely consumer demand, and the network effects that might be created by the spread of such access.

Demand and Diffusion

Chapter 2, by Bruce Owen, raises the questions of why broadband Internet technology inspires heated policy debate and why many observers believe that there are barriers to the diffusion of such access. Owen concludes that residential access has spread as rapidly as most other "successful" new consumer services and durables, such as cable television, videocassette recorders, and personal computers. To Owen, barriers to broadband access are more likely to be related to demand than to supply, including regulatory policy. Until important new uses for broadband Internet access develop, many potential residential customers may believe that the service is not worth its current cost (a view of the demand side supported by Paul Rappoport, Donald Kridel, and Lester Taylor in chapter 4). Owen admits that there is little theoretical justification for the asymmetric regulation of digital subscriber line (DSL) and cable modem service but points out that such anomalies are common due to the political economy of regulation.

Demand for broadband Internet access is addressed in chapters 3 and 4. Hal Varian, in chapter 3, provides evidence from a marketlike controlled Internet demand experiment (INDEX) conducted at the University of California, Berkeley, in 1998–99. Participants in INDEX were given the choice of symmetric and asymmetric speeds of service, up to the now rather slow 128 kilobits a second, at prices that varied over time. The variation in prices across bandwidths and over time allowed Varian and his associates to estimate the price sensitivity of demand for speed in connecting to the Internet. He concludes that the demand for speed is quite sensitive to price; estimated own-price elasticities are in the range of –2.0 to –3.1 for the higher speeds. The most surprising result, however, is that most of the Berkeley participants were willing to pay no more than $0.02 a minute, or $1.20 an hour, for the time saved by high-speed connections to the Internet. Varian suggests that the delays encountered elsewhere on the Internet and the lack of applications that require high-speed connections are likely to explain this apparently low value of connection speed. It is also important to note that Varian's results are from several years ago, an ancient era in Internet time.

Rappoport, Kridel, and Taylor (chapter 4) provide more recent estimates of broadband demand. They compare a sample of narrowband and broadband subscribers' use of the Internet in mid-2001 and discover that broadband subscribers are heavier users of the Internet at all hours of the day, visit more Internet sites, but spend less time at each site than narrowband users. Their study finds that the price elasticity of demand for broadband is approximately –1.0, a much lower value than that indicated by Varian's INDEX project. Perhaps the proliferation of Internet applications is making high-speed service more attractive.

Technology

Chapters 5 and 6 deal with the technology of broadband delivery through fixed wires and by wireless connections. Charles Jackson, in chapter 5, describes the two rival wire-line technologies: digital subscriber lines and cable modems. Jackson demonstrates that these technologies are similar in structure and in cost. Digital subscriber lines use part of the spectrum on copper telephone wires to provide high-speed service, while cable modems use part of the spectrum on the coaxial cable that distributes cable television. Because both services are offered over networks designed for other services, the carriers offering the services must make substantial investments in electronics and plants. The sharp decline in the cost of electronics has allowed both services to become more affordable in recent years.

Jackson points out that much of the cost of delivering broadband service is in the conversion of optical signals to electrical signals. Digital subscriber line and cable modem services are both delivered over a fiber backbone to an optical network interface, which converts the signal to an electrical signal for distribution over wires. The length of the wires in local telephone networks serves as a barrier to digital subscriber lines, while the number of subscribers sharing the fiber to the node, where it is converted from an optical signal to an electric signal, limits the capacity of cable modems. In the future, extremely high-speed service could be obtained through either system by extending optical fiber all the way to the subscriber, but each subscriber would then have to convert the optical signal to an electrical signal compatible with the equipment in his or her home.

Jerry Hausman, in chapter 6, provides a review of the current wireless broadband technology, often described as third-generation technology. Hausman begins with a review of the evidence on the substitutability of wireless (cellular) telephony for ordinary voice services delivered over the traditional wired telephone network. He concludes that wireless is rapidly becoming a full-fledged substitute for these narrowband services in many countries but that the wire-line networks do not yet face meaningful competition from third-generation wireless for broadband services due to its lack of market penetration. Hausman identifies spectrum availability as one of the major obstacles to the deployment of third-generation technology. In the United States the federal government has not yet released and auctioned sufficient spectrum for the deployment of third-generation services. As a result, there is no evidence on the cost of building these networks, on the ability of consumers to cope with the hand-held devices, on the interfaces required to access wireless broadband service, or on the likely price of this service. Once the spectrum problem is solved, Hausman foresees the evolution to a world in which numerous wireless carriers compete with existing telephone and cable television networks, obviating the need for regulation.

Regulation

A major issue in current discussions of broadband Internet service is the role of regulation in encouraging or inhibiting its diffusion. Jerry Hausman, chapter 7, provides a critical assessment of the current regulatory regime, which mandates wholesale unbundling of telephone company networks and retail price controls while largely exempting cable from retail or wholesale regulation. Hausman shows that Korea now leads the world in broadband deployment by a wide margin and that far more Korean households have digital-line connections than have cable modems. In the United States, by contrast, cable modems outnumber digital subscriber lines by more than two to one. Hausman asserts that one reason for this disparity is that the Korean telephone company is not required to unbundle its local lines to allow other companies to use its facilities to deliver digital service. On the other hand, cable modem providers can use Korea Electric's infrastructure to offer cable modem service without regulation. Other reasons for the success of broadband Internet service are lack of government regulation, the service's low price, and the built-in access to the service in Korea's numerous modern high-rise apartment buildings. Hausman provides an economic analysis (based on the Hausman-Sidak test) of the need to unbundle the facilities used for delivering broadband in Korea and the United States. Because in both countries there is competition in providing the service and rivals are able to duplicate the incumbents' facilities, Hausman concludes that unbundling is not required in either country. Finally, Hausman shows that the incentives for telephone company deployment of broadband are particularly attenuated in the United States by the low total-element, long-run incremental cost of unbundled elements leased to rivals. At these low rates, entrants are provided a free option, and facilities-based entrants are unfairly penalized.

In chapter 8, Howard Shelanski shows that the case for unbundling depends on setting the correct wholesale prices, including an option price for avoiding the risk of stranded sunk facilities. He cites SBC's experience in unbundling: providing co-location at remote terminals when it deployed Project Pronto, its version of digital subscriber line service. Shelanski concludes that there is at best a tenuous case for unbundling anything more than the conventional loops. Similarly, he finds the case for open-access regulation of cable modem services unpersuasive, because such regulation would provide disincentives for investment by cable operators.

Thomas Hazlett, chapter 9, provides an analysis of the effects of regulating the vertical integration of carriers delivering innovative services. Mandatory unbundling or access rules discourage investment in these risky activities by encouraging firms to wait and simply lease others' sunk investments at regulated rates. Hazlett attributes the cable television companies' reluctance to dedicate more than six megahertz of their systems' capacity to cable modem service to a fear that opportunistic would-be entrants without their own facilities would petition regulatory authorities for mandated access to this additional capacity. Hazlett concludes that there is already sufficient competition in the delivery of broadband to allow regulators to refrain altogether from regulating the service. Proponents of regulating cable or telephone companies' delivery of broadband are competitors seeking to raise their rivals' costs. A firm that would benefit from greater output of broadband services, such as Intel, is opposed to regulation of either service.

Gerald Faulhaber, in chapter 10, questions whether regulatory policy is indeed "in the way" of broadband development and, like Bruce Owen, finds little in residential broadband use to lead him to conclude that regulation is impeding the deployment of the service. Instead, the telephone companies' own internal problems in provisioning digital subscriber lines, he claims, are retarding growth in residential digital service. Moreover, he feels that DSL is only a stopgap technology, which will eventually be replaced by fiber. But even if regulation is not the cause of the incumbent carriers' lagging behind cable television systems in the broadband race, Faulhaber finds no reason to impose wholesale unbundling on the telephone companies' investment in new facilities, such as digital subscriber line access multiplexers or other equipment at remote terminals deployed in the architecture of the new generation digital loop carrier described in chapter 5.

An empirical analysis of the financial effects of broadband regulation by George Bittlingmayer and Thomas Hazlett, chapter 11, finds that the threat of new or continued regulation in three areas—open-access regulation of cable television, regulation of incumbent telephone companies' digital-line services, and bans on the participation of regional Bell operating companies in inter-LATA (local area transport and access) services—reduces the returns to major competitors' securities. The threat of open-access requirements on cable systems has adverse effects on Internet-related companies. On days when positive news appeared about the

Tauzin-Dingell legislation (which would reduce regulation of incumbent local exchange carriers' broadband services and facilities), competitive local exchange carriers' stocks enjoyed positive returns. Finally, positive news on the lifting of the restrictions of section 271 of the 1996 Telecommunications Act was not negatively associated with the stock returns on Internet, semiconductor, or Internet equipment. However, setbacks for the lifting of these restrictions had negative effects on the values of Cisco, Sun Microsystems, and Level 3 (a large competitive supplier of transmission capacity). Bittlingmayer and Hazlett conclude, therefore, that neither new regulation of cable systems nor continued regulation of incumbent telephone companies provides a benefit to new entrants into telecommunications.

Subsidies and Broadband Deployment

Chapter 12, by Austan Goolsbee, addresses the question of whether and how to subsidize the deployment of broadband services to residential subscribers. Using 1999 consumer survey data on willingness to pay for broadband service, Goolsbee constructs a demand function for broadband services. This demand function is then used to estimate the value of encouraging broadband deployment through public subsidies. Goolsbee shows that the most cost-effective (and welfare-enhancing) subsidy is one that funds the start-up costs for the deployment of broadband in unserved markets. Subsidies focused on attracting additional subscribers in markets in which broadband services are already deployed necessarily attract new subscribers who do not value the service at its current price. On the other hand, subsidies that induce firms to expand services to new markets facilitate the enrollment of subscribers who value the service highly but have not had the opportunity to signal their preferences through the market.

In the concluding chapter, Robert Crandall, Robert Hahn, and Timothy Tardiff show that any estimate of the likely benefits of broadband deployment to consumers depends crucially on the assumed form of the demand function. Nevertheless, any of several potential functional forms provides very large estimates of the value of broadband when it achieves universality, that is, when 94 percent or more of all households subscribe. The danger is that regulation may postpone the achievement of universal broadband service, much as earlier regulatory policies postponed or otherwise reduced the value of cable television, cellular telephony, voice messaging, and network television programming.

Conclusion

Broadband Internet services have been available to dispersed residences and small businesses for only a few years. As a result, there is little accumulated evidence on the likely uses for such services, their potential value to consumers, or even the best technologies for bringing them to households and small businesses. The leading players in the broadband game have been companies with networks not designed for the delivery of such services: cable television and telephone companies. These companies have deployed these services in differing regulatory environments. Cable companies were virtually deregulated by the 1996 Telecommunications Act, but incumbent telephone company regulation was substantially expanded by the act. Because regulated telephone companies have had less market success than the unregulated cable companies, they blame regulation for a large share of their problems. The chapters in this volume do not provide much empirical support for the theory that regulation is inhibiting the growth of digital subscriber lines, but neither is there a compelling case made for continuing this asymmetric regulatory policy. Jerry Hausman provides an a priori argument that asymmetric regulation is impeding digital service in the United States, and George Bittlingmayer and Thomas Hazlett show that such regulation is not apparently enhancing the prospects of new entrants into the market. Bruce Owen and Gerald Faulhaber comment on the lack of evidence linking regulation to the slow deployment of digital service, but neither concludes that regulation of new investment in broadband facilities is a good idea. In summary, the papers in this conference volume provide little support for the asymmetric regulatory policy that now governs broadband.

BRUCE M. OWEN

2 | *Broadband Mysteries*

The theme of the conference whose participants contributed to this volume was overcoming barriers to the diffusion of broadband communications. This is a public policy issue because Congress made it so. The 1996 Telecommunications Act provides in part that "the commission and each state commission with regulatory jurisdiction over telecommunications services shall encourage the deployment on a reasonable and timely basis of advanced telecommunications capability to all Americans (including, in particular, elementary and secondary schools and classrooms) by utilizing, in a manner consistent with the public interest, convenience, and necessity, price cap regulation, regulatory forbearance, measures that promote competition in the local telecommunications market, or other regulating methods that remove barriers to infrastructure investment."[1]

I do not question the wisdom of Congress's desire in 1996 to encourage broadband deployment. Promotion of commerce in one form or another, after all, has always been an accepted role of government. I focus instead on exploring some of the mysteries that surround the recent debates about barriers to broadband deployment.

Monique Fuentes, Peter Owen, and Greg Rosston provided helpful comments on drafts of this chapter.
1. 47 USC, sec. 157.

The first mystery is how the broadband debate can continue at full volume with no generally accepted definition of the term *broadband* and certainly no accepted list of services unique to broadband.

The second mystery is why it is so generally assumed that there are significant barriers to broadband deployment. The available data appear to demonstrate that broadband availability is already widespread after a period of extremely rapid growth, even in low-income areas, and that household penetration of broadband exceeds 20 percent of households with personal computers, with no evidence of slowing growth. How could broadband deployment reasonably be expected to take place more rapidly than it has?

The third mystery is why this seemingly rapid deployment has taken place despite the absence of any definable service that requires broadband for its provision and in the absence of any compelling applications that might be expected to drive broadband demand.

The fourth mystery is why principal barriers to development of broadband are assumed to involve access obligations. What explains the fact that the vast bulk of the advocacy, discussion, research, and political activity in this narrow area is directed to access issues (specifically, competitive access to cable modems and local loops) rather than, say, problems related to demand, product innovation, intellectual property protection, tax incentives, or technical standards?

The fifth mystery (although there may well be many more) is why so much intellectual energy and corporate treasure is now devoted, in all apparent seriousness, to the problem of classifying broadband into one or another (or none) of the regulatory categories used to describe older technologies or services.

In this chapter I explore the evolution of broadband policy issues in the context of political economy. My basic claim is that neither communications policy in general nor the evolution of the present policy issue—nor indeed this conference volume itself—can be explained by appeal to the rationality of substantive policy. Communications policy seldom makes sense and is almost never consistent. It is the product neither of an inspired solon nor a benign invisible hand. Communications policy is best understood simply as the accumulated outcomes of a series of struggles among contending economic interests to obtain favorable treatment by government.

Accepting this view, unfortunately, makes my task like that of a sportswriter faced with a story deadline on a baseball game at the end of the fifth inning with no rain in sight. It is too soon to write the story of this game, much less the story of the season or the series.

What Is Broadband?

There is a story about an executive attempting to hire an accountant. She asks each candidate CPA, "How much is two and two?" Most of them reply, "Four." But the one who gets the job is the fellow who answers, "What would you like it to be?" *Broadband* as a term has even greater flexibility than the CPA. Indeed, broadband is regularly defined in such a way as to promote the ends of whatever speaker is using the term.[2] The Supreme Court of the United States may decide this question forever, just as the Court found it necessary to answer the question, What is golf?[3]

Meanwhile, the term *broadband* refers to a poorly defined set of services, facilities, and providers. It has been defined as a medium of communication that contains more than the usual amount of information transmission capacity, wherein information can be used rigorously in its statistical sense.[4] Information capacity in a medium results from a design trade-off among bandwidth, power, the computational power of terminal devices, and other factors of production. For a given choice of production technology or factor proportions, bandwidth and transmission speed have a fixed ratio, so that capacity can be stated either as the range of frequencies used in hertz (Hz) or, in a digital system, as the number of bits a second that can be transmitted. Thus *broadband* and *high speed* are synonymous. Broadband's broadness, or speediness, is relative—by comparison with older media.

Curiously, however, neither a telephone channel (3,000 Hz) nor a television channel (6 million Hz) nor even a traditional cable television service (upward of 750 million Hz) is considered in the current policy debate to be broadband. Broadband requires high-speed transmission capacity both to *and from* the home. The term also tacitly excludes media that are not consumed or interactive in real time but that may otherwise be func-

2. See Hausman and others (2001a).

3. Justice Scalia, dissenting in *PGA Tour Inc.* v. *Martin,* 121 S. Ct. 1879 (2001) points out that in agreeing to decide whether the PGA rule against use of golf carts in tournaments was "fundamental" to the game of golf the court risked bringing ridicule upon itself. The majority thought deciding whether golf carts were fundamental to golf was required of them in order to interpret the hazy statutory phrase "reasonable accommodation."

4. Shannon and Weaver (1964).

tionally identical to real-time broadband. (These media include print and DVD, for example.) Finally, the present context requires that the focus be on the characteristics of residential rather than commercial end users or on upstream network services such as the fiber-optic packet-switched (Internet Protocol) backbones.

Specific examples of consumer-oriented broadband media are digital cable television systems capable of offering two-way, high-speed, Internet access and interactive video (cable modem service, for brevity); digital subscriber lines (DSL); fixed, wireless, multipoint, multichannel, distribution systems such as those now used by SPRINT and WorldCom to offer two-way broadband Internet access in a number of cities; hypothetical third-generation fixed or mobile wireless systems; and direct broadcast satellite systems, such as Starband, offering two-way, Ku-band, Internet access. Of course, no one today would think of any medium as broadband if it did not provide Internet access.

In offering examples of what most of us mean by broadband in today's policy context, I do not want to give the impression that the definition makes any sense; it has been created by the political players to serve their current interests and generates a demand for consulting services, policy papers, and academic conferences. No one knows whether broadband by this definition ever will be associated with any important consumer products or services. By way of illustration, Jerry Hausman and colleagues, arguing for the imposition of open-access requirements on cable systems for Internet service providers, list applications that can be supported "only by high-bandwidth connections." These include "real-time video programming, on-demand video, customized music and video libraries, home networking, real-time radio programming, interactive, multiplayer gaming, high-speed telecommuting, and interactive advertising and e-commerce."[5]

These examples are disappointing; all of them exist, but none requires broadband advanced services as currently defined. Real-time video, for example, is what you get when you watch a football game on television. On-demand video does not require two-way broadband. Customized music and video libraries do not require two-way broadband or for that matter any form of electronic transmission. Home networking was used to connect computers, printers, and analog modems in the homes of the pluto-techno elite long before there was broadband service to the home. Interactive, multiplayer gaming has existed for many years in a narrow-

---

5. Hausman and others (2001b, pp. 137–38). See also Hausman and others (2001a).

band world. Indeed, I dimly recall playing in a multiuser dungeon from a remote terminal connected to a mainframe through an acoustic coupler attached to a rotary-dial telephone. High-speed telecommuting is tautological as a defining example. Interactive advertising and e-commerce have flourished without broadband, both on the Internet and on home-shopping channels.

As to formal legal definitions of broadband, the Telecommunications Act as amended in 1996 established a national policy of encouraging the development of "advanced telecommunication capability." The act defines the term *advanced services* as "high-speed, switched, broadband telecommunications capability that enables users to originate and receive high-quality voice, data, graphics, and video telecommunications using any technology."[6] The term *broadband* itself is not defined.

The Federal Communications Commission (FCC) uses the terms *broadband, high-speed,* and *advanced services* more or less interchangeably and adopts ad hoc definitions of each to suit its needs of the moment. In its First Report (in 1999) the FCC defines *broadband*—and in effect advanced telecommunications capability and advanced services—as "having the capability of supporting, in both the provider-to-consumer (downstream) and the consumer-to-provider (upstream) directions, a speed (in technical terms, *bandwidth*) in excess of 200 kilobits per second (kbps) in the last mile."[7] In its Second Report (August 2000) it focuses on "infrastructure capable of delivering a speed in excess of 200 kbps in *each* direction." However, it distinguishes as high speed those services capable of delivering transmission speeds in excess of 200 kilobits a second in at least *one* direction. Advanced telecommunication capability and advanced services thus are a subset of the larger high-speed category."[8] Note that the term *broadband* does not appear in this definition, which is retained in the August 2001 Common Carrier Bureau report on high-speed services.[9] In its September 2000 Notice of Inquiry regarding Internet service provider access to local cable systems, the FCC defines *broadband* quite narrowly as "cable modem service."[10]

In December 2000 the commission looked into "advanced broadband" services defined to include "cable telephony and Internet Protocol

6. 47 USC, sec. 157.
7. FCC (1999c, para. 20).
8. FCC (2000b, para. 8).
9. FCC (2001d).
10. FCC (2000c, para. 1 and n. 1).

telephony, Internet access through cable modems, digital video, video-on-demand, near-video-on-demand, and interactive guides—interactive programming."[11] This attempt to define broadband by example ran into the same difficulties that Jerry Hausman seems to have faced in attempting to provide concrete examples of the new services that only broadband can provide. None of the FCC's specific advanced broadband services meets the definition of advanced services from its Second Report. Neither Internet telephony nor cable telephony requires 200 kilobits a second to *or* from each subscriber. Both video on demand and near-video-on-demand require far more than 200 kilobits a second in one direction (downstream) and much less in the other. Interactive guides (to television program schedules) are available today using narrowband channels (analog modems or even vertical blanking intervals) and local caching.

Note also that the exemplary services examined in the December 2000 FCC proceeding are indeed services in the usual sense of the word (that is, outputs of value to consumers), while both the Telecommunications Act and the FCC otherwise use *service* in this context to refer either to providers or to technologies. Because there seem to be no convincing examples of the consumer benefits of broadband (as broadband needs to be defined to distinguish it from older technologies), it is easy to fall into confusion. (The government might be better off defining the benefits of broadband in dimensions other than consumer services, as it did with the Dwight D. Eisenhower system of interstate and defense highways or ARPAnet.[12]

In its June 2001 Notice of Inquiry regarding cable television competition, the commission asks for information about direct cable competitors (overbuilders) "including the types of companies (for example, open video system operator, broadband provider, telephone company) that are overbuilding."[13] This leaves the nature of a broadband provider unclear but apparently distinguishes such providers from both cable and telephone companies. Although possible candidates include third-generation wireless and direct broadcast satellite services, one suspects that the FCC has in

11. FCC (2001c, n. 11).

12. "The [Federal Highway Administration] is committed to improving the nation's national defense mobility by improving the capacity and operation of the highway system. Highways are critical links for mobilizing and deploying military forces from U.S. bases to railheads, seaports, and airports. In fact the Department of Defense relies on commercial providers to meet over 90 percent of its passenger and freight needs during peacetime and times of war." Federal Highway Administration (1999, p. 12).

13. FCC (2001b, para. 7).

mind, to paraphrase Justice Scalia, a platonic broadband provider, one that meets the definition even if it does not exist.[14]

Broadband, for purposes of current policy debate, excludes essentially all the older media for which there are well-established answers to the relevant policy questions. Thus by beginning the discussion with this ill-defined word, the possibility that the laws and rules applicable to newspapers, television broadcasting, telephony, or spectrum licensing have any relevance is discounted. Notice too that the demarcation of broadband media relies chiefly on technology (at least 200 kilobits a second in each direction) rather than on functions, economic production characteristics, or substitutability in consumption. If this discussion of broadband were in an antitrust context, it surely would not be described as a market. Although the 1996 act was conceived in the context of alleged technological convergence of technologies and gives lip service to being technology neutral, the act in fact continues the regulatory tradition of treating different technologies differently.[15]

A definition of broadband could be arbitrary and still useful. The key point is that those engaged in debate and research agree on the same definition. Otherwise, everyone may as well be speaking a different language. Nevertheless, it is convenient in the current climate that everyone can use the word loosely—so convenient that there is a sort of conspiracy of silence about it.

What Barriers?

Although this volume considers what the barriers to broadband infrastructure investment are and what can be done about them by adjustments in what the Congress quaintly calls "regulating methods," no one has made a convincing case that underinvestment in broadband actually exists. The excesses of the technology stock market and related activity in the late 1990s suggest the opposite. Indeed, in 2000 the FCC reported that broad-

14. Justice Scalia characterizes as silly the Court's attempt to decide which PGA rules are "fundamental" to golf. For Justice Scalia these fundamental rules define "Federal Platonic Golf" (see *PGA Tour Inc.* v. *Martin*). Of course, in deciding what is essential to the game of golf the Court is doing nothing different from what it does in deciding whether the facts of any case fall within an intentionally vague standard set by Congress. It may be a silly job, but someone has to do it.

15. Rosenbloom (1994) reviews the legal history of the regulatory distinction between communication common carriers and broadcasters.

band "competition is emerging, rapid build out of necessary infrastructure continues, and extensive investment is pouring into this segment of the economy."[16] In December of that year AT&T claimed that investment in broadband infrastructure was proceeding at "breakneck" pace.[17] The apparently extraordinarily rapid deployment of broadband infrastructure is confirmed by numerous studies. The FCC in August 2001 reported, based on survey data from December 2000, that:

> Subscribership to high-speed services increased by 63 percent during the second half of the year 2000, to a total of 7.1 million lines (or wireless channels) in service. The rate of growth for the full year was 158 percent.
>
> . . . High-speed ADSL [asymmetric digital subscriber lines] in service increased at the fastest rate, 108 percent, during the second half of the year, to 2 million lines. High-speed lines in service over coaxial cable systems (cable modem service) remained more numerous, increasing 57 percent, to 3.6 million lines. The rates of growth for the full year were 435 percent and 153 percent, respectively.
>
> Subscribership to the subset of high-speed services that the commission defines as advanced services (that is, delivering to subscribers transmission speeds in excess of 200 kilobits a second in each direction) increased by 51 percent during the second half of the year, to a total of 4.3 million lines (or wireless channels) in service. Advanced service lines provided by means of ADSL technology increased by 107 percent, and advanced service lines provided over coaxial cable systems increased by 49 percent.
>
> As of December 31, 2000, there were about 5.2 million residential and small business subscribers to high-speed services. By contrast, there were approximately 3.2 million such subscribers six months earlier, and about 1.8 million a year earlier.
>
> Providers of high-speed ADSL services report serving subscribers in forty-nine states and the District of Columbia, as do providers of high-speed services over coaxial cable systems. High-speed service providers who use wire-line technologies other than ADSL, or who use optical carrier (that is, fiber), satellite, or fixed wireless technologies in the last few feet to the subscriber's premises report serving subscribers in all fifty states.
>
> At the end of the year 2000, subscribers to high-speed services were reported in 75 percent of the nation's zip codes. Multiple providers reported having subscribers in 51 percent of the nation's zip codes. . . . Over 96 percent of the country's population lives in the 75 percent of zip codes where a provider reports having at least one high-speed service subscriber.

16. FCC (2000b, p. 6).
17. AT&T (2000, p. 43).

As of December 31, 2000, high-speed subscribers are reported to be present in 97 percent of the most densely populated zip codes and in 45 percent of zip codes with the lowest population densities. The comparable figure for the least dense zip codes was only 24 percent a year earlier.

High-speed subscribers are reported in 56 percent of zip codes with the lowest median family income, compared to 42 percent a year earlier.[18]

In August 2001 the Yankee Group reported similar findings with respect to actual subscribership. Table 2-1 summarizes the group's estimate of the overall last-mile Internet access landscape as of the first quarter of 2001.

Further support for the idea that broadband deployment has been rapid can be found on the cable industry association's website, which claimed in August 2001 that cable modem service was available to about three-quarters of all U.S. households and that cable companies spent over $12 billion in 2000 and over $41 billion since 1996 (over $600 per subscriber) on "infrastructure upgrades."[19]

Given these data regarding services that by current definitions hardly existed five years ago, it is not clear what basis there is for concern about barriers to broadband infrastructure investment. In any event, that concern appears to be misplaced. Even if the data on the current availability of infrastructure are discounted for overstatement (both digital subscriber lines and cable modem providers have been known to report that broadband is "available" in an area where as a practical matter it is not available to many households), the infrastructure numbers remain impressive. Broadband infrastructure growth apparently is significant even in low-income areas. As for the actual number of subscribers to broadband services, that appears now to be roughly comparable to the number of direct broadcast video subscribers, having gone from essentially none to around 10 million in half a decade. While direct broadcast satellite video has penetrated around 12–15 percent of households with television, broadband appears to have penetrated roughly 20 percent of households with personal computers.[20] This is an enviable showing, not matched by many new con-

---

18. FCC (2001d). Footnotes and table references omitted. See also GAO (2001).

19. National Cable Telecommunications Association (www.ncta.com/industry_overview [March 12, 2002]).

20. There is no generally accepted number for the numerator or the denominator of this ratio because both have been changing and official data are considerably behind the times. According to GAO (2001) there were 12 million broadband subscribers as of April-May 2000. The number of households with personal computers has been estimated at anywhere from 50 million to 70 million. The 20 percent figure is based on dividing 12 by 60.

Table 2-1. *Last-Mile Residential Internet Access Media,*
First Quarter 2001

Medium	Residential Internet subscribers	
	Millions	*Percent*
Dial up (analog modem)	56.5	88.9
Digital subscriber line (DSL)	2.2	3.5
Competitive local exchange carrier	(0.2)	(0.4)
Incumbent local exchange carrier	(2.0)	(3.1)
Cable modem	4.7	7.4
Satellite and wireless	0.2	0.3
Total	63.6	100.1

Source: Yankee Group, see *New York Times,* August 6, 2001, p. C-1. Figures are subject to round-ing error.

sumer product or service offerings. Indeed, it is a surprising showing, given the absence at present of any particular landmark service associated with residential broadband.

How can it be that both broadband infrastructure investment and actual broadband subscriptions are growing rapidly while Washington worries that there are barriers to broadband deployment? Is there some-thing wrong with the numbers, something that the government and indus-try insiders know about that is not apparent to the rest of us?[21] Should we be expecting growth rates even more remarkable than the numbers suggest?

Although broadband has been growing rapidly both in availability and in subscriber reach, it is hard to know how fast it "should" be growing. As a logical matter, however fast broadband has grown, there could still be barriers that have prevented it from growing faster still. Nevertheless, the faster that broadband has grown, the less likely it is that there are signifi-cant barriers.

One way to put this issue into perspective is to compare the growth of broadband with the growth of other electronic innovations aimed at con-sumer markets. Pictures showing the cumulative percentage of users that have adopted a particular innovation over time are called diffusion, or logistic, curves. Figure 2-1 displays diffusion curves for various consumer

21. Concern about broadband deployment antedated the beginning of the 2001 recession but coin-cided roughly with the crash of NASDAQ technology stocks and the evaporation of the dotcoms.

Figure 2-1. *Diffusion Curves, Various Telecommunications Media, 1950 to 2000*

Percent of households

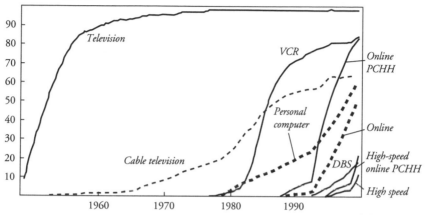

Source: TVB, Inc. (www.tvb.org/tvfacts/trends/tv/tvhouseholds.html [March 11, 2002]); (www.tvb.org/tvfacts/trends/tv/cable.html [March 11, 2002]); Paul Kagan Associates (2000, 2001); Warren Publishing (2000); National Science Foundation, 00-314 (March 31, 2000); NTIA (2000).

electronic and communication innovations, including household high-speed Internet connections.[22] (The household products and services chosen for the figure are enough alike to make them interesting to compare, but there remain obvious and potentially important factors differentiating them. Thus figure 2-1 offers questions, not answers.)

Television is by far the most successful consumer product shown in the figure. It diffused rapidly and now reaches about 98 percent of all households—a greater percentage than have telephones or indoor plumbing. In contrast, cable television has diffused much less rapidly and is currently stable at just over 60 percent penetration of households. The recent success of Ku-band direct broadcast satellites (such as DirecTV) is part of the reason for cable's flagging diffusion. Video cassette recorders and personal computers became available to households at roughly the same time, but videocassettes have been much more successful than personal computers.

Perhaps the most successful of the recent innovations shown in the figure is the simple analog modem Internet connection (Online, in the figure). This success is even more striking if considered in terms of diffusion

___

22. The figure could be drawn in such a way that all the curves start from the same point. This might facilitate comparisons, but what year should be chosen as the starting point for each series is subject to debate.

among households with personal computers (Online PCHH) rather than among all households. Normalizing for computer households is a more appropriate way to compare online services to cable, videocassettes, and direct-broadcast satellite, because television households are essentially the same as all households. Normalizing in the same way, it appears that high-speed online service (High-speed online PCHH) is diffusing at a rate that compares favorably to direct-broadcast satellite, a successful recent innovation that offers more channels and better picture quality than cable television. Direct-broadcast satellite arrived on the scene a year or two earlier than broadband and was immediately available to most television households. In contrast, broadband has only gradually become available and currently reaches only about 80 percent of all households. In spite of this, broadband penetration of households with personal computers now exceeds direct-broadcast satellite penetration of television households.

The evidence seems consistent with the view that there are no barriers to broadband deployment, or if there are they have been trivial in their effects. Nevertheless, for analytical purposes possible demand-side and supply-side barriers to broadband deployment are explored below.

Demand-Side Barriers

As indicated, there do not appear to be significant barriers to broadband, as evidenced by the fact that broadband is already widely available. But assuming there are barriers, what might they be? Lack of consumer demand for broadband seems an obvious starting point in the search for explanations. In 2001 the president of AT&T admitted that, at that time, consumers did not have much reason to get broadband.[23] Not the least of the reasons for low consumer demand is the lack of any—much less any attractive—consumer products and services that require broadband media for their delivery. Certainly Internet access alone is not a sufficient basis for this demand. Residential personal computer penetration has stalled.[24] And although many residential web surfers would like their pages to load faster, enhancing the speed of last-mile connections is neither the only nor necessarily the cheapest method to improve matters. The speed at which web

---

23. Henderson (2001).

24. Angwin (2001). There is no consensus on the fraction of households with personal computers or Internet access. Press reports, based largely on industry-sponsored research with a possible upward bias, suggest that household penetration of personal computers is about 50 percent. Angwin (2001) reports residential Internet access at 63 percent, the highest number I have seen.

pages load is influenced by many factors other than last-mile bandwidth.[25] These include Internet latency, server capacity, web page design, compression technology, local or nearby caching capacity, and the use of methods such as Java to recreate content locally.

It is useful to distinguish broadband video from other broadband services. Broadband video has captured the imaginations of many, but consumers have never seemed excited about it. Ralph Lee Smith and others wrote in the 1970s about the wonders of broadband, and as early as the 1950s policy mavens were debating such "regulating methods" as common carrier status for cable.[26] But thirty years of commercial experimentation with two-way video services failed to produce a product that consumers find attractive at a price that covers costs. It is hard to know what changes in regulating methods might stimulate consumer demand or permit popular innovations in product space. It is not that the FCC has not tried. Even if local telephone and cable companies are assumed to have been comatose or incompetent regarding two-way video service innovation, several other innovations—leased cable access, video dial tone, and open video systems—have been offered. As to video, many consumers seem content with POTV—plain old TV.[27] Things may be different today, of course, given the opportunity to add Internet services to video within a broadband offering, but it is not encouraging that one cannot readily list many (or even any) potentially popular Internet services that require two-way, last-mile broadband.

It is true that broadband might make any service listed by Hausman, for example, better or at least faster, but as Hal Varian's chapter in this volume makes clear, there is no basis to assume that such improvements will generate significant increases in consumer willingness to pay. And from a policy perspective there seems to be no market failure problem or spillover effect that would justify government promotion of any of these services at the expense of other objectives, such as achieving optimal levels of environmental pollution or installing a missile defense. (Network externalities might qualify as a spillover benefit of broadband investment, but the network effects card has been played so often in recent years that its effect on policy analysis now is hardly greater than the influence of the labor theory

25. See Varian, this volume.

26. See Smith (1972); Owen (1970). On regulating methods, see FCC (1959).

27. Indeed, although consumers obviously have been willing to pay for huge increases in the number of plain old television channels, surveys report them to feel less satisfied with television than in the past. Owen (1999, pp. 10–13).

of value.) Both Hausman's list and similar FCC lists of services are embarrassments. All they lack to make them look like the gee whiz wish lists of the 1970s is telemedicine.[28]

If it is true that if there are barriers to broadband deployment, they are due primarily to lack of demand (or lack of attractive products). What alterations in regulating methods, then, would be helpful? This is not a challenge beyond the capabilities of the FCC. For example, between 1968 and 1978 the commission suppressed cable television growth in an avowed effort to make ultrahigh-frequency television stations more profitable by denying consumers superior alternatives, although it turned out that powerful very-high-frequency stations got more benefits. A generation earlier, the commission literally wiped out the entire FM (frequency modulation) radio industry to make it easier for the influential CBS and NBC radio networks to expand into television broadcasting. The FCC's prime-time access rule (1972–95) created demand for cheap game shows by forbidding broadcast networks to offer programming between 7 and 8 p.m., programming that viewers preferred. The commission knows how to make consumers "demand" what is good for them.

The government also knows how to promote the status of a consumer service into an entitlement. Measurement of and agitation over the "digital divide" has occupied policymakers for several years.[29] One motivation for the promotional aspects of the 1996 Telecommunications Act was the notion that new telecommunications technology would improve public services such as education. Accordingly, the act provides explicitly for subsidies for service to rural areas, schools, and health facilities. Moves to further subsidize consumption of broadband service by defining it as a universal service entitlement are already under way.[30]

Lack of demand would be perhaps the most plausible explanation of any failure of broadband to thrive, but because the evidence shows that broadband is thriving, talk of demand barriers to the deployment of broadband may reflect little more than the desire of the industry to obtain more

28. Telemedicine has been a favorite service of futurists promoting the wired nation since or even before the time of Smith (1972). See, more recently, National Research Council (2000).

29. NTIA (1995, 1998, 2000); Noll and others (2000).

30. 47 USC, sec. 254 provides for "universal" service through cross-subsidies. On August 22, 2001, the FCC released a notice soliciting comments on expanding the definition of universal service. The notice states: "We also invite comment on whether any advanced or high-speed services should be included within the list of core services." See FCC (2001a). Expansion of the definition would increase prices for nonbroadband services in order to transfer billions of dollars of subsidies to broadband services.

federal subsidies than it already has, supported by regulatory taxes and transfers from consumers of other services.

Supply-Side Barriers

What are the possible supply-side barriers to investment in broadband deployment? Until 1999 it certainly was not lack of favorable capital markets. The problem, some claim, is access. Internet service providers (and especially the online service providers such as AOL, before it acquired Time Warner and its extensive cable holdings) claim that they will risk vertical foreclosure at the hands of local cable monopolists.[31] Online and Internet service providers want access to cable subscribers on the same terms as vertically integrated cable operators for purposes of selling online portal and content services. Cable operators respond that their incentive to invest in broadband hardware will be reduced, perhaps fatally, if they cannot appropriate all the spillover effects in terms of demand for online portals and content. (There is no evidence that blocking consumer access to any Internet or online service provider or to the Internet directly is of practical benefit to cable operators, or even that it occurs. The argument on the level of general principles is that it might be and that, hence, to forbid it reduces a priori expected returns.) Meanwhile, local telephone companies complain that they are being forced to give rival digital subscriber line providers use of telephone company property at prices below cost, thus deadening their own incentive to invest in new broadband hardware, such as fiber loops to the home.

The heart of these access issues is whether potential monopolists should be permitted to deny competitors access to essential facilities. This is by no means a trivial question. There are powerful and convincing economic arguments on both (or all) sides. Complicating the matter for partisans is the necessity of finding a way to distinguish their answers: You should be regulated but I should not. For an economist, this means that the theoretical, or welfare, argument that leads to a given conclusion must be the same in the two cases, while the facts that matter to the theory must

31. There is a smidgen of empirical evidence on the magnitude of this danger. Excite@Home was the company, owned in part by AT&T, that it was feared would be the beneficiary of vertical foreclosure by AT&T of competing online service providers. Excite@Home provided an Internet Protocol backbone, local servers, and an interface to enhance the technical quality of high-speed Internet service to cable subscribers. Excite@Home declared bankruptcy in October 2001.

be so different that the result is quantitatively reversed. Life is perhaps easier for lawyers, who need simply to find any fact that is different (not the same statute, for example, or not the same technology) and then a way to define that fact as a fundamental distinguishing factor. Different courts have classified cable Internet access service as belonging in different parts, and also in no part, of the FCC's jurisdiction.

How does the access issue relate to the provisions of the act concerned with promoting the rapid development of advanced services? The relationship has to do with investment incentives. The story goes that new technology is expensive and risky. More rapid development is encouraged if the risk-adjusted rate of return is increased, as with the patent system, by facilitating the appropriation of spillover benefits. Conversely, there is a negative effect on investment incentives from a potential reduction in the appropriability of the gains from investment. Monopolists, or incumbents without access obligations, will tend to appropriate more of the gains from their investments in new technology.[32] However, there is a negative effect on investment incentives from protecting incumbent firms from competition, thus deadening initiative, and also a negative effect from confronting potential entrants with a greater threat of incumbent anticompetitive behavior.[33] These are all respectable arguments. In addition, some advocates (often slanderously citing Schumpeter) say that because monopolists do not face competitive risks their risk-adjusted rate of return is higher and they have a greater incentive to make risky investments, so all that is needed to unleash the potential of the incumbent is freedom from the shackles imposed by access policies designed to benefit feckless entrants.

Respectable or not, the arguments about the incentive effects of access requirements suffer from a common affliction of economic policy analysis: We may get the sign of the effect right but seldom have much to say about its magnitude. Aside from some controversial event studies regarding competitive local exchange carriers and focused on the Tauzin-Dingell bill, I am not aware of any empirical research on these incentive effects.[34]

32. Owen and Rosston (1998); Hausman (1997).

33. Hausman (1999).

34. James K. Glassman and William H. Lehr, "The Economics of the Tauzin-Dingell Bill: Theory and Evidence" (www.techcentralstation.com); Glassman (2001). But see Hazlett (2001). Jeffrey K. MacKie-Mason, however, estimates that because broadband cable infrastructure investment increases cable system returns by 60–250 percent, "any" reduction in incentives caused by a regulatory taking of cable operator property through access requirements would be inconsequential. See his "Investment in Cable Broadband Infrastructure: Open Access Is Not an Obstacle" (www-personal.umich.edu/~jmm/papers/broadband.pdf).

Political Economy

Different treatment for different technologies is deeply imbedded in communications policy, even when it comes to constitutional freedoms.[35] Consider for example the vastly disparate First Amendment protections of the various media: print media and cable television have roughly the same strong protection from government regulation of content; wireless broadcasters have far less protection. These striking policy inconsistencies are possible because the law is content with distinctions based on technology—or nearly any other criterion that is a sufficiently bright line and not too close to a slippery slope. As Oliver Wendell Holmes and Ronald Coase would say, all that matters is that courts make the application of law predictable so that private parties can get on with their contracting.[36] Coase would add, of course, that in the real world, with its transactions costs, there should be an efficiency basis for the distinctions drawn by the courts. Perhaps the affirmation of political-economic outcomes can be linked to efficiency. Of course, "legal realists" and "critical legal scholars" will recognize these policies as consistent at least insofar as they reflect and codify the outcomes of political-economic struggles among contending interest groups.

Today's economic interest groups' ability to move political actors is based partly on the notion that a new technology can benefit consumers only if the barriers to its development are minimized. Barriers can be reduced, for example, through consumption or production subsidies, through exemptions from costly taxes or regulations that might otherwise be applicable, through protection from threatened competition, or through protection from nearby monopolies. The Internet has been promoted as such a new technology. Any interest group with a colorable connection to the Internet climbs aboard for the ride. What chiefly distinguishes today's information superhighway from Ralph Lee Smith's phantom wired nation is the Internet connection.

The political attractiveness of viewing broadband as embodying new technology, and especially Internet-related new technology, helps explain the otherwise puzzling observation that, to a great extent, broadband is the same old wires and radio channels operated by the same old companies. The digital subscriber lines that promise to provide high-speed, last-mile Internet connections to some residential telephone customers are the very

---

35. Rosenbloom (1994).
36. Holmes (1897); Coase (1960).

twisted copper wires used for phone calls and first installed a century or more ago. The high-speed digital cable modems that promise to provide last-mile Internet connections to some residential cable television customers use the same coaxial cables used for the past half-century to provide community antenna service and, more recently, cable television service. The high-speed, fixed, wireless, multichannel, distribution system, Internet services offered by SPRINT and WorldCom are nothing but microwave radios and antennas.

To be sure, new equipment is hung on the ends of these links to offer the new services, which are digital rather than analog, and new investments are also required in facilities upstream from the last mile. But broadband is, by definition, the last mile itself, and these last-mile lines have the same physical and economic characteristics they have always had. They are the same wires. Not surprisingly, the policy issues that arise today in broadband bear a remarkable resemblance to policy issues that arose in the past with respect to these very wires. But calling the wires by a new name opens the possibility of a different outcome, one reflecting today's interest group struggles rather than the battles of yore.

Conventional wisdom holds that most of the policy issues surrounding barriers to broadband communications are framed by the collision of dynamic technologies and new business models with the government's outdated and inflexible jurisdictional and policy reference points and categories. But demonizing government regulators is unfair; it ignores the fact that policy reference points, classifications, and categories are not defined by regulators in a political or economic vacuum. They are the product of generations of clever and industrious lawyers whose job has been to rationalize, regularize, and enforce the resolution of political struggles among economic interest groups. (The word *rationalize* is not intended to be pejorative. Rationalization may serve as a proxy for interests not represented at the table and may help make the political process more predictable.) Some of these interest groups have become defunct or have lost their former power, while new ones have appeared. The process unfolding in broadband communications is the attempt by policymakers to understand and to rationalize the evolving political equilibrium among the current set of economic interests.

These remarks do not arise from cynicism. It is possible to recognize substantive policy outcomes as imperfect while recognizing that a democratic form of government encourages and perhaps requires the process that produces them. I am not persuaded by Justice Breyer's argument that our current process should be exchanged for the rule of policy mandarins impervious to the cajolery of economic interest groups.[37] Further, whether a particular political outcome is capable of rationalization often plays some role in determining the outcome of the political debate. Other things equal, policies that are difficult to rationalize lose out to policies that are not. That is one reason that so much distinguished academic brainpower is in thrall to commercial interests.[38] The interest groups are willing to pay well for demonstrations that the policies they advocate are capable of being rationalized.

The data on the rate of broadband deployment are difficult to reconcile with the degree of concern that appears to exist in Washington about barriers to broadband deployment. The chief concern that motivates Washington, to be blunt, is that the cable industry will get ahead of the telephone industry, or vice versa, in developing broadband services unless the federal government varies the pressure of its thumb on the scales of competition. This, together with the common interest of the communications industry and Silicon Valley in promotions and subsidies for broadband deployment, explains much of the broadband mystery.

The Evolution of the Access Issue

Current issues in broadband communication raise essentially every policy question that has ever arisen in connection with communication: freedom of expression, freedom of access, competition versus monopoly versus regulation, subsidization, cross-subsidization, taxation, privacy, exposure of children to pornography and obscenity, junk mail, and so on. Many of these issues are both important and difficult and need to be revisited periodically. The arrival of new (or even allegedly new) technology is as good an occasion as any to think them through again. Rawlsian fetuses gathered here would want to debate, for example, the trade-off between the role of the state and the role of individual initiative in the provision of media content.

This volume has no such high purpose. Everyone knows that the central issue in broadband concerns chiefly the political struggle between cable

---

37. Breyer (1993).
38. See for example "Reply Declaration of Kenneth J. Arrow, Gary S. Becker, and Dennis Carlton," in Verizon (2001, appendix A).

television companies, telephone companies, and their competitors and suppliers, each to free themselves from regulatory constraints while retaining or imposing such constraints on each other. An economic analysis of investment incentive effects provides a useful link to the statutory policy objective and thus a rationale for regulatory action or inaction.

Each of the contending groups is allied with fellow travelers who share their objectives either because they are paid to do so or for their own independent reasons.[39] How did the access issue come to the fore as a salient public policy controversy? When it comes to regulatory policy, economic history and political history are the same thing. Access rose to prominence during the boom in technology stocks, when

—It appeared that the market believed that rapid growth of Internet usage might result in significant consumer demand for services requiring greater last-mile capacity.

—Significant subsidies for construction of broadband facilities were made available, financed by government-mandated, nontax taxes on telephone use.

—Excess capacity began to accumulate in the upstream networks due to overinvestment in fiber backbones, leading suppliers to seek assured downstream markets so as to better weather the coming storm.

—No single technology emerged as clearly the most efficient way to provide local consumer broadband service, setting up a potential competitive battle among cable, telephone, and perhaps other media.

From an economic point of view the access issue is essentially identical to the essential facilities debate. There is nothing about this debate that is unique to broadband, unless it is that the word *broadband* itself permits a new resolution of the old arguments, which it may do. Since 1992 cable legislation has provided two remedies for potential vertical foreclosure of video programmers and rival carriers. First, cable operators are required to make a certain amount of video capacity available for "leased access."[40] Second, program suppliers (like Home Box Office) owned by cable operators are required to make their video programming available to media that compete with cable (for example, direct-broadcast satellite).[41] The FCC has specific regulations implementing both safeguards.[42]

---

39. See for example Center for Democracy and Technology (2000b); Competitive Access Coalition (2000); Mercatus Center (2000).

40. 47 USC, sec. 532.

41. 47 USC, sec. 548.

42. See for example 47 CFR, sec. 76.1003.

In the telephone industry, the 1984 decree breaking up AT&T focused on access by equipment sellers and long-distance companies to the facilities of local exchange carriers, based on the premise that the local facilities were natural monopolies.[43] In the initial settlement agreement, future vertical integration by the divested local telephone companies was forbidden, minimizing incentives to engage in vertical foreclosure. The 1996 Telecommunications Act uprooted this framework, replacing it with one in which the policy objective was the establishment of local competition in concert with the elimination of restrictions on vertical integration. To accomplish this local companies were required to unbundle the components of their services, offering each component separately for use as inputs by new entrants.

In contrast to the cable television leased-access provisions, which had no significant political or interest group support, the telephone unbundling requirements are supported by a vociferous and contentious crowd of competitive local exchange carriers and allied long-distance competitors, such as AT&T. Since 1984 the Bell companies, of course, have focused their political energies on removing the restrictions that keep them out of the long-distance business. The unbundling mandate produced endless FCC proceedings and litigation in the years after 1996, as incumbents and entrants struggled to impose regulatory and other costs on each other. But these battles had to do with telephone service, not consumer access to broadband services.

On the telephone front, digital subscriber line technology dating from the late 1960s continued to stay in the residential broadband game as a potentially cost-effective rival to digital cable systems, despite the inability of the technology to provide useful service to customers more than a few miles away from the central office. But the ponderous Bell companies did little to promote digital service. Some of the competitive carriers, however, saw that their access to the booming dotcom capital market might be enhanced if they leased unbundled local loops from the Bells and offered digital Internet access supported by heavy advertising expenditures (aimed perhaps as much at investors as at consumers).

An interesting controversy then arose over how the Bells should price the unbundled loops. Digital subscriber lines on a local loop do not preclude use of the same loop for ordinary analog telephone service because different frequencies are used. Thus the incremental cost of a local loop for

43. *United States* v. *AT&T*, 552 F. Supp. 131, 189–90 (DDC 1982), Consent Decree, Modified Final Judgment.

digital service, given that the loop is already installed for telephone use, is close to zero.[44] The pricing standard for unbundled network elements is forward-looking incremental cost. Therefore, the wholesale price for digital loops should be low. So the competitive carriers want digital access at low prices, while the incumbents complain about the unfairness of having to provide their own facilities at zero cost to competitors. The FCC resolved this issue in 1999 by ordering the incumbent local carriers to provide shared-line bandwidth to competitive carriers' digital providers at the same low incremental cost they charged their own unregulated digital subsidiaries.[45] Unresolved is the pricing of bandwidth on fiber and other new, as opposed to existing, loops. Of course, following the end of the technology stock bubble, such major digital-oriented competitive carriers as Northpoint entered bankruptcy proceedings, so this issue may now be moot.

Meanwhile, America Online emerged as the most successful consumer Internet service provider, interface provider, content aggregator, and portal. (Vertically integrated Internet service providers that provide a proprietary interface and other content are sometimes called online service providers.) AOL was slow to offer features compatible with high-speed access, such as a dedicated high-speed backbone and content caches near end users; its position would have been threatened if competitors had offered such features. AOL saw that its strategic position would be best served in a world in which a potentially highly concentrated last-mile service industry such as cable was prevented from integrating vertically and thus competing with AOL services. Failing that, AOL decided to seek safeguards to forestall discrimination against itself by integrated last-mile suppliers. Obviously, AOL preferred the telephone common carrier model to the cable model, in which most cable operators provided their digital customers with Internet access that included a proprietary interface or portal. Thus around 1998 AOL began a campaign to incite local franchise authorities and libertarian user groups to impose Internet service provider access requirements on cable operators.[46] AOL soon found allies in the incumbent local exchange carriers, which suggested that their broadband competitors be subjected to burdensome regulations, if only to keep the broadband race fairly handicapped.

At the same time, the 1996 act's relaxation of ownership restrictions led to a series of mergers among communication companies, such as

---

44. However, there are some up-front costs associated with line conditioning.
45. FCC (1999a).
46. Center for Democracy and Technology (2000a, p. 46).

AT&T's 1998 acquisition of TCI, the largest cable operator. As the FCC commonly uses its power to review these transactions as leverage to impose conditions on the parties, AOL and its allies urged the commission to make Internet service providers' access a condition of approval of any transaction involving a cable company.[47]

Finally, overlying the specific disputes involving access to local loops and Internet service providers' access to digital cable systems, there is a broader and increasingly frantic industrywide focus on promotion of broadband by any means, spurred by the hope that the availability of such transmission capacity will be accompanied by the development of new products that are attractive to consumers. If successful, this would address two major industry problems: finding ways to absorb the huge quantities of redundant backbone capacity created during the technology stock bubble; and reinvigorating the flagging residential demand for personal computers and related electronic equipment.

Access to Broadband

The issue on the cable television front is whether cable television operators who add Internet access to their consumer services should be required to provide equal or reasonable or some other level of access to companies like America Online, the leading online service provider. The issue on the telephone front is whether local telephone companies should be required to rent their copper wires running to residential units on favorable terms to any company that wishes to offer digital high-speed Internet access service. This issue—and of course it is the same issue from an economic point of view—has arisen in several courts, at the FCC, and in Congress, none of which acknowledges or treats it as the same issue.

The antitrust faction calls this the essential facilities question and has debated it for a century. It has been at the heart of regulatory policy debates, especially those related to vertical integration. Closely related issues were part of the development of English statutory and common law for several hundred years before that. The FCC itself has addressed the question again and again in the last thirty or forty years, in many forms. It is not a new problem. Three specific examples are

—Pole attachments. Telephone companies, power companies, and cable operators often share space on "telephone" poles. It would be

47. See for example FCC (2000a).

inconvenient and costly to have multiple poles. Should pole owners have to sell space to anyone who wants to buy it? At what price? Does the answer depend on who owns the pole? Does the answer depend on which companies are demanding access? Or on the services they provide? Despite decades of litigation and legislation on these somewhat prosaic questions, the Supreme Court itself declined to say how to classify broadband services and upheld the FCC's right not to decide the issue.[48] Finally, on March 15, 2002, the commission issued a declaratory ruling that "cable modem service" was an "information service" rather than a "telecommunications service" and immediately instituted new parallel proceedings to decide whether to force cable operators and telephone companies to offer access to Internet service providers.[49]

—Cable television. In 1972 (when cable television offered only local and a few distant broadcast signals, most systems had only twelve channels, and cable television penetration was around 35 percent of households with television) the Cabinet Committee on Cable Communications recommended that cable television systems be required to offer substantial amounts of capacity on a common carrier basis in order to avoid a need for federal regulation of cable content.[50] Current law contains a "leased access" requirement for video programming descended from that recommendation.[51]

—The (first) dissolution of AT&T. A federal judge agreed in 1982 that AT&T, then the owner of "bottleneck" local telephone companies, had the incentive and ability to use, and had used, that control to block entry by firms seeking to compete with AT&T's long-distance division and AT&T's equipment manufacturing division. AT&T agreed to divest its local companies, which became today's regional Bell operating companies and incumbent local exchange carriers.[52] (Today, in its disputes with the

48. *National Cable and Telecommunications Association* v. *Gulf Power Company,* 122 S. Ct. 782, 788 (2002).

49. FCC (2002a, 2002b).

50. Office of Telecommunications Policy (1974). At the time, the FCC regulated the content of broadcasters through its fairness doctrine (now defunct) and other means. The courts had upheld the constitutionality of this apparent First Amendment violation, relying on public ownership of the airwaves and the "scarcity" of broadcast frequencies. See *Red Lion Broadcasting* v. *FCC,* 395 U.S. 367 (1969). The Cabinet Committee hoped to avoid possible future federal regulation of content on cable systems by ensuring that many entities controlled cable content. This rationale for access is no longer relevant.

51. 47 USC, sec. 532 (leased access).

52. *United States* v. *AT&T,* 552 F. Supp. 131, 189–90 (DDC 1982), Consent Decree, Modified Final Judgment.

Bells, AT&T has adopted the Justice Department's old arguments as its own.)

The same access issue has arisen frequently in energy markets, where for example competing electricity-generation firms often complain of anti-competitive exclusion by vertically integrated electricity transmission monopolists; and in transportation markets, in which gas producers face integrated pipeline monopolists and coal producers face integrated monopoly railroads. Because this is an old story, there are widely accepted economic analyses of the problem:

—A vertically integrated monopolist may, but need not, have incentives to discriminate against rivals who require access. The effects of such discrimination may either increase or decrease consumer welfare.[53]

—A special case of the incentive to discriminate arises when a monopolist is subject to a binding regulatory constraint. Such a monopolist may increase profits by engaging in permanent predation or other anti-competitive behavior to ease or escape the regulatory constraint. Both consumers of the monopoly service and its rivals are worse off.[54]

—A quarantine of the monopoly service through prohibition on vertical integration (or divestiture if it already exists) eliminates or reduces the incentive problem but runs the risk of sacrificing economies of vertical integration. (Less convincingly, a quarantine eliminates a potentially efficient competitor—the original monopolist—in the nonmonopoly market.)

—Any binding access regulation will tend to reduce the incentive of the bottleneck owner to invest both in the bottleneck facility and in the upstream or downstream competitive activity. However, the incentive of competitors to invest will increase. The net effect on investment requires a case-by-case analysis.

The Ultimate Policy Questions

Is broadband an essential facility to which access should be mandated? Or will such access instead retard broadband deployment? The nebulous definition of *broadband* makes these questions unwieldy. For one thing,

---

53. Chipty (2001). Chipty reviews the foreclosure literature and reports on original empirical research, concluding that, in video, cable operators have engaged in vertical foreclosure that has improved consumer welfare.

54. Noll and Owen (1994).

broadband is not itself a single facility. Digital subscriber line service is one minor way of using a pair of copper telephone wires. Cable modem service is one minor way of using digital cable systems. In each case the underlying facilities have been regarded as essential facilities for earlier, well-established services. Broadband services are different from these established services in three important ways:

—They are new. Consequently there is little history of discrimination or other anticompetitive behavior on the part of the owners of the supposed essential facility that would support (in an antitrust context anyway) mandated access. Because of the significant risks that accompany such an intervention, it is sensible to wait until a problem arises before moving to solve it.

—Neither digital subscriber line nor cable modem service are yet monopoly services (that is, consumers have substitutes), even though the services are supplied by facilities that may be, or have been, the source of monopoly in other services. Digital cable systems and digital telephone systems are still contenders to supply this ill-defined new service, for which there may be no great consumer demand. Cable modem and digital services are competitors, not monopolists. If digital subscriber lines compete with cable modem service, clearly it is not an essential input to broadband service production, and vice versa. Therefore, the most basic condition required to regard a facility as essential is not met.

—Not only do digital and cable modem services compete with each other, but both incumbent carrier digital and cable modem services face competition from technologies that challenge their underlying dominance of transmission facilities. Facilities-based competitive carriers are making progress in attacking the incumbents' local loop monopoly. Direct-broadcast satellite providers are making substantial progress in competition for video subscribers at the expense of cable operators.

In the end, it is impossible to see a credible case for mandatory access to cable systems. Even in their purported monopoly service (video distribution), satellites now undeniably provide effective competition for cable, with DirecTV at the 10-million-subscriber mark and DISH network at about 4 million, and with both offering essentially all cable networks as well as many local television stations.

The digital issue is more difficult. Unfortunately, digital subscriber line service makes use of some of the same facilities that are essential to non-facilities-based competitive local carriers offering services other than digital subscriber lines. Does it make sense to say that incumbent local carriers should have no obligation to offer unbundled loops to competitive carriers offering digital subscriber lines while simultaneously insisting that incumbent carriers must offer unbundled loops and other elements to competitive carriers not offering digital subscriber lines? What about competitive carriers that offer both digital and other services? Is the long history of anticompetitive behavior by the incumbent carriers a sufficient reason to distinguish them, in the present context, from cable companies?

A perennial answer to questions about incumbent carrier participation in potentially competitive markets, such as digital subscriber lines, is the separate subsidiary. The idea is for the monopolist to sell monopoly services to itself at arm's length, an approach that may ease regulatory monitoring problems but does nothing to reduce anticompetitive incentives. The FCC adopted this approach in its predivestiture computer inquiry proceedings.[55] It was also the focus of the abortive attempts in 1980 and 1981 (labeled "Quagmires I and II" by participants) to settle the antitrust case against AT&T. A firm dedicated to the task can find effective ways to discriminate against competitors using shared facilities, whatever accounting rules may be in place. My own view is that only effective facilities-based competition provides a satisfactory answer.[56]

Conclusion

There is no evidence of barriers to broadband development worthy of the name. As to access, clearly it is necessary to wait until an essential facility exists before deciding on its regulation, and at the moment there is competition in the provision of broadband services, with no winner in sight. In the telephone context, regulation of access and access pricing is an unfortunate byproduct of incumbent carriers' historic monopoly of the local loop; in fact, regulation should be eliminated as rapidly as the growth of facilities-based competitors permits, in line with the objectives of the 1996 act. Finally, can the real issues at stake in the current debates—the use of government power to favor one competitor over another and to promote one set of services at the expense of consumers of other services—be resolved in a way that advances social welfare?

55. See FCC (1966, 1980, 1986).
56. According to the FCC (2001e), at the end of 2000 about 35 percent of competitive carrier customers were served by facilities owned by the carrier. Telephone customers of these carriers numbered about 16.4 million in December 2000, about 8.5 percent of the total.

References

Angwin, Julia. 2001. "Has Growth of the Net Flattened?" *Wall Street Journal*, July 16, 2001, p. B-1.

AT&T. 2000. Comments. Docket 00-185, p. 43.

Breyer, Stephen. 1993. *Breaking the Vicious Circle: Toward Effective Risk Regulation.* Harvard University Press.

Center for Democracy and Technology. 2000a. "Broadband Backgrounder: Public Policy Issues Raised by Broadband Technology." Washington.

————. 2000b. Comments. FCC Inquiry Concerning High-Speed Access to the Internet over Cable and Other Facilities. GN Docket 00-185.

Chipty, Tasmeen. 2001. "Vertical Integration, Market Foreclosure, and Consumer Welfare in the Cable Television Industry." *American Economic Review* (June): 428–53.

Coase, Ronald H. 1960. "The Problem of Social Cost." *Journal of Law and Economics* 1 (October).

Competitive Access Coalition. 2000. Comments. FCC Inquiry Concerning High-Speed Access to the Internet over Cable and Other Facilities. GN Docket 00-185.

FCC (Federal Communications Commission). 1959. CATV and TV Repeater Services. 26 FCC 403.

————. 1966. Regulatory and Policy Problems Presented by the Interdependence of Computer and Communication Services and Facilities. Notice of Inquiry. 7 FCC 2d 11 (Computer I). Docket 16979.

————. 1980. Amendment of Section 64.702 of the Commission's Rules and Regulations (Second Computer Inquiry). Final Decision. 77 FCC 2d 384 (Computer II). Docket 20828.

————. 1986. Amendment of Section 64.702 of the Commission's Rules and Regulations (Third Computer Inquiry). Report and Order. 104 FCC 2d 958 (Computer III). CC Docket 85-229.

————. 1999a. Deployment of Wire-Line Services Offering Advanced Telecommunications Capability and Implementation of the Local Competition Provisions of the Telecommunications Act of 1996. Third Report and Order. CC Docket 98-147. Fourth Report and Order. CC Docket 96-98.

————. 1999b. Staff Report to William E. Kennard, October.

————. 1999c. Deployment of Advanced Telecommunications Capability to All Americans in a Reasonable and Timely Fashion and Possible Steps to Accelerate Such Deployment Pursuant to Section 706 of the Telecommunications Act of 1996. Report, 14 FCC Rcd 2398. CC Docket 98-146.

————. 2000a. Applications for Consent to the Transfer of Control of Licenses and Section 214 Authorizations from MediaOne Group, Inc., Transferor, to AT&T Corp., Transferee. Memorandum Opinion and Order. FCC 00-202. CS Docket 99-251,

————. 2000b. Deployment of Advanced Telecommunications Capability to All Americans in a Reasonable and Timely Fashion and Possible Steps to Accelerate Such Deployment Pursuant to Section 706 of the Telecommunications Act of 1996. CC Docket 98-146.

————. 2000c. High-Speed Access to the Internet over Cable and Other Facilities. GN Docket 00-185.

————. 2001a. Notice. FCC-01J-1A1.

————. 2001b. Annual Assessment of the Status of Competition in the Market for the Delivery of Video Programming. CS Docket 01-129.

————. 2001c. Annual Assessment of the Status of Competition in the Market for the Delivery of Video Programming. CS Docket 00-132.

————. 2001d. Industry Analysis Division, Common Carrier Bureau. High-Speed Services for Internet Access: Subscribership as of December 31, 2000.

————. 2001e. Industry Analysis Division, Common Carrier Bureau. Local Telephone Competition: Status as of December 31, 2000.

————. 2002a. High-Speed Access to the Internet over Cable and Other Facilities. GN Docket 00-185. CS Docket 02-52.

————. 2002b. Appropriate Framework for Broadband Access to the Internet over Wire-Line Facilities. CC Docket 02-33.

Federal Highway Administration. 1999. *Connecting America: 1999 Report to the Nation.* FHWA-HCM-00-002.

GAO (General Accounting Office). 2001. Characteristics and Choices of Internet Users. GAO-01-345.

Glassman, James K. 2001. "A Dangerous Fantasy." Statement submitted in legislative hearings on HR 1542, Committee on the Judiciary, House (June 5).

Hausman, Jerry A. 1997. "Valuation of the Effects of Regulation on New Services in Telecommunications." *BPEA, Microeconomics:* 1–38.

————. 1999. Investment and Consumer Welfare in Broadband Internet Access. Ex parte submission on behalf of AOL Time Warner. CS Docket 98-178 (January 14).

Hausman, Jerry A., and others. 2001a. "Cable Modems and DSL: Broadband Internet Access for Residential Customers." *American Economic Review* 91 (May): 302–07.

————. 2001b. "Residential Demand for Broadband Telecommunications and Consumer Access to Unaffiliated Internet Content Providers." *Yale Journal on Regulation* 18:129.

Hazlett, Thomas W. 2001. "Broadband Deregulation and the Market: Correcting the Fatal Flaws of Glassman-Lehr." American Enterprise Institute (July).

Henderson, Peter. 2001. "AT&T's Dorman Says Broadband Still a Tough Sell." Reuters (August 22).

Holmes, Oliver W., Jr. 1897. "The Path of the Law." *Harvard Law Review* 10.

Mercatus Center. 2000. Regulatory Studies Program. Comments. FCC Inquiry Concerning High-Speed Access to the Internet over Cable and Other Facilities. GN Docket 00-185.

National Research Council. 2000. Computer Science and Telecommunications Board. *Networking Health:Prescriptions for the Internet.* National Academy Press.

Noll, Roger G., and Bruce M. Owen. 1994. "United States v. AT&T: The Economic Issues." In *The Antitrust Revolution*, edited by John E. Kwoka and Lawrence J. White. Scott Foresman.

Noll, Roger G., Dina Older-Aguilar, Gregory L. Rosston, and Richard R. Ross. 2000. "The Digital Divide: Definitions, Measurement, and Policy Issues." Stanford Institute for Economic Policy Research (December 9).

NTIA (National Telecommunications and Information Administration). 1995. "Falling through the Net: A Survey of the 'Have Nots' in Rural and Urban America" (July).

————. 1998. "Falling through the Net II: New Data on the Digital Divide" (July).

————. 2000. "Falling through the Net: Toward Digital Inclusion" (October).

Office of Telecommunications Policy. 1974. Cabinet Committee on Cable Communications. *Report to the President*.

Owen, Bruce M. 1970. "Public Policy and Emerging Technology in the Media." *Public Policy* 18 (Summer): 539.

————. 1999. *The Internet Challenge to Television*. Harvard University Press.

Owen, Bruce M., and Gregory L. Rosston. 1998. Cable Modems, Access, and Investment Incentives. Ex parte submission on behalf of the National Cable Television Association, CS Docket 98-178 (December 10).

Paul Kagan Associates. 2000. "Kagan Media Index, December 28, 2000." In *Economics of Basic Cable Networks*.

————. 2001. "Kagan Media Index, January 31, 2001." In *Economics of Basic Cable Networks*.

Rosenbloom, Joel. 1994. "On the Sixtieth Anniversary of the Communications Act of 1934." *Federal Communications Law Journal* 47 (2).

Shannon, Claude E., and Warren Weaver. 1964. *The Mathematical Theory of Communication*. University of Illinois Press.

Smith, Ralph Lee. 1972. *The Wired Nation: Cable TV, the Electronic Communications Highway*. Harper and Row.

Verizon Communications. 2001. Reply Comments. FCC GN Docket 00-185 (January 10).

Warren Publishing. 2000. *Television and Cable Factbook, 2000.*

HAL R. VARIAN

3 | *The Demand for Bandwidth: Evidence from the INDEX Project*

The Internet Demand Experiment (INDEX project) was a set of experiments designed to estimate how much people were willing to pay for various levels of Internet service, most prominently bandwidth. The INDEX designers built the system to provide these various quality levels on demand and to record the usage of each level by user. Users could change their service instantly and as often as they wished; they were billed monthly for their usage.

From April 1998 to December 1999 the INDEX team provided approximately seventy people at the University of California, Berkeley, with residential ISDN (integrated services digital network) service. This chapter summarizes some of the results of the study and relates these results to the current discussion about broadband deployment in the United States. In sum, the study finds that people are not willing to pay much for bandwidth, at least with the currently available applications; that those willing to pay the most for bandwidth are technical and professional workers who work at home at least some of the time; and that people are willing to pay a substantial premium for flat-rate, as opposed to metered, service.

This work was supported by the National Science Foundation grant "Demand for Quality-Differentiated Network Services." I would like to thank Karyen Chu and Jorne Altmann for help with data extraction and manipulation and the entire INDEX team for helpful discussion and critiques. My special thanks go to Pravin Variaya and Richard Edell for designing and implementing the INDEX experiments.

Figure 3-1. *Typical Menu of Choices*

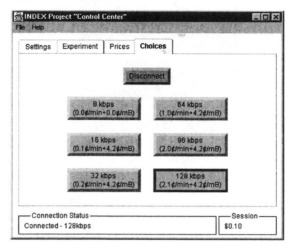

The Experimental Design

Users were given always-on, 128-kilobits-a-second ISDN lines provided by Pacific Bell. These gave them direct access to a high-speed switched ethernet in a UC Berkeley laboratory, which in turn was connected to the campus's fiber backbone and the public Internet.

Users' packets were routed through a billing gateway, which had two functions. First, it measured certain aspects of user behavior, which were recorded in a database. Second, it could offer various qualities of service by selectively degrading how the packets were handled. For example, even though the actual ISDN bandwidth was always 128 kilobits a second, the billing gateway could buffer packets so that actual throughput was any desired speed less than this. The experiments were limited to six speeds: 8, 16, 32, 64, 96, and 128 kilobits a second. Once a month each user's credit card was charged based on the aspects of his or her recorded usage. Users could access their billing records at any time and could view the charges as they accumulated in real time.

A small software application was written that by default ran in miniaturized mode but that could be opened any time with a mouse click. This application showed the choices facing the user at that time, which choice was operative, and what charges were being incurred. The actual layout of the choices varied with the experiment. Figure 3-1 shows a typical set: A user could choose one of eight bandwidths and incur different charges by doing so. The bottom of the user's computer screen showed the connection status and the charges being incurred in the current session. Clicking on the session window switched it to charges for the month or charges for the day.

Note that the users could change their bandwidth instantaneously, simply by clicking one of the buttons. Hence the INDEX project allowed users more flexibility in bandwidth choice than if they had signed up for a high-speed Internet provider and paid a flat monthly fee.[1]

Description of Experiments

A number of experiments were run over the twenty months that the project lasted. A typical experiment would begin on a Sunday evening. Users were generally given a week to experiment with the various service quality levels without incurring charges. This week was followed by six weeks of priced service with that particular set of choices, varying the prices for the choices each week. We ran the following experiments:[2]

—*Symmetric bandwidth.* Users paid the same prices for bandwidth used for upload and download.

—*Asymmetric bandwidth.* Users paid different prices for bandwidth used for upload and download.

—*Buyout pricing.* Users were presented with a set of prices for band width and a rate at which they could buy out from the metered pricing. At the start of the week they could choose whether they wanted to use the metered schedule or purchase the unmetered schedule.

—*Volume pricing.* Users were charged for the cumulative bytes transferred over the course of the week.

—*Fixed mixtures.* Users were charged based on a weighted average of bytes transferred and bandwidth chosen, with the weights chosen by the experimenters.

—*Variable mixtures.* Users were charged based on a weighted average of bytes transferred and bandwidth chosen, with the weights chosen by the users at the start of each week.

---

1. For discussion of why and how the INDEX experiment was created, see Edell and Varaiya (1999) (www.path.Berkeley.edu/~varaiya/papers_ps.dir/networkpaper.pdf [May 27, 2002]). For a detailed description of the technology that went into the experiment, see Edell (2001).

2. An experiment intended to measure the willingness to pay for always-on service by offering users varying delays to connect was not implemented.

Users ran through experiments asynchronously, so that each user started with the first experiment, regardless of when they were recruited. Users were recruited by advertisements posted around campus and run in campus newsletters. An attempt was made to get a balanced mix of faculty, staff, and students, but all of the users had to be part of the Berkeley community in order to use the campus Internet service. In general the subjects were experienced and heavy users of the Internet, compared to the population as a whole, as indicated by the following statistics:

—91 percent had used the Internet for more than three years (in 1998).

—86 percent had used computers for more than five years.

—58 percent characterized their Internet use as above average.

—56 percent considered themselves computer professionals.

These users are clearly not representative of the population as a whole but may be representative of early adopters of new technology. The users, of course, were volunteers. They found participation in the experiment attractive since a portion of the costs were subsidized. In particular, they did not have to pay for the ISDN modems, they did not have to pay a setup charge to Pacific Bell, and they were, on average, charged below market rates for the service. The equipment and setup charges amounted to several hundred dollars, and the rates were chosen to be, on the average, around 75 percent of the market price. The actual rates were typically chosen randomly, subject to a monotonicity requirement that higher quality cost as least as much as lower quality.

Users filled out surveys before their service was started. Several of the questions were identical to the CommerceNet-Nielsen survey, which claims to be a representative sample of the U.S. population, so we could determine how different the Berkeley users were from the national averages. In particular, users reported their occupation, Internet experience, income levels, and the payer of the service (that is, whether they were spending their own money for access or whether someone else paid for their access).

The Demand for Bandwidth

In the experiments designed to measure the willingness to pay for bandwidth, users were offered the choice of the six bandwidths described above (from the 8-kilobits-a-second bandwidth, which was free of charge, to the 128-kilobits-a-second bandwidth). Users could choose the free service at any

Figure 3-2. *Bandwidth Usage*

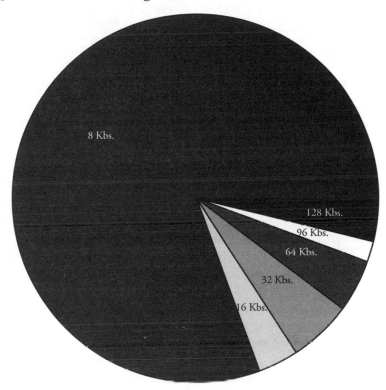

time. Each Sunday a new set of prices was chosen for the other bandwidths, ranging from $0.01 to $0.12 a minute. The INDEX system measured how much bandwidth the users consumed at each price, allowing experimenters to estimate demand for each bandwidth as a function of price.[3] About 75 percent of the usage was with the 8-kilobit service. Since this service was free, users tended to keep it on all the time. Usage was roughly equally divided among the five priced bandwidths, as shown in figure 3-2. Table 3-1 depicts the output of regressing the log of total minutes used at each bandwidth on the log of the five prices. Observations with zero usage were

---

3. For a more detailed econometric analysis of this data set, see Varian (2001) (www.sims.berkeley. edu/~hal/people/hal/papers.html [June 11, 2002]). The following description is taken from this analysis. For a more detailed structural approach to estimation, see Beckert (1999) (www.sims.berkeley. edu/~hal/index-project [May 26, 2002]).

Table 3-1. *Reduced Form Estimates*

Bandwidth	p*128*	p*96*	p*64*	p*32*	p*16*
128	−2.00*	+0.80	+0.25	−0.02	−0.16
96	+1.70*	−3.10*	+0.43*	+0.19	+0.18
64	+0.77	+1.80*	−2.90*	+0.59	+0.21
32	+0.81	−1.00	+1.00*	−1.40*	+0.15
16	+0.20	−0.29	+0.04	+1.20*	−1.30*

*Significant at 95 percent.

omitted. No attempt was made to restrict coefficients across equations since this regression is intended only to show the patterns of demand.

Note that the diagonal terms (the own-price effects) are all negative and statistically significant. The subdiagonal terms are the cross-price effects for slower bandwidths. The positive numbers indicate that one-step slower bandwidths were perceived as substitutes for the chosen bandwidth. This sign pattern is quite plausible. Note also that the implied elasticities are rather large. The regression for the 96-kilobit service implies that a 1 percent increase in the price of this service level led to a 3.1 percent drop in demand. A 1 percent increase in the 128-kilobit service led to a 1.7 percent increase in the demand for the 96-kilobit service. We ran these regressions with and without dummy variables for individual users, with little change in the estimated coefficients. Table 3-2 depicts the R^2s for these regressions.

Roughly speaking, about 20 percent of the variance in demand is explained by price variation, about 75 percent is explained by individual specific effects, and about 5 percent is unexplained. These fits are remarkably good, giving some confidence that the users were behaving in accord with the traditional economic model of consumer behavior.

Structural Demand Estimates

Reduced-form estimates suggest that the users behaved in an economically sensible way. Hence it makes sense to model their choice behavior in more detail so as to extrapolate to other environments. Assume that users got utility from the bits transferred, $u(x)$, and the time, t, it took to transfer them. The cost of transfer time has two components: the subjective cost of time, c, which varies according to users and circumstances, and the dol-

Table 3-2. *Regression R²s with and without Individual Specific Effects*

Bandwidth	With ISE	Without ISE
128	.95	.11
96	.93	.25
64	.92	.18
32	.95	.14
16	.90	.17

lar cost, which depends on the price of the chosen bandwidth, $p(b^*)$. If b^* is the chosen bandwidth, optimization implies that

$$u(x) - [c + p(b^*)]t - u(x) - [c + p(b)]t$$

for all bandwidths, b. Since bandwidth is by definition bits for each unit of time, we have $t = x/b$. Making this substitution and canceling the xs, we have

$$[c + p(b^*)]\frac{1}{b^*} \leq [c + p(b)]\frac{1}{b}$$

for all bandwidths, b^2.

It follows from simple algebra that

$$\min_{b^* < b} \frac{p(b^*)b - p(b)b^*}{b^* - b} \geq c \geq \max_{b^* > b} \frac{p(b^*)b - p(b)b^*}{b^* - b}.$$

This gives observable upper and lower bounds for the user's subjective cost of time, c. Figure 3-3 depicts these bounds graphically.

Define the total cost of time by

$$K(c) = [c + p(b)]\frac{1}{b},$$

and plot these affine functions for each bandwidth, b. A user with subjective time cost, c, will choose the bandwidth with the lowest total cost. Conversely, an observed choice of b implies that the time cost must be bounded above and below, as indicated in figure 3-3. Note that a choice of the lowest available bandwidth yields only an upper bound on time cost and that a choice of the highest available bandwidth yields only a lower bound on time cost.

Figure 3-3. *Upper and Lower Bounds*

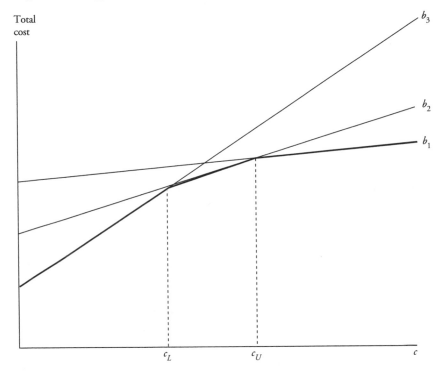

The Value of Time and the Distribution of Time Costs

Assume that the user's time cost was a random parameter, drawn from a distribution $p(c)$. Sometimes users were in a hurry, which meant they had a high cost of time. Sometimes they were patient, which meant they had a low cost of time. Distribution of time cost is summarized by the probability distribution, $p(c)$. The objective is to estimate this distribution. Each weekly menu of prices and bandwidths provided a set of upper and lower bounds. Since the frequency with which users chose each bandwidth, b, during a week is known, a histogram can be constructed for each user for each week illustrating the implied time costs. An example for a particular user in a particular week is given in figure 3-4.

Table 3-3 shows the frequency with which the upper and lower bounds fall in a given range. For example, thirty-nine of the users, or about 60 percent, had an average upper bound on the time cost of less than \$0.01 a minute; eight of the users, or about 12 percent, had an average

Figure 3-4. *Time Cost for a Particular User in a Particular Week*

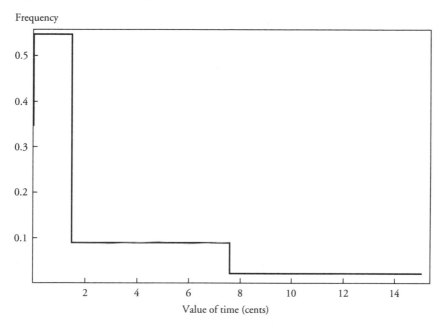

Frequency

Value of time (cents)

upper bound greater than \$0.01 a minute but less than \$0.02 a minute; and so on. The last line in the table is the distribution of a simple average of the upper and lower bounds, which is a rough-and-ready nonparametric estimate of the distribution of time cost across users. Figure 3-5 depicts the same information in a bar chart.

The remarkable thing about table 3-3 and figure 3-5 is the low value that users place on their time. Most users had a time cost of less than \$0.01 a minute, with only a few users having higher time costs. The obvious question is whether it can be predicted which users have a higher time value. Relevant variables available are occupation, income, and whether the employer or the user paid for the service. Occupational dummies explain the time costs using the following regression:

c = 0.86 professional + 2.40 technical + 7.02 administrative + 0.91 student.

All coefficients are statistically significant, and the R^2 for the regression is .646. Adding in both income and the payer yields an R^2 of .652, a negligible increase, suggesting that the best predictor of willingness to pay is

Table 3-3. *Frequency of Time Cost, by Range*

Boundary	Range (cents/minute)															
	1	2	3	4	5	6	7	8	9	10	11	12	13	14	15	16
Upper	39	8	3	4	1	2	2	1	2	0	3	0	1	2	1	2
Lower	67	3	0	0	1	0	0	0	0	0	0	0	0	0	0	0
Average	47	7	2	3	3	3	1	3	1	1	0	0	0	0	0	0

occupation. Figure 3-6 shows the distribution of time values by occupational classification, which tells essentially the same story as the regression.

To sum up: Users placed a remarkably low value on their time, on the order of $0.005 per minute. However, users who classified themselves as being in technical and administrative jobs tended to place a significantly higher value on their time. It appears that many of the technical and administrative users were telecommuting, suggesting that these users had either low demand elasticities or high time costs and, therefore, a relatively high willingness to pay for broadband.

Figure 3-5. *Average Time Costs*

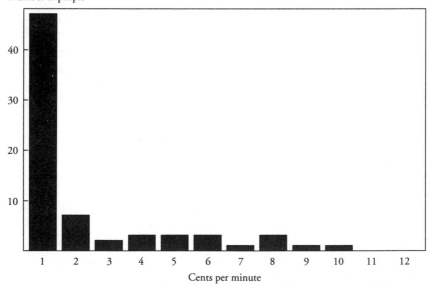

Figure 3-6. *Time Cost and Occupational Category*

Cents per minute

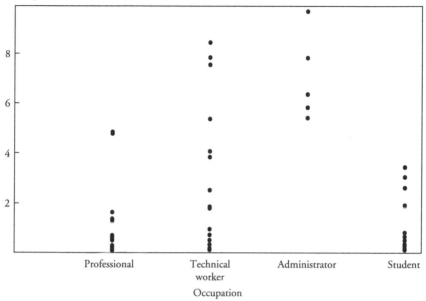

Why Is the Time Cost So Low?

The estimated time costs seem remarkably low, and it is worth considering why this is so. Several hypotheses suggest themselves.

—Nonrepresentative users. This is likely part of the story. The users were volunteers, many were students, and it is apparent from figure 3-6 that certain occupations had much higher time valuations than the representative user. However, the fact that the users volunteered for broadband and that they were drawn primarily from a university population suggests that, if anything, these users should have a higher value for broadband than the population as a whole.

—Use of waiting time for other activities. Not all of the time spent waiting for a download is wasted, since it is common to engage in other activities. Users in this project tended to leave the eight-kilobit service on all the time so that e-mail could be downloaded in the background. Because of this multitasking capability, the value of time saved could easily have been lower than one might think. A closely related point is that certain activities, such as web surfing, tend to involve bursts of activity followed by a period of time spent in absorbing the acquired material. In this situation, bandwidth as such is not necessarily the constraining factor in acquiring and absorbing information.

—Service quality on the rest of the Internet. The experiment controlled quality of service only on the link from the user's residence to the Internet service provider. It had no control over bandwidth elsewhere on the Internet. If the user was accessing a congested site, an increase in speed on the residential Internet link could have had no value, since it would not have increased overall throughput.

—Truncation at the high end. The experiment could not charge more than commercially available ISDN services, and the methodology (or any methodology) cannot determine how much more users would have been willing to pay than the highest price offered. Hence high-end users' willingness to pay might be underestimated. However, there were no observations at the high end of the distribution (see table 3-3), so this explanation does not appear to be a strong one.

—Limits on measurements. Only the value of the existing mix of applications could be measured. If the user had access to high bandwidth at low cost, there could easily be applications that were infeasible at current bandwidths that the user could have found valuable. The value of such hypothetical applications could not be measured using the methodology described. Note in particular that the experiments were run before Napster became popular in college communities. If broadband were widely deployed, new and compelling applications might well emerge.

Buyout Pricing

Another interesting set of experiments examined how much people were willing to pay to avoid being metered. Earlier evidence shows that a substantial fraction of local telephone users prefer flat-rate service, even when they would have been better off under metered service. It has often been argued that the same thing is true of Internet users.[4] There is a psychological cost to being metered, and it is of interest to know how much

4. Earlier evidence, as summarized in Odlyzko (2001) (www.research.att.com/~amo/doc/networks.html [May 27, 2002]), shows that a substantial fraction of local telephone users prefer flat-rate service, even when they would be better off with metered service.

Table 3-4. *Buyout from Metering Experiment*

Kilobits per second	Cents per minute	Buyout fraction
16	0.4	0.125
32	0.8	0.250
64	1.6	0.500
96	2.4	0.750
128	3.2	1.000

people are willing to pay to avoid facing this cost. The experiment designed to examine and quantify this issue was ten weeks long. Users faced the price schedule shown in table 3-4. Each week prices were drawn in a range from $1 to $20, which measured the cost to the users of purchasing unlimited use of the 128-kilobit service. The column labeled "Buyout fraction" in the table shows how much it cost to buy unlimited service up to and including other speeds. For example, if it cost $10 to buy unlimited 128-kilobit speed, it would cost $5 to buy unlimited 64-kilobit speed (since the buyout fraction for 64 kilobits was 0.5). If users wanted to consume higher bandwidth than they had bought, they could do so by incurring the indicated per minute charges.

A preliminary analysis by Karyen Chu of data generated by an INDEX experiment using forty subjects with 337 person-weeks shows that users chose the buyout option during roughly 80 percent of the 337 weeks.[5] Of the weeks that were bought, about 26 percent of the users would have been better off with the metered pricing, given their ex post behavior. If the buyout premium is the total amount paid for Internet access during a given week (usage plus buyout charge minus the minimum cost of purchasing that same pattern of use), the buyout premium ranged from a high of $9.00 down to $0.65, with a median of about $2.00. The median expenditure a week was about $4.00, so $2.00 was quite a large premium relative to expenditure.

The buyout premium can be viewed either as an optimization error or as the additional benefit that users felt from not being metered. Since the demand studies suggest that users seemed to have done a good job at optimization, the latter interpretation seems correct. Behavior was quite different between the metered and the unmetered weeks. The volume of data transferred during the 265 bought-out weeks was about eleven megabytes

5. Chu (1999) (www.sims.berkeley.edu/~hal/index-project [May 27, 2002]).

a day, while the volume of data transferred during the 72 non-bought-out weeks was roughly one and a quarter megabytes a day. Revenue collected was higher during bought-out weeks, but the revenue from each megabyte transferred was much lower: roughly $0.8 a megabyte during bought-out weeks and $0.30 a megabyte during non-bought-out weeks. Whether flat pricing or metered pricing is more profitable for the provider depends critically on the assumed cost structure. The total amount of bytes transferred was roughly nine times larger during the bought-out, flat-priced weeks, but users were willing to pay, on average, a 50 percent premium for a flat price.

Findings

The implications of the INDEX experiments discussed in this chapter are the following.

—Users were not willing to pay for higher bandwidth, at least for applications available in 1998–99.

—Administrative and technical users who appeared to be telecommuting were willing to pay a significantly higher price than the average user.

—Users were willing to pay a substantial premium for unmetered pricing, but they also placed larger demands on the system than when they were metered.

According to the General Accounting Office, roughly 50 percent of Internet users had access to broadband in the fall of 2000, but only 12 percent of those purchased the service.[6] This fact, along with the INDEX findings, suggests that the problem with broadband is not access but applications. Ordinary users need a good reason to pay a premium of roughly $25 a month for broadband access.

Much has been made of the fact that in South Korea 50 percent of households use broadband. Less known is the fact that the incremental cost of broadband in South Korea is less than $23.00 a month, about the cost of dial-up service in the United States.[7] Additional evidence for significant price sensitivity comes from Charter Communications, a U.S. cable television company owned by Microsoft billionaire Paul Allen. Charter offers cable modem service at 256 and 512 kilobits a second at prices of $23.00

6. General Accounting Office (2001) (www.gao.gov/docdblite/form.php?entry=1 [May 27, 2002]).

7. For a discussion of the early days of the Korean experience, along with the experiences of OECD countries, see Paltridge (2001) (www.oecd.org [May 27, 2002]).

and $39.95, respectively, with 60 percent of subscribers choosing the lower priced service.[8] The estimated price elasticity for U.S. cable modem at $29.95 a month is 1.075, while at $49.95 a month it is 1.793.[9] These estimates demonstrate considerable price sensitivity, particularly at the high end. Unfortunately, this is the direction in which prices appear to be moving. Given the applications available today, it appears that users are not willing to pay a big premium for broadband. What are the prospects for new applications increasing demand?

The available studies are inconclusive. According to one study, broadband users spend 27 percent more time on line and average 37 percent more sessions a month than users without broadband.[10] The same study finds that broadband users spend proportionally less time on the web than when they had only narrowband access; they spend more time on e-mail, in chat rooms, and downloading music. However, music downloads dropped dramatically after Napster suspended operation. This study also finds that the use of game websites significant increases. However, another study shows that time spent on the Internet by broadband and narrowband users is not significantly different.[11] It may be that the difference in usage patterns found by these two studies is due to Napster and games. The studies suggest that users do not change their behavior dramatically when switching to broadband, particularly now that Napster is gone.

The fact that usage patterns are relatively stable suggests that the results from INDEX remain valid: Users are not willing to pay much of a premium for broadband, given the applications currently available. Of course, it may well be that a compelling application will arise when broadband is sufficiently widespread. There is a chicken-and-egg problem with broadband deployment: Telecommunications providers do not want to pay for network upgrades if the demand is not there. But if the infrastructure is not there, software developers have little reason to deploy broadband applications and content. When such indirect network externalities are prominent, it makes sense to offer low penetration prices to get the positive feedback going.[12] Unfortunately, prices in the United States appear to

---

8. Blumenthal (2002).

9. Estimates by Kridel, Rappoport, and Taylor (2002).

10. Joseph Berchtold, Veit V. Dengler, Bonnie M. Johnson, and Srividya Prakash, "What Do Broadband Consumers Want?" (www.mckinscyquarterly.com [May 27, 2002]).

11. Rappoport, Kridel, and Taylor, this volume.

12. For discussions of business strategy in the presence of network effects, see Shapiro and Varian (1999) and Rohlfs (2001).

be heading higher. According to one study, cable broadband prices rose about 12 percent in 2001, from $39.40 a month at the beginning of the year to $44.22 a month by the end of the year. Prices for digital subscriber lines (DSL) rose approximately 10 percent over the same period, from $47.18 to $51.67.[13]

These trends lead to the conclusion that, unless new compelling applications are forthcoming or the price of broadband connectivity falls significantly, a surge in demand for broadband in the United States should not be expected.

The Implications for Internet Service Providers

What can be done about this relatively pessimistic forecast? The INDEX study estimates can be used to make rough calculations about demand. As noted, dial-up access costs about $25 a month, and broadband access currently costs about $50 a month, which indicates that the marginal broadband user is apparently willing to pay at least $25 for the additional utility provided by broadband.

The Government Accounting Office figures cited above indicate that about 12 percent of Internet users have signed up for broadband. If this group values their time at about $1.20 an hour (roughly four times the average in the INDEX population), and if broadband saves them each month roughly twenty hours of waiting (an hour each business day), the $25.00 premium for broadband makes economic sense. However, the average user in the INDEX population values time at only $0.36 an hour. If they save twenty hours of waiting time a month, this would imply a willingness to pay only a $7.20 premium for broadband, which is much lower than current rates. These numbers are for metered service. The premium that people are willing to pay for flat-rate service may be as high as 50 percent, which would make these figures significantly larger. The question facing those who wish to sell broadband and complementary services is, What can be done to make broadband more economically attractive to users and providers?

First, since technical and administrative users appear to have the highest willingness to pay for broadband, Internet service providers would be

---

13. See Sam Ames, "Study: Broadband Fees Climbed in 2001," *CNET News.com* (news.com.com/ 2100-1033-818013.html [May 27, 2002]).

well advised to target this market. One approach is to offer a range of premium services that appeal primarily to this group of people. Examples are virtual private networks, which provide secure connection to the corporate intranet, online backup services, and home office support. This may be the best route to profitable deployment of broadband. Second, those who wish to see more rapid deployment of broadband should nurture the development of new applications. The INDEX study was conducted before Napster became popular. The evidence suggests that this single application dramatically increased the demand for bandwidth on college campuses and among users of cable modems and digital subscriber lines. Of course, both the bandwidth and the content was free to end users, so little about actual willingness to pay for online music can be inferred. Providers mention a $9.95 monthly subscription fee for content alone, so music fans might be willing to pay an extra few dollars for broadband downloading of music.

If compelling content and applications that have mass market appeal become available, and if the price for the service declines, the prospects for broadband could change dramatically.

References

Beckert, Walter. 1999. "Estimation of Stochastic Preferences: An Empirical Analysis of Demand for Internet Services." Technical Report. Department of Economics, University of California, Berkeley.

Blumenthal, George. 2002. "High Speed Internet Access Is All about Price, Not Bandwidth." NTL Powerpoint Presentation.

Chu, Karyen. 1999. "User Reactions to Flat-Rate Options under Time Charges with Differentiated Quality of Access: Preliminary Results from INDEX." Technical Report, Department of Economics, University of California, Berkeley.

Edell, Richard. 2001. "Internet Demand Experiment: Technology and Market Trial." Ph.D. dissertation, University of California, Berkeley.

Edell, Richard, and Pravin Variaya. 1999. "Providing Internet Access: What We Learn from the INDEX Trial." *IEEE Network* 13 (5): 1–17.

General Accounting Office. 2001. "Telecommunications: Characteristics and Choices of Internet." Report 01-345.

Kridel, Don, Paul Rappoport, and Lester Taylor. 2002. "The Demand for High-Speed Access to the Internet." In *Forecasting the Internet: Understanding the Explosive Growth of Data Communications*, edited by David G. Loomis and Lester D. Taylor. Boston: Kluwer.

Odlyzko, Andrew. 2001. "Internet Pricing and the History of Communications." In *Internet Services: The Economics of Quality of Service in Networked Markets,* edited by Lee W. McKnight and John Wroclawski. MIT Press.

Paltridge, Samuel. 2001. "The Development of Broadband Access in OECD Countries." Technical Report. Directorate for Science, Technology, and Industry, OECD.

Rohlfs, Jeffrey. 2001. *Bandwagon Effects in High-Technology Industries*. MIT Press.

Shapiro, Carl, and Hal R. Varian. 1999. *Information Rules: A Strategic Guide to the Network Economy*. Harvard Business School Press.

Varian, Hal R. 2001. "Estimating the Demand for Bandwidth." In *Internet Services: The Economics of Quality of Service in Networked Markets,* edited by Lee W. McKnight and John Wroclawski. MIT Press.

PAUL N. RAPPOPORT
DONALD J. KRIDEL
LESTER D. TAYLOR

4

The Demand for Broadband: Access, Content, and the Value of Time

T he purpose of this chapter is to take a detailed look at the relationship between residential Internet usage and the form of Internet access that is demanded. The information analyzed is derived from real-time, click-stream data for a group of residential customers of Internet service providers located in ten cities across the United States. The data set consists of Internet usage data for two groups of households: one group with regular dial-up access to the Internet, the other group with access by digital subscriber line (DSL) or cable modem.[1] Click-stream data for each group provides details on the websites visited, time of day of the visit, and the minutes spent at each site. Our goal is to provide a first step in identifying the factors that cause some households to choose low-speed access to the Internet and other households to choose high-speed access. Obviously, the relative costs of access ought to be one of the most important of these factors. However, the nature of broadband service—its speed and its always-on feature—provides value that is likely to vary across households. Therefore, we developed proxies for such potential value and incorporated those measures into the models.

We wish to thank Kevin Babyak of the Plurimus Corporation for providing the click-stream data and for his helpful and insightful comments.

1. See Charles Jackson, this volume, for a discussion of the various broadband delivery services.

In general, we analyze the demand for broadband from three inter-woven perspectives: the form of access (narrowband or broadband), sites visited (as a reflection of a user's choice of content), and time spent in an Internet session (as a measure of the value of time). All of the analyses refer to households that already had access to the Internet (either by narrowband or broadband). Nationally, at the present time, it is estimated that over 50 percent of American households are connected to the Internet in some form or another and that approximately 9 percent of these households have access through broadband services.[2] Our focus is accordingly on the char-acteristics that distinguish broadband users from narrowband users, rather than on what distinguishes Internet users from nonusers.

Background and Motivation

In view of the tender age of the Internet as a mass phenomenon, it should come as no surprise that there is not a well-established literature on the demand for Internet services. Little is known about the structure of the demand for access, and even less is known about the structure of the demand for usage.[3] In developing a methodology for analyzing Internet demand, it is natural to take the standard framework for analyzing tele-phone demand as a point of departure.[4] This framework consists of two stages. In the first stage, a demand function for telephone usage is specified, conditional on access. A discrete-choice model is then specified in the second stage, in which the demand for access is a function of the consumer surplus from usage relative to the price of access as well as other variables, such as income, age, and household size.

Unfortunately, there are at least two important complications in apply-ing this framework to household Internet demand. The first of these is that differences in end use are much more important for Internet demand than they are for conventional telephone demand. While there are clearly many end uses in conventional telephony, in none of these is speed (or band-

2. See Marketing Systems Group omnibus survey, Centris (www.m-s-g.com).
3. In addition to our own efforts, other Internet demand studies include Madden and Simpson (1997); Madden, Savage, and Coble-Neal (1999); Eisner and Waldon (2001); Madden and Coble-Neal (2000). Also see chapter by Hal Varian in this volume. Our own efforts include Rappoport and others (1998); Kridel, Rappoport, and Taylor (1999, 2001b); and Rappoport and others (2003). The focus of these studies is on either access per se or type of access. The present study is, as far as we know, the first to take a serious look at Internet usage.
4. Compare Taylor (1994, chapter 2).

width) of any real significance. Internet use is different. Speed may be of little importance for conventional e-mail transmission but not for the origination or receipt of large data files, videos, graphics, or photographs. In conventional telephony, real minutes are the appropriate measure of output; however, for most Internet end uses, bits per second (that is, speed) are important. Among other things, this means that the modeling of Internet demand requires that much greater attention be paid to end uses.

This leads to the second complication in modeling Internet demand, namely, the determination of the capacity of the access pipe. With traditional telephony, a need for increased voice capacity can be met by adding more lines (or their equivalent in the form of trunks). With many Internet end uses, however, more speed can be obtained only by increasing the capacity of the incoming pipe, not by simply multiplying the number of pipes. The implications of these complications for modeling Internet demand in an access-usage framework are accordingly as follows:

—Demand must be measured in both usage (minutes on line or sites visited) and kilobits a second, rather than in terms of raw minutes, as in the demand for regular telephony.

—The consumer surplus from usage must, at least in principle, be measured over all end uses.

—The demand for access must be approached in terms of a menu of different types of access (regular dial-up, a digital subscriber line, a cable modem), or more simply, narrowband (dial up) versus broadband (everything else).

Our intent is to adapt to these imperatives in the modeling of Internet access demand and usage. The two groups of households constituting the data set were drawn in such a way that they represent samples drawn at random from the population of households having Internet access: One group was selected from the set of households with dial-up access, while the other group was selected from the households with cable modem access. Since all households in the sample had both narrowband and broadband access available, we postulate and estimate a logit model of access choice, in which the choice menu consists of dial-up and cable modem access. The extension to a discrete-continuous choice model seeks to further explain a household's choice of type of access while explicitly taking into account household preferences, as measured by the amount of time spent on the Internet and the number and type of sites visited.

We begin with a descriptive analysis for the purpose of isolating those characteristics most likely to be associated with the choice of access. From this descriptive analysis, it is hoped that, among other things, we might be able to identify significant factors or "thresholds" with respect to income, total minutes of usage, and usage of bandwidth-intensive end uses that induce households to demand access pipes of greater capacity.

In the end, greater bandwidth allows household Internet users to economize on time. In general, time affects Internet usage in two important ways: through impatience and as a real opportunity cost.[5] A ten-second wait for an image or graphic to appear on a screen may seem trivial in the abstract but not when it is known that high-speed access could reduce the wait virtually to zero. Impatience of this form usually has a subjective opportunity cost. However, low-speed access involves real opportunity costs as well, for in many cases time is indeed money. A telephone line that is tied up for a half-hour (say) in retrieving a large data file, for example, cannot be used to retrieve another file that is complementary to the first nor to make or receive traditional telephone calls. It is clearly to be expected that both a household's income and a measure of the value of the activity to the household will be important determinants in the decision to demand high-speed access: income and derived value in relation to the price of access for cases of pure impatience, but income pretty much by itself for those cases in which an actual loss of income is involved.

The first section of the chapter provides a detailed descriptive analysis of the characteristics of Internet users. At the most basic level, there is a question as to the role that household variables such as age, income, and education play in the decision to move to broadband services. Whereas it is readily understood that age and income are highly correlated with Internet access (of whatever form), it is less certain that these demographic measures affect the choice of the type of access. Click-stream data afford the opportunity to look at a household's choice of content. Content is measured in terms of the type and number of sites visited, the length of time spent at any one site, and the frequency of returning to a site. An important general question is whether broadband users are different from dialup and narrowband users, as measured by their online Internet activity. For example, is there an increase in the probability that a household is a broadband subscriber if the principal online activity of the household is downloading MP3 files?

5. The presence of an impatience factor is inferred from observing a large number of broadband users who have low levels of activity. This subjective form of opportunity cost can be contrasted with a more substantive measure of opportunity cost, in which one observes broadband activity increasing with income.

The second section focuses on the specification and estimation of models for Internet choice and usage. Two related analyses are undertaken. The first entails a classical discriminant analysis designed to test the proposition that households can be classified according to the type of access that they demand. The second is a conditional discrete-choice model of Internet demand, in which choice is assumed to be a function of the price of access and the opportunity cost associated with Internet usage. Both models draw on the richness of information regarding Internet activity available in click-stream data.

The final section seeks to put the analyses and models into both a marketing and policy perspective.

Profiles of Internet Users

A major concern among policymakers in the United States and other countries has been whether it is appropriate for access to the Internet to be bifurcated into two user groups, one group with high-quality broadband access and another group limited to low-quality narrowband access. This issue has been captured by the phrase *the digital divide*.[6]

The results of this survey suggest that, with respect to Internet access, income, education, and ethnicity are key demographic factors. Based on the strength of these factors, a case is offered supporting the existence of a digital divide, even though all socioeconomic groups were increasing their usage of the Internet. The report notes that Internet access rates are lower for low-income households as well as for nonwhite households. While the survey indicates that geographical variation in terms of narrowband access to the Internet has all but disappeared (although some areas still require a long-distance telephone connection), this is clearly not the case for broadband access. There remains a substantial gap in the availability of high-speed access between rural and nonrural areas.[7]

6. The most recent analysis of the digital divide is reported in National Telecommunications and Information Administration, "Falling through the Net: Toward Digital Inclusion" (www.ntia. doc.gov/ntiahome/fttn00/contents00.html [April 5, 2002]). The focus of this report is more on access than on usage and, accordingly, only partially examines how people use the Internet. In addition, small samples limit the analysis of Internet users based on speed of access. The NTIA report is based on Current Population Supplemental Survey (www.bls.census.gov/cps/cpsmain.htm [April 5, 2002]). The executive summary can be found at (www.ntia.doc.gov/ntiahome/digitaldivide/execsumfttn00.htm [April 5, 2002]).

7. It is not clear that, in and of itself, this rural-urban difference has much (if any) social significance. It might have had some fifty years ago, when most people living in rural areas had to do so because they

While the unavailability of high-speed access to the Internet is obviously a sufficient condition for the existence of a digital divide, the question that appears to trouble many policymakers is whether such a divide is forming on purely sociodemographic grounds; that is, whether, in areas in which both low-speed and high-speed Internet access services are available, the difference between the access rates can be explained by standard sociodemographic factors such as age, education, and income. If the answer is yes, then a case can be made for the existence of a broadband digital divide. On the other hand, if the answer is no, then it is necessary to look beyond simple demographics to the formal structure of Internet usage: total minutes on line, the number and nature of sites visited, time of day of online usage, and average times spent at the various sites. If it can be shown that the form of Internet access can be explained by end-use preferences and usage factors, the broadband version of the digital divide question would appear to need reexamination.

There are other reasons to study the linkage between the choice of access and usage. For Internet service providers, the focus is on the size of the potential broadband market. Market sizing requires the ability to classify households into narrowband or broadband groups. The estimation of minutes on line by time of day provides input into network sizing in terms of the demand for bandwidth. Also, knowledge of a household's pattern of use may lead to innovative time-of-day or peak-pricing programs. Finally, knowledge of a household's demand for usage in terms of the type of sites visited can provide valuable information to content providers and their advertisers.

Household Demographics

Household data was obtained for 3,900 dial-up customers and 600 broadband customers. The raw data amounted to over 20 million spe-

---

made their living from agriculture. Now, however, residence in rural areas is often a matter of choice, because of perceived positive attributes of "country living." Why society ought to subsidize high-speed Internet access in this situation is not obvious. The issue, in our view, is really one of cost of supply and whether, in an unsubsidized market, willingness to pay is sufficient to induce broadband suppliers to make high-speed access universally available on a local-area-by-local-area basis. An argument for local area subsidization cannot be made, in our opinion, on the basis of consumption (or network) externalities, at least as these are usually interpreted, because the benefits of broadband access are not shared among users.

cific Internet activities. An activity is a unique link that includes the time stamp denoting when activity was initiated and terminated, the location (URL) of the activity, and all page-view information associated with the activity.[8] Data were obtained from ten cities for the month of August 2001. The households in the sample were randomly drawn from narrowband and broadband households in the specific city.

The following set of stylized facts can be adduced from the data:

—High-speed access is positively related to income (table 4-1) and education (table 4-2).

—Households with high-speed access both are heavier users and have higher variance of usage than households with low-speed access (table 4-3).

—Households with high-speed access visit more sites, on average, than households with low-speed access (table 4-4). The difference is especially marked for households visiting more than two hundred sites a week (figure 4-1).

—Households with high-speed access are notably heavier users during the hours 6 p.m. to midnight and are uniformly more likely to be on line during all hours of the day and night (figure 4-2).

—Households with high-speed access visit many more sites than narrow-band households (table 4-4). Nevertheless, a not insignificant percentage of broadband users clock low activity, and a sizable number of narrowband users show extensive activity.

—Households with high-speed access spend less time, on average, than households with low-speed access at a site (table 4-4).

Demographic variables such as income and level of education appear to be more correlated with Internet access as such than with type of access (tables 4-1 and 4-2). Indeed, once Internet subscription is chosen, household demographic variables are not the most significant variables in the modeling of choice of access, suggesting that other factors explain the choice of access speed. These results underscore the importance of digging further into the click-stream data to explore the relationship, if any, between specific activities and choice of access.

---

8. Click-stream data are collected by a number of entities, including Comscore, Jupiter, Media Metrix, and Plurimus. The data analyzed here were obtained from the Plurimus Corporation of Durham, North Carolina. Unlike most collectors of click-stream data, Plurimus does not rely upon panels but obtains information directly from Internet service providers. Census block group demographics were assigned to each household in the Plurimus database. Specific household demographics were not available. Therefore, care should be used in interpreting the demographic tables and figures.

Table 4-1. *Distribution by Income Level*
Percent

Income (thousands of dollars)	Narrowband	Broadband	No Internet
< 15	15.5	1.0	83.5
15–25	23.3	1.7	75.0
25–35	33.8	2.2	64.1
35–50	44.2	3.4	52.3
50–75	56.2	5.3	38.5
75–100	63.4	8.1	28.5
> 100	65.7	12.6	21.8

Source: M-S-G Centris national omnibus random survey of more than 50,000 households (2001).

Table 4-2. *Distribution by Educational Level*
Percent

Education	Narrowband	Broadband	No Internet
Less than high school	4.3	3.9	15.1
High school	32.0	25.2	46.9
Some college	31.3	31.0	22.2
College graduate	32.4	39.9	15.8

Source: See table 4-1.

Table 4-3. *Minutes of Internet Use a Month, by Type of Access*

Measure	Narrowband	Broadband
Mean	1,013	1,536
Median	495	870
Standard deviation	1,563	2,261

Source: Plurimus click-stream data for August 2001.

Table 4-4. *Number of Sites Visited, by Type of Access*[a]

Measure	Narrowband[b]	Broadband[c]
Mean	434	824
Median	207	466

Source: See table 4-3.
    a. A site is a unique URL. Visits to portals such as yahoo.com are not included in this computation, eliminating possible double counting of sites. Plurimus adjusted the time computation to account for always-on broadband access.
    b. Average minutes per site, 2.75.
    c. Average minutes per site, 2.12.

Figure 4-1. *Distribution by Number of Sites*[a]

Percent

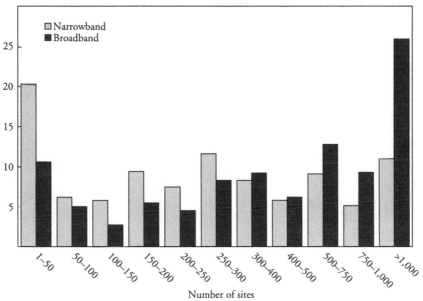

Number of sites

Source: Plurimus, August 2001.
a. Distributions are long tailed.

Usage

Two questions guide our analysis. First, does usage—such as hours a month spent on line—distinguish broadband users from narrowband users (figure 4-3)? Second, what measures of usage are most useful for classifying households? Usage for this analysis includes average number of minutes on line (table 4-3), minutes on line by time of day and day of week, type of site visited (figure 4-4), frequency of revisits to a site, and average time spent at a site.

On average, broadband users spend 50 percent more time on line than their narrowband counterparts. Both the narrowband and broadband usage distributions are long tailed, indicating that there are users who spend a lot of time on line independent of type of access. Since all households in this sample had both types of access available to them, why do a significant number of narrowband users spend so much time on line? Two points are worth emphasizing.

Figure 4-2. *Distribution by Time of Day*[a]

Percent

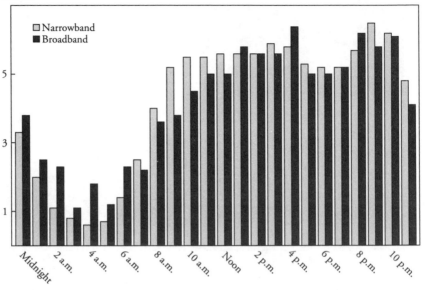

Source: Plurimus.
a. Distributions are long tailed.

First, about 55 percent of narrowband subscribers were on line less than ten hours a month. About 40 percent of broadband users spent less than ten hours a month on line. The fact is that, independent of type of access, a large number of Internet users fall on the lower side of the usage distribution.[9]

Second, 2 percent of the narrowband users were on line more than a hundred hours a month, compared to nearly 5 percent of broadband users. This presence of long tails is expected for the broadband group but not as expected for the narrowband group, given the hypotheses associated with opportunity cost and the implicit value of online activity. From the narrowband perspective these results are surprising. Why, given the availability of broadband services for all households in this sample, is there a large portion of narrowband customers showing heavy use? Is this a result of the price dif-

9. This finding is consistent with the analysis of long-distance telephone traffic, in which a large proportion of households consume small numbers of minutes. See for example TNS Telecom's bill harvesting data (www.tnstelecomms.com).

Figure 4-3. *Distribution by Hours a Month*[a]

Percent

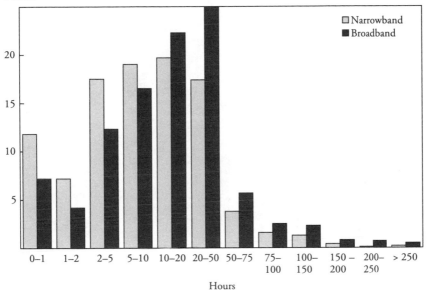

Hours

Source: Plurimus.
a. Distributions are long tailed.

ference between broadband and narrowband services?[10] Is it an income effect? Or might there be other, essentially random, factors accounting for the narrowband long tail? Finally, is it simply a matter that narrowband users focus on low bandwidth applications such as chat rooms and e-mail?

Another indicator of usage is found in the number of sites (specific URLs) visited (figure 4-4). The differences between narrowband and broadband users in the number of sites visited is even more striking. Broadband users visit, on average, 90 percent more sites. They also tend to spend 23 percent less time at a site. A large proportion of both narrowband and broadband users visit fewer than 50 sites a month, or less than 2 sites a day. The difference appears to be more significant for users who visit a large number of sites. For example, for users at the higher end of the number-of-sites-visited distribution, broadband users are likely to visit between two and three times as many sites than narrowband subscribers.

10. The difference in the price of broadband and narrowband service was approximately $30. The presence of a second line could not be obtained from the Plurimus data.

Figure 4-4. *Distribution by Type of Site*[a]

Percent

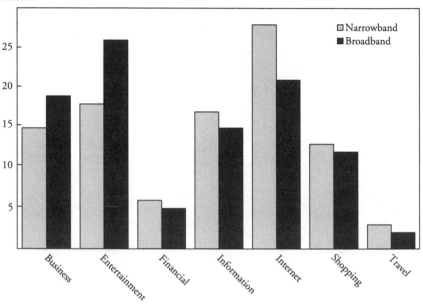

Source: Plurimus.
a. Distributions are long tailed.

The following picture of Internet usage appears to be emerging. The distribution of Internet activity in terms of sites visited and time on line is clearly a long-tailed, or skewed, distribution in that there appears to be a significant number of heavy users for both narrowband and broadband households. A large percentage of users regularly visit more than a thousand sites a month (figure 4-1). The usage of broadband users diverges from that of narrowband users as the number of sites increases. If intensity of use, as measured by the number of sites visited or the amount of time spent on line, were the determining factor in access choice, one would expect to see significant differences in the usage distributions by type of access. However, the similarity between the usage distributions for narrowband and broadband users suggests that overall usage appears to play only a minor role in differentiating the majority of narrowband users from broadband users.

Does hour of the day help differentiate narrowband from broadband users (figure 4-2)? Interestingly, broadband customers are heavier users from midnight through 6 a.m., while dial-up customers are heavier users from 6 a.m. through noon. Afternoon and evening usages are similar for both types of customer.[11]

Site Content

Are there differences between broadband users and narrowband users in type of site visited or minutes spent on line at specific sites? Generally, click-stream data are not organized by site type. Plurimus, however, has created a classification table that separates URLs into broad categories.[12] The scheme is similar to the conventional standard industrial code (now North American industrial classification system, or NAICS) used in classifying industries and their products. Within each level-one category (analogous to the standard industrial code at the one-digit level) there are further delineations (analogous to the standard industrial code at the two-digit level). Following the Plurimus categories, the click-stream site information was aggregated into seven major (level-one) categories:

—Business and companies: sites related to business products, computers, clothing, consulting, electronics, general merchandise, marketing, medical services, music, real estate, software, telecommunications, and vehicles.

—Entertainment: sites related to adult services, arts, astrology, events, gambling, games, movies, music, personal pages, radio, sports, sweepstakes, and television.

—Finance and insurance: sites related to banking, credit, finance, insurance, and online trading.

—Information services: sites related to classified advertisements, health, jobs, law, local portals, maps, news, organizations, politics, science, special interest, technology, and weather.

—Internet services: sites related to a variety of Internet services, including chat, community, e-cards, e-mail, subscriptions, hosting, incentives, Internet telephony, portals, search, security, streaming media, web design, and web applications.

—Online shopping: sites related to auctions, books, business products, clothing, computers, electronics, flowers, food, general merchandise, music, software, sporting goods, toys, vehicles, and video.

---

11. Average minutes on line are for households that were on line for at least ten minutes in that hour and who visited at least two sites.

12. Plurimus classifies URLs into two levels of similar activity.

Table 4-5. *Number of Visits a Month, by Type of Access and Level-1 Category*

Category	Narrowband	Broadband
Business and companies	31	87
Entertainment	57	154
Finance and insurance	14	21
Information services	42	67
Internet services	92	102
Online shopping	31	48
Travel and places	4	8

Source: See table 4-3.

—Travel and places: sites related to airlines, hotels, rental cars, places, and cruises.

The Internet services category is confounded, since it includes visits to portals as well as use of e-mail, e-cards, and search engines. Portals are avenues to other sites. From this perspective, a visit to a portal provides little information on the demand for a class of sites. Accordingly, percentages are computed by first omitting visits to portals.

The distribution of visits depicted in table 4-5 shows that broadband users have noticeably higher visiting propensities than narrowband users for two of the seven categories. The higher broadband share for entertainment is expected, given the increased propensity for users to download large MP3 files or streaming video files.

Broadband users tend to spend more time on line than narrowband users (table 4-6) but spend fewer minutes at any site (table 4-7). This tendency in terms of time or number of sites visited varies within level-one categories. For example, broadband users spend twice the amount of time at entertainment sites, on average, than their narrowband counterparts, whereas they spend less time on the Internet category than narrowband users (tables 4-8, 4-9). The differences between broadband and narrowband users are largest for the entertainment and the business and companies categories (tables 4-8, 4-10).

Summary

The demographic results displayed in the tables and figures are not surprising. First, income and education levels are evident in the choice of

Table 4-6. *Minutes a Month, by Type of Access and Level-1 Category*

Category	Narrowband	Broadband
Business and companies	92	184
Entertainment	185	360
Finance and insurance	47	42
Information services	136	163
Internet services	197	175
Online shopping	116	124
Travel and places	17	20

Source: See table 4-3.

type of access (even though a significant number of narrowband users fall into high-income and high-education categories). Second, broadband users are on line more, both in terms of minutes and in terms of the number of sites visited. This tendency, however, does not always apply to specific sites and categories. Broadband customers tend to be above average users of sites associated with intensive use.

Models of Classification and Choice

Two models are described, the discriminant model and the discrete-continuous choice model. The discriminant model seeks explanatory variables that can classify households into either a narrowband or broadband category. This model is primarily data driven, in that the specification of the model depends less on the theory of why households might choose one

Table 4-7. *Minutes a Visit, by Type of Access and Level-1 Category*

Category	Narrowband	Broadband
Business and companies	2.97	2.12
Entertainment	3.26	2.34
Finance and insurance	3.39	1.99
Information services	3.23	2.44
Internet services	2.14	1.72
Online shopping	3.77	2.59
Travel and places	4.37	2.46

Source: See table 4-3.

Table 4-8. *Minutes a Visit and Number of Sites, by Type of Access and Level-1 Entertainment Category*[a]

	Minutes		Sites	
Entertainment category	Narrowband	Broadband	Narrowband	Broadband
Adult Services	112.84	126.43	51	124
Arts	13.34	7.43	6	4
Gambling	15.20	47.04	3	6
Games	79.27	109.24	22	48
Movies	14.65	10.69	5	5
Music	47.40	68.01	10	15
Radio	18.11	34.92	6	11
Sports	67.52	89.51	23	42
Sweepstakes	25.06	42.00	9	18
Television	21.01	32.01	6	13

Source: See table 4-3.

a. Averages are computed for those households that had positive visits to at least one entertainment site during the month of August.

form of access over the other than on the correlation of a household's specific activity and type of access. The conditional, discrete-continuous choice model is based on an underlying economic rationale of choice.[13] Thus variables of interest are access price, the value of time, measures of content, and opportunity cost, as well as demographic factors.

The Discriminant Model

The discriminant model uses socioeconomic and demographic characteristics and end-use characteristics for the two user groups (broadband and narrowband). Classical discriminant analysis provides a statistical vehicle for answering the question, Can a function be developed that predicts which of the access modes a household will choose?[14] A discriminant

13. While discriminant analysis has a long history of use in economics and the social sciences, this is to the best of our knowledge the first time it has been applied in a context such as the present one. The model has many instances of use in telecommunications demand analysis, although often the first stage is only estimated in order to create an inverse Mill's ratio for use in a second-stage continuous model. See for example Hausman (1991); Rappoport and Taylor (1997); Kridel, Rappoport, and Taylor (2001a).

14. Of the many references for discriminant analysis, *Discriminant Analysis and Clustering*, published by National Academy Press in 1988, is especially useful, because the entire book is available on line (www.nap.edu/catalog/1360.html [April 5, 2002]).

Table 4-9. *Minutes and Number of Sites, by Type of Access and Level-1 Internet Category*[a]

	Minutes		Sites	
Internet category	Narrowband	Broadband	Narrowband	Broadband
Chat	94.30	84.45	48	43
E-mail	111.57	158.46	59	92
E-cards	19.18	25.87	9	17
Hosting	29.25	63.45	16	37
Incentive site	9.54	18.59	1	3
Internet service provider	59.48	33.20	27	21
Search	56.76	45.06	42	38
Security	9.19	6.79	5	4
Web design	7.44	9.11	4	7

Source: See table 4-3.

a. Averages are computed for those households that had positive visits to at least one Internet site during the month of August.

analysis can be thought of as a regression model in which the dependent variable is a zero-or-one indicator for each category. The independent variables are the discriminators, which provide the weights used to score individual observations. Reorganization of the scores provides the basis for assessing the accuracy of the function.

The output associated with the estimation of a discriminant function provides insight into the strength of the classification function. Typical output options include the structure matrix; the table of standardized, canonical, discriminant function coefficients; classification function coefficients; and a summary table. The structure matrix displays the within-group correlations between each predictor variable and the canonical function. Based on the structure matrix, the age and income variables have the highest within-group correlations, which is hardly surprising given the descriptive results. However, usage measures such as the amount of time spent on line and type of location visited are also correlated with the canonical function. The role of the usage variables can be seen by comparing the discriminant model using demographic and usage predictors with a discriminant model using only demographic variables.[15] The additional

15. The discriminant function based solely on demographic variables performed poorly, suggesting that the classification of households into narrowband or broadband categories cannot be accomplished

Table 4-10. *Minutes a Visit and Number of Sites, by Type of Access and Level-1 Business and Companies Category*[a]

Business and companies category	Minutes		Sites	
	Narrowband	*Broadband*	*Narrowband*	*Broadband*
Books	5.52	4.17	2	2
Business products	11.04	11.50	4	5
Computers	11.52	17.13	4	8
Consulting	4.39	4.99	2	3
Electronics	8.80	6.95	3	4
Food and drink	8.36	7.54	3	4
General merchandise	6.71	8.29	2	4
Real estate	24.70	30.63	8	12
Software	71.79	184.59	28	82
Vehicles	12.59	14.57	4	7

Source: See table 4-3.

a. Averages are computed for those households that had positive visits to at least one business site during the month of August.

explanation provided by the usage metrics is critical to the success of the classification analysis. The standardized, canonical, discriminant function coefficients provide a means for comparing each variable on a similar scale of measurement.

Explanatory variables used in the discriminant function include measures that reflect the price of access and the expected value of an online session. The price of access is represented by the access price of broadband and the access price of narrowband. These prices were obtained directly from the participating Internet service providers. The prices do not reflect any nonrecurring charge (if any). All narrowband households in the sample paid a recurring monthly price. There were no per-hour charges. The price of broadband represents the recurring charges for either cable modem or digital subscriber line service. For this analysis, the two services were combined into a broadband group. In those areas in which both digital subscriber line and cable modem service were available, the resulting broadband price was an average price. Broadband demand is likely to be driven by the value placed on speed and the number of bytes to be downloaded.

---

with demographic measures alone. The only discriminant function had an eigen value of 0.3 and a canonical correlation of 0.2.

The expected value of an online session is proxied by the variable "opportunity cost."[16] This variable represents a crude effort to capture an expected time cost of the byte-intensive usage of an online subscriber. The measure assumes that the search and surfing pattern of a broadband user was established when the user had only dial-up access. This household-specific pattern is then adjusted by the expected activity at the site (bytes transferred or time spent); the expected activity measures were obtained from information outside of the current sample.[17] The more intensive the expected activity, the higher the opportunity cost of dial-up access and hence the increased likelihood of demanding broadband access. The assumption underlying this view of expectations is that broadband users previously experienced long delays in downloading information or were thwarted in their tasks by slow response times and thus increasingly valued broadband. The opportunity cost measure is also predicated on a user's pattern of use, implying that users who spend more time at entertainment sites implicitly have the ability to compare broadband access and dial-up access for specific entertainment applications.

The ability to discriminate users into two distinct groups is summarized by the eigenvalue (3.3), the Wilk's lambda (0.233), and the canonical correlation coefficient (0.876). A high eigenvalue (typically over 1) implies that the classification into groups can be obtained from the set of variables. A low eigenvalue implies that no classification can be obtained using the available data. Wilk's lambda tests for the differences in the means of the discriminant score. A low value suggests that the independent variables are able to differentiate groups. The square of the canonical correlation coefficient is the same as the degree of fit (R^2) from the regression in which the dependent variable is an indicator of either narrowband or broadband. These summary measures suggest that the explanatory variables are able to classify households by type of access. The importance of individual variables in the discriminant function can be assessed through the standardized canonical coefficients. These coefficients give the partial contribution of a variable to the discriminant function, controlling for the other independent variables in the equation. The

16. Opportunity cost as a measure of the value of time is typically proxied by income. The measure of opportunity cost used in the modeling focuses on the expected intensity of a visit, so two households with the same income could have different levels of this measure.

17. Plurimus computed the average number of bytes downloaded for each household between March and August 2001. These averages (assumed to represent the expected value of bytes transferred) were used as fixed parameters in the computation of opportunity cost.

Table 4-11. *Standardized Canonical Discriminant Function Coefficients*[a]

Variable	Canonical coefficient
Opportunity cost	0.907
Income > $100k	0.312
Income $75k–$100k	0.253
College graduate	0.207
Income $50k–$75k	0.178
Income $35k–$50k	0.154
Broadband price	−0.096
High school	−0.108
Visits	0.088
Age 40–49	0.080
Income $25k–$35k	0.076
Hours 100–150	0.046
Age 50–59	0.046
Hours 50–100	0.037
Price of dial-up access	−0.035

a. Eigen value = 3.3; Wilk's lambda = 0.233; and the canonical correlation is 0.876.

largest standardized discriminant function coefficients are shown in table 4-11.[18]

A review of the standardized canonical discriminant function coefficients in table 4-11 underscores the importance of price and click-stream information in classifying households by type of access. Whereas the function of discriminant analysis is classification, the signs and the magnitudes of the standardized canonical coefficients provide insight into the determinants of choice of access. For example, the strongest predictor is the measure of opportunity cost (table 4-11). Opportunity cost is a composite variable incorporating the intensity of a visit (expected number of bytes to be transferred) and the distribution of sites visited. Note that the broadband price has a higher correlation than the dial-up price. Further, increasing levels of income have importance.[19] Within-sample predictions appear to be strikingly good: 98 percent of narrowband households and 84 percent of broadband households were correctly classified (table 4-12).

18. Standardized coefficients are obtained by standardizing the discriminant score when that score is the value resulting from applying the discriminant function formula to the data on a case-by-case basis. These coefficients accordingly will lie between −1 and 1. Variables with higher canonical coefficients have more explanatory power.

19. Keep in mind that the information in table 4-11 is similar to beta weights in a standardized regression model. The coefficients cannot be used for incremental analysis.

Table 4-12. *Predictions of Group Membership*

Measure	Group	
	Narrowband	Broadband
Number		
Narrowband	3,802	80
Broadband	97	504
Percent		
Narrowband	98	2
Broadband	16	84

The Discrete-Continuous Choice Model

The discrete-continuous nature of the data offers a textbook circumstance for the use of a classical Tobit model. That is to say, there is a self-selected discrete choice (broadband or dial-up access), with a continuous variable (Internet usage) observed for that choice. Unlike many Tobit settings, however, usage is observed under each of the choice regimes, rather than just one or the other. The model that is estimated here therefore is a joint discrete-choice, continuous model for choice and usage, which is known in the literature as a type-5 Tobit model.[20] The model may be written in latent form as follows:[21]

$$y_{1i}^* = x_{1i}'\beta_1 + u_{1i},$$
$$y_{2i}^* = x_{2i}'\beta_2 + u_{2i},$$
$$y_{3i}^* = x_{3i}'\beta_3 + u_{3i},$$

$$y_{1i} = 1 \quad \text{if } y_{1i}^* > 0,$$
$$y_{1i} = 0 \quad \text{if } y_{1i}^* \le 0,$$
$$y_{2i} = y_{2i}^* \text{ if } y_{1i}^* > 0,$$
$$y_{2i} = 0 \quad \text{if } y_{1i}^* \le 0,$$
$$y_{3i} = y_{3i}^* \text{ if } y_{1i}^* \le 0,$$
$$y_{3i} = 0 \quad \text{if } y_{1i}^* > 0,$$

20. See Amemiya (1985); compare Maddala (1983).
21. Lee (1978).

where the subscript i denotes the individual household, the subscript 1 corresponds to the choice of broadband or dial-up access, the subscript 2 corresponds to broadband usage, and the subscript 3 denotes dial-up usage.[22]

The model may be viewed as an extension of the standard Heckman selectivity model, in which the continuous variable is observed under both regimes. In this case, an additional explanatory variable (the inverse Mill's ratio, or hazard rate) is added to each usage equation. In the broadband usage equation, the inverse Mill's ratio is calculated as $-f(\psi) / F(\psi)$, where f is the normal density, F is the cumulative normal distribution, and ψ is the index (or utility difference) from the access-choice model.[23] The variable takes the form of $f(\psi) / [1-F(\psi)]$ in the dial-up usage equation. A two-step, Heckman-type procedure is used. In the first step, a probit model for access choice is estimated by maximum likelihood. The two inverse Mill's ratios are calculated and then used as independent variables in semilog specifications for the usage equations.

Since only limited demographics are available in the data sets, the specified models are necessarily parsimonious. The variable set for the first-stage choice equations include price and opportunity cost and age, income, and education demographic measures. The number of visits or time on line are not available as determinants in the choice model due to issues associated with using right-hand-side variables that are endogenous. Table 4-13 presents the results for the estimated probit model for access choice.[24] As is to be expected, income and household size affect positively the likelihood of purchasing broadband service. Somewhat surprisingly, the same is true for age (a result that may simply reflect an artifact of the sample or, alternatively, a confounding relationship between age and income).[25]

Price is reflected in the variables D_INTENSITY, which is the opportunity cost of broadband users minus the opportunity cost of narrowband users based on intensity of use, and PRICE DIFFERENCE, which is the difference between the costs of broadband and dial-up access. The coeffi-

22. Lee (1978) used this model to study the effect of unionism on wages; Kridel, Rappoport, and Taylor (2001a) used it to examine telephone carrier choice.

23. See Maddala (1983, chapter 6).

24. The estimated access-choice model is conditional on households already having Internet access. In an effort to remove this conditionality, a model was estimated that included an "extraneous" inverse Mill's ratio calculated from the data set employed in Kridel, Rappoport, and Taylor (1999). The coefficient, however, was insignificant.

25. Household demographic measures were derived by Plurimus using census block distributions and third-party provider information. The demographic measures were not obtained from a survey or from a panel.

Table 4-13. *Access Choice Equation*

Independent variable	Coefficient	t-statistic	Mean
CONSTANT	−8.28823	−7.7	1.00
INCOME[a]	0.00443	5.3	51.63
AGE[b]	0.08408	16.7	37.32
HHSIZE	1.43545	13.5	2.43
D_INTENSITY	0.0003	7.4	12,502.1
PRICE DIFFERENCE	−0.01101	−2.8	30.64

Log likelihood function (slopes = 0): −8,247.9
Log likelihood function (final betas): −1,316.0
R**2, uncorrected: 0.2805; corrected: 0.2796
Number of residuals > .5: 479
a. INCOME is the average household income.
b. AGE is the average age of the head of the household.

cients for both of these variables are negative, as expected. In terms of statistical significance, *t*-ratios are all in excess of 5 (in absolute value), with the exception of that for PRICE DIFFERENCE, which is −2.8. The price elasticity implied in the coefficient for PRICE DIFFERENCE (−0.01101) is −0.47.[26] The difference in this elasticity and previous estimates of broadband elasticities appears to be at least partially explained by the presence of another measure of cost (D_INTENSITY).

The results for the two usage equations are given in tables 4-14 and 4-15. As expected, the variable VALUE OF TIME (defined as INCOME divided by the standard number of work hours in a year) negatively affects usage for broadband subscribers. For broadband households, usage is negatively affected by age and (somewhat surprisingly) by education. The variable VALUE OF TIME has an effect on households with dial-up access opposite to that for households with broadband access. The effect of education is negative for dial-up users, while age is of little consequence. The significance of the two LAMBDA variables supports the direct linkage between access choice and usage. (LAMBDA_1 is the inverse Mills ratio for the broadband access choice and LAMBDA_2 is the inverse Mills ratio for the dial-up access choice).

26. This compares with a value of −0.985 obtained using survey data by Rappoport and others (2003). The price elasticity of −0.40 is obtained by simulation, using a 10 percent change in the price difference.

Table 4-14. *Broadband Usage Equation*

Independent variable	Coefficient	t-statistic	Mean	Elasticity
CONSTANT	9.62447	14.4	1	
VALUE OF TIME	–0.42718	–2.6	0.6712	–0.2867
AGE	–0.04138	–3.4	41.486	–1.7166
EDUC	–0.11245	–1.4	2.6007	–0.2924
LAMBDA_1	0.68892	4.7	–2.0272	–0.8269

$R^{**}2$, uncorrected: 0.0493; corrected: 0.0428
Standard error: 1.4803
Sum squares, error: 1295.12; regression: 67.11; total: 1,362.24
$F(5,590)$: 7.657

While the results are interesting and suggestive, it is probably best to be somewhat humble in interpreting their quantitative significance. Despite the limitations of the measure of the opportunity-cost-of-time, it seems clear that impatience, intensity of use, and time cost are important empirical drivers of broadband demand. The price of broadband is also an important factor in determining broadband demand, but because of the complex relationship between the out-of-pocket cost of broadband access and the opportunity costs of time, not a great deal of significance can be attributed to the value of the price elasticity (–0.47). Until more direct measures of these opportunity costs can be devised, it is best to simply state that the price elasticity of broadband access is falling and is less than –1.

Table 4-15. *Dial-Up Usage Equation*

Independent variable	Coefficient	t-statistic	Mean	Elasticity
CONSTANT	7.03163	36.0	1	
VALUE OF TIME	–0.83029	–4.5	0.3735	–0.3101
AGE	–0.02498	–4.8	36.6676	–0.9161
EDUC	–0.01336	–0.4	2.5224	–0.0337
LAMBDA_2	–1.38687	–6.0	0.1888	–0.2618

$R^{**}2$, uncorrected: 0.0115; corrected: 0.0104
Standard error: 1.548
Sum squares, error: 9148.259; regression: 16.1565; total: 9254.415
$F(5,3817)$: 11.076

Conclusion

A number of insights can be drawn from the data sets analyzed here. The most important finding is that although socioeconomic and demographic factors are clearly important determinants of broadband Internet demand, they are not the only factors. Internet end-use factors are also important.

A second important finding is that the decision to use broadband access is not a simple matter of monotonic relationships but rather a complicated matter involving end uses in conjunction with the opportunity costs of time. The value of time appears to be a factor not only in terms of real cost but also in terms of intensity of use (impatience). However, sorting out the relationships involved will require not only the development of appropriate measures of opportunity cost but also a definition of *usage* in terms of information transfer per unit of time.

What are the implications of these results with regard to the so-called digital divide? In general, our view is that if a digital divide exists, it is far more likely to be a geographic phenomenon (rural versus urban) rather than one formed by socioeconomic and demographic factors. What the click-stream data show is that, depending upon the volume and distribution of their end use, middle- and low-income households can be just as strong demanders of broadband access as high-income households. The problem will most likely be one of availability, for there are some areas of the country—even high-income ones—in which digital subscriber line and cable modem service are not going to be available at any time in the foreseeable future absent a substantial supply subsidy or technological innovation. The big policy question is, accordingly, whether society ought to provide this subsidy.

References

Amemiya, Tareeshi. 1985. *Advanced Econometrics.* Harvard University Press.
Crandall, Robert W. 2001 "Bridging the Divide Naturally." *BPEA* 2:38–43.
Eisner, James, and Tracy Waldon. 2001. "The Demand for Bandwidth: Second Telephone Lines and Online Services." *Information Economics and Policy* 13 (September): 301–10.
Hausman, Jerry. 1991. Phase II IRD. Testimony of Jerry A. Hausman before the Public Utility Commission of California. September 23.
Heckman, J. 1976. "The Common Structure of Statistical Models of Truncation, Sample Selection, and Limited Dependent Variables and a Simple Estimator for Such Models." *Annals of Economic and Social Measurement* 5:475–92.

Kridel, Donald, Paul Rappoport, and Lester Taylor. 1999. "An Econometric Study of the Demand for Access to the Internet." In *The Future of the Telecommunications Industry: Forecasting and Demand Analysis*, edited by David Loomis and Lester Taylor, 21–42. Boston: Kluwer.

———. 2001a. "Competition in Intra-LATA Long Distance: Carrier Choice Models Estimated from Residential Telephone Bills." *Information Economics and Policy* 13:267–82.

———. 2001b. "The Demand for High-Speed Access to the Internet: The Case of Cable Modems." In *Forecasting the Internet: Understanding the Explosive Growth of Data Communications*, edited by David Loomis and Lester Taylor. Boston: Kluwer.

Lee, Lung-Fei. 1978. "Unionism and Wage Rates: A Simultaneous Equations Model with Qualitative and Limited Dependent Variables." *International Economic Review* 19 (June): 415–33.

Maddala, G. S. 1983. *Limited-Dependent and Qualitative Variables in Econometrics*. Cambridge University Press.

Madden, Gary, and Grant Coble-Neal. 2000. "Advanced Communications Policy and Adoption in Rural Western Australia." *Telecommunications Policy* 24 (4): 291–304.

Madden, Gary, Scott Savage, and Grant Coble-Neal. 1999. "Subscriber Churn in the Australian ISP Market." *Information Economics and Policy* 11 (July): 195–208.

Madden, Gary, and M. Simpson. 1997. "Residential Broadband Subscription Demand: An Econometric Analysis of Australian Choice Experiment Data." *Applied Economics* 29 (8): 1073–78.

Rappoport, Paul, and Lester Taylor. 1997. "Toll Price Elasticities Estimated from a Sample of U.S. Residential Telephone Bills." *Information Economics and Policy* 9:51–70.

Rappoport, Paul, Lester Taylor, Donald Kridel, and W. Serad. 1998. "Demand for Access to Online Services." In *Telecommunications Transformations: Technology, Strategy, and Policy*, edited by Erik Bohlin and S. Levin. Amsterdam: IOS Press.

Rappoport, Paul, Donald Kridel, Lester Taylor, K. Duffy-Deno, and J. Alleman. 2003. "Forecasting the Demand for Internet Services." Vol. 2. *International Handbook of Telecommunications Economics,* edited by Gary Madden. Cheltenham, England: Edward Elgar.

Taylor, Lester D. 1994. *Telecommunications Demand in Theory and Practice*. Boston: Kluwer.

CHARLES L. JACKSON

5 | *Wired High-Speed Access*

This chapter examines several key technologies for residential high-speed Internet access, focusing on the two alternatives—cable modems and digital subscriber lines (DSL)—that are currently used by several million households in the United States. The chapter provides the nonengineering reader a basic understanding of the capabilities, limitations, and cost structure of the major high-speed access technologies and an appreciation of the key uncertainties associated with each of these technologies. It also ventures to predict the evolution of these technologies and addresses some demand issues related to the technical issues. The chapter does not discuss high-speed access over cellular and PCS (personal communications service) wireless telephone networks. Wireless access will be important in the future, and it deserves a full section of its own.[1]

Broadband technologies provide high-speed, always-on connections to the Internet. *High speed* is an imprecise term; today it simply means much faster than dial-up connections. A dial-up connection, using a so-called 56-kilobits-a-second modem, typically transfers data at about 40,000 bits a second. A transfer rate ten times as fast, say 400,000 to 500,000 bits a second, qualifies as high speed.[2] *Always on* refers to an Internet connection

1. That topic is addressed by Jerry Hausman, chapter 6, this volume.
2. FCC (2002) retains the FCC definition for advanced telecommunications capability as infrastructure capable of delivering at a high speed in each direction.

that is immediately available. With an always-on or always-available connection, the delay from the time that a user clicks on a web page icon to the time when the request for information is delivered to the user's server is measured in milliseconds. The alternative to always on is dial up or its equivalent, which requires that a connection be established before communications can proceed. Establishing a dial-up connection requires dialing a telephone, connecting the telephone to the terminating modem, synchronizing and training the modem, and logging onto the dial-up server. Typically, this process takes thirty to forty-five seconds or more. Always on is a bit of a misnomer. The key concept is that any lag created by setting up a connection to the Internet be sufficiently small that it has a negligible effect on the benefit consumers derive from the service.

Without an always-on connection, services such as instant messaging cannot be used until the user has taken the step of connecting to the Internet. Always-on connections are essential for certain applications, such as power-load shedding and security services. Always-on connections facilitate other services, such as e-mail. With an always-on connection, e-mail software downloads messages before notifying the user that mail has arrived. Consequently, e-mail can be browsed at the speed of the local machine. Always-on connections also increase the use of the Internet. If one has an impulse to check the web for data, using a connection that is already established rather than establishing a dial-up connection improves the response time by about a factor of ten.[3]

Technology

It is convenient to divide high-speed access technologies between those that use some form of wire or cable and those that depend on a radio link for the connection to the residence. The discussion below follows that division, with most of the emphasis on wire and cable. The fundamental architecture for a cable system extends fiber close to the customer's premises and then uses a metallic conductor the rest of the way or even extends fiber all the way to the customer's premises. When fiber is run all the way to the residence, the design is called fiber to the home. If a single fiber serves a few households, the design is called fiber to the curb. In the telephone indus-

---

3. The size of the improvement depends on how responsive the server is at the other end, the speed of the line, and the complexity of the page viewed.

try, this generic design is now sometimes referred to as fiber to the x, where x can be home, curb, pole, business, or remote terminal. These alternatives on the basic architecture are illustrated in figure 5-1.

The telephone and cable industries have already installed many billions of dollars worth of telephone wire and television cable. Therefore it is natural to design fiber-to-the-x systems that exploit these assets. The first such designs came out in the late 1980s and early 1990s and were used for one-way cable television and traditional telephone service.[4] In the cable industry such designs are called *hybrid fiber-coaxial* and in the telephone industry *digital loop carrier* or *interoffice fiber*.[5] With the proliferation of home computers and the explosion of the Internet, it was natural to expand these systems to provide data service.

The fundamental difference between the various types of fiber to the x lies in the sharing of the device that converts electrical signals to optical signals, and vice versa.[6] This device, often called *optical network interface*, will remain essential for decades, until computers, television sets, and videocassette recorders come with standardized optical ports and homes have built-in fiber networks. Linked to this sharing is the length of the metallic connection. Typically, the more users who share the interface, the longer the metallic connection to the interface.

The capacity of fiber transmission facilities is immense, even when fiber cable is paired with relatively low-cost electronics and the fiber is relatively long.[7] The capacity of metallic conductors is far more limited and shrinks relatively quickly with distance. Thus the metallic conductor establishes both the fundamental limits and the practical economic limits on the performance of fiber-to-the-x architecture. The basic rule is that the shorter the metallic conductor the greater the capacity. Figure 5-2 illustrates this trade-off between range and practical capacity for copper telephone wiring.

The capacity of a wire circuit in any specific situation depends on the nature of the specific copper wires, the nature of the signals in other wires in the same cable, and how much one is willing to spend on transmitting and receiving equipment.[8] Two points should be noted. First, the capacity

4. See Starr, Cioffi, and Silverman (1999, chaps. 2 and 3).
5. Earlier digital loop carrier systems were fed by copper cable.
6. Telephone calls and television signals travel on fiber-optic systems as photons (flashes of light). These light signals must be converted to electrical signals in order to travel over the wire to the home and to be compatible with equipment in the home.
7. See Green (1993).
8. For an overview of digital subscriber line technologies, see Starr, Cioffi, and Silverman (1999).

Figure 5-1. *Four Fiber-to-the-X Architectures*

Fiber to a central office

Central
office

Fiber
network

DSL (copper)

Many thousands of homes per fiber link

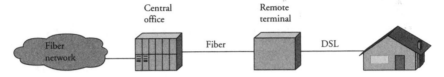

Fiber to a remote terminal

Central
office

Remote
terminal

Fiber
network

Fiber

DSL

Many hundreds of homes per fiber link

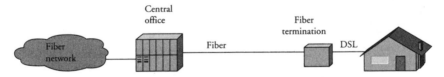

Fiber to the curb

Central
office

Fiber
termination

Fiber
network

Fiber

DSL

Ten or fewer homes per fiber link

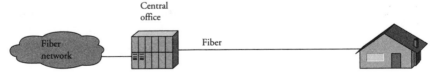

Fiber to the home or business

Central
office

Fiber
network

Fiber

One home per fiber link

of copper loops is much larger than the capacity of modems designed to work over voice-grade connections. A data rate of 5 million bits a second over a mile of copper wire can be achieved by practical systems. Second, the capacity of shorter runs of copper wire is quite large: A telephone wire a half mile long can carry about 50 million bits a second.

Figure 5-2. *Data Capacity of Copper Telephone Wiring*[a]

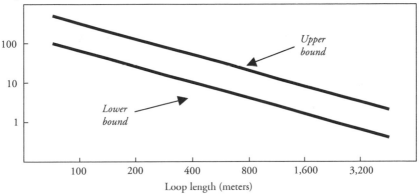

Megabits a second

Loop length (meters)

a. Figure is illustrative, not exact.

Cable

Cable modem service is the most widely used form of high-speed Internet access in the United States. According to one source, there were 7.1 million cable modem subscribers in the United States at year-end 2001; at the same time there were only 3.9 million DSL subscribers.[9]

Historically, cable systems used coaxial cable to distribute television signals from a single location, called a head end, to subscriber locations. Cable systems were one-way distribution systems built with coaxial cable and microwave radio systems. In the 1980s a new system design emerged that used fiber to the neighborhood and coaxial cable the rest of the way. This hybrid fiber-coaxial design improved the quality and reliability of cable systems and was put in place by many cable systems (see figure 5-3).

The design of the hybrid fiber-coaxial cable simplifies the design of broadband access systems in two ways. First, the substitution of fiber for coaxial cable on much of the path from the head end to the residence improves the quality of the signal delivered to the consumer. Second, the design shrinks the amount of coaxial cable in the upstream path, the path signals follow from the home to the network. Because the coaxial part of the network limits the capacity of the return channel, shortening the coaxial cable in the return path increases the capacity and reliability of the upstream path.

9. FCC (2002).

Figure 5-3. *Hybrid Fiber-Coaxial Cable System Architecture*

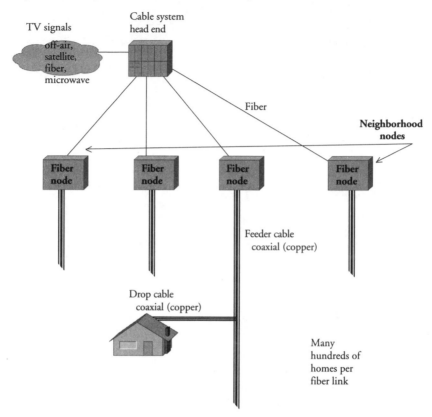

The cable industry and its suppliers experimented with many forms of two-way data communications over cable systems. In the 1990s a cable industry research consortium, CableLabs, developed a specification for data communication over cable systems (usually referred to by the acronym DOCSIS, standing for data-over-cable-service interface specifications; see figure 5-4).[10] These interface specifications have had a major impact on the cable modem market. Compliance with a single standard permits manufacturers to compete in the supply of compatible equipment. Further, a single standard permits retailers to efficiently stock cable modem gear and reduces or eliminates the risks that a consumer will be stuck with orphaned

10. The DOCSIS project was renamed the CableLabs® Certified™ Cable Modem project. The cable modem specifications are available at (www.cablemodem.com/specifications.html [March 14, 2002]).

Figure 5-4. *Data-over-Cable-Service Interface Specifications*

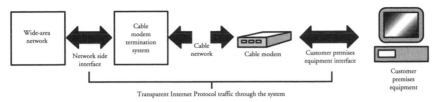

Source: CableLabs SP-RFI-I06-010829.

equipment or will be unable to move to another city and use the modem. The cable industry is now deploying cable modem service using predominantly equipment that is compliant with the standard. More than fifty manufacturers (including Motorola, Cisco, Toshiba, and 3Com) supply cable modems that comply with the standard, and retail stores such as CompUSA, Circuit City, and Radio Shack sell compliant modems.[11] Typical cable modem prices range from $125 to $250. The trade press reports that sales of such modems exceeded 2 million units in the second quarter of 2001.[12]

Corresponding to the cable modem at the customer's premises is a cable modem termination system located at the cable system's head end. Basically, cable modems and their termination systems use the preexisting cable network much as dial-up modems use the telephone network. Cable modems in the home can receive data at speeds as high as 40 million bits a second and can transmit at speeds up to 10 million bits a second. The next generation of cable modems is expected to transmit upstream at 30 million bits a second.[13] To implement high-speed access over a cable system, the system operator must dedicate some of the system's capacity, typically the equivalent of a single television channel, to the cable modem service. One television channel provides a pool of about 40 million bits a second of downstream capacity.

A fundamental problem for cable systems arises from the fact that the capacity of a single cable is shared by many subscribers. In a traditional cable network, the same signal is delivered to every household, and the

---

11. See (www.cabledatacomnews.com/cmic/docsiscm.html [March 14, 2002]).

12. "S-A Storms into DOCSIS Modem Market," CableDataComm News, September 1, 2001 (www.cabledatacomnews.com/sep01/sep01-2.html [March 14, 2002]).

13. CableLabs, "CableLabs® Creating Advanced Modem Spec to Enable 30 Mbps in Upstream," August 31, 2001.

tuner in the television set or in the set-top box selects the specific program that the subscriber views on the television set. Cable modems work the same way. The downstream data (from the head end to the subscriber) is broadcast over the cable just as a television signal is. The interface specifications include an encryption element to prevent anyone other than the subscriber from reading the data in these broadcast packets.[14] In a large cable system, say one with 100,000 subscribers, a downstream capacity of 40 million bits a second would work out to an average capacity of 400 bits a second per subscriber.

Hybrid fiber-coaxial cable networks permit different data streams to be sent to each neighborhood node. Thus if a cable system serves an average of 2,000 homes for each fiber node, the average downstream capacity would be 20,000 bits a second for each home. If only 10 percent of the homes have cable modems, then the average downstream capacity would be 200,000 bits a second. Broadband access over a cable modem system capable of delivering average traffic levels this high would result in an acceptable web-browsing service for most subscribers. The data capacity is not rigidly divided among subscribers. Rather, the capacity resides in a pool and is allocated as users need to communicate. Notice, however, that if many consumers choose to use the web in a fashion that requires continuous transmission—say downloading lots of music files or watching a video conference or a football game—the shared capacity will be exhausted.

When traffic levels grow, cable operators have two alternatives to expand capacity. One, they could dedicate more of the cable's transmission capacity to data services and less to television. The least-watched television channel of a hundred channels could be sacrificed to expand data capacity. Or, two, they could reduce the number of households served by each fiber node, essentially moving the fiber closer to the home.

Digital Subscriber Lines

Copper wires stretching from a telephone company's central office to the subscriber's premises serve the majority of telephones in the United States. Equipment much like an ordinary modem can transmit data over the copper wire running from the home or office to the central office. Such

---

14. See "Data-Over-Cable Service Interface Specifications Baseline Privacy plus Interface Specification SP-BPI+-I07-010829," Seventh Interim Release, August 29, 2001.

digital subscriber line modems can transmit data at far higher speeds than is possible over voice-grade connections because they can take advantage of capacity in the copper wire that is not used for voice communications. The term *asymmetric digital subscriber line* (ADSL) refers to a digital subscriber line system in which the transmission capacities in the two directions are different—a split that can be useful for web browsing or distribution of audio or video programming. Telephone companies promote ADSL to residential consumers as the preferred form of high-speed access to the Internet. It is designed to coexist with the loop for ordinary telephone calls. Thus by hooking extra equipment up at each end of the loop, the telephone company can deliver a high-speed access service (at least on those loops that are not too long and that otherwise qualify).

Digital subscriber line service is limited by loop quality, distance, and the use of digital loop carrier systems.[15] The connections can be restricted or even made unworkable if the copper loop is impaired. For example, loading coils, which improve voice transmission on longer loops, must be removed for ADSL to work. And, as discussed above, the ability of copper telephone loops to carry high-speed data signals declines with distance. Telephone equipment manufacturers produce a variety of incompatible digital equipment. Although there are standards, there are multiple standards, known by acronyms such as ADSL, G.lite, SDSL, HDSL2, SHDSL, and IDSL. These standards offer a mix of ranges and capacities and reflect the evolution of digital subscriber line services.

The telephone industry, unlike the cable industry, lacks the efficiency of a single standard. Typically, an ADSL permits downstream speeds of up to 8 megabits a second and upstream speeds of up to 640 kilobits a second. The communications speed actually achieved depends on the quality and length of the copper loop. ADSL modems automatically adjust the operating rate to deliver the best possible speed over a specific loop. These modems do not operate reliably over copper loops longer than about three miles.

To offer digital subscriber line service, a telephone company must install a modem at the customer's premises and at the central office (or the remote terminal). Usually the modem in a central office comes in assemblies of multiple modems, called digital subscriber line access multiplexers.

15. In digital loop carrier systems, a high-capacity digital transmission line is run to a remote terminal in the neighborhood. At the remote terminal, the digital voice signal is converted to analog and transferred to copper loops. Digital loop carriers save money by substituting one high-capacity transmission system for many lower-capacity copper loops.

The access multiplexer must then have a high-speed connection to the rest of the Internet. The multiplexer in a telephone network corresponds to the cable modem termination system in a cable system.

Digital Subscriber Lines from a Remote Terminal

For decades, local exchange carriers have used digital loop carriers to lower the cost of providing telephone service. Unfortunately, these systems do not provide a copper connection all the way from the telephone company's central office to the subscriber's location. The solution to this is to upgrade the capabilities of the digital loop carrier to enable the terminal to support ADSL service over the copper connection to the subscriber's premises.

Two upgrades are required. First, ADSL modems must be installed in the remote terminal, thus giving the terminal its own small digital subscriber line access multiplexer. Second, a high-capacity fiber connection must be provided from the remote terminal back to the central office. Remote terminals with such capabilities are sometimes called next-generation digital loop carrier. Typically, the areas served by a digital loop carrier have been designed so that the loops are less than about 18,000–20,000 feet in length—just at the outer reach of modern ADSL systems. This is no coincidence; these systems were designed with an understanding of the distribution of the lengths of copper loops in the United States. Thus fiber to the remote, where the remote is the current remote for voice service, can provide ADSL service to households that would otherwise not be able to get the service. However, fiber to the (current) remote does not provide service at higher rates than standard ADSL. To provide service at faster rates, new remote terminals would have to be put into neighborhoods.

Fiber to the Home

The prospect of extending fiber all the way to the home has excited futurists, engineers, and policy analysts alike. An Internet search on Google for the term *ftth* generates about 10,000 hits. (In contrast, an Internet search for AEI-Brookings generates about 5,000 hits.) Carriers have connected fiber to some large office buildings. However, in spite of a substantial research and development effort, running fiber all the way to detached residences has not yet proven economical. Fiber to the home stumbles over a few economic facts. First, there is little or no residential demand for services that require the speed delivered by fiber but not by other technologies. Second, existing household equipment—telephones, televisions, and computers—all came with an electrical signal interface. Even if fiber were extended to the home, the digital signal on the fiber would have to be changed to an electrical signal. If the equipment for converting optical signals to and from electrical signals displays even modest economies of scale—say, with a unit serving three homes costing only twice what a unit serving a single home costs—it may be more efficient for multiple subscribers to share optical-electrical interfaces.

The next generation of digital subscriber line technology will support communications over copper loops at data rates as high as 50 million bits a second at distances up to a few hundred meters. One optical-electrical interface in the middle of the block could supply services at speeds up to 50 million bits a second to all homes on the block.

Cable Modems versus Digital Subscriber Lines

Cable modem and digital subscriber line services account for the vast bulk of high-speed residential Internet access in the United States today. What can be discerned about the long-term competitive balance between these two technologies and industries? What are the long term prospects for fiber to the home replacing both of them?

Cable modems and digital subscriber lines each have unique advantages and disadvantages. The advantages of cable modems include ease of installation and the high (40 million bits a second) peak capacity for each subscriber. The disadvantages of cable modems include the relatively low average capacity provided to each subscriber, due to shared use of the transmission path, and the location of the cable connection—in many homes it runs only to the main television set and is some distance from the computers in the home.

These problems can be overcome. A cable system with 600 megahertz of cable capacity might be divided into 300 megahertz for downstream digital video, 200 megahertz for downstream Internet access, and 100 megahertz for upstream Internet access. A cable system with these specifications is easily within the reach of today's technology. Such a system could deliver 250–500 standard-definition video channels, about 100 high-definition television channels, or a mix of standard and high-definition channels, given the advances in signal-compression technologies. If each fiber node served 200 homes, the average downstream data capacity for each home would be about 6 million bits a second. Even if each fiber node served 2,000 homes, the average data capacity would be about 600 kilobits a second. This example should make it clear that a modern cable system can evolve into a capable broadband service provider without extensive rebuilding of the network nodes. Home networks would reduce or resolve the problem of an inconvenient cable modem location in the home.

A digital subscriber line has the advantages of higher average capacity and a more convenient location in the home—phone lines often run close to computers in the home. But telephone companies face a more complex upgrading process than cable companies face. Current-generation DSL modems have a peak data rate of about 8 million bits a second in the downstream direction and 800 kilobits a second in the upstream direction.[16] In most installations, the length of the copper loop from the telephone company facility to the residence prevents the digital subscriber line modem from operating at maximum speed. Telephone companies can increase the maximum data rate by installing, at significant expense, remote terminals closer to the subscriber. This process will work until the peak data speed at the residence reaches 8 million bits a second. At that point, any additional increase in peak data rate to a residence will require replacing the modem in the home.

Although fiber to the home appears to be a natural next step in communications, the timing of true fiber to the home is uncertain. The preconditions for the technology gaining marketplace acceptance are either that residential subscribers be willing to pay a premium for services at data rates well above 10 megabits a second or that the cost premium currently associated with fiber becomes insignificant. The mixed fiber-copper solutions, whether used by the cable industry or the telephone industry, have the ability to provide high-speed service up to data rates of perhaps 100 million bits a second without requiring any substantial rebuilding or reinstallation of the last thousand feet of their networks.

Comparing the Costs

Two of the significant cost elements, the modem in the home and the connection to the Internet, should be almost identical. Typically, both dig-

16. See for example the data sheet on the Alcatel speed touch home external ADSL modem for the residential market (www6.alcatel.com/products/productsummary.jhtml?_dargs=%2fcommon%fopg%2fproducts%2finclude%2fproductbrief.jhtml_a&_dav=%2fx%2fopgproduct%2fspeed_touch_home.jhtml).

ital subscriber lines and cable modems are built as small boxes with connections for electric power to local computers and to the communications network. Retail prices for both cable and ADSL modems are in the $100–200 range. Similarly, the cost of connecting the aggregated traffic from a digital subscriber line or a cable modem service provider to the Internet should be roughly equal. The broadband service provider must also provide a connection to upstream capacity. A 45-million-bit-a-second connection to the Internet costs about $8,000 to $10,000 a month and should provide enough capacity to serve 1,000 users, meaning that this cost for each user is about $10.[17]

Estimating the cost of the transmission plant used by the two services is more difficult. In both cases, the added cost of using the transmission capacity is relatively small. A digital subscriber line uses part of the transmission capacity in the loop that once went unused. However, putting this service into a telephone cable does restrict some of the other uses that could be made of the cable, reflecting an opportunity cost of this capacity.

Converting a cable system from a one-way to a two-way operation requires adding extra hardware, but this extra hardware can support multiple services, not just high-speed Internet access. Of course, taking away the least valuable channel on a modern cable system imposes relatively little cost. Whatever service is implicitly displaced by the system's cable modem service may be of little value to most subscribers.[18]

The cost structures at the telephone company's central office and at the cable system's head end do differ slightly. The cable system's modem termination system and the telephone company's digital subscriber line access multiplexers are parallel units; they not only contain the modems that communicate with the modems on the customers' premises but also have routing and administrative capabilities. Installing a digital subscriber line requires that the customer's telephone line be connected to equipment that separates (splits) the voice telephone signal from the DSL signal. Each customer's DSL signal must then be routed, via a pair of wires, to the access multiplexer. These wires must be manually installed for each customer. In contrast, the upstream signals from consumers of cable modem

---

17. The number of users served depends upon the average traffic for each user. Users are not active all the time, and when they are, are not always downloading web pages. A forty-five-megabit-a-second connection would provide average capacity of forty-five kilobits a second to each of 1,000 users—probably more than enough for typical web browsing and e-mail. However, if 100 of those 1,000 users are running the popular Morpheus or Napster servers, then the system will be overloaded.

18. See Thomas Hazlett, this volume.

service are combined into a single electrical signal. No physical rewiring is required at the head end for an added cable modem customer.

The cost of an access multiplexer is determined by the number of customer lines it serves. In contrast, the cost of a cable modem termination system is determined by the volume of traffic it carries. If each customer line generates the same level of traffic, then these two measures will be identical. Currently, access multiplexers and termination systems cost about $30 to $100 for each subscriber, depending upon the size of the system and the features purchased. The two biggest nonrecurring hardware costs are for the modems at each end of the broadband access link. These modems are electronic devices and should be expected to follow the same declining cost curves that have been seen in other electronic devices.

The remaining costs of digital subscriber line and cable modem service (such as the costs of marketing, installation, and customer support) are likely to be similar across the two platforms. Improved hardware and software should reduce the costs of installation and customer support.

The Recent History of Broadband Technology

Some people assert that digital subscriber lines and cable modems are relatively old technologies.[19] In fact, the progress of microelectronics has controlled their development. That is not to say that other developments were not also important, but modern high-speed modems require enormous arithmetic processing power. Modern modems process signals in digital rather than analog form—sampled data replaces currents and voltages, and arithmetic replaces capacitors, resistors, and inductors. The general technique is called digital signal processing. Implementation of a modern modem design for an asymmetric digital subscriber line requires a processor capable of performing a few hundred million instructions a second.[20] The development of such modern systems had to wait for the development of

19. "DSL technology . . . had been collecting dust on the shelves and in the warehouses of the Bell Companies for over six years." Testimony of Charles J. McMinn, "On the Internet Freedom and Broadband Deployment Act of 2001," House Committee on Energy and Commerce, April 25, 2001. "Although DSL technology was well known to the Bells and GTE, they let it sit on the shelf." Testimony of John Windhausen Jr., Hearing before the House Telecommunications Subcommittee on the Deployment of Broadband Technologies, May 25, 2000. Both assertions are misleading if not totally in error.

20. The Texas Instruments TNETD2200 ADSL Transceiver can perform 1,600 million instructions a second and supports two ADSLs when used as part of an access multiplexer. Thus with this specific digital signal processing architecture, a single line requires between 500 million and 800 million

semiconductor technology, which could implement at reasonable cost the complex designs required to wring data capacity out of the recalcitrant medium created by old telephone cables designed for voice signals.

The problems in implementing effective cable modems were similar, and today's cable modems are also based on digital signal processing cores capable of hundreds of millions of instructions a second. Development of the standard for data-over-cable-service interface specifications facilitated competitive markets in the supply of equipment and made it easier for consumers to invest in cable modems, knowing that they could reuse the modems if they moved. Figure 5-5 illustrates the decline in the price of cable modems; figure 5-6 shows the evolution of the price of modems for ADSL service.

The timing of standardization activities affected the timing of widespread residential deployment. The process of setting a standard (data-over-cable-service interface specifications) started in 1995 and delivered a standard in 1996.[21] The American National Standards Institute adopted the ADSL standard in 1995.[22] Examining the record makes it clear that asymmetric digital-line service and cable modem service could not have been deployed significantly earlier unless consumers were willing to pay equipment and service prices closer to $500 a month than the current $40 to $50 a month.

Limitations

Both cable television and telephone network high-speed access have significant limitations.

Cable

The shared downstream path in cable systems limits the use of a cable modem system for bandwidth intensive services such as streaming media. Telephone systems also have shared media, typically the connection from the central office back to the Internet. However, capacity on the telephone company's backhaul can be expanded at relatively low cost. For cable com-

---

instructions a second. If an ADSL required fewer than 500 million instructions a second, then this device could support three such lines. A modem chip set for an ADSL offered by Texas Instruments in 1998 could perform more than a billion mathematical operations a second. See Texas Instruments product bulletin SPAT007.

21. CableLabs, "Cable Industry Issues Specification for High-Speed Data Delivery," Anaheim, California, December 11, 1996.

22. ANSI T1E1 T1.413–1995, now replaced by T1.413–1998.

Figure 5-5. *Cable Modem Prices, 1990–2000*[a]

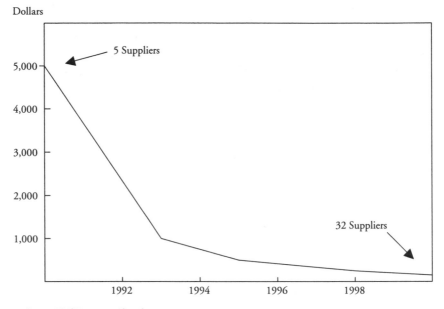

Dollars

Source: Neil Ransom, Alcatel.
a. Data are illustrative, not exact.

panies to double their streaming capacity, they must double the number of neighborhood nodes in the hybrid fiber-coaxial cable network or give up some of their video capacity. Doubling the number of nodes is expensive. However, as digital cable rolls out, transferring a significant fraction of the cable system's capacity from carrying video to carrying data may be possible with little curtailment of service.

Not every cable system can immediately deploy cable modem service. Rather, the cable system has to be upgraded to two-way capabilities. The shared downstream path also presents possible privacy problems. When the equipment is set up correctly, the encryption in the data-over-cable-service interface specifications should adequately protect a consumer. However, mistakes in the configuration of the encryption equipment can make traffic vulnerable to interception.

Telephone Network Systems

The biggest problem for high-speed access over the telephone network arises from the fact that a significant fraction of telephone loops are fairly

Figure 5-6. *Prices of Modems for Asymmetric Lines, 1990–2000*[a]

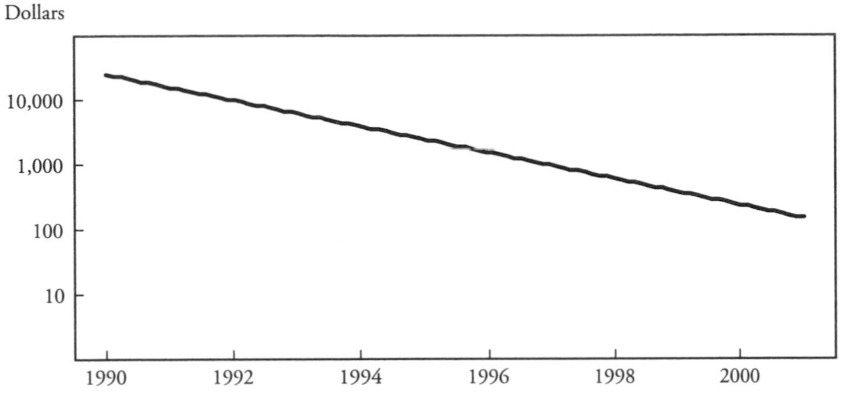

Dollars

Source: Author, using data points from Amati Prelude Modem, Computer Design, and Davis (1996).
a. Data are illustrative, not exact.

long and, consequently, cannot support extremely high speeds. Some loops will not support high-speed services at all. If telephone companies find that they need to increase the data speed delivered to all consumers, they must install remote terminals in order to shorten the length of the longest loops. In addition, the installed modems for asymmetric digital subscriber lines will not support the highest data rates made possible by shorter loops. Hence upgrading to the next step—to a version called very-high-speed digital subscriber loops—will require upgrading electronics in the home. In contrast, the cable industry does not face a change in home electronics if it makes comparable network upgrades.

Regulation also burdens telephone companies' provision of high-speed services. The Federal Communications Commission (FCC) has imposed on the incumbent local exchange carriers the obligation to permit others to install digital subscriber line equipment at the central office and to connect to the local carriers' loops. This obligation creates the necessity for the systems installed by these carriers and by new entrants to be compatible. Telephone loops (also called wire pairs) are bundled together into larger cables, made up of hundreds of wire pairs. Electrical energy leaks from a wire pair to nearby pairs in a cable. The services carried over wire pairs in the cable must be chosen or designed so that this energy leakage does not create unacceptable interference. Some of the new entrants providing digital services over the loops of incumbent carriers have already asked the FCC to consider limiting the incumbents' use of some older technologies that are not good neighbors in the cable to the current generation of equipment. The FCC, supporting the new entrants without quite ordering the incumbent carriers to change their equipment, says, "We strongly believe that industry should discontinue deployment of well-recognized disturbers, such as AMI T1. We further believe carriers should, to the fullest extent possible, replace AMI T1 with new and less interfering technologies. In the accompanying NPRM, we seek comment on methods by which to reduce or eliminate the deployment of AMI T1."[23]

Restating without the industry jargon, the FCC says that some technologies, long used by the incumbent carriers, should be eliminated in order to make life easier for firms using the incumbents' lines. Suppose that Lucent or Nortel develops a new technology that substantially expands the useful capacity of telephone cables. Suppose further that the new technology is incompatible with the use of current-generation digital subscriber lines in the same cable. If the incumbent carrier were the only firm using the cable, then the decision to adopt this new technology would be a decision to be made inside the firm. The carrier would trade off the benefits of the new technology against the costs of obsolescence. But in the unbundled-loop environment, one firm may get benefits while another firm bears some of the costs. In this environment, the incumbent will face substantial political constraints, which may prevent it from adopting the new technology. Of course, such an alternative is unlikely to happen. Equipment manufacturers are well aware of the situation and would be unlikely to invest in developing a technology that was difficult for incumbent carriers to adopt. Thus one result of the current unbundling is to restrict or redirect the innovation process for telephone equipment.

The unbundling obligations imposed by state and federal regulators also create market uncertainties. For example, SBC is deploying the technology for asymmetric digital subscriber lines from many of its remote terminals using next-generation digital loop carriers.[24] Competitors have asked regulators to allow the competitors to install their own equipment in SBC's remote terminals and even to place their own line cards in SBC's digital subscriber line access multiplexers. Installation of such competitor

23. FCC, First Report and Order, CC Docket 98-147 (June 15, 1999), para. 74 (www.fcc.gov/bureaus/common_carrier/orders/1999/fcc99048.txt [April 4, 2002]).

24. "SBC Launches $6 Billion Initiative to Transform It into America's Largest Single Broadband Provider," SBC, San Antonio, October 18, 1999.

equipment in next-generation digital loop carriers may alter the economics of the carriers' rollout. Such competitor equipment also becomes a fixed cost that will be protected by political means rather than efficiently traded off against other investments by SBC. Thus for example if SBC were to choose to split the region served by a digital-line concentrator into four smaller regions served by an even more advanced concentrator, competitors whose equipment would also need to be updated might well object to SBC's action. Such controversies might cause the incumbent carrier to delay its investment in asymmetric digital subscriber line technology or to abandon it entirely.

Demand

There was a time when 56 kilobits a second was considered high speed. The original high-speed office networking, Ethernet, ran at 10 megabits a second. Ethernet has been upgraded twice. Today, Ethernet cards that operate at gigabit rates over the standard Category 5 wiring used in many offices can be bought for less than $100.[25]

One can gain insight into residential demand by considering a few commonly used digital signals and objects. A medium-sized web page can be stored in 10,000 bytes. A web page with several complex embedded graphics may require 250,000 bytes. At 1 million bits a second, the 10-kilobyte web page will download in less that 0.1 seconds and the 250-kilobyte page in 2.0 seconds. A faster connection makes no significant difference for a person viewing the first web page. It may make a difference for the second web page, but that advantage will vanish as the connection speeds faster than 4 million bits a second. DVD-quality video requires about 10 million bits a second, high-definition television about 20 million bits a second. A compact disc can be transmitted over a 10-million-bit-a-second link in about ten minutes. So 50 million bits a second would support multiple live high-definition television (HDTV) channels or permit downloading a full compact disc in 2 minutes. It is difficult to imagine that households will be willing to pay significant premiums for data speeds in excess of about 20 million bits a second. But as the technology improves, the underlying cost for higher speeds will drop, new demands will develop, and households will be willing to spend for higher speed access.

25. These cards cheat. They use multiple wire pairs to gain the full 1,000-megabit-a-second capacity. But the transmission rate on each pair is a respectable 250 megabits a second. See IEEE Std 802.3, 2000 Edition (ISO/IEC 8802-3:2000[E]).

A second factor that may affect demand will be the move to integrated access. We operate separate voice and data networks today because high-speed data capabilities are being added to a network that already supports voice. At some point it will become economically efficient to combine voice traffic with data traffic and use a single, integrated, high-speed access service.[26] The adoption of integrated access service requires that high-speed access connections become as reliable as the telephone network is today. We also do not know how strongly consumers will value mobility. It may be that many will prefer to use wireless alternatives for most telephone calls.

Fixed Wireless and Satellites

Although wired systems appear to offer the most economical high-speed access for most consumers, there are important wireless alternatives. The term wireless encompasses satellite systems; cellular and personal computer services; multipoint, multichannel distribution bands; local point, multichannel distribution bands; and unlicensed bands. Unlike digital subscriber lines and cable modems, most of these technologies will require several years to develop and even longer to gain widespread use.

Satellite systems are the most widely used of the high-speed wireless options. Two firms, DirecPC and StarBand, provide two-way, satellite-based Internet access at data rates of about 400 to 500 kilobits a second.[27] Satellite firms appear to be targeting customers in rural areas who are not offered digital-line service or cable modem service. The next generation of satellite systems, due in orbit in about 2002 or 2003, will offer higher data rates and much more system capacity due to the use of spot beams.[28]

The FCC has licensed two radio services—the multipoint, multichannel distribution service and the local multipoint distribution service—that also can be used to provide wireless Internet access to fixed locations. The multipoint band is a radio service originally used to provide a wireless alternative to cable television. The technology can serve customers within a range of about fifteen miles of a base station and requires a line-of-sight path between the antenna at the residence and the antenna at the base station. The local

---

26. Crandall and Jackson (2001).

27. See (www.direct.com [March 21, 2002]) and (www.starband.com [March 21, 2002]).

28. For a description of one of these systems, Hughes Spaceways, see (www.hns.com/products/advanced_platforms/spaceway/inside_spaceway.htm [March 21, 2002]).

multipoint distribution service operates at frequencies ten times higher than those used by the multichannel, multipoint distribution service, so local point transmissions are strongly attenuated by rainfall.

Unlicensed radio bands provide yet another alternative for high-speed Internet access. The FCC has made several radio bands available for operation on an unlicensed basis, using low-power radios. Perhaps the best known of the unlicensed operators is Metricom, which offered its Ricochet service in several communities around the country. The original Metricom service ran at 56 kilobits a second; an improved version was being deployed that operates at 128 kilobits a second. (Metricom filed for bankruptcy in the summer of 2001.) A few hundred smaller Internet service providers have used unlicensed wireless to provide links to their customers. Typically, such systems run at data rates of about 1 million bits a second and can serve customers at ranges of up to about fifteen miles.[29] It is still unclear how successful unlicensed radio services can be for small business and residential Internet access. In rural areas, where the probability of interference is low, unlicensed radio may become a real competitor.

Short-range communications using wireless local area network (LAN) technologies are much less likely to suffer from interference than longer-range systems. There has been substantial interest in providing broadband Internet access at public points, such as airports and restaurants, using such technologies. For example, Starbucks has announced a program to put 11-million-bits-a-second wireless LANs in all 3,000 of its U.S. retail outlets.[30] Several airlines now provide wireless LAN connections in their airport lounges. These short-range services will probably not be used to provide access for homes or businesses, but they are an indication of the value that people attach to high-speed Internet access, and they will stimulate the adoption of high-speed Internet access more broadly.[31]

Conclusion

Cable and telephone systems can provide high-speed service at affordable costs to many—but not all—households. Some households will not

29. Several Internet service providers that use unlicensed radio channels for access are listed at (www.beagle-ears.com/lars/engineer/wireless/w-isp-list.htm [April 4, 2002]).

30. Bob Brewin, "Starbucks Takes Wireless Leap," ComputerWorld, January 8, 2001.

31. Some people envision a world in which many such short-range wireless LANs, by cooperatively sharing capacity and relaying messages to a backbone connection, could provide substantial Internet connectivity. See Flickenger (2001).

have the option to subscribe to wired high-speed access services because they are not near enough to either a telephone company providing asymmetric digital subscriber lines or a cable company providing cable modem service.

The ultimate architecture for high-speed access is unclear. Why would a residential user need access at speed greater than 100 million bits a second? Perhaps if such access is sufficiently inexpensive, consumers will buy it. Few could have believed a dozen years ago that households would use computer hard drives with capacities greater than 10 gigabytes. (The portable computer on which this chapter was written has a 20-gigabyte disk drive that is 75 percent full.)

Two important issues are not discussed above. One is the growth of home networking. Currently, homes have limited networks for voice and television and no network for data. The home telephone or power wiring can be used for data networking at speeds up to about 1 million bits a second. Wireless data networking, capable of speeds up to 10 million bits a second, now costs about $100 for each connection. The value of high-speed access is enhanced when that capability can be made available throughout the house via a home data network. Home networks are an important complement to high-speed access services. The second issue not considered is ease of use. Installing home networks that permit multiple computers to share a single high-speed access line is often difficult. Simplifying and automating equipment configuration will help with this task.

Larry Roberts, one of the pioneers of the Internet, has a time line of the Internet on his corporate website. Unlike most historical time lines, this one extends into the future as well. His entry for three years from now reads, "2005: The service quality and security on the Internet increases to the point where there is a major trend of both home and office users to use the Internet for their primary voice service, their high-quality television and radio service, as well as their data service. This trend will slowly eliminate all other communication nets like the current telephone network over the next decade."[32] Wired high-speed access will be an essential part of this evolution.

References

Crandall, Robert W., and Charles L. Jackson. 2001. "The $500 Billion Opportunity: The Potential Economic Benefit of Widespread Diffusion of Broadband Internet Access." *Criterion Economics*, July 16.

32. See (www.caspiannetworks.com/internethistory/timeline.shtml).

FCC (Federal Communications Commission). 2002. High-Speed Services for Internet Access: Status as of December 31, 2001.

Flickenger, Rob. 2001. *Building Wireless Community Networks: Implementing the Wireless Web*. Sebastopol, Calif: O'Reilly.

Green, Paul E., Jr. 1993. *Fiber Optic Networks*. Prentice Hall.

Starr, Thomas, John M. Cioffi, and Peter Silverman. 1999. *Understanding Digital Subscriber Line Technology*. Prentice Hall.

JERRY HAUSMAN

6 | *From 2G to 3G: Wireless Competition for Internet-Related Services*

Mobile (cellular) telephone is a relatively new product that has significantly affected how people live. Since its introduction in Europe and Japan in the early 1980s and in the United States in 1983, mobile telephone subscriptions have grown at about 25 to 30 percent a year. By the end of 2000 about 110 million mobile telephones were in use in the United States (see figure 6-1). More than 40 percent of Americans now use cellular telephones, and there are about 80 percent as many cellular telephones in the United States as regular (wire-line) telephones. Cellular penetration rates in Europe are significantly higher, with the penetration in a number of countries exceeding 60 percent and the number of mobile telephones often exceeding the number of wire-line telephones. Thus consumers and businesses find the mobile telephone to be one of the most significant innovations since 1950.

When mobile telephone began operation in the United States in 1983–84, the Federal Communications Commission (FCC) licensed two analogue providers in each large metropolitan statistical area. This analogue service is now referred to as 1G, or first-generation, service.[1] Beginning in 1996 the next-generation cellular technology was introduced in the United

Y. K. Kim provided helpful information on Korean telecommunications.

1. Analogue service used radio transmission similar to that used on the traditional wire-line network. Transmission voice quality improved markedly when second-generation, or digital, technology began operation.

Figure 6-1. *Cellular Subscribers, 1985–2000*

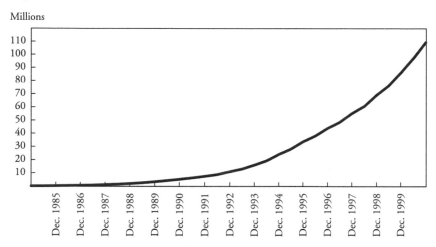

Millions

Source: CTIA (2001) (www.wow-com.com/2).

States when the FCC auctioned off a significant amount of additional spectrum. The carriers adopted digital technology, which is often called 2G, or second-generation, technology. As a result of the introduction of 2G, U.S. consumers have a choice among five or more mobile providers in most locations. Verizon Wireless (a joint venture between Verizon and Vodafone), AT&T Wireless, Sprint PCS, Cingular (a joint venture between SBC and Bell South), Voicestream, and Nextel all offer nationwide networks. Many other companies offer local or regional services.

Although mobile telephone has been a great success in the United States, it has been even more successful in other countries (figure 6-2). In Finland, Sweden, and Japan mobile penetration has now surpassed regular telephone (wire-line) penetration. The greater success of mobile services in Europe and Japan is explained in part by the higher monthly price for local wire-line telephone service, particularly when one includes the charges for local calls. Thus mobile is less expensive relative to wire-line service in these countries than in the United States.

In addition, in Europe and Australia a single 2G digital mobile standard was adopted, while in the United States three standards are in use, making the use of mobile telephones in nonlocal regions (called roaming) less convenient. Also, Europe and much of Asia have adopted a calling-party-pays framework, so that incoming calls to mobile telephones are not charged to the recipient of the calls. In the United States the recipient pays,

Figure 6-2. *Cost of Mobile Service for Consumers, Twenty-Nine Countries, August 2000*[a]

U.S. dollars

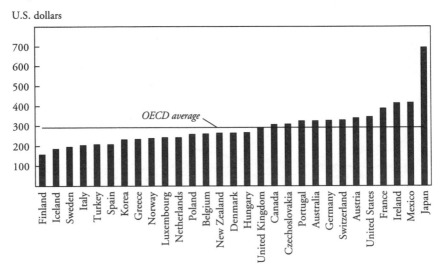

Source: OECD (2001a, 2001b).
a. The basket includes fifty minutes a month and excludes international calls. The OECD average is US$300.

resulting in less usage and a much lower proportion of mobile calls.[2] Finally, European and Japanese mobile services have employed more innovative marketing than have U.S. carriers. For example, prepaid calling cards have been highly successful in Europe, especially among young people.[3] In Japan NTT DoCoMo has introduced Internet-convenient mobile telephones, which have a special appeal to young people.[4] Indeed, mobile companies worldwide are attempting to develop technology that will allow convenient combined use of mobile telephone and the Internet.

Given that the mobile telephone and the Internet are the two outstanding telecommunications developments since 1950, one might ques-

2. In the United States many mobile telephone subscribers do not give out their mobile telephone number because they have to pay for incoming calls. However, this policy seems to be changing as more mobile subscribers use so-called bucket plans—buying a large number of minutes per month of mobile usage.

3. In many European countries (for example, Italy and the United Kingdom) greater than 80 percent of new subscribers are using prepaid service. In the United States only about 6 percent of subscribers use prepaid service. (Information supplied by carriers.)

4. In the first fourteen months after its introduction NTT DoCoMo's I-mode telephone, which connects to the Internet, achieved approximately a 5 percent penetration among the Japanese population. See *Wall Street Journal,* April 17, 2000, p. A25.

tion whether they will supplant wire-line telephone service. Modern digital mobile telephones are convenient to use, have good voice quality, are moderately secure, and the cost of using them is decreasing rapidly (see figure 6-3). Cellular rates in the United States declined rapidly after the removal of regulation in 1995 and the entry of the new providers in 1996. For example, carriers now offer monthly packages that cost approximately $0.10 to $0.15 a minute for combined local and long-distance service when large bundles of minutes are purchased. With a monthly landline residential subscription price that averages $20 a month and long-distance calls priced at approximately $0.07 to $0.09 a minute, landline telephone is still less expensive than mobile for most callers but lacks the convenience of anytime-and-anywhere service through a single number.[5] However, mobile prices would not have to fall too much farther before they could begin to have a significant substitution effect on landline telephone usage. Indeed, in a number of countries mobile usage has begun to supplant wire-line subscriptions.

Long-distance and local wire-line usage is already declining in countries in which consumers face charges for local calls. However, wire-line telephone service offers broadband (high-speed) Internet service, which mobile 2G technologies cannot currently offer. Current mobile technology has an upper range of about 19 kilobits a second, which is considerably slower than current wire-line narrowband connection speeds of 56 kilobits a second. Broadband wire-line connections are typically at speeds above 300 kilobits a second, with top speeds in the range of about 1.5–2.5 megabits a second. Thus although current mobile 2G technology provides a substitute for wire-line voice services, 2G cellular does not provide a substitute for data services. In the next several years third-generation (3G) wireless services may provide an adequate data substitute. If they do, the need for regulation for wire-line service is likely to disappear, along with the numerous economic distortions that such regulation creates.[6]

Broadband services for residential customers and small businesses are currently provided by digital subscriber lines (DSL) using traditional incumbent local exchange carriers, by broadband using competitive local exchange carriers, and by cable modems using hybrid fiber-coaxial cable networks operated primarily by cable television operators. In a number of countries, incumbent local exchange carriers are required to share their networks with

5. Each month a typical large user makes local calls totaling about 500 to 600 minutes, so the charge is still significantly less than mobile.

6. For research on these distortions, see Hausman (1998, 1999a, 1999b, 2000, forthcoming).

Figure 6-3. *Cellular Average Price Index, 1985–2001*[a]

Index, 1985 = 1.0

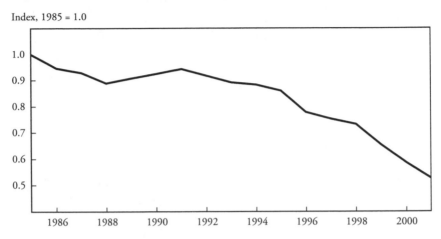

Source: Survey of cellular prices in the top thirty metropolitan statistical areas, 1985–98, from Hausman (1999b); Bureau of Labor Statistics (2001).

a. 2001 data are year to date.

competitive local exchange carriers through unbundling rules at prices set by regulation. However, cable providers have not been required to share their networks. This is an example of asymmetric regulation, a regulatory approach that has created significant economic distortions and has helped cause the bankruptcy of a number of broadband competitive local exchange carriers.[7]

In this chapter I analyze the potential of the next-generation (3G) wireless and consider whether future competition from this innovation could make the regulation of wire line unnecessary. But first I discuss the extent of 2G wireless substitution for wire-line voice service across countries and contemplate the added features that 3G technology offers.

Substitution of Cellular Voice Services for Wire-Line Voice Services

The voice quality of digital cellular voice service is already high, nearly equal to the quality of traditional wire-line telephone service.[8] For voice

7. See Hausman, chapter 7, this volume.

8. First-generation (1G) cellular is the original analog technology, which had voice quality significantly below wire-line quality. Second-generation (2G)—digital—technology is provided by GSM, CDMA, TDMA, and iDEN.

usage, cellular also has the advantage of mobility and a single number at which a person can be reached anytime and anywhere. As a result, substitution of cellular for wire line is beginning to be evident in wire-line usage data in countries such as Australia, which has current mobile penetration of about 53 percent.[9]

The Australian Data

Australia, unlike the United States, has a charge for local calls of about $0.20 a call.[10] As a result, mobile companies have begun to offer special local calling plans, which are competitive with this local calling fee. Hutchison, which markets under the Orange brand and has been highly successful in the United Kingdom and elsewhere, offers Orange One service, a combination of mobile and local service. Local calls made from a home zone are charged $0.15 and are untimed. Incoming calls from a fixed wire-line number have no termination charges, thereby eliminating the calling-party-pays framework.[11] The Australian data suggest that mobile services compete with fixed, wire-line services:

—Local calls using fixed access lines decreased by 1 percent a year between December 1997 and December 2000, from 95.5 a month to 94.1 a month.[12]

—The mobile customer base doubled over this period, from 27 percent to 53 percent of the population (see figure 6-4). Growth in mobile lines averaged 25 percent; that of Telstra's fixed-access lines was only 2.8 percent a year. The number of mobile services in operation, at 10.4 million, is approximately equal to—and beginning to surpass—the number of fixed lines.

—Growth in mobile, originating-call minutes was approximately 28 percent a year, whereas growth in fixed-to-fixed national long-distance minutes declined from 4 percent to 1 percent over those years.

Given the robust growth of the Australian economy over the same period (per capita gross domestic product growth of 3.6 percent a year) and a likely income elasticity of approximately 1, the decrease in the growth of fixed wire-line long-distance calls is especially noteworthy.[13] Only if wire-

9. The penetration of mobile and wire-line phones in Australia is now approximately equal.

10. Local calls are untimed. Dollar amounts used are in A$ (about US$0.50).

11. The calling party does pay the usual wire-line amount for the call (www.orange.net.au).

12. Based on traffic data in Telstra (1999–2000).

13. Income elasticity is based on U.S. empirical studies. For an evaluation of income elasticities for long-distance service, see Taylor (1994, pp. 265–66). Also see (www.rba.gov.au).

Figure 6-4. *Mobile Penetration Rate, Australia, 1997–2000*

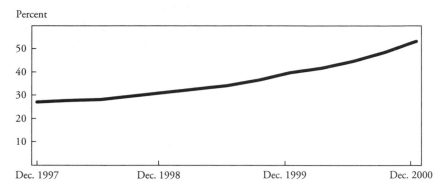

Percent

Source: Communications Research Unit, Department of Communications, Australia.

line long-distance prices increased or Internet telephony increased substantially could this decrease in growth be explained other than by significant mobile substitution. However, since long-distance prices decreased by about 16.1 percent between 1997 and 1999, or 5.7 percent a year, the evidence points toward mobile substitution for fixed long-distance calls.[14] Given an estimated price elasticity of –0.55, the expected growth rate of fixed long distance is 6.8 percent a year; the actual growth rate is 1 percent a year.[15]

The Communications Research Unit of Australia's Department of Communications finds similar evidence of mobile-for-fixed substitution for local calling (see figure 6-5).[16] Between 1997 and 2000 local calls for each access line on Telstra's fixed-line network decreased by 1 percent a year, from 95.5 a month to 94.1 a month, even though the price of local calls was decreasing.[17] The report finds that "local call prices declined by an average of 18 percent between 1999 and 2000, but the distribution of the declines was uneven." Over the 1998–2000 period, the number of local calls for each access line for residential users significantly decreased (more than 15 percent for capital city residential users). Revenue per call and revenue per access line for residential users also decreased by more than 15 percent.

14. ACCC (2000, p. 19).

15. Price elasticity estimate from "Review of Price Controls" (1998, p. 99). The corresponding elasticity estimated for the United States is –0.73, which would lead to an even higher expected growth rate.

16. Report by Collins, McCutcheon, and Osiowy (2001).

17. Based on data comparing local calls for each access line in fiscal year 1998–99 and in fiscal year 1999–2000. See Telstra (1999–2000).

Figure 6-5. *Consumption and Expenditure, Residential Local Calls, Australia, 1997–2000*

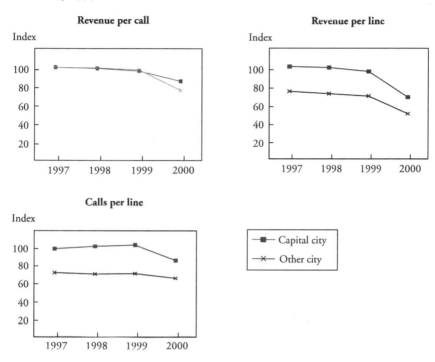

Source: Author's calculations based on data from the Communications Research Unit, Department of Communications, Australia.

The report suggests that the decline in local calling per access line was due to substitution of mobile for fixed services. "Residential users made fewer local calls per line in 2000 than 1999. The decline in the average number of local calls per line is most likely to have been partly due to the substitution of mobile telephony for local calls."[18] The data also demonstrate that fixed-line local calls are decreasing faster in large cities, a pattern that is consistent with the greater penetration of mobile telephones in these areas.

The Korean Data

Mobile penetration has also grown rapidly in Korea, to about 58 percent of the population. As a result, mobile penetration now exceeds

18. Collins, McCutcheon, and Osiowy (2001, p. 21).

wire-line penetration.[19] Between 1999 and 2000 (the last year for which data are available) fixed local calls, which are charged for in Korea, decreased by 16.1 percent, from 78.1 billion to 65.5 billion, and long-distance calls decreased from 13.5 billion to 12.2 billion, a decrease of 9.6 percent. Over the same period, mobile usage increased by 49.6 percent, and the price of mobile calls fell relative to the price of wire-line calls, which is consistent with a significant substitution from wire-line to mobile calling.

Data for the United Kingdom and the Republic of Ireland

Although survey data are not as good as usage data, they demonstrate significant and increasing substitution of mobile usage for wire line usage. Survey evidence published by the British regulator, Oftel, shows the percentage of mobile subscribers who substitute mobile calling for fixed-line calling in certain situations and attributes this phenomenon to the convenience and lower price of mobile usage.

> About half of U.K. adults . . . have both a fixed and mobile phone (dual-users). Only three in ten dual-users . . . were not substituting fixed phone usage with mobile. . . . Almost one in ten (8 percent) of these dual-users considered their mobile rather than their fixed line to be their main phone. . . .
>
> Six percent of U.K. homes . . . use mobiles instead of fixed phones, mainly a result of the flexibility and ability to control costs offered by prepay mobiles. These homes are spending as much each month on their mobile usage as other mobile owners and almost as much as the average fixed-phone owners spend. . . . Four in five of these mobile-only consumers use prepay packages, higher than the average 64 percent. Preference for the flexibility and convenience that mobiles offer, particularly prepay in relation to managing costs, are the main drivers behind this trend.[20]

In the Republic of Ireland wire-line minutes decreased by 1 percent between June 2000 and June 2001, as only Internet (narrowband) use was growing.[21] Non-Internet wire-line minutes, including international long distance, declined by about 18 percent. Over the same period, mobile penetration grew significantly, to 70 percent of the population, well in excess of wire-line penetration.

19. Data as of November 2000. See Korea Ministry of Information and Communication (www.mic.go.kr). Other Korean data from (www.rapa.or.kr).

20. Office of Telecommunications (2000).

21. Office of the Director of Telecommunications Regulation (2001).

The U.S. Data

Data on substitution of mobile for wire line in the United States is more difficult to analyze, because most residential usage (apart from New York City) is untimed (local calls being "free" after payment of a monthly fee). Nevertheless, the data demonstrate that the growth rate of wire lines has decreased significantly. After a period of growth from 1988 to 1999 (about 3.5 percent a year), the number of residential lines decreased slightly between 1999 and 2000 (by about 0.3 percent).[22] Between 2000 and 2001 the number remained approximately constant (Verizon at 62.9 million and SBC at 61.3 million).[23]

Although the growth in mobile telephone usage is likely one cause of this decrease in residential access lines growth followed by an absolute decline, there are other causes, such as a reduction of second residential lines previously used for Internet access as consumers shift to digital subscriber lines or cable modems.

Mobile Use and Wire-Line Prices

To determine if mobile service is a substitute for fixed wire-line service, one needs to analyze whether fixed-line operators could profitably increase the price of a local call. To measure the potential competitive effect of the growth of mobile usage on wire-line prices, assume that the price of a fixed wire-line local call is $0.20. Suppose one wants to determine if price is as much as 5 percent above the competitive level. What percentage of subscribers would need to shift to make the current price uneconomic? The critical share loss, which just makes the 5 percent price above competitive level unprofitable, follows from the equation:[24]

$$Q_2 (1.05p - c) = Q_1 (p - c),$$

where Q_1 is the quantity sold before the price increase, Q_2 is the quantity sold after the price increase, p is the price before the price increase, and c is marginal cost.

Using a U.S. estimate for marginal costs and converting these costs to Australian currency, c would equal A$0.038. Solving, find $Q_2 / Q_1 = 0.941$.

---

22. FCC (1999–2001).

23. These carriers are by far the largest incumbent local exchange carriers in the United States, with more than 75 percent of all access lines. 1999 and 2000 data from company 10-Ks; 2001 data from 10-Qs.

24. Also see appendix 6A, and Hausman, Leonard, and Vellturo (1996).

Thus if 5.9 percent of Australian consumers shifted their local calls from fixed to cellular service, an attempted price increase would not be profitable.[25] For long-distance calls the marginal cost is well below the price of the calls; therefore, for an attempted 5 percent price increase, only a relatively small amount of usage would need to shift to make the increase unprofitable.

In the United Kingdom, mobile use for local calls that replace fixed-line calls appear to be approaching this range. Thus one could conclude that mobile is currently constraining wire-line prices, or nearly so. As mobile calls become less expensive relative to wire-line calls, this constraint should become even more important. Thus only a relatively small share of wire-line usage needs to shift to wireless usage to have a significant constraining effect on wire-line pricing. Once a significant constraining effect exists, the need for wire-line regulation begins to disappear.

However, current 2G mobile service is not an adequate substitute for wire-line Internet usage for either narrowband or broadband Internet content. Advances in 2.5G mobile service are likely to make mobile service approximately equivalent to narrowband Internet access. An important issue remains: whether wire-line service will need to continue to be regulated because of its ability to provide broadband Internet access.

From 2G to 3G

Broadband Internet access over 2G (or 2.5G) cellular service is not competitive with either digital subscriber lines or cable modems. Will 3G cellular service be competitive? That is, will it deliver sufficient speed to provide broadband Internet access? A summary of the several generations of the technology is presented in table 6-1.

The mobile communications industry has evolved in three stages, from analog (1G) through digital (2G) to broadband (3G). Both 1G and the early implementations of 2G mobile systems were designed for circuit-switched services. Wire-line voice calls use circuit-switching technology, which establishes a link for the duration of the call. By contrast, 3G systems use packet-switching technology, through which the information is split into separate but related packets before being transmitted and reassembled at the receiving end. Packet-switched data formats are much more common than their circuit-switched counterparts, the best example

---

25. For slightly higher or lower values of marginal cost, the percentage changes little.

Table 6-1. *Generations of Technology and Service*

Generation	Type	Year	Description
1G	Analog	1980s	Voice centric, multiple standards
2G	Digital	1990s	Voice centric, multiple standards; data at 9.6 kilobits a second; short message service; e-mail
2.5G	Higher-rate digital	2001	High-speed circuit-switched data, 14.4–43.2 kilobits a second; general packet radio service; 10–115 kilobits a second and enhanced data rates for global evolution; 144 kilobits a second for mobile; 384 kilobits a second for stationary
3G	Digital broadband	2001–03	Voice- and data-centric, single standard, with multiple modes; maximum data rates from 144 kilobits a second (high-speed mobile) to 2 megabits a second (stationary)

being the Internet Protocol. The Internet is packet based, and it is expected that most 3G applications will be Internet based. Packet-switched systems also have an always-on characteristic, so data can be sent or received at any time in a manner similar to that provided by digital subscriber lines and cable modems. The transition from 2G to 3G has resulted in hybrid circuit- and packet-based services; this hybrid is often referred to as 2.5G. The basic evolution has been

—Analogue 1G could be used only for voice calls.

—Digital 2G mobile phone systems added fax, data, and messaging services.[26] However data transfer speeds are at 19.6 kilobits a second, significantly slower than current wire-line, narrowband, data-transfer speeds of 56 kilobits a second.[27]

---

26. Short messaging services have become extremely popular in Europe and Asia, but they have not gained wide usage in the United States. Much of European usage is among young people, who purchase prepaid cards and who are quite price sensitive. This U.S. population has not used cellular to the extent that its European and Asian counterparts have.

27. Claims have been made that 2G networks can be upgraded to data speeds of 180 kilobits a second. See (WSJ.com [February 21, 2001]). Whether these speeds can be achieved outside a laboratory with reasonable economics is doubtful.

—Broadband 3G services add high-speed data transfer to mobile devices, allowing new video, audio, and other applications through mobile phones. Data transfer speeds are available up to two megabits a second, or 200 times higher than 2G and similar to the broadband data-transfer speeds of digital subscriber lines and cable modems. Voice capacity also increases significantly with 3G technology for a given amount of spectrum.[28]

Carriers are beginning to deploy 3G communications systems outside the United States. Indeed, NTT DoCoMo in Japan began service on October 1, 2001, offering voice, video, graphics, audio, and other information. Speeds of up to 2 megabits a second are achievable with 3G. Data transmission rates depend upon the environment in which the call is being made. Only in stationary environments will the highest data rates be available. For high mobility, data rates of 144 kilobits a second are expected to be available, a rate about three times the speed of today's wire-line narrowband modems. For stationary applications, a subscriber can use a universal appliance, such as an evolved laptop computer, in any place that has access to broadband.[29]

Next-generation wireless, or 3G, facilitates applications not previously available.[30] These applications range from web browsing to file transfer to home automation (remote access of, and control of, home appliances and machines). Because of bandwidth increase, these applications will be even more easily accessed with 3G than they are with interim technologies such as GPRS (2.5G). From an economic perspective, the question is whether sufficiently compelling applications will arise to generate the revenue required to fund the development of 3G networks. To date, 2G applications that attempt to offer web-based services such as wireless applications protocol have been unsuccessful, in part due to slow speed and small screen size. 3G services will have to overcome these problems. Little of 2G networks can be reused in 3G networks, so the cost of a 3G network is substantial.[31] The major uncertainty regarding 3G is whether it will achieve

---

28. In Japan the 3G communications system NTT DoCoMo began service on October 1, 2001. It offers voice, video, graphics, and audio. The firm expected to attract 150,000 customers (mostly business) in the first six months of 3G deployment. See "Joy of Text" (2001, p. 55).

29. Broadband stationary wireless networks are being deployed in airports and other locations using WiFi technology (802.11b standard technology). However, WiFi technology does not offer mobile applications.

30. Data speed for 2.5G is thirty kilobits a second (www.iii.co.uk/isa [May 18, 2001]).

31. In Norway one of the recipients of a 3G spectrum has returned the spectrum to the government (www.iii.co.uk/isa/ [August 13, 2001]). A number of European countries are considering allowing

speeds high enough and cheap enough to attract consumer demand.[32] To use 3G, users will need

—A mobile phone or terminal that supports 3G. To date, equipment manufacturers have encountered difficulties in producing terminals in sufficient numbers.[33]

—A subscription to a mobile telephone network that supports 3G. Automatic access may be allowed by some mobile network operators; others will charge a monthly fee and require a specific opt-in to use the service (as is done with other nonvoice mobile services).

—Knowledge of how to send and receive information using their model of mobile phone, including software and hardware configuration. This creates a customer service requirement.

—A destination to send or receive information.[34]

Third-generation mobile Internet technology represents a significant departure from earlier generations of mobile technology:

—People will look at their mobile phone as much as they hold it to their ear.

—Data (nonvoice) uses of 3G will be as important as, but different from, the traditional voice business. Indeed, data uses of 3G are crucial for the economic success of 3G because it offers only limited voice quality improvement over 2G networks.

—3G will be similar to 2G in its capability for fixed communications. Thus many people will likely have *only* a mobile phone or appliance. This last point is crucial for the evolution of competition in telecommunications.

Third-generation technology will offer voice and data services of similar (or better) quality than wire-line services. It is packet-switched

---

facilities to be shared among 3G service providers to lower required network construction costs. British Telecom and Deutsche Telekom plan to institute a policy of sharing 3G network facilities with the expectation of a 30 percent savings in investment costs (//news.ft.com/ft/gx.cgi/ftc? [September 21, 2001]).

32. Initial broadband deployment will be at speeds significantly below 2 megabits a second. (www.iii.co.uk/isa/ [September 6, 2001]). Reports suggest initial rollout speeds for 3G data of between 64 to 384 kilobits a second. Speed appears to be a significant issue regarding 3G performance. Vodafone has stated that the slower speed of 64 kilobits a second will occur only on the edge of coverage areas, while 384 kilobits a second will be the common speed at rollout. NTT DoCoMo's 3G service, introduced on October 1, 2001, has data speeds of 384 kilobits a second. (Data can be obtained from author.)

33. A similar equipment manufacturing problem has arisen for GPRS (2.5G).

34. Web pages need not be altered, as in current protocol applications (www.iii.co.uk/isa/ [May 18, 2001]).

technology with always-on capability. However, 3G mobile will have advantages over wire-line networks because it will offer a single number with high-speed data capabilities. Thus a 3G user will not have to navigate multiple networks when shifting from the workplace, to home, to traveling through and to airports and hotels. Security problems should decrease as well. However, cost and spectrum availability will be important factors in its adoption.

Spectrum Availability for 3G Technology

A number of European and Asian countries have already auctioned spectrum for 3G. The April 2000 auction in the United Kingdom raised approximately $35 billion for the government.[35] In August 2000 Germany completed its auction, raising approximately $46 billion.[36] A number of other European countries, such as the Netherlands and Italy, have also completed 3G auctions, as have Australia and Hong Kong. While spectrum prices have decreased from their earlier high levels, companies continue to bid for the spectrum and will begin the service in 2002–03.

The United States, on the other hand, is encountering difficulty in arranging an auction of spectrum for 3G, in part because of insufficient available spectrum. This problem has been created by regulation. The U.S. authorities (the FCC and the Department of Commerce) have given away spectrum and have specified its usage. As a result, large amounts of spectrum suitable for 3G are currently used by local governments and by the Defense Department. These government agencies have no incentive to use the spectrum in an economically efficient manner. Indeed, most local government use is extremely inefficient because it employs analog technology.[37] These government entities refuse to surrender some of their spectrum and claim they cannot afford to switch to more spectrum-efficient technology.

A market solution exists for this problem of contrived scarcity. An auction could be held for much of this spectrum. Local governments (and the

---

35. The United Kingdom reserved one of five frequency bands for a new entrant.

36. Per capita auction amounts for the United Kingdom and Germany are extremely close, with the United Kingdom slightly higher.

37. The shift from analog (1G) to digital (2G) technology in cellular led to an efficiency improvement of approximately 300–1,000 percent. Astoundingly, in its recent plan to shift ten channels of ultrahigh frequency television spectrum to other uses, the FCC reserved 40 percent of the spectrum for further local government use.

Defense Department) could compete in the auction as bidders, and a portion of the resulting auction proceeds could be returned to those government entities that currently use the spectrum.[38] The government entities could use the excess revenue (after buying considerably less spectrum than they currently use) to implement digital technology, which is much more spectrum efficient than the technology they currently use. This market approach to solving the spectrum problem is likely to lead to a more efficient outcome than that achieved by regulators. It is doubtful that the FCC can implement this economically efficient policy on its own. Therefore, congressional action is likely to be necessary.

Another problem unique to the United States involves earmarking the spectrum for small companies' personnel communications systems (PCS) (2G) and allowing the winning bidders to defer their payments for a number of years. This political favor has allowed a number of winning bidders to default on their payments to the U.S. government when it appeared that they had overbid for the spectrum and to try to keep the spectrum when they emerged from bankruptcy. The most notorious example is Nextwave.

The FCC auction rules, as interpreted by the bankruptcy court and subsequent appeals courts, gave Nextwave a free option, that is, the right but not the obligation to purchase the spectrum. Nextwave bid for the spectrum and then declared bankruptcy when it was unable to raise the necessary capital. If the price of the spectrum increases, as it has, Nextwave can sell the spectrum and realize a profit with little or no risk. If the price of the spectrum decreases, Nextwave could liquidate (chapter 7 bankruptcy), with no financial obligation to pay. It now appears that Nextwave may sell the spectrum for approximately $10 billion more than its winning bid if congressional approval can be obtained.[39] Thus the outcomes of the political favor by Congress are a huge windfall gain and enormous delays in using the spectrum. So even the auction process can be distorted by political interference.

Whether Congress and the FCC can solve the spectrum problem in the near term is problematical. Powerful vested interests, such as the Defense Department and local governments, are loath to give up their free spectrum. However, if 3G proves successful in other countries, this demonstration effect is likely to force a political solution, as happened with the original cellular technology, which began operation in Europe

---

38. The proportion returned to the government entities would be significantly less than one.
39. The Nextwave controversy was still mired in the courts as this book went to press.

significantly earlier than in the United States as the result of FCC inaction.[40] As with 1G cellular, delaying 3G in the United States will entail a welfare cost of billions of dollars a year and may cause U.S. suppliers of broadband content to suffer significant delays compared to European and Asian providers.

3G and the Regulatory Problem

Significant regulatory problems have existed in the United States since the AT&T divestiture in 1984. First, a federal district court judge controlled U.S. telecommunications for a decade. This experiment in judicial regulation was far from a success, as regulatory delays and the absence of residential long-distance competition cost consumers billions of dollars a year.[41] In 1996 Congress passed the Telecommunications Act of 1996, which was supposed to modernize the regulation of telecommunications. This objective has not been achieved, given that in late 2001 all but seven states were still lacking long-distance competition between local carriers and long-distance companies, a policy that every other country worldwide has adopted and that leads to lower prices for consumers.[42] Furthermore, most of the companies that entered local telecommunications to provide voice services, traditional data services, or competitive broadband services are in extreme financial difficulty, with a number of the largest now bankrupt or liquidated.[43]

The FCC's policy of asymmetric regulation of broadband, including incumbent local exchange carriers' wholesale rates for unbundled elements at levels that are below cost, has created severe regulatory distortions.[44] This latter policy is a principal cause of the economic disaster that has befallen the U.S. telecommunications industry—this and the failure to construct a more modern telecommunications infrastructure, as called for in the Telecommunications Act of 1996. This deficiency in infrastructure investment is an outcome of government regulation, a fact that FCC Chairman Michael Powell recognizes.[45]

40. See Hausman (1997) for a description of this delay and the subsequent welfare loss to U.S. consumers of billions of dollar a year.

41. See Hausman (1995, 1997); Hausman, Leonard, and Sidak (2002) for estimates of consumer welfare losses.

42. See Crandall and Hausman (2000) for an analysis of the Telecommunications Act of 1996.

43. See Hausman, chapter 7, this volume, for an analysis of these outcomes.

44. For a demonstration that such wholesale rates have been set below cost by regulators, see Hausman, (1997, 1999a).

45. Michael K. Powell, chairman of FCC, "Digital Broadband Migration," pt. 2, October 23, 2001 (www.fcc.gov/speeches/powell/2001).

3G cellular, which will be largely unregulated by the government, has the potential to solve the regulatory problem, the severe economic distortions, and the billions of dollars of annual losses in consumer welfare caused by telecommunications regulation. As the price of cellular continues to decrease and the younger generation matures, voice usage of mobile will become increasingly important. However, the wire-line network currently also provides Internet access, both narrowband and broadband, which 2G cellular cannot provide. Once 3G technology proves successful, it may provide sufficient competition to constrain wire-line providers and to eliminate government-induced distortions through its regulatory practices.

Competition and Regulation

Regulators attempt to direct a framework of regulated competition (an oxymoron), but the harm to consumers is easily in the tens of billions of dollars—if not hundreds of billions of dollars—a year.[46] Economists generally agree that the purpose of regulation is to correct market failure (in this case, the potential ability of a wire-line local exchange carrier to distort competition because of potential market power), not to favor competitors. Thus regulation is needed only to prevent the exploitation of market power.[47] A sufficient increase in competition from 3G mobile would likely remove the economic rationale for regulation of incumbent local exchange carriers.

As current and new mobile users become increasingly comfortable with forgoing wire-line telephone service, incumbent local exchange carriers will not have the potential to distort competition. Substitution of 3G for wire-line service will depend on features and price. However, substitution with 2G technology is already occurring in countries that do not subsidize local wire-line service to the same extent as in the United States. As prices for mobile continue to decrease, the substitution of wire line by mobile will increase because of the change in relative prices and demographics.

46. See Hausman (1997, 1998, 2000); Hausman and Shelanski (1999); Hausman, Leonard, and Sidak (2002) for quantitative estimates of consumer harm. Long-distance prices for residential customers and small businesses are estimated at 15–20 percent less if the regulatory restriction on the Bell operating companies' provision of long-distance service were eliminated.

47. Regulation might still be needed for universal service reasons. However, a tax system could solve this need. See Hausman (1998).

Note that, according to the critical share analysis discussed above, only a relatively small group of marginal customers needs to shift to mobile to create a competitive constraint on wire-line providers. A shift of perhaps as little as 10 percent would constrain the pricing behavior of wire-line carriers. However, given the experience of eliminating regulation of cellular in 1994, it is unlikely that regulators will eliminate their jobs. Despite evidence that state cellular regulation led to higher prices for consumers, it took an act of Congress to eliminate cellular regulation.[48] The self-interest of regulators seemingly takes precedence over the interests of consumers, as public choice theory suggests. However, it is still possible that a competitive outcome, absent regulation, is likely to occur, albeit with a longer lag than necessary.

The recent past of telecommunications is replete with new technology predictions that never succeeded. 3G mobile could be another example. In 2000–01 cellular providers paid hundreds of billions of dollars in auctions to purchase 3G spectrum.[49] In Europe mobile operators paid over $125 billion for 3G spectrum. Successful auctions for 3G spectrum took place in 2001 in Australia and other countries, although at lower prices. Thus market activity predicts that 3G technology will succeed. Numerous technological problems occurring in 2001—such as a lack of handsets and a variety of software problems—delayed deployment of 3G. British Telecom canceled a 3G rollout in the summer of 2001 because of these problems.[50] These problems are likely to be transitory events with little effect on the long-term outcomes.

Two developments are required for the widespread adoption of 3G mobile technology. First, sufficiently attractive applications need to be developed to cause people to shift from their current combined use of 2G mobile and wire-line narrowband (or digital subscriber lines or cable modems) to broadband Internet access. Second, 3G technology must provide broadband speeds. The market may solve the potential applications problem, even though uncertainty about broadband data speed remains. In addition, two conditions necessary for 3G to provide sufficient competition to the wire-line network to allow regulation to wither away are widespread deployment of 3G networks with broadband capabilities and sufficient spectrum to permit the deployment to occur.[51] With sufficient

48. See Hausman (forthcoming) for further discussion.
49. Hausman (forthcoming) discusses the auction results.
50. See (www.iii.co.uk/isa/ [May 14, 2001]).
51. Potential problems of decreased competition in rural areas might be handled by requiring uniform prices for residential customers for a transitory period.

spectrum and a full rollout of facilities, there would be no need for the continuation of wire-line regulation.

The End of Regulation?

Regulation has been a feature of U.S. telecommunications since the 1960s. Despite the technological changes over this period, regulators have failed both to promote a timely introduction to consumers of new technology and to allow telecommunications prices to reflect underlying costs. In addition, regulation-induced distortions in the U.S. economy have been extremely large. The one successful deregulatory episode in telecommunications is the deregulation of cellular created by congressional action in 1995. Cellular prices have decreased significantly since then.[52]

A similar outcome could occur in wire-line telecommunications if 3G is successful. The barriers to entry created by the significant sunk costs in constructing a competing wire-line network would not matter in a rapid-growth industry such as cellular telephony. Only a relatively small share of wire-line users, on the order of 10 percent, needs to shift to alternative technologies such as 3G (or cable networks) to provide a competitive constraint on wire-line providers such that regulation becomes unnecessary. The process could be lengthy and contentious, but the end of regulation may be a glimmer on the horizon, with potential gains to the economy in the tens of billions of dollars a year.

Conclusion

Widespread substitution of 2G mobile services for wire-line voice services is beginning in a number of countries. However, for Internet access, wire-line-based digital subscriber lines or cable modem access are essentially the only technologies available.

The potential outcome from the adoption of 3G technology could be to create conditions that would allow an end to telecommunications regulation. A combination of voice and data applications with mobility, broadband access, and always-on features is likely to be sufficiently attractive to a sufficient number of customers to provide a competitive constraint to wire line. This competitive constraint would make regulation redundant. Regulation

52. In the United Kingdom regulation of cellular continues, with significantly higher prices than in nonregulated countries such as the United States and Australia.

would then disappear, along with market distortion. This outcome would create a large gain in economic efficiency and consumer welfare.

Appendix 6A. The Relevant Product Market and Critical Share

The 1992 U.S. *Merger Guidelines* specify that relevant markets for merger analysis may be defined for classes of customers on whom a hypothetical monopolist of the merging firms' products would likely impose a discriminatory price increase.[53] The task of defining the relevant product market when price discrimination is not feasible involves identifying the smallest set of products for which a hypothetical monopolist could profitably raise price a "significant" amount (typically 5 percent) above the competitive level for a "nontransitory" period of time (normally assumed to be two years). Thus a potential market definition is too narrow if, in the face of a 5 percent price increase, the number of customers who would switch to products outside the market is large enough to make the price increase unprofitable.

Customers who decide not to purchase the product (or to purchase less of the product) at the increased price are "marginal" consumers. For small price increases, they switch from the products inside the putative market. Not all customers, however, are marginal customers. Indeed, in the typical case most customers would continue to purchase the product despite the higher price because their willingness to pay for the product exceeds the raised price. These customers are "inframarginal" consumers.

In the presence of high demand elasticity and high supply elasticity, a firm cannot exercise unilateral monopoly power by attempting to decrease its supply. Demand elasticity is captured by a customer's willingness to switch to competing suppliers as relative prices change. Thus a broad range of available substitutes implies a high own-price elasticity of demand. Following the same logic as the market definition criteria, the guidelines provide a concrete test for evaluating the competitiveness of a market as captured in the idea of market power, which is the ability of a single firm unilaterally to increase price above the competitive level for a nontransitory period of time.[54]

---

53. FCC (1992).

54. The *Merger Guidelines* emphasize own-price elasticity of demand, while other analyses focus on the cross-price elasticity of demand. But the two elasticity measures are closely related.

Because competition takes place at the margin, only a small proportion of the customers of the incumbent local exchange carrier need to defect to defeat its attempted price increase. It is possible to calculate that necessary proportion. Suppose that the local exchange carrier attempts to increase prices for end-user access by 5 percent. How much traffic would that carrier need to lose before the increase would be unprofitable? The formula to calculate that critical share is

$$Q_1 (p - c) < Q_2 (1.05p - c).$$

An important empirical fact for network elements is that fixed costs are a large component of the overall cost, so that marginal cost is a relatively small component. Assume, for example, that the ratio of marginal cost to price, c/p, is 0.2. Then Q_2 would be $0.94Q_1$, so that the critical share is 6 percent. Thus if the carrier were to attempt to raise its price by 5 percent, and if as a result it were to lose more than 6 percent of its traffic, the attempted price increase would be unprofitable and thus unilaterally rescinded.[55]

References

ACCC. 2000. "Telecommunications Charges in Australia." April.

Bureau of Labor Statistics. 2001. *Cellular Telephone Service Consumer Price Index, 1998 to 2001 (Year to Date).*

Collins, Peter, Marion McCutcheon, and Eve Osiowy. 2001. *Benefits to Consumers of Telecommunications Services in Australia, 1995–96 to 1999–2000.* Communications Research Unit, Department of Communications, Australia.

Crandall, Robert, and Jerry Hausman. 2000. "Competition in U.S. Telecommunications Services Four Years after the 1996 Legislation." In *Deregulation of Network Industries: What's Next?* edited by S. Peltzman and C. Winston. Brookings.

CTIA (Cellular Communications and Internet Association). 2001. "Semiannual Wireless Industry Survey." *Economist,* September 15.

FCC (Federal Trade Commission). 1992. *Department of Justice and Federal Trade Commission Horizontal Merger Guidelines.*

———. 1999–2001. *Statistics of Communications Common Carriers 1998; 1999; 2000.*

Hausman, Jerry. 1995. "Competition in Long-Distance and Equipment Markets: Effects of the MFJ." *Journal of Managerial and Decision Economics* 16:365–83.

———. 1997. "Valuing the Effect of Regulation on New Services in Telecommunications." *BPEA, Microeconomics*: 1–38.

———. 1998. "Taxation by Telecommunications Regulation." *Tax Policy and the Economy* 12:29–48.

---

55. For a more extensive discussion of critical share, see Hausman, Leonard, and Vellturo (1996).

————. 1999a. "The Effect of Sunk Costs in Telecommunication Regulation." In *The New Investment Theory of Real Options and Its Implications for Telecommunications Economics*, edited by James Alleman and Eli Noam, 191–204. Boston: Kluwer.

————. 1999b. "Cellular Telephone, New Products, and the CPI. "*Journal of Business and Economics Statistics* 17:188–94.

————. 2000. "Efficiency Effects on the U.S. Economy from Wireless Taxation." *National Tax Journal* 53:733–43.

————. 2001. "Competition and Regulation for Internet-related Services: Results of Asymmetric Regulation." Mimeo. MIT.

————. Forthcoming. "Mobile Telecommunications." In *International Handbook of Telecommunications,* edited by Martin Cave and others. MIT Press.

Hausman Jerry, Greg Leonard, and J. Greg Sidak. 2002. "Price Effects of BOC Provision of Long-Distance Service in New York and Texas." *Antitrust Law Journal* (forthcoming).

Hausman, Jerry, Greg Leonard, and Chris Vellturo. 1996. "Market Definition under Price Discrimination." *Antitrust Law Journal* 64:367–86.

Hausman Jerry, and Howard Shelanski. 1999. "Economic Welfare and Telecommunications Welfare: The E-Rate Policy for Universal Service Subsidies." *Yale Journal on Regulation* 16:19–51.

Hausman Jerry, and J. Greg Sidak. 1999. "A Consumer-Welfare Approach to the Mandatory Unbundling of Telecommunications Networks." *Yale Law Journal* 109:417–505.

"Joy of Text." 2001. *Economist,* September 13.

OECD (Organization for Economic Cooperation and Development). 2001a. *Communications Outlook, 2001.*

————. 2001b. *Basket of Consumer Mobile Telephone Charges.*

Office of the Director of Telecommunications Regulation (U.K.). 2001. *The Irish Communications Market Quarterly Review* (September 6).

Office of Telecommunications (U.K.) 2000. "Consumers' Use of Mobile Telephony: Summary of Oftel Residential Survey."

"Review of Price Controls on Telstra." 1998. *Access Economics* (August): 102.

Taylor, Lester. 1994. *Telecommunications Demand in Theory and Practice.* Boston: Kluwer.

Telstra. 1999–2000. Annual Reports.

Woroch, Glenn. 2001. "Demand, Competition, and Regulation of Fixed and Mobile Services." Mimeo. University of California, Berkeley.

JERRY HAUSMAN

7 | *Internet-Related Services: The Results of Asymmetric Regulation*

B roadband services for residential customers and small businesses are currently provided by digital subscriber lines (DSL) using traditional incumbent local exchange carriers, by broadband using competitive local exchange carriers, and by cable modems using hybrid fiber-coaxial cable networks operated primarily by cable television operators. In a number of countries, incumbent local exchange carriers are required to share their networks with competitive local exchange carriers through unbundling rules at prices set by regulation. However, cable providers have not been required to share their networks. This is an example of asymmetric regulation, a regulatory approach that has created significant economic distortions and has helped cause the bankruptcy of a number of broadband competitive local exchange carriers.[1]

This chapter explores the implications of asymmetric regulation and asks if it serves the interests of consumers, comparing the experience of Korea, a country without such a regulatory regime, with that of the United States. It also examines the experience of the competitive local exchange carriers in providing these services and their subsequent financial distress.

Research support from KIET is gratefully acknowledged. Dr. D. H. Lee and Mr. Y. K. Kim provided helpful information on Korean telecommunications. C. Miu and A. Sheridan provided excellent research assistance. The editors provided helpful suggestions.

1. A digital subscriber line is an asymmetric line through which data moves downstream at significantly faster speeds than it moves upstream. See Charles Jackson, this volume.

In addition, it addresses the effects on investors of asymmetric regulation. I begin with an examination of the recent experience of various countries in securing broadband access for their businesses and consumers.

Broadband Internet Access across Countries

Korea has by far the largest penetration of high-speed, broadband, Internet access, on a per capita basis, of any country. Korea had 4.32 million broadband Internet connections in November 2000, with about 64 percent using digital subscriber lines and the other 36 percent using cable modems.[2] Korea had 9.2 broadband Internet connections for every 100 inhabitants in 2000, or a penetration equal to 9.2 percent of its population. Canada was next, with a 4.5 percent penetration, and the United States was third, with a 2.2 percent penetration. Surprisingly, U.S. penetration was less than one-fourth that of Korea. Thus the runner-up countries were far behind Korea. Some advanced economies had extremely low penetration rates, such as Germany at 0.2 percent and the United Kingdom at 0.09 percent (see figure 7-1).

Korea has no unbundling requirements like those of the United States and Canada (to allow competitive local exchange carriers to compete with incumbent local exchange carriers). However, the United Kingdom and Germany do require network unbundling.[3]

Of course, important demographic differences exist among the countries. In Korea a high proportion of people live in apartments, which increases population density and decreases the cost of providing a wired telecommunications network.[4] However, Hong Kong, which also has a high proportion of people living in apartments, had a penetration ratio of only 3.5 percent.[5] Also, the United States, Canada, Germany, and the United Kingdom are among the richest countries as measured by per capita gross domestic product or income. They also have high computer pene-

2. Organization for Economic Cooperation and Development database. At the end of June 2001 the number of subscribers had increased to 6.25 million subscribers. See Korean Ministry of Information and Communication: (http://www.mic.go.kr [June 2001]).

3. Both the United Kingdom and Germany have high levels of computer penetration and narrowband Internet access.

4. For further discussion see W. Blois, "Broadband in a Time of Financial Crisis," talk given at IDATE conference, November 2001 (www.IDATE.fr).

5. Hong Kong OFTA, "Hong Kong: Fact Sheet 2000, Telecommunications" (www.ofta.gov.hk/frameset/press_index_eng.html [August 2000]). Hong Kong requires regulatory network unbundling.

Figure 7-1. *Broadband Connections per 100 Inhabitants, Eleven Countries, 1999*

Subscribers per 100 inhabitants

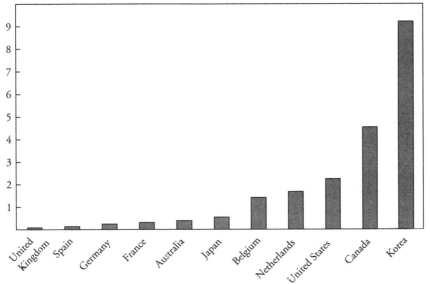

Source: OECD Telecommunications Database, 2001.

tration ratios, which should also increase demand for broadband Internet connections. Thus Korea being first in this area—and by a wide margin—is remarkable. An important factor may be that Korea does not have a regulatory requirement for network unbundling, as do the United States, the United Kingdom, and Germany.

An econometric investigation on penetration rates across countries for the years 2000 and 2001, using data on broadband penetration, the broadband access price, the narrowband access price, and gross domestic product per capita provides additional insights on the determinants of broadband penetration.[6] Included also is a variable for regulation, which equals 1.0 if the regulators require unbundling as in the United States, the United Kingdom, and Australia. Unfortunately, the sample is not especially large, with just twenty-six observations and even smaller subsamples for certain of the regressions. Overall, the findings are that broadband

---

6. I was unable to collect data on Internet subscriptions per capita. However, the use of gross domestic product per capita should control for this variable.

penetration depends significantly on gross domestic product per capita, with an elasticity of approximately 1.0.[7]

Neither the narrowband nor the broadband access prices are statistically significant, an outcome consistent with the fact that Korea, with by far the largest broadband penetration, had among the least expensive narrowband access prices and broadband prices higher than those in both Australia and Canada, which have significantly lower broadband penetration. (This comparison may no longer hold, as Korean broadband prices have since fallen.) The elasticity of broadband penetration with respect to broadband price is estimated at about −1.5 and is statistically significant at the 10 percent level. Another variable estimated to have an important (but not statistically significant) effect is regulation, which leads to a decrease in broadband penetration of approximately 70 percent. Thus per capita gross domestic product, broadband price, and regulation appear to have the largest effects on broadband penetration. However, given the small sample and the absence of strong statistical significance of the estimated coefficients, these results should be interpreted as suggestive, rather than as definitive.

Narrowband and Broadband Prices

It might be argued that narrowband (dial-up) Internet access is actually a close substitute for broadband access, so that focusing on broadband access alone is misleading.[8] Yet the two types of access and the services they support have important differences. Cable modems and digital subscriber lines offer access speeds about ten to thirty times higher than dial-up access. Many of the services supported by broadband connections are not available through narrowband connections. The demand for applications that can be supported only by high-bandwidth connections suggests that the product markets for narrowband and broadband access are distinct. A quantitative analysis of U.S. data supports this conclusion.[9]

Although the price of connection for broadband and narrowband access (when adding the price of a second line) may be similar, the quality-

7. This elasticity is estimated to be 1.16, the broadband access price is estimated to be −0.98, and the regulation variable is estimated to be −0.71. The R^2 of the regression is 0.32.

8. This section is taken largely from Hausman, Sidak, and Singer (2001b).

9. The estimated coefficient for narrowband access price has the incorrect sign in a number of the regression specifications.

adjusted price is not. In particular, a second line is not always "on," is subject to congestion, and cannot simultaneously support several broadband applications, such as streaming video and video conferencing. Second, many heavy Internet users who own a wireless telephone can avoid the cost of a second line.[10] If the choice to subscribe to wireless is made before the decision to obtain Internet access, as would seem likely for many Internet users, the monthly price of the wireless connection should not be included in the price of narrowband access. Third, if the price of a second telephone line should be included in the price comparison, then certainly the installation cost of a broadband connection (typically $150 for a cable modem) should be incorporated as well.[11] Under any reasonable comparison, the prices of broadband and narrowband access are different and hence support the notion of distinct product markets.

An additional indication that narrowband and broadband Internet access are in separate product markets arises from the "natural experiment" of individual states setting their own narrowband prices. The data demonstrate that prices of second telephone lines vary greatly across regulatory jurisdictions, while the price of broadband access remains relatively constant. These data support the hypothesis that narrowband access does not constrain the price of broadband access.[12]

The definition of the product market can also be established empirically. If it can be shown that narrowband prices (including the access charge plus the price of a second telephone line) do not constrain broadband prices, then a hypothetical monopoly provider of broadband access could more easily sustain a 5 percent price increase.[13] This would confirm the existence of a separate broadband market.

The econometric analysis is based on August 1999 price data from forty-one states and fifty-nine cable television multiple-system operators who were offering either @Home or Road Runner.[14] For cable subscribers, the broadband access price varied from $34.95 a month to $64.95 a

10. Many college students and singles with roommates reportedly use home telephone lines for their computer modems only and make voice calls on digital cellular telephones.

11. Some cable providers provide free or low-cost cable modems. Amortized over a thirty-six-month period, the results are not sensitive to whether the cable modem price is included.

12. Paul Rappoport, Donald Kridel, and Lester Taylor (this volume) also support the separate-market hypothesis.

13. This test is the approach to market definition commonly used by antitrust authorities in the United States, the European Union, and Australia. See Department of Justice (DOJ) (1992).

14. A partial resurvey was conducted in August 2001 to recheck the data, and similar conditions were found.

month.[15] The installation fee varied from $50 to $150, which was amortized over different periods for various regression specifications, depending on the predicted churn rate for broadband customers. The narrowband data were collected from the incumbent local exchange carriers providing service in the areas served by the local cable provider.[16] Prices for second telephone lines (used, for instance, by many America Online customers) varied from $7.70 to $47.62 a month.[17] Installation costs for a second telephone line varied from $16.90 to $55.30, a cost that was amortized over its expected service life.[18] The standard price for @Home cable service was $40 a month, but the price for narrowband access varied considerably because the monthly price of a second line varied, from $8 to $48.

These data indicate that, under the Department of Justice (DOJ) test for market definition, narrowband access is in a separate market from broadband access, because narrowband prices vary by a factor of over 300 percent, while broadband prices vary much less.[19] Thus variations in the price of narrowband access cannot explain the variations in the price of broadband access. Otherwise, one would expect to observe a decrease in the price for broadband access service when second telephone line rates are low, and vice versa. There is no significant relationship of this kind, a result that demonstrates the existence of separate product markets for antitrust purposes.[20] This conclusion is confirmed by a benchmark regression (see table 7-1).

The estimated coefficient for the narrowband access price is essentially zero (−.003) and far from statistically significant. Thus the hypothesis that the price of narrowband access does not affect the price of broadband

15. Prices for noncable subscribers are typically $10 a month higher. Consideration of these prices for customers who do not subscribe to cable had no significant effect on the results.

16. These data cover the price of monthly telephone access, not the price to the Internet service provider. Although @Home and Road Runner provide both services in their price, because many narrowband service providers provide national service at a single price, the price of Internet service was included in the intercept coefficient in the regression specification.

17. For residential customers who do not use a second (or higher) telephone line, the marginal price of access is zero (everywhere but in New York City) as long as a local network node exists. I use different weighted averages for use of first and second telephone lines in some of the regression specifications, but the results are not sensitive to the particular weights used.

18. The installation cost captures only the connection fee and does not reflect the costs of rewiring the telephone jack.

19. DOJ (1992). The standard price of broadband Internet access over cable has increased to $50 a month. The price of America Online has increased to $23.95 a month.

20. Some narrowband Internet customers do not use a second telephone line. The data using a weighted average of customers who use a first or second telephone line was analyzed. The results do not differ significantly.

Table 7-1. *Benchmark Regression of Broadband Internet Access Prices on Narrowband Internet Access Prices (estimated)*[a]

Log price of broadband access	Coefficient	Standard error	t-statistic
Intercept	4.03	.090	47.7
Log price of narrowband access	−0.003	.026	−0.102
Road Runner indicator	−0.116	.013	−8.64
Addendum			
Number of observations	59		
Standard error of regression	.011		
R^2	.572		

a. The price of a second telephone line is treated as predetermined in the regression specification because it is set by regulation, not by market forces. Also, a Hausman specification test (Hausman [1978]) does not reject exogeneity. Furthermore, regulation requires that tariffs of incumbent local exchange carriers be identical across a service area.

Broadband access price is the natural logarithm of cable broadband access price plus amortized monthly cost of installation. Narrowband access price is the natural logarithm of the price of a second telephone line plus second-line fees plus amortization of the installation cost.

access (transport) and Internet service is not rejected: Lower narrowband prices do not constrain the prices charged for broadband access. Because the price of America Online is not included in any explanatory variable, its effect is contained in the estimate of the intercept coefficient.

The findings are uniform across specifications corresponding to varying definitions and amortization periods for installation costs. The estimated coefficient of the narrowband price variable is always small and statistically insignificant. The Road Runner indicator variable, however, is about −11.6 percent and highly statistically significant, with a *t*-statistic of 8.6. Thus Road Runner is priced significantly below @Home, on average.

When the regression specification is expanded to include median household income, average population density, the cost of the calls from the residence to the Internet service provider, and age of the population, these variables are not statistically significant. Moreover, the coefficient of principal interest—the effect of narrowband access price—does not change in any meaningful way.[21] The coefficient of the estimated logarithm price of narrowband access is the same whether or not demographic variables are included.[22] The results of three additional regressions with different specifi-

21. The *p*-values for an *F* test are .105 and .235 for the two regression specifications. Both *p*-values are well above normal significance levels.

22. The *p*-values for an *F* test for the use of demographics is 0.63 for the first specification and 0.84 for the second specification. Neither *F* statistic is near the 0.05 significance level.

cations are presented in appendix 7A. All of these results confirm the conclusion that the price of narrowband access does not constrain the price of broadband access. Broadband Internet access is a separate product market.

Asymmetric Regulation

If the goal is to have actual competition that benefits consumers, the following questions must be addressed. Should network elements be unbundled so that competitive local exchange carriers can provide broadband Internet access using incumbent local exchange carriers' network elements? Should similar regulations exist for hybrid fiber-coaxial cable networks? Finally, is the current situation of asymmetric regulation appropriate? The following analysis demonstrates that if regulators require the entire local telephone network to be unbundled, as the Federal Communications Commission (FCC) has done in the United States, the likely outcome will be less competition.

The principal concern in this analysis is the effect of regulation on consumer welfare.[23] The appropriate goal is not a competitor welfare goal, as regulators often seem to believe, but a consumer welfare goal. The FCC regulates under a public interest rule, which should translate into a consumer welfare rule, but the FCC has used the public interest standard to provide it wide latitude in its decisions, often resulting in consumer harm in the billions and tens of billions of dollars a year.[24]

The Telecommunications Act of 1996 established the basic principles for the unbundling of network elements.[25] Sections 251 and 252 provide a framework for the pricing of interconnection, resale, and unbundling. Section 251(c)(3) requires any incumbent local exchange carrier (other than certain rural carriers) to offer competitors access to its network elements on an unbundled basis. In turn, Section 251(d)(2) requires that the FCC, when determining whether to mandate the unbundling of the local exchange carrier's network elements under Section 251(c)(3), consider whether "access to such network elements as are proprietary in nature is

23. See Hausman (1998); Hausman and Shelanski (1999); and Hausman and Sidak (1999). The Australian regulator, the ACCC, has explicitly established this goal for their approach to telecommunications regulation. The ACCC refers to the goal as the "long-term interests of end users."

24. See Hausman (1997, 1998); and Hausman and Shelanski (1999). See also Crandall and Waverman (1995).

25. See Hausman and Sidak (1999).

necessary" and whether "the failure to provide access to such network elements would impair the ability of the telecommunications carrier seeking access to provide the services that it seeks to offer." Together, those two subsections are known as the "necessary" and "impair" requirements.

Consumer Welfare

The implementation of the necessary and impair requirements should be based on the goal of furthering overall competition not merely the economic interests of individual competitors. If overall competition is increased, consumer welfare and economic efficiency will also generally increase.

Consumers benefit from competition because it leads to greater innovation and lower prices. However, the FCC's public interest standard, although central to the interpretation of telecommunications regulations, has not always been aligned with consumers' interests. The primacy that economists ascribe to economic efficiency and to the maximization of consumer welfare has a related benefit: It harmonizes economic regulation and antitrust (competition) law. In 1996 Congress endorsed this view when it emphasized in the Telecommunications Act that the improvement of consumer welfare was the new legislation's overarching purpose.

Suppose that substitutes outside the incumbent local exchange carrier's network are available and are being offered by competing firms. The availability of the competing services occurs because some firms have made the rational economic decision that they can efficiently provide these services. Two conclusions follow from this situation. First, the element as provided by the incumbent carrier cannot be essential for competition because competition is already occurring without its provision by the carrier. Thus the network element cannot be labeled an essential facility, and its availability to competitors at regulated prices is not necessary for the development of competition. Nor would a decision not to mandate unbundling at a regulated price impair the competitive supply of telecommunications services. Second, competition will not be adversely affected if a competitive local exchange carrier cannot procure the unbundled element from the incumbent carrier. Other firms are providing substitutes outside that carrier's network, and so, in the absence of diminishing returns to scale, increased demand for the element can be met at the same or lower economic cost.

One approach to the necessary and impair standard within a consumer welfare framework is termed the Hausman-Sidak test.[26] The definitions of *necessary* and *impair* rely on the competitive analysis of demand and supply substitution that provides the primary basis for other areas of regulatory economics and, more particularly, the analytical basis for modern antitrust and competition law. The Hausman-Sidak test consists of the following five necessary elements for the FCC to mandate unbundling:

—It is technically feasible for the incumbent carrier to provide the competitive carrier unbundled access to the requested network element in the relevant geographic market.

—The incumbent carrier has denied the competitive carrier use of the network element at a regulated price.

—It is impractical and unreasonable for the competitive carrier to duplicate the requested network element through any alternative source of supply.

—The requested network element is controlled by an incumbent carrier that is a monopolist in the supply of a telecommunications service to end users and that employs the network element in question in the relevant geographic market.

—The incumbent carrier can exercise market power in the provision of telecommunications services to end users in the relevant geographic market by restricting access to the requested network element.

To implement the fifth element of the Hausman-Sidak test, one modifies the DOJ's test for unilateral market power only slightly, examining whether an incumbent carrier's refusal to sell a particular unbundled network element to a competitive carrier at a regulated price would impair competition. This part of the test is based on a critical-share analysis of the possibility of exercising unilateral market power.[27]

Intuitively, the impairment test asks whether the incumbent carrier can exercise market power when restricting access to a particular network element to the competitive carrier in a particular geographic market. If the carrier cannot exercise market power in the output market when declining to offer a particular network element at a total-element, long-run, incremental-cost price, all of the consumer benefits associated with a competitive outcome have already been secured, and the regulator should not order the network element in question to be unbundled. The Hausman-Sidak test is focused on protecting competition as opposed to competi-

---

26. Hausman and Sidak (1999).
27. The critical-share test is discussed in the appendix to chapter 6.

tors. If market forces can protect consumers from the harms of monopolization, then the regulators should not impose mandatory unbundling.

A network element should be unbundled only when the incumbent can exercise monopoly power in the absence of unbundling. When the incumbent has such power, competition is harmed by the denial of the unbundled element, and consumer welfare is decreased because consumers will pay a supracompetitive price for the final service (barring further regulatory distortions). This conclusion is closely related to the essential insight of the economic approach to regulation. Regulation should be used only in the situation of market failure—in this case, the exercise of unilateral monopoly power.

South Korea

Broadband Internet access is assumed to be a separate product market in Korea, as it is in the United States. The technology and economics of narrowband access in Korea are similar to those in the United States.[28] In Korea significant competition currently exists in the delivery of broadband access, even though Korea Telecom (its incumbent carrier) has not been required to provide unbundled elements to competitive carriers. Cable modem suppliers enjoy a similar freedom from mandated unbundling. Thus no open-access regulation or unbundling requirements have been implemented to date in Korea.

Hanaro Telecom, a competitive carrier, was the first provider of digital subscriber lines in Korea, connecting apartments to local stations via fiber-optic cable. In Korea about half of all households live in apartments; therefore, access to Korea Telecom's local loop is not indispensable in Hanaro's providing digital subscriber lines. In the case of the households not in apartments, Hanaro can provide broadband service through cable modems.

Cable infrastructure that is capable of broadband Internet service is owned mostly by the Korea Electric Power Corporation. However, although Korea Electric is the owner of the cable infrastructure, it does not provide cable television service or broadband Internet access. Cable service providers use the Korea Electric infrastructure to provide both cable television and broadband Internet cable modem service. Thrunet is the largest cable modem provider, but other operators also provide cable modem

---

28. The major difference is that telephone calls are charged for by the minute in Korea, so that unlimited local calling for a monthly fee does not exist as it does in the United States.

service. Although there is no regulation for open access, de facto open access exists for cable modem services because cable service providers offer open access using the common infrastructure of the Korea Electric network. Prices of cable modem service, and entry into the field by service providers, are not subject to government regulation. Table 7-2 illustrates the 2001 penetration of digital subscriber line and cable modem access. Digital subscriber lines account for 64 percent of Korea's broadband access subscribers (the reverse of the U.S. situation).[29]

When the Hausman-Sidak test is used to determine whether unbundling should be implemented in Korea to increase consumer welfare, the answer appears to be no:

   —*It is technically feasible for the incumbent carrier to provide the competitive carrier unbundled access to the requested network element in the relevant geographic market.* Since Korea does not have regulation-mandated unbundling, this factor is not applicable.

   —*It is impractical and unreasonable for the competitive carrier to duplicate the requested network element through any alternative source of supply.* Hanaro Telecom has provided broadband Internet access both by providing its own facilities and by using the cable network infrastructure of Korea Electric.

   —*The requested network element is controlled by an incumbent carrier that is a monopolist in the supply of a telecommunications service to end users and that employs the network element in question in the relevant geographic market.* To the contrary, broadband Internet access is provided by seven additional providers, in addition to Korea Telecom.

   —*The incumbent carrier can exercise market power in the provision of telecommunications services to end users in the relevant geographic market by restricting access to the requested network element.* The critical-share test demonstrates that Korea Telecom does not have unilateral market power in the provision of broadband Internet access.

The overall conclusion, based on a consumer welfare standard, is that the incumbent carrier should not be required to unbundle its network for competitive carriers to provide broadband Internet access. Competition in the market is substantial, output is high, and Korea Telecom cannot exercise unilateral market power. Thus no role for regulation to protect consumers is evident.

---

29. In 2000 cable modems accounted for 64.3 percent of U.S. broadband Internet subscribers in the FCC estimates. In the first quarter of 2001 cable modems accounted for about 70 percent of broadband access (*Telechoice*, June 25, 2001).

Table 7-2. *Broadband Internet Access, Korea, May 2001*

Type of broadband	Millions of subscribers	Market share (percent)
Digital subscriber lines		
Korea Telecom	2.4	46.8
Hanaro Telecom	0.75	14.6
Others	0.15	2.9
Total	3.3	64.3
Cable modems		
Thrunet	1.0	19.5
Hanaro Telecom	0.52	10.1
Others	0.31	6.0
Total	1.8	35.6
Total broadband	5.13	

Source: Korea Ministry of Information and Communication (www.mic.go.kr).

The United States

In most areas of the United States broadband Internet access is available over digital subscriber lines and is offered by two types of local exchange carrier: incumbent carriers, which use their own networks, and competitive carriers, which typically rent network elements from incumbent carriers at prices set by regulators below economic costs.[30] Broadband Internet access is also offered over cable hybrid fiber-coaxial cable networks, which pass over 95 percent of U.S. residences. Cable operators are essentially unregulated and are not required to share their networks with competing firms. Thus U.S. broadband access is subject to asymmetric regulation: Incumbent carriers are highly regulated and are required to share their networks, while cable operators are unregulated and not required to share their networks.

Cable operators have refused to permit competing broadband Internet access providers to use their networks. Moreover, the largest cable operators have signed exclusive contracts with Internet service providers that tie their high-speed broadband Internet access to the use of cable-owned Internet service providers. Thus if cable customers want to use a noncable-owner internet service provider, they must pay twice—once for Internet access and use of the cable-owned service and again for the independent service provider.

30. See Hausman (1997, 1999a, 1999b).

In the first quarter of 2001 about 6.9 million households in the United States subscribed to broadband Internet access. About 70 percent of subscribers used cable modems and 30 percent used digital subscriber lines. Of the digital-line customers, 84 percent were served by incumbent carriers, 15 percent by competitive carriers, and 1 percent by long-distance carriers.[31] Cable modems' recent growth rate has been approximately equal to the growth rate of digital subscriber lines, at about 23 percent a quarter.[32]

Currently, AT&T is the nation's largest cable multiple-system operator. AT&T also controlled Excite@Home, the largest provider of residential broadband service, with approximately 3.3 million subscribers in July 2001. Before declaring bankruptcy in 2001, Excite@Home had exclusive contract rights to provide residential broadband service over the cable facilities of its three principal equity holders—AT&T, Comcast Corporation, and Cox Communications—which collectively accounted for over 35 percent of the nation's cable subscribers.[33] AOL Time Warner is the second largest cable provider and has an exclusive contract with Road Runner, the second largest provider of broadband Internet service, with 1.1 million subscribers in November 2000.[34]

The application of the Hausman-Sidak test to the U.S. broadband market is summarized as follows:

—It is technically feasible for U.S. incumbent carriers to provide competitive carriers unbundled access to the requested network element in the geographic market. Also it is technically feasible for the cable operator to provide access to its hybrid fiber-coaxial cable network in the geographic market.

—Incumbent carriers have not denied competitive carriers use of the network element at a regulated price; however, unregulated cable operators have refused access to competing broadband access providers and to nonaffiliated multiple-system operators.

—It is impractical and unreasonable for competitive carriers to duplicate the requested network element, the customer loop, through any

---

31. *Telechoice,* August 10, 2001. Incumbent carriers have a much larger percentage of residential customers than small business customers; competitive carriers are in the reverse position.

32. *Telechoice* estimates that digital growth declined from 23 percent in the first quarter of 2001 to 14 percent in the second quarter.

33. Excite@Home declared chapter 11 bankruptcy. It cut off AT&T's customers and has now terminated operations.

34. As a settlement with the Federal Trade Commission to receive approval of Time Inc., America Online agreed to provide service to three nonaffiliated Internet service providers when it begins to offer broadband service over the Time cable networks.

alternative source of supply in certain geographical areas. However, in other geographical areas economic duplication is possible. For cable modems, in most areas of the United States it is impractical and unreasonable for a competitive Internet service provider to duplicate the hybrid fiber-coaxial cable network. In certain areas duplication is possible for both incumbent carriers and competitive carriers. RCN has constructed a competing fiber optic network on the East Coast and the West Coast in certain urban areas. However, RCN has curtailed its expansion because of financial stringencies.[35]

—The requested network element is not controlled by an incumbent carrier that monopolizes the supply of a telecommunications service to end users and that employs the network element in question in the relevant geographic market. In most geographic markets the incumbent carrier is not a monopolist in the provision of broadband Internet access. Instead, the incumbent carrier competes with the cable operator's hybrid fiber-coaxial cable network, over which broadband Internet access is provided. Indeed, in July 2001 about 70 percent of broadband customers purchased broadband Internet access over cable networks and about 30 percent purchased such access using digital subscriber lines over incumbent carrier networks. Similarly, in most geographic markets cable modems have a competitor in digital subscriber lines.

—Incumbent carriers cannot exercise market power in the provision of telecommunications services to end users in the relevant geographic market by restricting access to the requested network element. These carriers could not exercise unilateral market power because sufficient marginal customers would shift to competing cable modem providers to make the attempted price increase unprofitable. The critical-share test (see appendix 6A) demonstrates that the incumbent carrier does not have unilateral market power in the provision of broadband Internet access. Whether the cable modem operator has unilateral market power is discussed below.[36]

The relatively slow deployment of digital subscriber lines has limited the incumbent carrier's ability to discipline any price increase by cable-based providers of broadband Internet access. Digital subscriber line deployment is constrained by technical impediments, because it is sensitive to the distance that transmissions must travel between the home and the

35. RCN had about 985,000 customers as of April 2001.
36. Cable companies sometimes claim that incumbents have market power for the supply of T1 lines. However, these carriers do not typically provide residential broadband service with T1 lines. Further, neither cable companies nor typically competitive carriers buy T1 connections from incumbents.

central office. These lines do not work (or work well) if the copper segment of the customer's line exceeds approximately three miles, which encompasses about 25–35 percent of incumbent carrier customers. Also, digital subscriber lines cannot be provided on a telephone that uses digital loop technology, which includes a large part of the southern United States, without substantial investment in electronics at remote terminals.

Even if digital-subscriber line providers were to overcome these technological limitations, significant regulatory barriers prevent them from competing effectively against cable broadband providers. The regional Bell operating companies, which are the primary providers of digital subscriber lines, operate within an entirely different regulatory environment than their cable competitors. First, they are excluded entirely from the core backbone market because of their exclusion from inter-LATA (local area transport and access) services under section 271 of the Telecommunications Act. These companies also face separate subsidiary requirements, which may make it more expensive to provide Internet search engines or content of any kind, and the Telecommunications Act requires the Bell companies to unbundle their network. The FCC has even indicated its intent to extend unbundling requirements to broadband Internet services, which decreases the economic incentives to provide these services.[37] Finally, the Bells' retail broadband rates are often regulated; cable modem rates are not. This asymmetric regulation prevents digital subscriber lines from being an effective competitor in the broadband Internet access market for residential customers.[38]

Thus under current regulation multiple-system cable operators are able to exercise unilateral market power, a conclusion consistent with the cable operators' ability to tie their broadband Internet access to customers. In the absence of such market power one would expect a sufficient proportion of marginal cable-modem customers to shift to digital subscriber lines and to force cable operators to provide customer choice for a nonaffiliated Internet service provider. The ability of cable operators to require these customers to "pay twice" demonstrates their market power.

A further difference exists between incumbent local exchange carriers and multiple-system cable operators: Incumbents do not provide content (the material downloaded by subscribers), so they do not have an economic incentive to distort competition for content. Cable operators provide con-

37. See Hausman (1997).
38. Satellites will not provide significant constraining competition to cable providers for broadband Internet access in the next few years. According to the FCC, as of December 31, 2000, satellites provided about 1.6 percent of high-speed Internet connections.

tent (video programming) both over the cable channels that they own and over their affiliated cable systems. Indeed, cable operators exercise significant monopoly power.[39] Internet video streaming competes—and will compete even more in the future—with video programming offered by cable systems. Cable system broadband Internet providers currently place significant restrictions on Internet video streaming to limit its use.

Competition among Content Providers

Full-service broadband providers integrate four services, or inputs:[40]

—Broadband content (for example, streaming video and audio, movies, video conferencing, interactive games.

—The aggregation of broadband content and complementary services (for example, chat rooms, instant messaging) by a broadband portal.

—Connectivity to the Internet supplied by a broadband Internet service provider.

—High-speed transport from the home to the Internet service provided by a cable operator, telephone company, or other broadband conduit provider.

A vertically integrated firm, offering both broadband transport and portal services, could profitably pursue two anticompetitive strategies. First, an integrated provider could engage in *conduit discrimination,* insulating its own conduit from competition by limiting its distribution of affiliated content and services over rival platforms. Conduit discrimination could involve a range of anticompetitive strategies, from refusing to distribute an affiliated portal over competing conduits to making popular content available only to customers using an affiliated conduit. Second, an integrated provider could engage in *content discrimination,* insulating its own affiliated content from competition by blocking or degrading the quality of outside content. Content discrimination could involve a range of strategies, from blocking outside content entirely to affording affiliated content preferential caching treatment.

Both of these strategies are potentially costly, but the benefits could outweigh the costs in certain situations. For example, a firm engaging in

---

39. The most straightforward evidence of this market power is that when RCN entered the cable market to compete with multiple-system operators, prices typically decreased by 10–20 percent. Cable operators moved premium channels into the basic tier, so that customers no longer paid extra for the premium channels.

40. This section has previously appeared in Hausman, Sidak, and Singer (2001a).

conduit discrimination will forgo revenues from content distribution over rival platforms. However, there are potentially countervailing benefits, because with conduit discrimination, customers will perceive the cable conduit as more valuable. This, in turn, will increase the demand for cable transport relative to other forms of transport. Hence a cable broadband provider will engage in conduit (or content) discrimination if the gain from additional access revenues from broadband users offsets the loss in content revenues from narrower distribution. To the extent that cable transport providers compete against digital subscriber line services and other broadband transport providers, the reduction in revenues from lost customers will be greater.

There are several ways in which a vertically integrated broadband provider can discriminate against unaffiliated content providers. First, it can give preference to an affiliated content provider by caching its content locally. Such preferential treatment ensures that affiliated content can be delivered at faster speeds than unaffiliated content. Second, a vertically integrated broadband provider can limit the duration of streaming videos of broadcast quality to such an extent that they can never compete against cable programming. For example, a vertically integrated firm like AT&T can block any competing content that it wants to (AT&T and other cable providers currently limit video streaming to less than ten minutes). Third, a vertically integrated firm such as AT&T and AOL Time Warner could impose proprietary standards that would render unaffiliated content useless. The academic literature on standards and network externalities provides theoretical and empirical support for the conjecture that AT&T could impose proprietary standards that would raise the switching costs for its subscribers and stifle competition in vertically related software markets.

AT&T's (and previously TCI's) traditional cable strategy has been to use its market power in the delivery of programming to expand its control over the programming itself. Time Warner used a similar strategy to limit competition in programming.[41]

Is Asymmetric Regulation Appropriate?

The current asymmetric regulation framework—requiring incumbent local exchange carriers to sell their network elements to competitive local exchange carriers at below-cost prices while cable modem operators are not

---

41. For example, see Shapiro and Varian (1999).

regulated—has no reasonable economic basis. This conclusion flows from the Hausman-Sidak test and from evidence that demonstrates that cable modem operators have the economic incentive and the ability to exercise unilateral market power and to discriminate against competitive content providers. In most geographic markets, one might conclude that no regulation is necessary since digital subscriber lines and cable modems compete against each other. However, the preferred outcome is to require both incumbent carriers and cable modem operators to provide access to their networks (without unbundling) where technically feasible. Prices would be determined by commercial negotiation between the parties.

Regulated Prices for Unbundled Elements: The FCC Approach

The legislative framework for incumbent carrier network unbundling was established in the 1996 Telecommunications Act. The FCC has since instituted numerous regulatory rules to implement the act, the most important of which is the Local Competition and Interconnection Order of August 1996.[42] The FCC, however, has established the basis for setting the prices of unbundled elements incorrectly, leading to less competition rather than to the desired increased competition.[43]

One way to analyze the problem of setting appropriate regulated prices for unbundled elements is to examine a new investment by an incumbent carrier. Suppose a competitor wants to buy the unbundled elements associated with such an investment. The carrier could offer the competitor a contract for the economic life of the investment—say ten to twenty years for investment in the local loop. The price of the unbundled element would be the total investment cost plus the operating costs each year for

---

42. FCC, "First Report and Order, CC docket No. 96-98 and 95-185," August 1, 1996. The FCC is being challenged by the incumbent local exchange carriers in federal court. The U.S. Supreme Court reversed and remanded for further consideration the FCC's regulatory approach in January 1999. See *AT&T Corp.* v. *Iowa Utils. Bd.,* 119 S. Ct. 721 (1999). In July 2000 the 8th Circuit Court of Appeals invalidated the FCC approach of basing its cost estimates on a hypothetical network rather than on the actual network in use. See *Iowa Utils. Bd.* v. *FCC,* 96-3321 (2000). The Court decision requires the FCC to modify its approach to cost estimation. The Supreme Court in 2002 reversed the Circuit Court of Appeals and upheld total-element, long-run, incremental cost. Further legal proceedings are likely.

43. For further discussion, see Hausman (1997, 1999a, 1999b).

the unbundled element. If demand did not materialize or prices fell, the new entrant would bear the economic risk of this outcome.[44]

However, regulation by the concept of total element, long-run, incremental cost as applied by the FCC typically allows the new entrant to buy the use of the unbundled element on a month-by-month basis. Thus if demand does not materialize or if prices fall, the incumbent carrier bears the risk. This carrier is required by regulation to give a free option to the new entrant to lease the use of the unbundled elements. The new entrant, however, is under no obligation to purchase or to continue purchasing the elements. So the monthly price of the unbundled element should be significantly higher than the total element, long-run, incremental cost so as to reflect the risk inherent in the sunk investments—or equivalently the value of the option.

Under the 1996 act the FCC mandated forward-looking, cost-based prices for competitors to use unbundled local exchange carrier facilities. The FCC does not permit any markup over cost to allow for the risk associated with investment in sunk assets; instead, it uses a total-element, long-run incremental cost approach, which is supposed to allow for recovery of the cost of investment and the variable costs of providing the service over the economic lifetime of the investment. However, this approach makes no allowance for uncertainty or the sunk and irreversible nature of telecommunications investment. The FCC assumed a "perfect contestability" market, in which no sunk costs exist. The perfect contestability standard is not the appropriate model to determine correct economic incentives for efficient investment when technological and economic uncertainty exist.

The concept of total-element, long-run, incremental cost assumes that all capital invested now will be used over the entire economic life of the new investment and that prices for the capital goods or the service being offered will not decrease over time.[45] With changing demand, changing prices, or changing technology, these assumptions are not necessarily true. Incremental cost assumes a world of certainty, whereas the actual world is one of uncertainty. Significant economic effects can arise from the uncertainty and the effects that the sunk nature of investment has on the calculation.

44. The contract (or regulation) could allow the new entrant to sell the use of the unbundled element to another firm if it decided to exit the business.

45. In contracts between unregulated telecommunications companies, such as long-distance carriers and their customers, significant discounts are given for multiyear contracts. This discussion follows Hausman (1997, 1999a, 1999b). For the options approach to investment in telecommunications, see Alleman and Noam (1999) See also Laffont and Tirole (2000).

Total-element, long-run, incremental cost calculations make the following assumptions:

—The investment is always used at full capacity.

—The demand curve does not shift inward (or outward) over time.

—A new or improved technology does not appear that leads to lower cost of production.

Of course, these conditions are unlikely to be valid over the life of the sunk investment. Thus uncertainty needs to be added to the calculation because of the sunk nature of the investment.[46]

Given the fundamental uncertainty and the sunk nature of the investment, a "reward for waiting" occurs because, over time, some uncertainty is resolved. The uncertainty can arise from at least four factors: demand uncertainty, price uncertainty, technological progress (input price) uncertainty, and interest rate uncertainty.[47] The fundamental decision rule for investment becomes

$$P^s > \frac{\beta_1}{\beta_1 - 1}(\delta + \lambda)I = m(\delta + \lambda)I,$$

where P^s is the output price net of operating costs, δ is the exponential depreciation rate, and $\lambda = r + \alpha$ is the sum of the risk-adjusted interest rate and the expected change in the price of output. The extra term that arises from sunk costs is the markup term $m = \beta_1 / (\beta_1 - 1) > 1$, since $\beta_1 > 1$. The term $(\delta + \lambda)I$ is the usual term in an investment rule that takes account of discounting and expected price changes (economic depreciation). The parameter β_1 takes into account the sunk-cost nature of the investment coupled with inherent economic uncertainty.[48] Parameter m is the markup

46. See Alleman (1999).

47. The FCC incorrectly assumes that taking account of expected price changes in capital goods and economic depreciation is sufficient to estimate the effect of changing technology and demand conditions. Thus the FCC implicitly assumes that the variances of the stochastic processes that determine the uncertainty are zero, that is, that no uncertainty exists. Under the FCC approach the values of all traded options should be zero (contrary to stock market fact), since the expected price change of the underlying stock does not enter the option value formula. It is the uncertainty related to the stochastic process as well as the time to expiration that gives value to the option, as all option pricing formulas demonstrate (for example, the Black-Scholes formula).

48. This equation is the solution to a differential equation. For a derivation see Dixit and Pindyck (1994). The parameter β_1 depends on the expected risk-adjusted discount rate, r, expected exponential economic depreciation, δ, the net expected price, α, and the amount of uncertainty in the underlying stochastic process. Note that this result holds under imperfect competition and other types of market structure—not just under monopoly, as some critics have claimed incorrectly. See Dixit and

factor required to account for the effect of uncertain economic factors on the cost of sunk and irreversible investments. Note that the markup factor equals unity, $m = 1$, for fixed, but not sunk, investments because such investments can be moved easily to other uses. Thus this equation

$$\frac{P^s}{m} > (\delta + \lambda)I,$$

which demonstrates that the value of the investment is discounted by the factor m to account for the sunk costs, compared to the fixed (but not sunk) cost case of $m = 1$. Investments that result in sunk costs must have higher threshold present values than investments that result in fixed but not sunk costs.[49]

Using the appropriate parameters for various components of incumbent carrier networks, accounting for the decrease in capital prices due to technological progress, and allowing for the expected negative change in (real) prices of most telecommunications services given the decreasing capital prices, the value of m is around 3.2 to 3.4. Thus a markup factor must be applied to the investment cost component of total-element, long-run, incremental cost, to account for the interaction of uncertainty with sunk and irreversible costs of investment. Depending on the ratio of sunk costs to fixed and variable costs, the overall markup on the incremental cost will vary, but the markup will be significant given the importance of sunk costs in most telecommunications investments.

When the markup for sunk and irreversible investment is applied, it should be used only for assets that are sunk, that is, potentially stranded. Investments that are fixed but not sunk would not have the markup. Applying this methodology to transport links and ports, which are treated as unbundled elements by U.S. regulation and whose proportion of sunk costs is 0.59, results in a markup factor for the overall investment of approximately 2.35 times the total-element, long-run, incremental cost. This estimated markup would be close to the appropriate markup for the regulated price of unbundled elements for digital subscriber lines, which mainly compose the loop from the central office to the customer premise. Thus FCC regulation has set the regulated price for unbundled loops at less than half the economically correct price when the sunk-cost nature of

---

Pindyck (1994, chapter 8). Imperfect competition is the expected competitive outcome in telecommunications because of its significant fixed and common costs.

49. See Hausman (1997, 1999a, 1999b).

loop investment is taken into account.[50] Failure by the FCC to set correct regulated prices has led to economically inefficient investment incentives in local broadband infrastructure in the United States.[51]

By contrast, the proportion of sunk costs for ports is about 0.10, so that the markup factor becomes 1.23 times the long-run incremental cost. The markup over this cost that takes account of sunk costs and uncertainty is the value of the free option that regulators force incumbent providers to grant to new entrants; for example, 1.35 times that cost for links and 0.23 times that cost for ports. This calculation demonstrates that the proportion of sunk costs has an important effect on the correct value of regulated prices.

Regulatory Failure: The Demise of U.S. Broadband Competitive Carriers

Soon after passage of the 1996 Telecommunications Act and the implementation of the FCC regulations on network unbundling, a number of competitive local exchange carriers began operations to provide digital subscriber line broadband Internet access. These carriers typically did not build network infrastructure to any significant degree. Instead, they used the incumbent local exchange carriers' loops, for which they paid prices based on the total element, long-run, incremental cost.

At their peak, each of the three largest carriers—Covad, Northpoint, and Rhythms—had a market valuation in excess of 1 billion dollars.[52] All three have now filed for chapter 11 bankruptcy.[53] The carriers had ready access to capital markets until 2001, when financing became more difficult due to the deterioration of the profitability of telecommunications markets and the increasingly large cash-flow losses of each of the companies. A major reason for these companies' failure against the background of rapid overall market growth is FCC regulation, which caused the carriers to engage in a wasteful business strategy.

50. When considering this result, one should realize that a new copper loop investment over its fifteen-to-twenty-year expected economic lifetime will likely compete with wireless 3G networks offering speeds of two megabits a second. These 3G networks are beginning to be implemented. Indeed, the next generation of wireless, 4G, is being developed with planned speeds of ten megabits a second.

51. This is an outcome of government regulation, as FCC Chairman Michael Powell recognized in 2001. See Michael K. Powell, "Digital Broadband Migration," pt. 2, October 23, 2001 (www.fcc.gov).

52. Crandall and Hausman (2000).

53. HarvardNet, a large regional provider, also filed for bankruptcy; it ceased offering digital subscriber lines in late 2000.

To provide digital subscriber lines, each company faced a "rent or buy" decision. Did it make more economic sense to rent the unbundled elements from the incumbent carrier or to buy (invest) in network infrastructure? Because the FCC set the price of renting unbundled elements well below the economic cost of the elements, the answer was to rent. Essentially, the companies were exercising their free options, provided to them by the regulators.

Given the lack of required investment, the economic incentive for these companies was to expand as fast as possible. But none of them had a sustainable competitive advantage, because they were "playing with the house money"—the free options granted to them by the FCC. They spent large sums of money on marketing, but customer churn remained high because none of the companies had a superior product to sell. Indeed, the quality of the service was determined primarily by the quality of the loops, many of which were quite old, since copper loops are rarely replaced except when service interruptions occur. Similarly, the incumbent carriers did not have an economic incentive to invest in improving the quality of their loops, since the FCC had set prices for their loops well below the correct economic level.

The equity values of the three companies—Covad, Northpoint, and Rhythms—plummeted, and capital markets became closed to them. The result was bankruptcy. Faulty regulation led to a large expenditure of money with little remaining in terms of real assets.[54] Neither consumers, who had significant service disruptions when the competitive exchange carriers ceased operations, nor investors, who have little or nothing remaining from their investments, benefited from FCC regulation.[55] The results of the FCC's asymmetric regulation policy must be considered a failure, with an economic waste of billions of dollars.

Conclusion

Korea is number one by a wide margin in broadband Internet access. It is notable that Korea has not required regulatory network unbundling or

54. This outcome is different from the outcome in long-haul markets, where new providers constructed fiber-optic networks. A number of these long-haul providers have experienced financial difficulty, but their networks continue to be used, so that real assets remain from the investment. To the contrary, when Northpoint ceased operations, AT&T did not acquire any of its network assets. A similar outcome occurred for Rhythms.

55. Of course, investors are supposed to be able to look after their own interests, without the need of FCC regulation.

regulated prices. Broadband Internet access is a separate product market from narrowband access (in which the incumbent carrier is dominant). Only when a firm can exercise unilateral market power is regulated network unbundling necessary. Korea does not satisfy the conditions of the Hausman-Sidak test for deciding when regulated network unbundling should occur. Thus regulated network unbundling should not be required in Korea.

In the United States it is not clear that the conditions for regulated network unbundling are satisfied, since digital subscriber lines provided by incumbent carriers compete with cable modem service. Indeed, cable modems have a significantly larger customer share than digital subscriber lines. Given cable operators' superior technology (for now) and their demonstrated ability to distort competition, the current asymmetric regulation—in which incumbents carriers are regulated but cable operators are not—does not make economic sense. Both incumbents and cable operators should provide access to their networks. However, the price for access should be unregulated and should be established by commercial negotiation.

The correct regulatory rules for setting regulated prices of unbundled elements requires an allowance for the role of sunk costs. Yet regulators have ignored the effect of sunk and irreversible investments when using total element, long-run, incremental cost to set these prices. As a result, prices are then set below correct economic levels, and a free option is given to competitive carriers.

The result of this mistake in regulation has been to distort the broadband access market and, in particular, the provision of digital subscriber lines. Competitive carriers did not benefit from the policy. To the contrary, the largest three broadband carriers have gone into bankruptcy, with two of the three ceasing operations. Misguided regulatory policy has led to the waste of billions of dollars of investors' funds. This outcome is hardly a victory for regulation and the goals set by Congress when it enacted the Telecommunications Act of 1996.

Appendix 7A. Alternative Specifications of Regression of Broadband Access Prices on Narrowband Access Prices

Table 7A-1. *Specification 2. Left-Hand-Side Variable: Log of Excite@Home Access Price plus Amortized Monthly Cost of Installation (estimated)*

Variable	Coefficient	Standard error	t-statistic
Intercept	3.98	.107	37.2
Log price of narrowband access[a]	0.012	.031	0.382
Addendum			
Number of observations	43		
Standard error of regression	.002		
R^2	.004		

a. Narrowband access price is the log of the price of a second telephone line plus second-line fees plus amortization of installation cost.

Table 7A-2. *Specification 3. Left-Hand-Side Variable: Log of Cable Broadband Access Price plus Amortized Monthly Cost of Installation (estimated)*

Variable	Coefficient	Standard error	t-statistic
Intercept	4.86	0.564	8.62
Log price of narrowband access[a]	−0.029	0.033	−0.877
Log population density	0.001	0.010	0.057
Log median household income	−0.028	0.064	−0.433
Percent population age 65 and older	−0.006	0.006	−1.16
Percent population age 35 to 54	−0.009	0.009	−0.979
Percent population under age 5	−0.016	0.022	−0.757
Road Runner indicator	−0.114	0.014	−8.07
Addendum			
Number of observations	59		
Standard error of regression	0.002		
R^2	0.600		

a. Narrowband access price is the log of the price of a second telephone line plus second-line fees plus amortization of installation cost.

Table 7A-3. *Specification 4. Left-Hand-Side Variable: Log of Excite@Home Access Price plus Amortized Monthly Cost of Installation (estimated)*

Variable	Coefficient	Standard error	t-statistic
Intercept	4.81	0.653	7.36
Log price of narrowband access[a]	−0.0003	0.041	−0.007
Log population density	0.006	0.012	0.506
Log median household income	−0.077	0.083	−0.929
Percent population age 65 and older	−0.001	0.007	−0.157
Percent population age 35 to 54	−0.001	0.011	−0.112
Percent population under age 5	0.002	0.028	0.110
Addendum			
Number of observations	43		
Standard error of regression	0.002		
R^2	0.056		

a. Narrowband access price is the log of the price of a second telephone line plus second-line fees plus amortization of installation cost.

References

Alleman, James. 1999. "The Poverty of Cost Models." In *The New Investment Theory of Real Options and Its Implications for Telecommunications Economics*, edited by James Alleman and Eli Noam. Boston: Kluwer.

Alleman, James, and Eli Noam, eds. 1999. *The New Investment Theory of Real Options and Its Implications for Telecommunications Economics.* Boston: Kluwer.

Crandall, Robert, and Jerry Hausman. 2000. "Competition in U.S. Telecommunications Services Four Years after the 1996 Legislation." In *Deregulation of Network Industries: What's Next?* edited by S. Peltzman and C. Winston. Brookings.

Crandall, Robert, and L. Waverman. 1995. *Talk Is Cheap: The Promise of Regulatory Reform in North American Telecommunications.* Brookings.

Department of Justice. 1992. *Department of Justice and Federal Trade Commission Horizontal Merger Guidelines.*

Dixit, Avinash, and Robert Pindyck. 1994. *Investment under Uncertainty.* Princeton University Press.

Hausman, Jerry. 1978. "Specification Tests in Econometrics." *Econometrica* 46 (6): 1251–71.

———. 1997. "Valuing the Effect of Regulation on New Services in Telecommunications." *BPEA, Microeconomics:* 1–38.

———. 1998. "Taxation by Telecommunications Regulation." *Tax Policy and the Economy* 12:29–48.

————. 1999a. "Regulation by TSLRIC: Economic Effects on Investment and Innovation." *Multimedia Und Recht:* 18:22–26.

————. 1999b. "The Effect of Sunk Costs in Telecommunication Regulation." In *The New Investment Theory of Real Options and Its Implications for Telecommunications Economics,* edited by James Alleman and Eli Noam. Boston: Kluwer.

Hausman, Jerry, and Howard Shelanski. 1999. "Economic Welfare and Telecommunications Welfare: The E-Rate Policy for Universal Service Subsidies." *Yale Journal on Regulation* 16:19–51.

Hausman, Jerry, and J. Greg Sidak. 1999. "A Consumer Welfare Approach to the Mandatory Unbundling of Telecommunications Networks." *Yale Law Journal* 109:417–505.

Hausman, Jerry, J. Greg Sidak, and H. Singer. 2001a. "Cable Modems and DSL: Broadband Internet Access for Residential Customers." *American Economic Review,* 91:302–07.

————. 2001b. "Residential Demand for Broadband Telecommunications and Consumer Access to Unaffiliated Internet Content Providers." *Yale Journal on Regulation* 18:131–73.

Laffont, Jean, and Jean Tirole. 2000. *Competition in Telecommunications.* MIT Press.

Shapiro, Carl, and Hal Varian. 1999. *Information Rules: A Strategic Guide to the Network Economy.* Harvard Business School Press.

HOWARD A. SHELANSKI

8 | Competition and Regulation in Broadband Communications

The market for retail broadband communication services differs from the markets for local telephone and cable television services in an important respect: It is emerging in an environment of competition rather than monopoly. Unlike the telephone network (which began as a patent monopoly and, after a brief period of competition, reached maturity as a regulated "natural" monopoly) and unlike cable television systems (which enjoyed decades of unrivaled and protected franchise monopolies), every broadband provider has from the beginning faced actual or imminent competition. Broadband in its current, early state thus seems more analogous to wireless telephony, which was born as a duopoly, than to either cable video or voice telephony. Instead of inheriting the comparatively deregulatory legacy of the wireless industry, however, broadband providers have found themselves the recipients of a host of rules and policy proposals relevant to a regulated monopolist.

The telephone-based broadband technology, digital subscriber line service (DSL), has been subject to the Federal Communication Commission's (FCC's) unbundling regulations under the Telecommunications Act of 1996, which requires that incumbent local exchange carriers provide network access to competitors on nondiscriminatory, cost-based terms. Yet these are regulations designed for a market in which incumbent local telephone carriers for most of the twentieth century faced no competitors.

Meanwhile, the cable-based broadband technology, cable modem service, faces calls for open-access rules under which exclusive vertical agreements between cable operators and Internet service providers (ISPs) would be prohibited and access to cable networks for unaffiliated ISPs would be mandatory. Yet this regulation echoes rules designed to prevent monopoly cable operators from obtaining too great a control over programming and to allow access to cable networks for unaffiliated program producers. There is something awkward about debating whether to apply concepts relevant to restraining a firm that operates as a monopoly to firms that face competition.

That awkwardness, heightened perhaps by an accumulated understanding of the practical difficulties of regulating even in clear cases of market failure, has prompted two adamant responses in the broadband regulation debate. The first is that, if cable modem and digital subscriber line services compete head to head to provide consumers with broadband data connections (*inter*modal competition), then there is no reason for regulatory intervention that tries to introduce competition within either of those platforms (*intra*modal competition). The second is that, if the two platforms do indeed compete, then there is no basis for regulating one of them but not the other. These two arguments are powerful and may be right, but they have not quelled the fervent policy debate over regulating digital subscriber line and cable modem services.[1]

The FCC has initiated separate proceedings to examine the regulatory status of cable modem service and digital subscriber line service. So far those proceedings have moved in a deregulatory direction. The FCC has declared cable modem service to be an information service rather than a "cable" or a "telecommunications" service, the latter of which would be subject to common carrier requirements under the Communications Act. The commission proposes classifying digital subscriber line service the same way, which would remove it from the purview of the network unbundling provisions of the Telecommunications Act of 1996. But such classification does not itself eliminate the regulation of the respective broadband services. Indeed, the classification of cable modem service as an information rather than a cable service is in at least one respect double-edged: Were cable modem access a cable service, the FCC would be barred

---

1. One only has to look to the FCC's pending proceedings involving cable open access and digital subscriber line reclassification to see that there are substantial differences among interested parties and an open question in the minds of regulators as to the regulation of both cable modem and digital-line services. See FCC (2002b, 2002c).

by the Communications Act from imposing common carrier obligations on cable modem services. More generally, the FCC still has discretion to regulate either service as an information service.

Deregulatory arguments based on rivalry between digital subscriber line service and cable modem service have therefore not yet carried the day, in part because proof of broadband competition does not suffice theoretically to prove that regulation of cable modem or digital lines cannot be beneficial for market performance. Consider the critical question of whether the competition between the two modalities is sufficient to warrant deregulation of digital subscriber line facilities and forbearance from regulation of cable modem facilities. Even if there is vigorous competition between the two services, regulation of one or the other might in theory still reasonably be considered. Such competition so far has principally involved two players: the local cable operator and the regional incumbent local exchange carrier.[2] So the most general presumption one can make is that the unregulated broadband market is a duopoly. And duopoly is not a market structure that economists or policymakers usually presume to perform terribly well for consumers. Regulations that facilitate additional competition therefore might, in principle, produce benefits. The hard question is whether any such regulatory proposals will, in the particular context of digital subscriber line and cable modem services, be likely to yield net competitive benefits that improve upon an unregulated duopoly. This question cannot be answered without looking beyond the threshold question of competition to the specific proposals at issue.

Nor is it self-evident that regulating one competitor in a market but not the other is illogical, especially when the competing firms deploy substantially different underlying networks or technologies, as cable modem and digital subscriber line providers do. The distinct regulatory histories of cable and local telephony, by which telephone carriers have come to face regulations to make their networks more open to competitors while cable operators face no such rules, has put regulatory parity at the heart of current policy discussions about broadband regulation: If digital subscriber line service provides enough competition to cable modem service that cable networks need not be regulated, why does cable modem service not, in

---

2. Of the 4,363,846 digital subscriber lines found by one source to be in service at the end of the fourth quarter of 2001, 88 percent were provided by incumbent local exchange carriers and 12 percent by competitive local exchange carriers. See TeleChoice, Inc. (www.xdsl.com/content/resources/deployment_info.asp [April 22, 2002]).

return, provide sufficient competition to digital subscriber line service that local phone networks need not be regulated for broadband purposes? And if it does not, should not cable modem providers be regulated too?

Regulatory parity, however, is not in itself a terribly helpful concept in deciding whether any individual regulatory proposal for broadband should be implemented. Level-playing-field arguments do not have much force if the rules purported to equalize regulatory burdens have distinct purposes or have effects that vary across networks. Indeed, regulations might affect different aspects of the two carriers' respective networks or services. Or it might be technically feasible to regulate one network but not the other. When competing networks involve distinct cost structures and technologies, the comparative costs and benefits of regulation may differ significantly between two networks. Net social benefits could theoretically result from regulating one but not the other, and it might be possible to regulate one of two rival carriers without significantly affecting competition between them. Assessing the costs and benefits of individual regulatory proposals is thus a necessary precedent to any economic argument for regulatory parity. Again, the threshold question of broadband competition, although important, cannot dispose ex ante of the need for further analysis.

The point of the above discussion is not to suggest that competition in broadband services is unimportant to the question of broadband regulation. It is extremely important and should raise presumptions against regulatory intervention. Rather, the point is to suggest, first, why the debate over broadband regulation persists despite competition between digital subscriber line and cable modem services and, second, what further inquiry is necessary to move the debate forward. Indeed, a recognition that competition between cable modem and digital subscriber line services does not necessarily eliminate the case for broadband regulation means that the broadband policy debate cannot be resolved without examining the various regulatory proposals for broadband and judging them individually on their merits. The history, technology, and economics of the networks at issue could, in principle, make some rules appropriate while rendering others, even apparently similar ones, inadvisable. Without such case-by-case analysis, the debate over broadband regulation proceeds at too abstract a level to produce helpful policy prescriptions.

If the analysis of individual regulatory proposals leads to the conclusion that regulation is in some cases warranted ceteris paribus, then the analysis must go one step further and examine the potential interaction effects of all the regulations taken together. For example, it might be that regulating cable modem service looks like a good idea in isolation. But if such regulation would place cable operators at a competitive disadvantage to local telephone companies, then one might reconsider regulating cable. The economic calculation at this stage would require determination of three factors:

—The extent of intermodal competition (that is, cable versus telephone).

—Whether intramodal regulation (that is, regulation specific to digital subscriber line or specific to cable) is likely to produce specific net benefits that would not also result from intermodal competition.

—Whether intramodal regulation will affect the development of intermodal competition.

The Broadband Networks

Broadband communication depends on a complex of systems and services that consist of multiple layers and of alternative networks within each layer. For simplicity, broadband networks can be divided into four parts:

—The last mile, which connects to end users and gives them high-speed access to the Internet.

—Internet service providers, which receive and translate Internet-bound data and help customers obtain online information from the Internet.

—High-speed fiber backbones and middle-mile pipes, which connect computers into networks, connect those networks into the complex that constitutes the Internet, and deliver traffic among Internet service providers, content providers, online service companies, and other customers.

—Providers of content and services for which consumers and businesses use the Internet in the first place.

The industry layers distinguished above may be integrated in a single firm but need not be. Moreover, each layer may itself be segmented. The last-mile market, for example, is divided among several alternative platforms, the two most prominent currently being cable television networks and local telephone networks, although both satellite and terrestrial wireless systems are potential providers of broadband access as well. The ISP layer consists of multiple providers that offer somewhat differentiated services, ranging from simple access to a full array of content, applications, and such other user services as hosting and website design. The backbone layer consists of multiple networks, some with ubiquitous national (and even global) coverage and others of more regional scope. Content and services are offered by an enormous number of diverse firms. Although the focus in this chapter is on the last-mile layer (in which digital subscriber line and cable modem services operate), it is important to keep in mind that each layer and platform relevant to broadband may have distinct economic properties and raise distinct regulatory issues.[3]

The Technological Characteristics of the Two Services

Digital subscriber line and cable modem services are the principal mass-market alternatives for broadband access. They represent the level of infrastructure where most individuals and businesses have their interface with high-speed data networks. The services are similar in that each provides a customer with transport from its on-premises equipment—a computer, telephone, television, or web PC—to an ISP that will translate and route data to and from the customer. Despite this functional similarity, the technical and architectural aspects of digital subscriber line and cable are quite distinct.[4]

The architectural difference between them has been particularly important in the broadband regulation debates. Digital subscriber line service operates mostly over local loops unique to each end user. Cable service, in contrast, operates over a shared network: Data travels from the head end to a customer not over a channel unique to that customer, as on a telephone network, but through a common trunk that connects only at the end to a customer-specific "drop." Whereas the telephone network is often portrayed as a hub-and-spoke architecture, with each customer having its own spoke, the cable network is a tree-and-branch architecture, with traffic traveling most of its route in a common trunk. Cable modem service thus has certain potential efficiencies, such as less infrastructure per customer, but also certain potential costs, such as data rates that vary with usage and lower security for individual communications. These architec-

3. With respect to Internet backbones, for example, there has been debate over whether market competition among top-tier backbones will be sufficient to ensure adequate transport and interconnection for smaller Internet service providers and regional networks. With respect to the service providers, some commentators have expressed concern that large providers should be prohibited from making exclusive deals with developers of broadband content and applications.

4. For a thorough description of these networks, see Charles Jackson, this volume.

tural differences are evolving as local exchange carriers move to an increasingly distributed architecture, in which some switching and other functions move from the telephone company's central office to terminals closer to subscribers. But even with such changes there are no signs that the underlying architectures of cable and digital will converge.

Comparative Economic Characteristics of Digital Subscriber Line and Cable Services

Both services share important economic characteristics, although there are specific differences in technology investment and cost structure.

COST STRUCTURE. Perhaps the most salient feature that the two services have in common (and that has attracted regulatory attention) is that both are delivered over networks whose construction requires large, upfront, fixed costs and which then are capable of serving additional customers at modest marginal cost. The underlying networks—the local telephone exchanges and cable systems—were of course developed for services other than high-speed data transmission. It is possible that once those networks are in place, the incremental cost of adding broadband capability is modest. But the point is that if a new entrant wishes to offer broadband service, it would have to build an entire distribution network and not just the broadband-specific facilities that an existing carrier can add incrementally to the system it already has for distributing video or telephone calls. Both services thus inherit the economies of scale of the networks on which they run.

Because of the economies of scale in telephony and cable video, both the cable networks that support cable-modem broadband Internet access and the regional telephone networks that underlie digital subscriber line broadband Internet service have, at some point in their histories, been considered natural monopolies in their respective core service markets. Both have therefore been subject over time to retail price regulation. Price regulation of cable video services for the most part ended in 1999. Rates for local telephone service continue to be regulated by both the FCC and state public utility commissions.

Cost-based barriers to entry have also led both cable and local telephone networks to be subject to various access regulations. Telephone companies are classified as common carriers that must, under title II of the Communications Act, serve all end users on nondiscriminatory terms. The Telecommunications Act of 1996 imposes additional service obligations on incumbent local exchange carriers. They must, for example, interconnect with rival local carriers so that customers of one network can exchange calls with customers of a competing network. In addition, incumbents must allow new entrants into the local telephone business to have access to network facilities (called unbundled network elements), without which competitors would find their entry "impaired." Part of the theory behind the unbundling of local telephone networks appears to be to allow the market to sort out what, if any, parts of local telephony in fact have natural monopoly properties by letting new competitors see which components they can provide for themselves and which confer a cost advantage on the incumbent that competitors cannot, without access, reasonably overcome.

Cable carriers also face access regulation. Under the Communications Act, cable companies cannot be subjected to common carrier obligations. They nonetheless have specific obligations to carry certain kinds of programming that, in the judgment of Congress, might not reach cable viewers in an unregulated market. For example, under the must-carry provisions of the 1992 Cable Act, cable operators must grant carriage to a certain number of local broadcasting stations in each market. Cable operators must in addition make a small proportion of their capacity available for "leased access" and for access by public, governmental, or educational institutions.

Finally, the historic monopoly positions of cable operators and local telephone carriers have led to regulations that limit vertical or horizontal growth and conduct by the two networks. After the divestiture of AT&T in 1984, for example, local exchange companies were prohibited from entering the long-distance business, from manufacturing network equipment, and from providing data processing or other "information services." The concern was that local carriers would use their monopoly bottlenecks to discriminate in favor of their own subsidiaries and therefore leverage their monopoly over local telephone service into monopoly over vertically related, competitive lines of business. The incumbent local exchange carriers remain able to enter the long-distance market only conditionally under the 1996 act and must meet structural separation requirements for entering the equipment business.[5]

Cable operators have long been limited in their relationships with program suppliers and in their ability to favor programming in which they

---

5. The 1996 act does not itself require structural separation. However, with the adoption of 47 C.F.R. sec. 64.1903, incumbent carriers must now use a separate corporate entity to provide in-region, interstate, interexchange services. See FCC (1998a).

have a proprietary interest. The most important remaining vertical regulation on cable is the channel occupancy rule, which limits a cable operator to using 40 percent of its channel capacity for its own programming. Cable operators also face specific restrictions on their horizontal activities. In the 1992 Cable Act Congress required the FCC to consider a "reasonable limit" on the percentage of cable subscribers a single cable operator could service nationwide. The commission is currently reviewing its horizontal ownership rules following the U.S. Court of Appeals' remand of the commission's earlier 30 percent limitation.[6]

INVESTMENT IN TECHNOLOGY.   Cable and telephone networks both operate in technologically dynamic environments and both require sustained levels of investment to maintain and improve their underlying infrastructure. To be sure, much of the investment in cable plant was to provide digital video service and was not broadband specific. Similarly, not all investment in telephone networks is motivated by demand for high-speed data access. But broadband communications are certainly an important motivation for current telecommunications investment. Network infrastructure needs to be upgraded to handle larger amounts of data more quickly and, in the case of cable, to ensure that a system initially designed for one-way delivery of video can handle two-way delivery of data. The steady growth in demand for broadband service means that those network upgrades will have to proceed quickly and on a geographically broad scale. The required network investment is, moreover, not likely to be a one-time cost. It seems a reasonable assumption that, as technology changes and as applications become more demanding of bandwidth, recurring network expansion and deployment of new technology will be necessary.

Data published by the FCC show the growth in scale of broadband services and the accompanying investment that cable modem and digital subscriber line providers have made in their networks.[7] Broadband consumption grew from an estimated 160,000 digital subscriber lines and about 1 million cable modems in mid-1999 to at least 3 million digital subscriber lines and 5.2 million cable modems in mid-2001. That growth outpaced projections of between 4 million and 6 million cable modem subscribers by 2002.[8] As broadband subscribership has increased, so too has its geographic coverage.

6. *Time Warner Entertainment Co., L.P.* v. *FCC,* D.C. Cir. (240 F.3d 1126) 94-1035, 3/2/01 (holding that the commission's 30 percent horizontal limit for cable companies violated the First Amendment).

7. FCC (2002a).

8. FCC (1999c, pp. 25, 26, 27; 2002a, pp. 44, 49–52).

Although estimates of availability vary, at least 75 percent of households had access to either cable modem or digital subscriber line service by the end of 2001. By 2005, 94 percent of U.S. households will have broadband access and 40 million of those will subscribe to high-speed service.[9] And these figures do not include business subscribers. The empirical evidence thus implies that cable modem and digital subscriber line providers have been, and will continue to be, investing heavily in their networks.

Actual investment figures confirm that conclusion. In 2000 incumbent local exchange carriers invested $29.4 billion in their networks, over $6 billion (22 percent) of which was specifically for high-speed data services; investment was even higher in 2001. Cable operators spent over $10 billion to upgrade their plants in 1999 and approximately $15 billion in both 2000 and 2001.[10] Although the cable figures do not distinguish investment for broadband from cable digitization generally, the commission finds the cable operators' investment to have directly benefited cable modem service, which requires upgrades such as digitization and improved two-way capability of its underlying infrastructure.

The fact that high-speed communications services require sustained investment in new technologies has factored into regulatory decision-making. Both digital subscriber line and cable modem providers argue that the commission should be sensitive to the impediments that regulation could impose for deployment of network improvements needed for broadband access. The argument has generally been one for forbearance from regulating in any manner the facilities that carriers use to provide broadband service. The legal framework for broadband regulation is provided by section 706 of the Communications Act, which directs the FCC (and state commissions) to "encourage the deployment on a reasonable and timely basis of advanced telecommunications capability to all Americans" and to conduct regular inquiries to ensure that such deployment is occurring. Should an FCC inquiry determine that this advanced capability is not being offered to all Americans in a reasonable and timely fashion, section 706(b) further commands the FCC to "take immediate action to accelerate deployment of such capability by removing barriers to infrastructure investment and by promoting competition in the telecommunications market."

Section 706 thus places the issue of innovation and investment at the center of the regulatory debate. Congress's command that the FCC

9. FCC (2002a, p. 21, secs. 61, 63).
10. FCC (2002a, p. 21, secs. 69, 65).

encourage the deployment of advanced telecommunications services empowers the FCC to consider a broad range of regulatory tools, including price cap regulation, regulatory forbearance, promotion of local competition, and according to section 706a, "other regulating methods that remove barriers to infrastructure investment." Section 706 thus appears to give the FCC discretion to extend existing regulations to advanced services or, alternatively, to exempt such services from existing regulations, depending on which will better encourage deployment of advanced network services and more generally further the public interest. Not surprisingly, there has been ardent debate over which path the commission should take.

NETWORK ECONOMIC EFFECTS.   Both digital subscriber line and cable modem services have the potential to create network externalities or feedback effects that benefit consumers. On the demand side, the most significant economic feature of network goods or services is that the value of a product or system increases with breadth of use. Each new subscriber to telephone service is one additional person whom existing subscribers can reach through the system, thus marginally increasing the network's value to current and future subscribers. Each additional person using a compatible word-processing program or e-mail system is another person with whom existing and potential users can easily exchange documents. This value that new users add to network goods is usually labeled a network externality, a demand-side effect on the value of certain goods and services.

Network effects have been ascribed to a broad array of products not limited to the relatively straightforward cases of communication systems or systems in which communication is an element. Any good whose usefulness depends on complementary products may increase in value to individual users as adoption broadens. A more widely used product may attract greater competition in the provision of complements than a relatively less-used product. This is the hardware-software phenomenon, in which, over time, software compatible with more widely used hardware platforms will have greater variety and lower prices than software compatible with less widely used hardware platforms.[11] The same can be said of the development of applications for high-speed data networks.

Adoption effects can to some degree be differentiated from the positive externalities typically produced by communications networks. In the case of the latter, the network benefit is the additional user. In the case of the former, the benefit may not be the new user but rather the response of a market to that new user. If I buy a copier, I want others to buy the same

11. Katz and Shapiro (1994, p. 97); see also Shapiro and Varian (1999).

one not because I care that others make copies but because I want the benefits that will arise from broader use of the copier, namely, a cheaper supply of after-market spare parts. This distinction has led some commentators to distinguish between network effects and feedback effects, the latter arising solely because of breadth of adoption and not because additional users are a direct part of a system's value to other users.

Cable modem and digital subscriber line services are unlikely to create direct network externalities for consumers. The last mile is not the level on which communicative interaction with others connected to the Internet depends. Whether one Internet user can send an e-mail to another or whether that user can gain access to a particular Internet-based service, business, or application depends instead on backbone and middle-mile interconnection and on decisions about compatibility and interconnection made by ISPs. If one broadband subscriber cannot send an instant message to another, it is because their respective ISPs do not have compatible or interconnected instant messaging services, not because the two parties subscribe to different broadband access providers. A consumer may care that she can send messages, particularly an instant message, to more rather than fewer people and choose her Internet service provider accordingly. But she probably cares little whether those other users get access to the Internet through her particular cable or digital network.

Although digital subscriber line and cable modem services may not give rise to communication externalities whereby one user of a service or network benefits directly from additional users of the same service or network, they may exhibit certain feedback effects that nonetheless depend on breadth of use. Thus if there are differences in the way online applications are developed for the respective technologies, comparatively widespread use of one over the other might lead to a greater range of complementary applications for that more popular service such as instant messaging. As the number of potential consumers of such applications grows, the more intensive their development becomes, making the underlying access technology yet more popular—a dynamic feedback relationship. This feedback relationship will arise not only for complementary applications and services but also for innovation and improvements in the underlying broadband access technology itself.

The usual regulatory concern regarding network effects is that if one service obtains an early lead in the marketplace the market may tip to monopoly by virtue of conferring on every potential new customer a network externality greater than any rival can offer. The early leader might, then, benefit from a self-reinforcing cycle: It will attract a comparatively large share of new customers because of the larger network externality it offers. Those new customers will, in turn, make the network yet more attractive to every subsequent consumer in the given market, and the network will become dominant. In that way a particular carrier could obtain a monopoly in the absence of anticompetitive behavior even if its technology or services turn out not to be superior to or even as good as those of its early rivals.

The tipping phenomenon and its particular regulatory challenges do not, however, readily apply to the broadband market. One platform's lead in number of subscribers will not attract new customers away from rivals because there is no direct network externality from having other users on one's system. The feedback effects that could lead to tipping are less visible and direct for consumers and, more important, have not so far been evident. Applications developers for the most part still appear to target all Internet users, or at least all broadband users, and not develop technologies unique to one platform or another. Of course, this broadly targeted development could change if one particular platform or Internet service provider became sufficiently powerful to foreclose access to content valuable to customers of a competing conduit or ISP. But as long as consumers detect no difference in their access to services and applications from one broadband technology to another, tipping is unlikely. Nonetheless, network economic considerations have given rise to arguments that vertical relationships among access providers, Internet service providers, and broadband applications providers should be regulated, or at least monitored, to ensure that one system does not gain an advantage over another and so foreclose competition and innovation.[12]

The Competitive Characteristics of the Two Services

The evidence strongly suggests that digital subscriber line and cable modem services compete head to head for broadband subscribers. The FCC estimates that by June 2001 subscribers to high-speed data services numbered approximately 10 million (a 400 percent increase over the 1999 level); 8 million of the 10 million were residential. More than half of the 10 million (54 percent) were served by cable modems and 28 percent were served by digital subscriber lines. More advanced forms of digital subscriber line and other telephone-based broadband technologies accounted

12. See FCC (1999b); see also Bar and others (forthcoming).

for an additional 11 percent. Thus while cable modem service grew from 51 to 54 percent of broadband subscribers, digital subscriber line service grew from 13 percent to 28 percent.

Besides being the main service providers in the broadband market, the two services have similar prices and geographic availability. Subscription prices are about $40 a month; setup charges are also comparable.[13] With respect to availability of digital subscriber lines, incumbent local exchange carriers' estimate for 2001 was 64 percent availability; the FCC estimate for 2001 was between 45 and 64 percent.[14] With respect to availability of cable modems, analysts estimated that by the end of 2001 close to 78 percent of homes could receive cable modem, and the FCC estimated that the service was available to about 70 percent of American homes.[15] Overall, broadband services were available in 78 percent of U.S. zip codes, which contain 97 percent of the population.[16]

For most users, cable modem and digital subscriber line services are fully substitutable. Some DSL versions offer much higher speeds than cable is capable of and may therefore be uniquely suitable at this time for certain business uses. More than 1 million subscribers use high-capacity, telephone-based broadband services like T1 transmission or advanced forms of digital subscriber lines.[17] Cable modem service is heavily oriented toward the residential market, with 96 percent of subscribers being residential or small business consumers.[18] The basic broadband services that the cable and telephone platforms provide both afford consumers download speeds in the neighborhood of 1 megabits a second and upload speeds of 128–384 kilobits a second.[19]

The Implications of Regulation for the Two Services

The data discussed above show only a snapshot of the market structure for broadband access services. All the trends, however, are toward rapid

13. "*CNET, DSL* vs. *Cable:* The Final Analysis" (www.cnet.com/internet/0-3762-7-2643122.html [May 30, 2002]).

14. FCC (2002a, secs. 1, 70).

15. FCC (2002a, secs. 65, 46).

16. FCC (2002a, sec. 28).

17. FCC (2002a, sec. 52).

18. FCC (2002a, sec. 45).

19. Although the major players in the broadband access market are cable modem and digital subscriber line services, other technologies provide actual and potential competition to those platforms. Fixed terrestrial wireless and satellite-based services each serve between 50,000 and 150,000 lines (see FCC [2002a, sec. 55]). These services are not currently significant, and the future of wireless and other broadband technologies remains uncertain for the foreseeable future.

growth and a narrowing of differences between cable modem and digital subscriber line services. The evidence convincingly demonstrates that these services compete in the same geographic and product markets. Even if there are some pockets in which one or the other has an advantage, for most households and small businesses the two services already compete. There seems little likelihood, however, that another major platform will enter the market in the near future to increase the level of competition beyond this duopoly.

But even in an economic environment of duopoly, the comparative institutional virtues of market forces versus regulation, or of general antitrust laws versus sector-specific rules, will differ from the comparative benefits of those alternative institutions under monopoly conditions. The effects of regulation are likely to differ depending on whether the underlying market structure is one of monopoly or duopoly. The marginal benefits of regulation, measured in terms of improvements in price and output for consumers, are likely higher in monopoly settings than in a setting in which competition delivers such benefits in the absence of regulation. Where there is any market competition, there may be less (or no) justification for the administrative costs and productive distortions that regulation often entails. This is particularly true if regulation will in some way hinder the competition that does exist, perhaps by burdening one competitor relative to another. Thus while the duopoly in broadband access services is not enough on its face to render regulation of these services inefficient, it is enough to raise a presumption against such regulations and to place a burden of persuasion on those who argue that regulation will improve the social benefits of the unregulated, though concentrated, market. The next step, once this presumption is established, is to analyze individual regulatory policies and proposals that apply to either digital subscriber line service or cable modem service.

Regulating Digital Subscriber Line Service

The regulatory debate relevant to broadband using the local telephone network focuses on access by competitors to the wires (or loops) that connect end users to a local telephone company's central switching office. The central question for regulators has been the degree to which incumbent local exchange carriers should have to unbundle (that is, provide access on a piece-by-piece basis to their networks for new, competing local exchange carriers). The theory behind unbundling is that the high initial costs of building a competing network are prohibitive and that entry into local telephony will occur only if new carriers can use the incumbent's existing network facilities. The Telecommunications Act of 1996 accordingly mandates unbundled access to any incumbent's facility without which a new entrant would be competitively "impaired." Unbundled access is thus analogous to the essential facilities doctrine of antitrust law.

The question of unbundling facilities for broadband services is a subset of the more general issue of network unbundling for purposes of fostering local telephone competition under the 1996 act. But several of the most contentious unbundling issues are unique to digital subscriber line service: Should the packet routing equipment an incumbent carrier uses to provide digital lines be unbundled? Should the high-frequency portion of a customer loop be unbundled separately from voice frequencies to enable line sharing between a competitive digital subscriber line provider and the incumbent local voice carrier? In cases where there is not a copper line that connects an individual customer to an incumbent carrier's central office, must the carrier provide collocation at whatever point the copper loop does begin so that a competitor can provide digital subscriber line service to that customer? Or more radically, should the local exchange networks be divested from local service providers, such that the networks would be operated by regulated monopolists that are prohibited from selling retail services over the network and must deal as independent, nondiscriminatory sellers of network access to digital and other local service providers?

Some of these questions have been vigorously debated and seemingly resolved.[20] Others remain very much alive. At the moment, incumbent local exchange carriers need not unbundle and make available to competitors their digital subscriber line packet-switching facilities. They must, however, make local loops available on an unbundled basis. That requirement is not specific to broadband but was motivated by the 1996 act's mechanism for introducing competition in conventional voice telephony.

The FCC did, however, extend local loop unbundling in a manner specific to broadband and in 1999 ordered incumbents to make separately available to competitive carriers only the high-frequency portion of the loop, thus enabling a competitive carrier that wants to provide digital subscriber line service but not voice service to enter the market without paying the costs of an entire loop. The motivating regulatory concern was that,

20. For example, the FCC mostly rejected the unbundling of packet switching (see FCC [1999a], sec. 306]) but did order line sharing (see FCC [1999d, secs. 29–48]).

without line sharing, competitive carriers providing only digital subscriber lines would be caught in a price squeeze by the provision of both voice and digital lines by incumbent carriers: The incumbent could provide both over one loop, whereas a competitive carrier would have to purchase an entire second loop and thus try to compete while asking customers to pay the cost of two loops. Hence the FCC ordered line sharing to level the competitive playing field. Line sharing nonetheless remains highly contentious, and there is little doubt that it will continue to be debated as the commission periodically reviews its unbundling rules.[21]

With respect to unbundling new local loop technologies, the FCC has tried to maintain a balance. It has not required new fiber loop plants, known as digital loop carriers, to be unbundled. But it has required carriers to make it possible for at least some competitive local exchange carriers to serve customers served by such new technologies. Digital loop carriers promise several improvements in local exchange service. They can increase both the efficiency and quality of voice and data services. They shorten individual loops by running a single line from the carrier's central office to a remote terminal, where it then connects to the individual loops for customers in the area. Copper loops then run only between customers and their local remote terminal, rather than all the way to the central office, making traffic between subscribers and the central office move more efficiently, thus raising the quality of digital subscriber line service by reducing the distance that the transmissions travel over copper. Because digital loop carrier technology is relatively new and is used for new network construction, incumbent carriers argue with some force that they are in no better position to deploy the technology than any other carrier and hence should not have to unbundle their facilities. The FCC has so far declined to subject digital loop carrier facilities to unbundling.

The proposal that local telephone network operations be divested from local telephone service provision has been made periodically since passage of the 1996 act. The closest it came to actual implementation was in October 1999, when the Pennsylvania Public Utilities Commission ordered Bell Atlantic to structurally separate its Pennsylvania operations into a wholesale network company and a retail service company, the former of which would be obligated to sell access on nondiscriminatory terms to the latter and to any competitive local exchange carrier seeking to enter the local exchange market. In April 2001, however, the Pennsylvania PUC retreated

---

21. The D.C. Circuit Court remanded the FCC's line-sharing requirement in May 2002. *United States Telecom Association, et al.* v. *FCC*, 290 F.3d 415 (D.C. Cir. 2002).

and required only functional separation of the two divisions, and in December 2001 it removed even that requirement. No state or federal entity has since attempted such a divestiture. Others, however, have renewed the proposal, arguing that such separation would be the most effective way to ensure the growth of local exchange competition.[22]

A more modest version of a divisional separation requirement, but one more directly related to broadband, involves cordoning off an incumbent carrier's advanced service operations from its conventional local exchange operations. The FCC has never required such separation either structurally or functionally through its rulemaking authority. It did, however, impose such a separation requirement as one of the conditions under which it approved the merger between SBC and Ameritech. The FCC has granted an exception to that separation, however, where the facilities at issue involve new local loop technologies like digital loop carrier. As a condition of granting this waiver of the merger condition, the FCC ordered SBC to provide digital subscriber line transmission for competitors from the central office on routes where these lines are deployed and to provide collocation necessary for competitive digital subscriber lines to be provided on those routes.[23]

The FCC has opened an inquiry into the regulatory treatment of broadband over the telephone network, which could ultimately remove high-speed service over the local exchange network from the regulatory framework applicable to conventional voice service. Indeed, the commission has proposed classifying broadband services as information services rather than telecommunications services under the act, which would remove them from the common carriage, unbundling, and other regulations applicable to voice telephony. The public notice for this proceeding was released on February 14, 2002, and as of this writing the initial comment period is still under way. But the possibility has been opened for the commission to exercise much greater discretion in freeing telephone-based, high-speed technologies from regulation. The new classification would keep broadband services under the commission's jurisdiction and would not necessarily eliminate all regulation of digital subscriber lines. Under section 706 of the act the FCC would still have discretion to regulate these lines. But the notice is important because, should digital subscriber line service be reclassified as an information service, then even if the FCC finds

22. See Robert Hall and and William Lehr, "Rescuing Competition to Stimulate Telecom Growth," September 28, 2001 (www.sandhillecon.com/hlpaper.pdf [May 30, 2002]).
    23. FCC (2000).

that a competitive local exchange carrier is impaired in providing digital lines in competition with the incumbent carrier, the FCC would not be required under section 251 of the act to unbundle the facilities needed to overcome that impairment. The importance of the notice is thus not that it would eliminate the commission's discretion to regulate digital subscriber lines but that it would increase its discretion not to regulate them.

In sum, then, the regulations that apply to digital subscriber lines are those that provide for unbundled access to the incumbent network facilities necessary to provide high-speed data services. Notably, incumbent carriers must unbundle local loops or, if competitors wish, the upper frequencies of a loop necessary to provide broadband data transmission. These unbundling rules are designed to allow additional competitors to enter the digital subscriber line market, thereby ostensibly making the overall broadband access market more competitive. The costs and benefits of fostering intramodal competition among digital subscriber line services depend on a variety of factors, including the extent of competing facilities, the effects of unbundling on innovation and investment by incumbents and new entrants, and the cost structure of the digital subscriber line service.

The Benefits of Unbundling

The two primary benefits ascribed to network unbundling are that unbundling will serve as a needed transitional mechanism to facilities-based competition and that allowing entrants to use an incumbent's facilities at cost will encourage more efficient use of incumbent networks, speed the introduction of new services that can be carried over those networks, and reduce the incumbent's market power.

The high fixed costs required for a firm to enter the local exchange market lie behind the idea that transitional means for new firms to enter the market were necessary. The purpose of the 1996 act's unbundling provisions was to permit competition to develop on a wider scale than it would if only facilities-based entry was possible. Access to incumbent facilities thus offered a way for Congress to mitigate the chance that local competition would not arise or would arise only piecemeal. By using an incumbent's network elements, a new carrier can begin to provide service and develop its brand name without first incurring large, fixed costs. In this way a firm can limit the costs of any initial strategic errors in entering the local exchange market. Once a competitor has some of its own network plant, unbundling allows the entrant to extend the reach of that plant even before its own buildout is completed. In that way the pace of a competitor's growth need not depend on the pace of its network construction. Ideally, unbundling can therefore provide a transition to initial facilities-based entry and a mechanism by which a small entrant can cost-effectively expand the scale of its services.

These transitional benefits are not, however, certain to accrue, and if they do they will likely be temporary. The mere fact that a new entrant could not feasibly construct a network on a scale equal to the incumbent's does not mean that unbundled access to an incumbent's facilities is necessary to improve competition. Even if new entrants cannot offer full networks from the outset, they may be able to build out incrementally and to obtain interconnection with other carriers such that viable entry does not depend on unbundling. To the extent the choice is genuinely one between monopoly and competition through unbundling, however, requiring unbundled access for some period of time may be sound policy.[24] But the unbundling-as-transition argument cannot by its terms provide an enduring justification for such regulation. Once the transition to facilities-based competition occurs, or once it can be shown that it can occur without resort to incumbent networks, the potential benefits of unbundling for digital subscriber line market performance become remote.

The second potential benefit of unbundling is that it will allow existing facilities to be used more efficiently. Unrivaled incumbents might be slow to introduce new services that can run on existing networks. Permitting a competitor to use that network might create incentives for the introduction of new services that raise consumer welfare and put the incumbent's facilities to more valuable uses. Indeed, this argument has been raised with respect to digital subscriber line service with the claim that incumbent local exchange carriers become serious about deploying digital subscriber line service only when competitive local exchange carriers and cable companies begin to offer high-speed data services. Unbundling might also create the incentives—and the the possibility— for rival carriers to provide conventional services more cost-effectively than incumbent carriers do by using the incumbents' facilities.

---

24. It is not necessarily the case that unbundling will be preferred to monopoly, however. There are administrative costs to unbundling as well as productive inefficiencies—for example from possible reduction of investment incentives for the network owner—that could offset the benefits of competition through unbundled access. But it cannot be questioned that the case for unbundling is strongest where it can be demonstrated that there is no other likelihood of competitive entry.

The scope of such efficiency gains from unbundling is, however, limited. Even if one assumes that unbundling is successful and that numerous competitive providers of digital subscriber line service will enter the market using incumbents' facilities, practical and empirical factors suggest that the marginal benefits of such competition will be modest at best. Consider first the practical limits on the scope of competition through unbundling. The comparative dynamics of competition through unbundling and competition based on rival facilities show that the latter has much less potential to improve market performance. When two firms use the same network to provide service, they for the most part have the same minimum production costs. To be sure, they may have some costs that are independent, such as those of marketing or customer service. But the sharing of facilities necessarily reduces the scope of the carriers' abilities and competitive incentives to reduce production costs. In comparison, when rival facilities compete in the marketplace, they have distinct production costs, and each competitor has strong incentives to reduce the costs of producing its service in order to cut prices to consumers and to gain market share. All else being equal, facilities-based competition promises much greater price and output benefits for consumers than competition over shared network facilities does. As Justice Breyer plainly put it, "A totally unbundled world—a world in which competitors share every part of an incumbent's existing system, including, say, billing, advertising, sales staff, and work force (and in which regulators set all unbundling charges)—is a world in which competitors would have little, if anything, to compete about."[25]

Similarly, when firms use common facilities, the industry at issue is less likely to create or deploy innovative technologies or services. The fewer the competing networks, the smaller the possible set of alternative approaches to innovation. With fewer firms pursuing independent innovation efforts, the probability that new services will be introduced in a given time frame is less likely. More fundamentally, the incentive to engage in innovation in the first place declines when rival service operators use a shared network, for the innovator must share any benefits it creates with others using the network. The incumbent's investment in its network will in effect create a positive externality for users of unbundled network elements, and the operator's incentive to undertake such investments will diminish to the extent it cannot capture returns from that externality. Much of the incentive to innovate can come from a desire to gain an edge over rivals, which

---

25. See *Iowa Utilities Board* v. *AT&T*, 525 U.S. 366, 430 (1999).

is not possible if those rivals automatically get access to the innovation in question.

In contrast, when a carrier faces competition from rival networks, it will have incentive to cut its own costs and to offer new services to its customers as a means of gaining market share from its rivals. Indeed, over the history of U.S. telecommunications, deployment of new technology and services has occurred more quickly in markets containing competing networks than in markets with only one network.[26] An analysis by FCC staff, for example, attributes accelerated deployment of digital subscriber line service to pressure from cable networks' broadband offerings.[27] The use of fiber in the long-distance telephone sector, the virtues of which were appreciated by the late 1970s, accelerated only with the facilities-based entry of Sprint upon the implementation of equal interconnection for long-distance carriers and local exchange carriers after the AT&T divestiture in 1984.[28]

The limited competitive benefits from unbundled access might be sought if they were all that were economically possible. But even that small benefit comes into question when there is evidence that competitive digital-line providers are entering, or economically could enter, the market over their own networks. Empirical data in fact show that competitors capable of providing digital subscriber line service have entered certain local markets with their own network facilities. Where such facilities-based entry does or could occur, it becomes steadily less likely that competition through unbundling will further improve market performance. Data on entry into the local exchange market indicate that competition among digital subscriber line services in many markets does not depend on unbundling, and where it does it requires only minimal access to incumbent carriers' networks.

A piece-by-piece examination of local exchange facilities reveals that competitive carriers can reach a large share of the customers they seek to serve without using any part of the local incumbent's network. The interesting fact is that this lack of necessary resort to unbundled network elements applies not only to the electronics needed for digital subscriber line service or other local services but also to the loops between those electronics and individual customers. Indeed, there is little basis for arguing that a competitive exchange carrier is impaired in providing competing services without access to the incumbent's switches. This is particularly true when it comes to the packet switches that drive data networks. The number of known competitive carri-

26. See, for example, Shelanski (2000).
27. FCC (1999c).
28. Shelanski (2000, p. 116).

ers' packet switches doubled between 1999 and 2002 from 860 to 1,700.[29] The FCC has already declared packet switching sufficiently competitive that it should not be subject to mandatory unbundling.[30] Thus the unbundling debate has focused on customer loops and the collocation space for competitive carriers to attach their own electronics to those loops.

There are several kinds of loops, with distinct economic properties and differing degrees to which a facilities-based entrant into the local market can feasibly deploy them. There are differences, for example, in the structure of the market for high-capacity lines, which serve midsized and large business customers, and in the structure of the market for conventional copper loops, which typically serve residential and small business customers. There are also some differences in the market for lines to be newly constructed and lines serving existing customers. High-capacity loops are capable of transmitting information at speeds of 1.54 megabits a second (designated DS-1) and higher (DS-2 and DS-3).[31] High-capacity loops generally serve businesses or apartment buildings, where large aggregations of individual end users exist at a single location. Conventional voice loops, in contrast, serve most residences and small businesses with only a small number of separate lines.

It has been demonstrated that high-capacity loops are economically provided on a competitive basis and that incumbents have little, and diminishing, bottleneck control over customers that can be served over such facilities. Numerous competitive local exchange carriers have constructed their own DS-1 and higher lines to serve buildings in which businesses are concentrated. A conservative estimate is that competitive carriers serve over 20 percent of all business lines nationwide.[32] They also serve residential customers in multidwelling buildings through high-capacity lines. Data from a sample of only twenty of these carriers show that group alone to be directly serving several hundred thousand apartment and office buildings over their own connections.[33] The above figures actually understate the true state of competition in high-capacity loops, since they do not

29. FCC (1998b, 2002d, 2002e).

30. FCC (2000, secs. 306, 308). The FCC nonetheless retained a requirement that carriers must unbundle packet switching in remote terminals that do not have spare collocation space where they provide digital subscriber line service over a combination of fiber and copper but where no spare copper is available (sec. 313). Given the deployment of competitive packet switching, this requirement allows unbundling without impairment, even with the adopted limits. Indeed, this requirement is particularly pernicious because it discourages incumbent carriers' deployment of facilities in a market in which the carrier itself is a new entrant.

31. 47 C.F.R. sec. 51.319(a)(1). See FCC (1998a).

32. FCC (2002e, p. 4-2).

33. FCC (2002e, pp. 4-3, 4-4).

count the facilities of all of these carriers and do not include loops owned by third-party fiber providers and leased by the carriers.

The above data indicate that competition within the incumbents' networks is not necessary to achieve digital subscriber line competition for a large number of customers. They moreover imply that any competition achieved through unbundling in areas where there are facilities-based digital-line competitors will not enhance market performance over and above the competition already existing in those markets. Empirically, then, the potential benefits of unbundling will accrue to customers in areas in which competing broadband facilities do not exist. Yet that category of customer is shrinking as cable modem providers expand their coverage. Moreover, the fact that competitive carriers have not served such areas, even with the availability of unbundled loops and line sharing, suggests that it is the poor business case for entering such markets, rather than any competitive advantages for incumbent carriers, that has kept competitive carriers out. Where there are high concentrations of customers, competitive carriers have found little trouble in entering the local market using their own facilities.

In sum, for both practical and empirical reasons the benefits of unbundling for digital subscriber line services are likely to be small, even putting aside the competition from cable modem services. Rivals compete on fewer dimensions when they use common, as opposed to independent, facilities. And even if the use of an incumbent's facilities might yield some price and performance consumer benefits, it is unlikely to produce any additional benefit in markets where facilities-based digital subscriber line competitors are operating or could economically operate.

The Costs of Unbundling

Unbundling regulations for digital subscriber line facilities can impose two broad categories of cost. First, they can impose social costs by displacing facilities-based competition. Second, such rules can impose costs on incumbent local carriers that over time affect incentives and competition in a manner detrimental to consumers. Consider first the effect that unbundling may have on facilities-based competition, which has greater potential benefits than competition over a common network.

If unbundling substitutes for facilities-based competition, consumers lose on multiple fronts. First, they will receive fewer price and output-related benefits than they would receive from head-to-head competition among independent networks. Second, they will receive fewer long-term benefits from development and deployment of innovative technologies and services. Third, they will not have the robustness and security that comes from having multiple sources of local exchange service. Unbundling should not, therefore, be viewed as a harmless policy for fostering competition or as a mere backup to more conventional means of competitive entry. The backup can become the primary path and in so doing cause important social benefits to be lost. Unbundling thus needs to be understood for what it is: a risky policy that, if not carefully and selectively implemented, could deter innovation and displace superior improvements to market performance through conventional, facilities-based entry.

One might argue that unbundling will simply coexist with, and not supplant, facilities-based competition. From that standpoint unbundling is simply another entry path, which should be left open to entrants. This argument is flawed for several reasons. To begin with, even if unbundling were to substitute only marginally for facilities-based entry, the forgone consumer gains could be substantial depending on the comparative efficiency gains that can be achieved through each kind of competitive entry. Where facilities-based competition promises greater welfare gains, its displacement will be costly. Those costs will rise as the substitution of unbundling for facilities-based entry grows. There are, moreover, several reasons that such a substitution effect is likely to be more than merely marginal.

First, unbundled access may offer a new entrant certain advantages over facilities-based entry, even if the latter would better serve competition and consumers. For example, an entrant may perceive entry over the incumbent's facilities as less risky or more profitable than entry on a facilities basis, even where, absent the unbundling option, the entrant would have found it economical to build its own facilities. An entrant might also prefer to limit the competitive pressure that would result from facilities-based competition by opting for unbundled access. That option would free the entrant from having to engage in independent innovation and, moreover, afford it an option on any advance in the network implemented by the incumbent. Consumers bear the resulting costs in the form of reduced flow of cost-reducing advances in the network and reduced flow of innovative service options.

Second, unbundling requirements entail regulated rates for unbundled access, which add to the costs and economic risks of unbundling. The administrative difficulties of setting economically correct prices for network elements are not trivial. If rates turn out not to match costs exactly and instead to understate costs, then those rates will fail to accurately communicate to entrants the relative prices of alternative entry options. The costs of such inaccuracies are potentially high. In particular, if the prices of unbundled network elements understate the total costs of unbundled entry, they will systematically bias entrants toward unbundling and away from facilities-based competition.

At the same time, prices that are too low will deter incumbents from making investments in their own networks because they will share the benefits but not the full costs with competitors using their unbundled network elements. Moreover, to retain mandatory unbundling once there is no longer impairment would be to raise the possibility that the prices of the unbundled elements will undermine those competitive exchange carriers that have invested in their own facilities—for state or federal regulators must get pricing right not only initially but also each time they revisit and revise pricing. Even if the prices of the unbundled elements sent accurate signals for a time, they might later fall to the point that facilities-based competitive carriers would be at a comparative disadvantage to those competitive carriers using the unbundled elements (and even though the former may have more efficient networks). This problem of shifting price signals is not conjectural. Several states have already held multiple-pricing proceedings and in some cases, like New York, have radically revised the rates of unbundled network elements over just a couple of years.[34]

The point here is not to delve into the complex and contentious issue of the pricing of unbundled elements. The point is simply that a strong assumption of sustained accuracy in setting regulated prices is required before one can say with any confidence that an unbundling option will not affect incentives to build new, competing facilities or to improve existing ones. The results of differing state pricing proceedings make clear just how unlikely it is that regulators will set prices correctly. One would expect states with higher population densities to have shorter loops, and hence lower loop prices, than states with lower population densities, topography held constant. One would also expect states with similar population densities and topographies to have similar loop rates. But as table 8-1 shows, the relationship between unbundled loop prices and population densities is not systematic. Tennessee, for example, has challenging terrain and low population density, yet it has lower loop rates than New Hampshire, which

34. NYPSC (2002) (www.dps.state.ny.us/fileroom/doc11122.pdf [June 3, 2002]).

Table 8-1. *State Population Densities versus Loop Prices*

State	Population Density (pop./sq. mile)	Loop Price (dollars)
Georgia	142	16.51
Indiana	168	8.30
New Hampshire	136	21.10
North Carolina	155	15.88
Tennessee	136	14.92
Virginia	170	13.59

has the identical population density, and North Carolina and Georgia, which have higher population densities. It seems most improbable that these price differences can be explained entirely by cost differences. The more likely explanation is that rate setting is an extremely delicate exercise. If rates are not set accurately, then the unbundling rules have significant potential to displace facilities-based competition and to be costly for consumers.

The second category of potential costs from unbundling rules stems from effects on incumbent carriers' operating costs, investment incentives, and comparative competitive position with intermodal rivals like cable modem providers or facilities-based digital subscriber line rivals. At issue are not so much the administrative costs of unbundling as the costs that unbundling imposes in terms of risk, uncertainty, and volume of investment.

Any firm operating in a technologically dynamic industry, particularly one in which new services are being introduced, faces significant risk and the possibility that investments will be stranded as technology and demand change. This risk is particularly acute for investment in network elements for digital subscriber lines because competition in the broadband market renders retail demand less certain—indeed, the data discussed earlier show cable modem service to have a market-share lead over digital subscriber line service—while providing no assurance that new digital subscriber line entrants will continue to demand unbundled network elements (which incumbents are obligated to provide) for their own retail offerings. An unregulated firm must, in making forward-looking investment decisions, manage the risk that its market share will change and that its capacity investments today will prove inefficient tomorrow. An incumbent carrier subject to unbundling requirements faces that risk plus another: Its investments in facilities are not only for plant to provide its own retail offerings but also for network facilities its competitors might use for their offerings. The incumbent effectively has to build capacity that competitive carriers will use to serve their own retail customers, but these competitive carriers are free to abandon the facilities at any time. Thus even if the incumbent carrier perfectly manages the risk of changes in demand for its retail services, it might still wind up with stranded investment due to changes in the demand for its unbundled elements.

The added risk faced by incumbent carriers is similar to what major car rental agencies would face if they were required to lease cars to new competitors at incremental cost and could not bind those competitors to fixed, long-term contracts. The incumbent agency would run the risk that at any time (perhaps, for example, when a new car model comes out) the competitors might drop their leases, buy their own new cars, and leave the incumbent with an excess supply of cars on which it has not recovered its costs. This risk is in addition to the risk the incumbent faces with regard to losing market share to the new entrant (or any other competitor). The ability of the new rental companies to drop their leases at will and to purchase their own cars makes every car the incumbent agency buys to lease out to the competitor a risky investment. The same risk inheres in every bit of network capacity an incumbent installs in anticipation of competitive carriers' demand for its unbundled network elements.

The costs to incumbents—and ultimately to consumers—are likely to be especially high where new technology is at issue. Deployment of new infrastructure proceeds well in advance of demand. Substantial risk and uncertainty accompany any such investment. If incumbents must also contemplate having to unbundle such infrastructure to competitors at cost, the return on such investment becomes less certain and hence less attractive. This is particularly so where the amount of investment necessary to implement new technology is increased by the possibility of mandated access to that technology.

Consider the case of SBC's provision of collocation for electronics on the line side of a new digital-loop carrier plant. To comply with this requirement, SBC has reported in public documents it filed with the FCC that it has spent $20 million thus far and will be forced to spend an additional $30 million if it continues to deploy remote terminals in accordance with its original Project Pronto plans. SBC also states that it was required to reconfigure its network design so that the transmission component of its broadband service could be made available to competitors. This requirement forced SBC to deploy in its central offices optical concentration devices that would not otherwise have been necessary and that have added nearly $200 million to Project Pronto's network costs. In addition, SBC reports that state requirements that it provide splitters for line sharing have added another $107 million in costs. SBC says that it has been able to recover virtually none of these additional costs because, as it turned out, not a single competitive carrier has collocated in an SBC remote terminal or elected to use its broadband service (other than its own affiliate), and only 14 percent of the line splitters it deployed are being used.[35] SBC's reported experience illustrates why the costs of accommodating competitive access need not always be productive and can in fact cause substantial waste of resources. Regulatory mandates that such expenditures be made to enable unbundled access, well in advance of any demonstrable need and demand for the end-user service at issue, might thus raise costs without the likelihood of compensating social benefits.

The Balance between Benefits and Costs

The discussions above demonstrate that the case for net benefits from unbundling for digital subscriber lines is at best unclear. The lowest potential costs and highest potential benefits both attach to the unbundling of conventional residential loops. The costs of building such loops are high for competitors, and in many areas there is virtually no likelihood that anyone would replicate the distribution plant of the incumbent local network. The unbundling of such loops would therefore constitute the only way of introducing competitive digital subscriber line service into such markets and could potentially speed up the spread of this service. Although these benefits are speculative and perhaps marginal, particularly in light of the rapid spread of incumbent-provided digital lines, the costs of such regulation might be correspondingly modest. Unbundled access in areas where competing facilities are unlikely to be built would not supplant facilities-based competition in any significant way. Moreover, existing copper loops are not the locus of much innovation, so an obligation to lease them to competitors at cost would be unlikely to deter beneficial investment.[36]

Unbundling regulations that go beyond conventional loops or that apply to markets that facilities-based competitors have entered would pose much greater risk of creating costs that are not offset by any competitive benefits. Even line sharing on loops that might reasonably be unbundled raises concerns. If an incumbent carrier must undertake investment to

---

35. FCC (2001, p. 26; 2002g).
36. Rogerson (2000).

enable sharing on lines over which competitive carriers do not choose to provide digital subscriber line service or that competitive carriers abandon soon after attempting to provide such service, regulation will only divert the incumbent's resources from more productive use. But the ultimate point is that the potential benefits from unbundling are small even in the absence of the accompanying costs. Once the potential costs are taken into account, unbundling regulation on its own terms is a risky proposition from the standpoint of economic welfare and the deployment of broadband technology.

Regulating Cable Modem Service

One proposal has dominated the regulatory debate over cable modem service: open access to cable networks for Internet service providers unaffiliated with the operator that owns the network. The broadest version of this proposal would require cable operators to allow their customers to use any ISP in conjunction with the operator's cable modem service. A narrower proposal would bar cable operators from striking exclusive deals with an ISP and would require that cable networks support some degree of competition among service providers independent of the cable operator. The issue of ISP access to cable systems arose when specific providers of cable modem service decided to provide Internet access only through a single, affiliated ISP. Unaffiliated providers demanded that they too be able to reach these cable customers and, further, that they be able to do so on nondiscriminatory terms. The requested regulation has been labeled *open access*.

Open-access regulation for cable has had a turbulent history. The FCC early on declined to pursue cable open-access policies. In speeches by individual commissioners and in decisions not to condition approvals of cable system mergers on open access, the commission established a de facto policy of nonregulation with regard to cable modem service. The commission's reasons for not regulating had both legal and economic dimensions. On the legal side, it was unclear in what statutory basket cable modem services fall. Are they cable, telecommunications, or information services? Are they none of the above? The answer to that question has significant consequences for both whether and how cable modem services are to be regulated under the 1934 Communications Act. The commission has declared cable modem service an interstate information service, subject to FCC regulatory jurisdiction. The commission also found that cable modem service does not contain anything the agency could characterize as a telecommunications service and, therefore, is not subject to common carrier regulation under the Communications Act. On the policy side, it is unclear whether open-access regulation is desirable as a matter of economics. The commission took the position that the provision of Internet service over cable was in such an embryonic stage, and the investment needed to provide such services was so large, that imposing regulation was more likely to deter growth and deployment than to encourage competition or investment.[37]

Although the FCC classifies cable modem service as an information service, there is little question that open-access regulation remains contentious. Many ISPs favor some such requirement, while incumbent carriers claim that open access is the cable counterpart to unbundling regulations, to which the these carriers are already subject.

It is important to recognize that, as a threshold issue, open access to cable systems and the unbundling of the local telephone company's network address two fundamentally different things and raise distinct economic issues. Unbundling is aimed at increasing competition in the provision of last-mile facilities to consumers. It has nothing to do with other layers of the broadband industry. Open access, in contrast, has nothing to do with increasing competition in the market for last-mile access. Even under open-access regulation, the cable operator and no one else would offer consumers cable modem access over its network. Instead, open access is designed to preserve competition at the ISP layer of broadband service and, through such competition, prevent anticompetitive vertical strategies with regard to broadband content and applications.

The Benefits of Open Access

The most direct benefit that open-access regulation would theoretically provide is the preservation of competition among ISPs. In 1999, when broadband was beginning to penetrate the consumer market, approximately 5,000 Internet service providers were in operation in the United States.[38] They competed on prices and services and pursued a variety of business models, some of them even offering the service free to

37. Kennard (1999) (www.fcc.gov/speeches/kennard/spwek921.html [June 3, 2002]).
38. Kende (2000, p. 4) (hraunfoss.fcc.gov/edoc_public/attachmatch/doc-206157A2.pdf [June 3, 2002]).

subscribers who agreed to receive certain kinds of advertising (a broadcast television model). The vast majority of consumers who used these ISPs, however, did so through slow, dial-up connections. Because local telephone companies, as common carriers, could not deny any ISP a phone connection through which subscribers could reach them, these service providers could enter the market easily, and local exchange carriers could not discriminate by blocking consumers' access to any particular ISP.

Cable modem service differs in an important respect. Because consumers have no way to reach ISPs over cable networks directly, it is up to the cable operator to decide which ISPs are accessible to broadband subscribers on its network. This gate-keeping monopoly has led some commentators and policymakers to be concerned that cable operators might leverage their local cable modem access monopoly into a broadband ISP monopoly. This speculation was fueled, in part, by exclusive contracts between large cable operators like AT&T and Comcast with ISPs like Excite@Home. The direct consequence of such monopoly extension would be a reduction in the intense ISP market competition that developed with popular use of the Internet.

The leveraging argument has several problems. For one thing, before monopoly leveraging can be coherently argued, one needs to explain why the cable operator cannot take virtually all the combined profits from ISP service and cable modem access through the price it charges for cable modem service alone. Even if the one-monopoly-rent principle for some reason does not hold in this context, leveraging would occur only if the cable operator predicted that an exclusive arrangement with an ISP would be more profitable than allowing competing ISPs onto its system. Restricting cable modem subscribers to a single ISP could deter use by consumers who do not want to abandon their existing ISPs and drive them to continue using narrowband Internet access or else to using digital subscriber lines instead of cable modems for broadband service. Moreover, cable operators seeking to increase their share of the Internet access market would not lose the benefits of competition among ISPs on their system. Such competition could increase subscriptions by offering potential cable modem users lower rates and better, more innovative service at the ISP level.[39]

The above considerations are not purely hypothetical. The strategy of the largest cable modem service providers has changed from the initial days of exclusivity. AT&T and Comcast no longer have exclusive contracts with

39. Speta (2000a, 2000b).

the now-defunct Excite@Home but instead have signed open-access agreements with, respectively, Earthlink and United Online; Cox has similarly begun technical trials of a multiple-ISP system for its broadband subscribers.[40] AOL Time Warner, which was obligated to provide some degree of open access as a condition of its merger approval, offers its customers in twenty-four major markets a choice of three national ISPs.[41]

These changes are not surprising. Given the economics of cable modem deployment, cable operators have a strong incentive to attract consumers for whom, on the margin, ISP competition matters. Once an operator has incurred the fixed costs to upgrade its network to provide broadband access in a geographic area, it can serve individual subscribers in that area at comparatively low marginal cost. Each customer that does not subscribe for reasons of ISP choice is therefore one less customer from which the cable operator can recover its fixed costs through the markup over marginal cost built into the subscription price. If ISP choice is important to customers, the cable operator thus might gain more from the additional subscriptions that come from ISP choice than from extending its monopoly to the ISP level. Therefore, even if one assumes for the sake of argument that profits per subscriber can somehow be increased through vertical integration and exclusivity between cable modem access and ISP service, it does not follow that such monopoly extension increases profits overall for the particular cable system.

Many proponents of open-access regulations no doubt understand the arguments questioning the incentives or direct harms from ISP–cable operator exclusivity. Some parties, notably independent ISPs, certainly continue to argue that competition among ISPs is itself important and depends on open-access rules. But others advocate open access not because of concerns about the ISP market itself but because of how dominance at the ISP layer might affect the flow of content and applications on the Internet. One such argument is that cable operators could use a powerful ISP affiliate to introduce broadband services and applications tailored to cable architecture rather than to the Internet. The result would be a compromise of the end-to-end principle, whereby content and service innovations that occur at the periphery are technologically accessible to all Internet users and cannot be blocked or captured by proprietary technology. In this view, the need for open access comes from the incentive of a cable operator to use its proprietary ISP as a gateway through which

40. FCC (2002c, para. 28).
41. FCC (2002c, para. 26).

selected, perhaps proprietary, broadband services and applications would be accessible only to its own subscribers.

Some commentators argue that competition for cable modem subscribers among Internet service providers is essential to continued competition throughout the Internet itself and that preemptive regulation is necessary because of the speed with which users become locked in to a single broadband ISP (which in turn could exercise undue control over Internet applications and content).[42] These experts pose the regulatory question, Should cable modem providers be allowed to dictate acceptable Internet uses? They contend that, because the answer is obviously no, cable open access is an exception to the usual prescription of awaiting evidence of harm before initiating regulation.

Thus the less direct but potentially more costly effect of a cable modem monopoly over ISPs is a compromise of the flow of innovative services and applications to the Internet. This argument, however, faces many of the same counterarguments that the basic monopoly leveraging claim faces. It requires a supporting explanation of why a cable operator would want to limit subscribers to an exclusive set of content and applications at the very time that it is trying to expand its services and attract narrowband users to broadband. Just as ISP competition is likely to produce price and service benefits that attract new subscribers, so too is competition among applications providers.

Moreover, even if there are instances of exclusivity between an application provider and a cable operator's proprietary ISP, that relationship may be beneficial for consumers. Such exclusivity might create incentives for the development of broadband applications and services and does not foreclose relationships between other ISPs on other cable systems and other applications providers. So even putting aside digital subscriber line service for the sake of discussion, it is unclear that any harm would result even if cable modem operators had geographic broadband access monopolies.

Finally, the relationship between open access and preventing foreclosure of Internet content and applications is quite indirect. It is not necessarily true that competition among cable modem ISPs will prevent any one of them from gaining market power and either blocking some nonproprietary applications from reaching its subscribers or blocking access to

42. See Bar and others (forthcoming) (e-conomy.berkeley.edu/publications/wp/ewp12.pdf [June 3, 2002]).

its proprietary applications for subscribers of competing ISPs. An important, proprietary application or body of content might under certain conditions be enough to give one ISP a large or even dominant market share, especially if the application at issue creates a network externality that grows with breadth of use.

In the end, the potentially profitable, anticompetitive activities that open-access regulations could prevent can be divided into the categories of conduit discrimination and content discrimination.[43] Discriminating against competing conduits by restricting their access to proprietary content or applications will be profitable where the losses from narrower distribution of the operator's content are offset by the gains from new subscribers to the operator's conduit. Similarly, discriminating against competing content by blocking it from reaching the operator's customers or by giving preferential treatment to affiliated content can pay off when more customers consume the operator's affiliated content than leave. Through these two vertical discrimination strategies a cable operator could in theory come to have such a dominant share of the ISP market that it attracts an increasing share of new customers because of the feedback effects that arise when a dominant platform attracts increasing content and applications developed specifically for its network.

While open access for ISPs could in principle reduce the likelihood of such dominance and create incentives for applications developers to bring new products to market, open-access regulation is neither a guarantee against foreclosure nor a necessary condition for broadband ISP competition.

Commentators advocating open-access rules do not necessarily argue that foreclosure of Internet applications and content is highly probable or that such rules would necessarily prevent foreclosure. They argue instead that the costs of foreclosure are so high that even a speculative risk justifies preemptive open-access regulation.[44] The merit of such preventive-regulation arguments hinges, however, on the costs of the regulations themselves. When the harms to be prevented are highly speculative and when there are good reasons to believe they will not materialize, then regulation might be fine as long as its costs are merely nominal. But open-access regulation risks the creation of substantial costs.

43. Hausman, Sidak, and Singer (2001).
44. See Bar and others (1999) (e-conomy.berkeley.edu/publications/wp/ewp12.pdf [June 3, 2002]).

The Costs of Open Access

Open-access regulations would, like unbundling, involve significant administrative costs. Any open-access rule would have to entail some form of price regulation for access. Whether the FCC tried to ensure only that access prices were nondiscriminatory or tried to set actual rate levels, it would have to engage in substantial analysis of cable network costs. There is no reason to believe that price setting for cable open access would be any more accurate or procedurally efficient than setting prices for unbundled network elements for incumbent exchange carriers. In addition to rate setting, standards issues will also likely arise in interconnection between cable head ends and ISPs. Some degree of regulatory intervention into the evolving technology of cable modem service will thus also occur in the implementation of open-access rules.

The greater potential costs of open-access regulation, however, are generally claimed to result from the impact that such regulation would have on cable operators' investment behavior. Early on in the cable open-access debate, for example, some commentators argued that open-access rules would exacerbate the already substantial risks of investing in cable modem infrastructure and thereby reduce the pace of cable broadband deployment.[45] Cable operators continue to make such arguments in the regulatory proceedings on cable modem regulation at the FCC. For example, in responding to the commission's Notice of Inquiry Regarding Open Access, the major cable operators contend that depriving them of control over the network and over the terms of access for ISPs will have substantial economic and technical consequences.[46] On the economic side, cable operators raise concerns about how open access will affect investment risk and, in turn, reduce deployment and innovation incentives. On the technical side, they argue that open access will exacerbate the potential congestion problems on the shared cable trunks. They also emphasize their need to control access, not to discriminate or act anticompetitively, but to preserve and ensure quality and speed of access for subscribers.

In the end, arguments that claim open-access regulation would harm investment incentives and impede deployment are hard to assess. Because the cable networks are in a period of substantial upgrading and investment, one cannot take their claims lightly. Even a minor damper on investment could translate into a substantial marginal effect in the current broadband

45. Owen and Rosston (1998).
46. FCC (2002c).

environment. The risk of such a fundamental cost should factor into any policy decision.

On the other hand, the evidence also suggests that not every kind of open-access requirement would be inimical to investment. Indeed, some ISP competition is probably an important component of cable modem growth. The fact that the major cable system operators have elected to pursue a multiple-ISP strategy for their broadband services bears this conjecture out. Regulations that would do no more than ensure that cable operators do what they are already doing is thus unlikely to be costly. A simple prohibition on pure ISP exclusivity, for example, might be consistent with the market-driven decisions of the cable operators and cause no disruption to their business strategies. Thus there is probably little reason to fear open-access conditions like that in the AOL Time Warner merger approval. Regulators should be most wary, however, of moving beyond where the cable operators have themselves gone and of mandating a broader, perhaps common carrier-like rule.

Conclusion

When the regulations and regulatory proposals for digital subscriber line and cable modem service are considered independently, the case for regulation of either platform is thin. For digital subscriber lines some limited loop unbundling offers an entry path into markets in which facilities-based entry is not economically feasible. Similarly, for cable modem service some limited nonexclusivity provision might bring a wider range of content and applications to broadband users. In each case, however, there are significant costs. The cost-benefit tradeoff for broadband regulation is in close balance. Even in the absence of competition, regulators might therefore hesitate to regulate either cable modem or digital subscriber line service.

The fact that there is competition between the two services, however, makes it even less likely that the regulations at issue are worth the tradeoff. Not only might regulations burden competition between cable modem and digital lines but, more important, such intermodal competition will provide some of the same benefits that intramodal regulations aim for—and at lower social cost. For example, competition from digital subscriber lines makes it hard for a cable modem operator to foist its affiliated ISP on subscribers. If consumers do not want that ISP, they can opt for a digital subscriber line and obtain the ISP of their choice. Similarly, competition from cable modem service provides deployment incentives and downward price pressure for digital subscriber line service. Indeed, an analysis by FCC staff directly attributes accelerated deployment of DSL service to pressure from cable networks' broadband offerings.[47] In light of these competitive pressures, the expected benefits from introducing further competition over an incumbent carrier's own facilities through unbundling appear quite small. Competition from cable modem services thus reduces the potential benefits of unbundling, accomplishes what unbundling itself sought to achieve, and does so without introducing the potential social costs of such regulation.

Put more generally, competition from digital subscriber lines helps to achieve much of what open-access rules would accomplish, while competition from cable modem service addresses the principal objectives that local unbundling rules might achieve. Given that the cost-benefit balance for each of those intramodal regulations is at best close when considered without reference to competition from the other platform, the fact that there is competition between these two modalities should tip the balance decisively against regulatory intervention. Such competition diminishes the potential incremental benefits of either open-access or unbundling rules and makes it more likely that such regulations will create social costs and distort incentives to invest and compete in providing broadband services. The FCC and Congress should not pursue either kind of regulation in today's broadband market.

References

Bar, François, Stephen Cohen, Peter Cowhey, Brad DeLong, Michael Kleeman, and John Zysman. 1999. "Defending the Internet Revolution in the Broadband Era: When Doing Nothing Is Doing Harm." Working Paper. BRIE (August).
———. Forthcoming. "The Open Access Principle: Cable Access as a Case Study for the Next Generation Internet." In *The Economics of Quality of Service in Networked Markets,* edited by Lee W. McKnight and John Wroclawski. MIT Press.
FCC (Federal Communications Commission). 1998a. Regulatory Treatment of LEC Provision of Interexchange Services Originating in the LEC's Local Exchange Area. CC Docket 96-149.
———. 1998b. Implementation of the Local Competition Provisions in the Telecommunications Act of 1996. CC Docket 96-98.

47. FCC (1999c, p. 27).

———. 1999a. Implementation of the Local Competition Provisions of the Telecommunications Act of 1996. Third Report and Order. 15 FCC Rcd. 3696.

———. 1999b. Application for Consent to the Transfer of Control of Licenses MediaOne Group to AT&T Corp. Written ex parte of Professor Mark A. Lemley and Professor Lawrence Lessig. CS Docket 99-251.

———. 1999c. Staff Report to William E. Kennard, Broadband Today, October.

———. 1999d. Deployment of Wireline Services Offering Advanced Telecommunications Capability and Implementation of the Local Competition Provisions of the Telecommunications Act of 1996. 14 FCC Rcd. 20912.

———. 2000. Ameritech Corp., Transferor, and SBC Communications, Inc., Transferee. Consent to Transfer Control of Corporations Holding Commission Licenses and Lines Pursuant to Sections 214 and 310(d) of the Communications Act and Parts 5, 22, 24, 25, 63, 90, 95, and 101 of the Commission's Rules. Second Memorandum and Order. CC Docket 98-141.

———. 2001. Comments of SBC Communications, Inc. Deployment of Broadband Networks and Advanced Telecommunications Services. Docket 011109273-1273-01.

———. 2002a. Deployment of Advanced Telecommunications Capacity to all Americans in a Reasonable and Timely Fashion, and Possible Steps to Accelerate Such Deployment Pursuant to Section 706 of the Telecommunications Act of 1996. CC Docket 9814.

———. 2002b. Appropriate Framework for Broadband Access to the Internet over Wireline Facilities. Notice of Proposed Rulemaking. CC Docket 02-33.

———. 2002c. High-Speed Access to the Internet over Cable and Other Facilities. Declaratory Ruling and Notice of Proposed Rulemaking (discussing comments filed). GN Docket 00-1-85, CS Docket 02-52.

———. 2002d. Deployment of Wireline Services Offering Advanced Telecommunications Capability. CC Docket 98-47, pt. 2, p. 2.

———. 2002e. UNE Fact Report, 2002. Submitted by BellSouth, SBC, Qwest, and Verizon. Review of the Section 251 Unbundling Obligations of Incumbent Local Exchange Carriers. CC Docket 01-338.

———. 2002f. Implementation of the Local Competition Provisions in the Telecommunications Act of 1996. CC Docket 96-98.

———. 2002g. Ex Parte Letter from James Smith, SBC, to William Caton, Acting Secretary, FCC. CC Docket 96-98.

Hausman, Jerry, J. Gregory Sidak, and Hal J. Singer. 2001. "Cable Modems and DSL: Broadband Internet Access for Residential Customers." *AEA Papers and Proceedings* 91 (2): 302–07.

Katz, Michael L., and Carl Shapiro. 1994. "Systems Competition and Network Effects." *Journal of Economic Perspectives* 8 (2): 93–115

Kende, Michael. 2000. "The Digital Handshake: Connecting Internet Backbones." Working Paper 32. FCC Office of Plans and Policy (September).

Kennard, William E. 1999. "The Road Not Taken: Building a Broadband Future for America." Remarks before the National Cable Television Association, Chicago, June 15.

NYPSC (New York Public Service Commission). 2002. Order on Unbundled Network Element Rates, effective January 28.

Owen, Bruce M., and Gregory L. Rosston. 1998. "Cable Modems, Access, and Investment Incentives." NTIA Report, Docket 98-178, December.

Rogerson, William. 2000. "The Regulation of Broadband Communications, the Principle of Regulating Narrowly Defined Input Bottlenecks, and Incentives for Investment and Innovation." *University of Chicago Legal Forum* 85: 119–46.

Shapiro, Carl, and Hal R. Varian. 1999. *Information Rules: A Strategic Guide to the Network Economy.* Harvard Business Press.

Shelanski, Howard. 2000. "Competition and Deployment of New Technology in U.S. Telecommunications." *University of Chicago Legal Forum* 85.

Speta, James B. 2000a. "Handicapping the Race for the Last Mile: A Critique of Open-Access Rules for Broadband Platforms." *Yale Journal on Regulations* 17: 39–90.

———. 2000b. "The Vertical Dimension of Cable Open Access." *Colorado Law Review* 975: 1010.

THOMAS W. HAZLETT

9 | Regulation and Vertical Integration in Broadband Access Supply

And enough already with this water-torture Tauzin-Dingell bill, and the bleating about "high-speed Internet access." I am so sick of these insufferably relentless radio and TV ads. Vote for Tauzin-Dingell! Say no to Tauzin-Dingell! I have reached the point where I hate Tauzin, I hate Dingell—I even hate Bill. I don't give a rat's patootie about high-speed Internet access. At my age, the only high-speed access I want is to the restroom, thank you.
            —Tony Kornheiser, *Washington Post*, July 22, 2001

The intense policy debate over broadband regulation has spilled out into the public square, and many are puzzled by its contentiousness.[1] According to proponents of cable open access, local cable operators dominate the market for broadband Internet access in residential markets and must be forced to share their high-speed cable conduits with independent Internet service providers on regulated terms and conditions. The desired outcome is to have multiple firms competing to offer customers service, even as the rivals supply broadband access

The author wishes to thank George Bittlingmayer and Robert Crandall for abundant insights. It should also be acknowledged that Bruno Viani and Lydia Regopoulos provided excellent research assistance.
    1. Tauzin-Dingell refers to H.R. 1542, a bill to partially deregulate the data networks of Bell telephone companies. "'I think this is the most intense lobbying battle I've seen in my career; there are jokes on television about the commercials,' said Representative Chris Cannon, a Utah Republican on the Judiciary Committee who opposes [Tauzin-Dingell]." Lizette Alvarez, "In Capitol, AT&T and Bells Fight to Control Web Access," *New York Times*, August 29, 2001.

over the same physical platform. Proponents include broadband access suppliers, who may gain low-cost access to retail customers via such rules, and local telephone companies (both incumbents and new competitors) offering Internet access service competing directly with cable modems.

Similarly, proponents of extensive unbundling mandates for incumbent local exchange carriers argue that legacy telephone monopolies will stifle broadband competition unless regulations guarantee the sharing of systems delivering digital subscriber line (DSL) service to residential users. Indeed, some have ratcheted the argument up, saying that common carrier rules alone are insufficient to guarantee equal access to the facilities of incumbent local exchange carriers and that a complete structural separation of wholesale and retail incumbent carrier operations is called for.[2] This claim is made again by Internet service providers (who may link to subscribers by reselling Internet access over an existing network) and by competitive local exchange carriers and cable television system operators offering rival broadband modem service.

As for the economics of broadband access, early trends are visible. First, competing networks are vying for residential broadband market share.[3] The primary rivals are cable television systems upgraded to provide broadband Internet access and telephone lines sufficiently close to central offices of the local exchange carrier to provide digital subscriber line service. Also offering broadband services are competing ("overbuilt") cable systems, fiber-optic local area networks, fixed or mobile wireless service providers, and satellite access technologies.

Second, the deployment of residential broadband access is still relatively modest. Of 105 million U.S. households, only about 9 million subscribed to broadband service as of June 30, 2001 (see table 9-1). Broadband penetration lags far behind narrowband dial-up access to the Internet, which accounted for about 52 million subscribers in mid-2001.[4] Third, the broadband growth rate is high. Even with macroeconomic and sectoral conditions leading to a pronounced decline in telecommunications

2. Ron Cowles and Alex Winogradoff, "Structural Separation: The Final Solution for Advancing Local Competition?" Gartner, Inc. (www.gartner.com [April 10, 2001]); Yochi Dreazen, "AT&T Makes Headway with Lawmakers in Bid to Break Bell Companies' Markets," *Wall Street Journal*, August 28, 2001 (www.wsj.com).

3. This chapter focuses on residential broadband markets.

4. Lizette Alvarez, "In Capitol, AT&T and Bells Fight to Control Web Access," *New York Times*, August 29, 2001.

Table 9-1. *U.S. Residential Broadband Subscribership, June 30, 2001*

Platform	Subscribers (thousands)	Share (percent)	Cost to customer (dollars)		Maximum speed (approximate kilobits a second)	
			Initial	Monthly	Downstream	Upstream
Cable Modem	6,095	69.8	100	46	2,000	128–500
Digital subscriber line	2,467	28.2	100	50	768	90–256
Overbuilder (cable modem)	95	1.1	100	40	512	128–256
Satellite, 2-way	46	0.5	700	70	150–500	40–128
Satellite, 1-way	42	0.5	350	50	400	28–56
Wireless (AT&T via PCS, WCS)	32	0.4	0	40	512–1,500	150
Wireless (Sprint/ MCI via MMDS)	2	0.0	100	40	1,000	512

Source: Precursor Watch (2001).

growth in the first half of 2001, residential broadband subscribership rose 34 percent from the previous six-month period.[5]

While the broadband marketplace is just emerging, the regulatory debate is already roaring. For both cable modem service and the supply of digital subscriber lines, rules mandating third-party access to the infrastructure built by an incumbent service provider are at issue. In cable, such access rules would allow Internet service providers to use high-speed conduits owned by the cable operator, in effect prohibiting exclusive contracts with any Internet service provider (particularly one owned by the cable system) as has been standard practice. For digital subscriber lines, current regulations imposed by the Federal Communications Commission (FCC) and state regulatory commissions mandate that incumbent phone companies share elements of their networks—for instance, local loops connecting homes and small businesses to central offices—with other carriers, including rivals, at cost-based wholesale rates.[6] The contentious policy issue is

5. The 34 percent sequential growth rate equals an annualized rate of 80 percent. The growth rate in the second half of 2000 was 71 percent sequentially, 192 percent annualized. Precursor Watch, "Broadband Deployment Outlook" (www.precursorgroup.com [August 10, 2001]).

6. Retail rates for digital subscriber lines are also subject to regulation by state or federal authorities.

whether new investments extending or upgrading data networks should be subject to similar sharing obligations.[7]

The regulatory regimes applied to cable television and local exchange service providers differ, but the analysis of broadband access regulation is generally comparable. In their prototypical application, access mandates to separate (or unbundle) the transport function (supplied by the network owner) from the retail service (supplied by competitors, intermediate suppliers such as Internet service providers, or content owners). The question is often framed in terms of vertical integration, as communications services can be provided either by full-service networks or by layered contributions of independent suppliers. The essence of access regulation is to delink the layers, allowing multiple service providers to participate in the chain of production on terms subject to government control.

As outlined in the analysis to follow, mandated unbundling is likely to reduce broadband investment incentives without providing substantial stimulus to competition. This conclusion holds for both cable modem and digital subscriber line service. Moreover, rules limiting vertical integration are daunting to design, particularly given the rapid pace of deployment, the unsettled technology of emerging networks, uncertainty concerning consumer demands, and the extreme volatility of market structures. The same factors, however, make returns to rent seeking in broadband policy relatively high. Erratic oscillations in product and capital markets can both confuse regulators and mask the results of their work. This raises the returns to strategic investments in the procurement of rules that inhibit demand for rivals' services, and the high-growth phase of the broadband market makes this corporate behavior relatively profitable. A relatively high level of offensive and defensive lobbying is the result.

Vertical Integration and Efficiency

In offering goods or services to customers, a firm elects to provide some inputs directly and to rely on outsiders for the supply of others.

7. Morgan Stanley (2001, p. 10) estimates suggest that 49 percent of U.S. households had digital subscriber line service offered to them at year-end 2001. The corresponding level for cable modem service was 77 percent. To enlarge the potential universe of digital subscriber line service, the standard problem is the attenuation of data transmission over existing local loops; it is difficult to deliver inexpensive broadband access to digital users more than about three miles from a central office. The most straightforward fix is to run fiber-optic links to new nodes—outside the areas currently within the radius of easy data transmission—connecting additional homes to the high-speed network. The construction of such fiber links entails significant sunk costs. See Charles Jackson, this volume

Where this line is drawn was the fascinating query posed by Ronald Coase in his classic article and has been the subject of numerous economic investigations since.[8] The consensus view in the economics literature is that vertical integration is pervasive and generally benign. Yet, depending upon the circumstances of the particular market (including regulatory constraints), vertical integration may prove either efficient or anticompetitive.

Standard efficiencies identified in the literature include

—Tightening coordination through the chain of production to ensure quality.

—Improving information flows between input suppliers.

—Eliminating upstream or downstream monopoly, ending double marginalization.[9]

—Lowering the cost of capital by diversifying revenue sources.

—Lowering the cost of capital by guaranteeing fidelity to sunk investments.

—Exploiting network externalities.[10]

Standard anticompetitive motives for vertical integration include

—Increasing scale to raise entry barriers.

—Monopolizing a complementary asset to raise entry barriers.

—Transferring profits to evade rate-of-return regulation.

—Foreclosing competition from complementary products that could also become substitutes.[11]

Assume that a service is provided via two stages of production: wholesaling and retailing. Will consumers generally be better off where these functions are supplied jointly? Or will net benefits accrue by separating these inputs? Even when pronounced scale economies suggest monopoly to be the lowest-cost market structure, these functions can in theory be separated.[12]

8. Coase (1937); for an example of later scholarship, see Williamson (1979).

9. This occurs when two firms with market power are involved in a vertical chain of production. Either firm restricts output to drive up price; each firm loses profitability from the other's output restriction. The result is that vertical integration of two such firms tends to increase output. Put somewhat differently, there is only one monopoly profit to extract from a given product, and attempts by multiple firms in the chain of production to separately capture it raises product price above the monopoly level.

10. See Shelanski and Sidak (2001).

11. Krattenmaker and Salop (1986); Bresnahan (1999); Fisher (2001).

12. A further complication is that "separation" is not a (0, 1) variable. Separate firms performing complementary functions may be brought together by a spot market, short-term contracts, long-term contracts, or long-term contracts with complex enforcement provisions (for example, reciprocal dealing clauses). In the discussion below I differentiate between just two sorts of interfirm relationships, arm's-length dealing (analogous to spot-market transactions) and long-term contracting.

Businesses make profit-maximizing choices in this matter on two general levels. First, the firm selects an optimal scale.[13] Second, the firm selects a method by which to achieve that size. That is to say that any given level of scale can be created by multiple business structures, including internal production of a complete package or provision of components that consumers combine with complementary goods supplied by independent firms. The latter structure may be coordinated formally, through standards, licensing, franchise agreements, or partnerships, or informally, through the market. The limitations of contracting devices to yield payouts that properly reward the risks undertaken is a key consideration in selecting among the infinite number of options.

If markets were perfect, the future certain, and legal inputs abundant, contracts would be complete; firms could write all contingencies into an agreement and obtain the benefits of integration without having to combine asset ownership. While theoretically available in a zero-transaction-cost world, actual markets do not offer such solutions. Imperfect contracts may mimic, but do not perfectly duplicate, the distribution of rights and responsibilities embedded in equity owners. Businesses trade off the costs and benefits of contracts versus those of ownership.[14] This is the transaction-cost explanation for vertical integration.

When fixed costs are substantial and nonsalvageable, the long-run payouts are relatively uncertain, and the probability is high that the economic incentives of various "partners" will change over time (for instance, as they learn what consumers will pay for a service produced by a long-lived investment, firms tend to favor integration.) Common equity interests are often useful in binding investors when contracts among parties with disparate and changing interests are not. Of course, as the cost of devising and enforcing contracts rises, this incentive to vertically integrate rises pari passu.

In simple terms, investors in risky projects attempt to lower the possibility that their partners will free ride, appropriating gains when returns are positive but abandoning projects (and liabilities) when returns are negative. "A contract that requires a party to make significant contract-specific investments . . . renders that party vulnerable to appropriation of some or

---

13. This is a multidimensional choice variable, including product volume, geographic service area, and range of products (scope).

14. Purchasing inputs in spot markets, forward markets, or other organized exchanges is taken as a contractual arrangement in this discussion.

all of its investment by the other party if the costs or benefits of performing the contract unexpectedly change after the contract is signed."[15]

The effect of open-access rules, allowing independent operators to utilize cable or telephone networks at regulated wholesale rates, is to curtail the opportunity for certain forms of vertical integration. Links between complementary input suppliers that could be provided by common ownership are replaced by a price schedule setting forth terms and conditions of access pursuant to a regulatory proceeding (typically to deduce "efficient" or "reasonable" costs as the basis for access charges).

The result is that contracts are restricted from solving certain coordination problems important to investors. A simple example will illustrate. Suppose that AAA is considering the investment of $X, a substantial sum, to construct a resort lodge on a remote Alaskan lake. Suppose further that the lodge would offer two consumer attractions: fishing and bird watching. The latter would require no complementary services provided by the lodge (lodgers just sit and stare, or hike the rugged terrain on their own), but the former requires complementary inputs including guide services.[16]

AAA is uncertain as to how many visitors the lodge will attract or what proportion of lodge clients will demand fishing, but the expectation is that most customers will come for the fishing and demonstrate a high willingness to pay for boat rentals and guide services (ancillary services offered by the lodge for those guests who fish). On this expectation AAA believes that the project has a positive net present value.

In an unregulated environment, the standard market outcome is that AAA invests X *after* reasonably securing long-term fishing guide services. If the market for guide services is highly competitive, reliance upon the spot market may be sufficient. Here it is likely, however, that qualified guides in this remote location are relatively scarce. If so, some mechanism to ensure that such services will be available at competitive rates will be sought by AAA before sinking capital. This mechanism is likely to be either a long-term contract or a share of equity in the venture. In effect, the lodge vertically integrates.

The problem created by an alternative arrangement is apparent. Suppose AAA builds the lodge and, once the assets are in place, then attempts to purchase fishing guide services for clients. Those few local guides available possess specific capital and may exert market power in bargaining with

15. Ordover and Willig (1999, para. 57)
16. I assume that guide services must be provided to attract fishing or kayaking enthusiasts to the lodge, perhaps telegraphing my lack of confidence in the wild.

the lodge owner. To the extent customers demand such inputs, guides can appropriate quasi-rents (payback of fixed costs).

Even when AAA lacks market power, it seeks to guard against appropriation. Common protective devices bind suppliers of complementary services to particular long-lived projects. When regulators attempt to jump-start competition by requiring the sharing of such common facilities with independent service providers, an asymmetry of risks and rewards appears.

In this example, regulated access might grant fishing guides the option to purchase lodge rooms, docking privileges, and fishing boats at cost, reselling such services—with their guide services—at retail prices to customers. If fishing proves popular, the local guides will be able to make a killing, with the lodge owner collecting a competitive return as a wholesale supplier of infrastructure. If the fishing is poor, however, and few fishing customers are attracted, the independent fishing guides remain employed in their best opportunity—away from the lodge.

Meanwhile, the lodge owner experiences less demand than anticipated, and the investment project now realizes a negative capital value. Windfall losses, however, are not shared. The investor's consideration of this probabilistic payout stream—where favorable returns can be captured by rival service suppliers using the investor's network at cost-based rates, while the investor is left to absorb losses alone—clearly alters investment choices.

As a result of mandatory unbundling, those who commit capital to risky projects cannot protect themselves against free riding; in addition to the transaction costs limiting contract utility, rules now prevent burden sharing. Note that the "effectiveness of . . . contingency clauses . . . is limited by the powers of human foresight. . . . Economists have shown that requiring market participants to obtain critical inputs through contracts rather than merger is likely to result in underinvestment and insufficient new entry."[17] This insight can be extended: "contingency clauses are limited by human foresight" *and prohibited by unbundling regulation.*

Indeed, the purpose of mandated access is to make the network available to those who did not contribute to its creation and made no commitment to its profitability. Such users are granted the zero-cost option to use fixed, sunk resources should they elect to do so. Transferring the value of

17. Ordover and Willig (1999, para. 59). See Klein, Crawford, and Alchian (1978) for a detailed explanation of how the basic strategy in preventing opportunism is to avoid arm's length, "unbundled" transactions, tying partners to each other for long-run dealings. When such agreements are voided in, for instance, antitrust decrees, vertical integration often results.

such options from the investor to the user reduces ex post returns, driving up the ex ante cost of capital.[18] The offer of unbundled "elements" vests potential service providers with the opportunity to compete without building facilities, an offer underwritten by the investor in the physical network. Both the incidence of the benefit and the burden of the payment tend to lower incentives to sink capital in fixed infrastructure.[19]

Additional sources of free riding exacerbate this cost increase. By giving regulators discretion to determine the price at which users may purchase network inputs, firms investing in fixed assets face potential opportunism from policymakers. The latter seek to maximize political support, income potential in postagency employment, ideological goals, or some other function distinct from the profit maximand of the project investor. Because regulators cannot be bound by contracts in the same manner as private parties, and because future policymakers are free to revise determinations of the public interest, access rates may be lower than anticipated.

The regulated wholesale prices set by federal and state regulators to access local telephone networks have been identified as subsidizing entrants for political purposes.[20] Indeed, rates based on total-element, long-run, incremental cost have been explicitly set below the actual costs of incumbent firms (and for terms that are less than the life of the asset).[21] The expectation that such terms will be set by regulation creates a risk premium for new investment. This provides an additional investment disincentive, one likely to be highest in a market exhibiting high (and volatile) growth rates, uncertain product demand, and unsettled technology.

Mandatory access rules have spillover effects. To the extent that fixed capital is available to appropriate, the access regime signals rivals that the marginal trade-off between owning and renting has shifted in favor of renting. This effect is widespread, deterring investment in rival facilities (that is, competitive fixed assets) for three reasons.

First, firms not owning facilities are awarded zero-priced options to use the facilities of others. This makes risky investments to create such market

18. See, generally, Dixit and Pindyck (1994).
19. Hausman (1998).
20. Kahn (1998, 2001).
21. "Total-element, long-run, incremental cost" defines what the FCC believes a hypothetical, state-of-the-art, efficiently sized network would cost to operate over a given output. "Unbundled network elements-platform" is the sum of the network pieces, reassembled into a whole system, but costing only about half what a similar increment for the incumbent system costs. See Kahn (1998, pp. 89–99).

opportunities relatively less desirable. Second, rules that make the transmission infrastructure available at regulated wholesale prices cap future returns from fixed investments. Should supply of the service in question prove more profitable than currently anticipated, the ability of new entrants to utilize network capital at (or below) cost will limit the upside returns enjoyed by owners of any facility providing such service.[22] Third, competitive entrants face a nontrivial probability that they will be subject to similar network sharing mandates, particularly if they succeed in constructing advanced systems that win large market shares. Under current U.S. law competitive telecommunications facilities are not, in fact, exempt from sharing requirements (although such rules are less onerous than for incumbent local exchange carriers). And entrants investing in competitive local exchange facilities inform their shareholders that free riding by current or future rivals is a tax on investment: "These requirements also place burdens on new entrants that may benefit their competitors. In particular, the resale requirement means that a company can seek to resell services using the facilities of a new entrant, such as Cox, without making a similar investment in facilities."[23]

A large source of irony in the approach taken to unbundled communication networks is that it departs sharply from previous policies to encourage dynamic efficiency found both in the economics literature and in public policy. The Demsetz solution to natural monopoly, for instance, describes a competition for the monopoly that could be deployed in public franchising or in marketplace settings.[24] The essence of the approach is that, where monopoly provision is efficient, consumer gains can be extracted by the use of long-term contracts. Competition for these contracts can be arranged in franchising rounds (with formal requests for proposals) or via rivalry among firms to gain critical mass by offering consumers favorable terms.[25] The dynamic powering an efficient solution is the lure of a long-term monopoly market share (for the supplier) in exchange for competitive performance on price, quality, and innovation.

The unbundling solution retains the monopoly service provision for that part of the production function deemed noncompetitive by regulators,

---

22. There is another factor that may offset these incentives of facilities-based entrants, namely the ability to rent facilities of incumbents during build out, thus achieving market coverage (and some scale and scope efficiencies) while in transition to facilities-based competition. Of course, the premise of unbundling mandates is that the incumbent's facilities will not be soon duplicated by rival networks.

23. Cox Cable (2000, pp. 27–28).

24. Demsetz (1968); Baumol, Panzar, and Willig (1982).

25. Hazlett (1985).

making illegal long-term contracts allowing firms and consumers to discover competitive solutions in the market. Hence the monopoly position is supported by regulation, and the forces used to mitigate its anticonsumer effects are blocked. They are replaced by a wholesale price schedule devised by regulators that may or may not stimulate retail competition, which will tax investment in specific capital and which will render moot market forces devising long-term solutions exploiting scale economies without output restrictions.

Contrast, too, the network-sharing approach with the defense of franchise barriers.[26] Many restrictions on entry can be explained as devices to encourage investment of risk capital. This idea was quickly seized as an explanation of many market forms that had previously been attacked by antitrust enforcement authorities as anticonsumer: Restrictions on entry created via exclusive contracts, brand name capital, and other mechanisms actually yield improved incentives to create specific capital.[27]

The economic logic tracks the institution of patents and copyrights. Restrictions on free entry can have powerful dynamic consequences, motivating a degree of long-lived investment that fully compensates for the static losses that predictably accrue from restricting output in the short run. The nature of broadband markets today—high (and volatile) growth rates, technological flux, uncertain consumer acceptance—suggests that the benefits of proinvestment policies are important relative to the yields available from promoting steady-state efficiencies via an increase in the number of competitors using the same facilities. Both economics and law have developed theories driven by the dynamic properties of long-term contracts, vertical integration, and restrictions on entry to protect innovators. Mandatory network sharing initiatives conflict frontally with this approach.

The Broadband Race

The crucial role of vertical integration in dispersing broadband technologies is emerging. One key indicator is provided by the distinct regulatory regimes faced by the rival services. Cable modem service is being offered by local cable monopolies, firms not facing effective regulation of rates (for broadband or plain old cable service) or subject to open-access mandates. While the latter have been considered by several municipalities

---

26. See Goldberg (1976).
27. See Klein, Crawford, and Alchian (1978); Klein and Leffler (1981).

(in authorizing franchise transfers, pursuant to mergers of system operators, or renewals) and by the FCC, U.S. cable systems currently operate virtually without any such regulatory obligations.[28]

The degree to which cable systems face weaker regulatory constraints
than incumbent local exchange carriers shows up in the financial data. As
seen in table 9-2, cable systems sell for about four times the replacement
cost of capital. In contrast, local exchange carriers are valued at just about
the cost of capital. These market data reveal how much more lucrative
anticipated revenue streams are in cable than in telephony. Telephone systems, largely governed by common carrier rules, are supposed to receive
only a competitive rate of return, in effect capping the q-ratio at unity.[29]
Cable television systems are not subject to such constraints and are anticipated by investors to produce revenues far in excess of costs.

In this light, it is informative that cable modem service continues to
outpace digital service lines in the broadband race. Despite early warnings
that digital service would prove superior to its cable modem competition
(including a 1999 prediction by Cisco chief executive officer John Cham-
bers that digital lines would soon dominate the broadband access market),
cable modem subscribership remained more than double that for digital
subscriber lines through mid-2001 (see table 9-1). While competing explanations are possible, financial analysts note the reluctance of incumbent
local exchange carriers to sink resources in advanced networks. Cable television companies themselves note their greater degree of aggressiveness in
rolling out new broadband services.[30] This is a predictable implication of
the distinct regulatory regimes governing each.

As mandated by unbundling rules, the digital subscriber line supply
chain is modular. Therefore, connections often require the cooperation of
three independent firms: the incumbent local exchange carrier that owns
the network; the digital subscriber line provider, which often owns some

28. Pursuant to the merger of Time Warner and America Online, some Internet service providers'
access requirements were levied on Time Warner's cable systems offering AOL's high-speed service.
These obligations are not substantial. See Morgan Stanley (2001); Espin (1998, 2000); Bittlingmayer
and Hazlett (2002).

29. The q-ratio equals the market value of assets divided by the replacement cost of tangible assets.
It is a market measure of the degree of profitability associated with a given enterprise or industry. In a
highly competitive market, assets will sell for about their replacement cost, implying a q-ratio near 1.
When monopoly returns are anticipated by investors, q-ratios should be considerably higher. The
q-ratio analysis is used to gauge market power in telecommunications markets; for instance, by the
FCC in examining cable television systems. See FCC (1994); see also Katz and Summers (1989).

30. AT&T (1999).

Table 9-2. *Capitalized Rents in Regional Bell Operating Companies and Cable Television Networks, 1999*
Dollars, except as indicated

Asset	Market value (1999 mean)	Capital cost (1999 mean)	q-ratio
Regional Bells	2,931 a line	2,311 a line	1.27
Cable television	3,995 a subscriber	1,000 a subscriber[a]	4.00

Source: Legg Mason (2001, pp. 12, 42); FCC (2002, table B-5); FCC (1999, figure 2).
a. Includes cost of two-way digital.

facilities (such as digital switches located in the central offices of the incumbent carrier and fiber transport lines) but relies heavily on unbundled incumbent carrier network elements for the "last mile"; and an Internet service provider, providing a retail service interface with users. Successful interaction of these suppliers with each other and with the consumer has proven challenging; widespread customer confusion has resulted, severely impacting the rollout of service.[31] Cable operators, unburdened by sharing requirements and vertically integrated into retail service provision, enjoy clear lines of responsibility. One way in which this has ironically manifested itself is in cable's superior coordination in the modem equipment market. Without regulatory constraints, cable operators have established open (nonproprietary) standards for modems that invite multiple equipment manufacturers to compete on cost and quality. "Open" telephone industry providers of digital lines have lagged far behind this effort.[32]

While cable's regulatory status has assisted it in the broadband race, there is evidence that the mere threat of open-access rules for cable operators has negatively impacted investment incentives. This evidence is gleaned from financial markets, where open-access events are negatively correlated with returns not only for specialized cable Internet service

31. Among myriad reports documenting the difficulties digital subscriber line suppliers have in coordinating their activities, this is typical: "In theory, digital service promises large cost savings for companies of all sizes, compared to T1. But installation woes and poor performance render it more trouble than its worth. . . . 'Service-level agreement issues remain very fuzzy. Who is responsible when something goes wrong?' asks Andy Bose, CEO of New York-based research firm AMI Partners. . . . 'The local phone company called six distinct times to schedule installation. I kept telling them, 'Its installation has already been scheduled. You've already called. You've already installed it,' says Eileen Zimbler, AMI's production manager. Zimbler says she got about the same number of calls from the digital subscriber line provider and Internet service provider, both uncertain as to where AMI's order stood." Jennifer Jones, "DSL in Distress," *InfoWorld,* December 4, 2000, p. 40.

32. Bittlingmayer and Hazlett (forthcoming).

providers like @Home but also for Internet infrastructure and content providers. Event windows wherein open-access rules move forward show no statistically significant reaction among the infrastructure-content plays; events wherein open-access rules suffer setbacks exhibit positive infrastructure-content returns.[33]

More pointedly, the limited bandwidth afforded cable modem service by cable operators illustrates how nervous network creators are about common carrier-type regulation. Just 1 television channel (6 megahertz) of the standard 125-channel cable television system (750 megahertz) is devoted to downstream Internet access. On a revenue-per-megahertz basis, it appears that cable operators (and monopoly operators much more than overbuilders) tend to underallocate radio spectrum to high-speed access. While cannibalization of video revenues is the oft-cited rationale for such parsimonious commitment to the emerging technology, this explanation is incomplete: Digital cable, pay per view, and video on demand can also cannibalize (or compete with) other video revenues. Yet these other services are allotted far more bandwidth, absolutely or adjusting for service revenues, than Internet access.

The key distinction is regulatory: Only with Internet access does the cable operator open itself up to potential common carrier regulation. To limit this apparent source of appropriation, already visible in the open-access movement (attempting to subject cable modem service, but neither plain old cable service nor advanced cable services, to mandatory unbundling), cable operators select system architectures that rigidly underallocate radio spectrum to the at-risk service.[34] Consistent with this behavior, cable operators vehemently resist any legal designation as common carriers.[35]

The impact of open-access rules in slowing the creation of advanced services over local exchange systems is also becoming evident. While unbundling is required for plain old telephone service as per the 1996

---

33. Bittlingmayer and Hazlett (forthcoming).

34. OpenNET, the coalition lobbying for open-access rules, puts its case to the FCC this way: "Cable operators have chosen to become common carriers by offering a telecommunications service over their existing cable system infrastructure. The [1996 Communications] Act requires that the nature of the service, not the underlying facility nor the particular provider, determines a provider's regulatory classification. The Commission should act immediately and declare that the Title II nondiscrimination and interconnection obligations that govern telecommunications common carriers apply to all cable broadband providers offering broadband Internet transport, which is clearly a telecommunications service." OpenNET (2001, p. 4).

35. See, for example, AT&T (1999).

Telecommunications Act, the FCC has explicitly declined to extend these requirements to advanced services (such as high-speed data networks).[36] Of course, the unbundling and separate subsidiary requirements for Bell companies achieve some of the same limits on vertical integration and long-term contracting that explicit regulation of advanced networks would.[37] This is why the relaxation of existing rules for high-speed data networks is both highly prized by Bell companies and intensely opposed by others.[38]

The difficulties in regulated unbundling of telecommunications networks may be observed in the current experience in plain old telephone and plain old cable. Introducing competitive telephone service via network-sharing mandates is proving difficult to effect in foreign markets, particularly those throughout Europe.[39] Introducing cable television competition via Video Dialtone and Open Video Systems garners trivial subscribership and virtually no actual sharing of facilities despite FCC regulatory proceedings stretching from 1987 (bolstered by the 1996 Telecommunications Act). Leased access, a channel unbundling requirement for cable systems in effect since 1972, has proven similarly unsuccessful.

Perhaps the most vocal advocate of extensive unbundling requirements for local telephone systems is AT&T, a long-distance carrier with extensive cable television holdings.[40] It acquired these cable systems primarily in mergers with TCI and MediaOne. In arguing the public interest benefits

36. FCC (1999). See also Kahn (2001, pp. 11, 24).
37. See, generally, Huber, Kellogg, and Thorne (1999).
38. David McGuire, "Bells, Rivals Gear up for Battle," *Washington Post*, February 28, 2001.
39. "Local loop unbundling is almost dead. . . . This time last year, you may remember, the European Commission was getting very excited about mandating local loop unbundling right across the European Union. Local exchanges were to become low rent hotels. At reasonable cost, new entrants could drive up and apply for a room in the incumbent's abode. . . . At that time, Jack McMaster, chief executive of KPNKwest, had one of the more ambitious pan-European unbundling plans. By October 2000 he'd cancelled most of them. . . . 'What we got wrong was that we didn't realise how successful the incumbents were going to be at dragging their feet,' McMaster reflects. 'When we announced we were going to pull out, people asked what had changed in such a short space of time? The answer was we got the crap kicked out of us.' . . . If, as a potential unbundler, you are faced with the full obstinacy and immovability of an incumbent, unbundling of the local loop becomes a very tall order indeed. . . . Roughly a year ago more than forty operators were involved in a negotiation process with BT and Oftel to agree [to] the terms and conditions which would enable them to unbundle BT's copper. With what any other company might have viewed as a major commercial opportunity, BT adopted the foetal position, stuffed its thumb in its mouth, and regressed back to the 1970s." Ian Scales, "Bottom Line: Toothless Watchdogs," CI-Online (www.totaltele.com/view.asp?articleID=42417&pub=newci& categoryid=735 [April 4, 2002]).
40. AT&T's cable television systems have recently been the subject of a merger offer by Comcast.

created in the latter purchase before the FCC in September 1999, AT&T was careful to specify the economic advantages of vertical integration in providing cable telephony (using cable system infrastructure to provide facilities-based competition to an incumbent local exchange carrier). In considering whether AT&T could, as an alternative to merging with MediaOne and owning its cable systems, achieve the same economic benefits via a sharing agreement, it wrote:

> Any joint venture that contemplates the provision of services by one party over the facilities of another party raises difficult issues that are likely to lead to protracted negotiations. And in the current environment of rapid and increasingly unpredictable evolution and convergence in technologies and consumer demands, reaching agreement on a joint venture contract for the provision and marketing of telephony and other services over cable is inherently and especially difficult.
>
> Technologies and services are rapidly evolving and converging; hence, no one can reliably predict what business models, service offerings, or technologies are likely to emerge as successful even over the next few years. . . . This uncertainty makes it extremely difficult for a cable company that owns facilities potentially capable of providing multiple existing and future services, and a telephone company that wants to use those facilities to compete with the offerings of an [incumbent local exchange carrier] (whose facilities have multiple uses under one ownership), to agree in advance on limits on the services that the telephone company will offer and the amount of cable bandwidth it may use.[41]

On the question as to whether vertical integration between the network owner and the Internet service provider having responsibility for retail customer relations is efficient, AT&T wrote:

> The relationship between AT&T and @Home is highly interdependent, and the two parties have negotiated a revenue split that reflects not the cost of transport but rather the investments and expertise that each side brought to the table. . . . This unique relationship cannot be duplicated by government mandate.
>
> Pricing regulation is an extremely complex process, both procedurally and politically. A new regulatory structure, similar to the structure in place for telephone service, would need to be developed to handle the Internet—a regulatory nightmare that could take years to put in place. . . . Common carrier regulation is completely unnecessary, and actually harmful, if applied in a nascent, competitive marketplace like that for Internet services.[42]

41. AT&T (1999, p. 19).
42. AT&T (1999, pp. 105–06).

The symmetry with arguments against unbundling incumbent carriers' networks is striking. When investing, all firms are quick to cite the tax provided by network-sharing obligations. They anticipate that compliance costs (negotiations, litigation, regulatory process) will be high, that the uncertainty produced by rule changes adds substantial project risk, and that the availability of their capital for the use of rivals (at the option of the rivals) constitutes free riding. All factors discourage investment. Since the premise of such regulation is that only the firms selected for sharing requirements will build facilities (hence the need to open them to competitors), this generally implies that total investment in network infrastructure falls.

Rent Seeking to Raise Rivals' Costs

The positions advocated by firms signal the likely effect of public policies. Because managers are obligated to advance the interests of their shareholders, they reliably seek to enact rules awarding their firms advantages. These may enhance profitability either by lowering costs (say, decreasing taxes or increasing efficiency) or by increasing revenues. Regulations that asymmetrically burden rivals achieve the latter by allowing the successful petitioner to gain market share.[43]

The intense public policy debate in broadband has fleshed out a revealing—and symmetric—set of economic interests.[44] The campaign to establish unbundling requirements for cable television systems was spearheaded by GTE and AOL and then joined by a host of incumbent and competitive exchange carriers and Internet service providers. The Open-NET coalition was formed as an "AOL/ISP/phone-company" group to lobby for open access, soon to be joined by the "BOC-backed,

---

43. AT&T notes that when its direct competitors argue in favor of regulating AT&T (through antitrust or regulatory mandates) it reveals that such policies will produce benefits for such firms by reducing the efficiency of AT&T. Speaking of opponents to its merger with MediaOne, it writes: "The private interests of these firms, unlike the interest of the consuming public, are disserved by any increase in competition for their services. If the incumbent providers truly thought that the proposed Merger was unlikely to intensify the competition facing them, then their logical reaction would be private rejoicing at the folly of AT&T's costly undertaking." AT&T (1999, pp. 3 and 8).

44. "The country's regional Bell telephone companies and the cable giant AT&T are engaged in a furious fight on Capitol Hill over the rules managing the rollout of high-speed Internet access into Americans' homes, in the process reopening one of the most bitter lobbying clashes of the last decade." Lizette Alvarez, "In Capitol, AT&T and Bells Fight to Control Web Access," *New York Times*, August 29, 2001.

iAdvance."[45] AT&T, as the leading cable operator, responded by backing "Hands off the Internet."[46]

A mirror image appears in the battle over potential deregulation of telco broadband (digital subscriber lines). Here, Bell companies aggressively advance their agenda to limit unbundling obligations and structural separation rules by advocating passage of the Tauzin-Dingell bill. Countering this agenda is AT&T, spending heavily for campaign contributions, lobbying, consulting, and advertising aimed at undermining support for the measure.[47] Going further, AT&T launched a campaign in 2000 to lobby state regulators to force vertical divestiture of local Bell companies, quarantining local access in a separate wholesale service provider. Thus far, twelve states are considering this structural separation proposal, although none has yet adopted it.[48] AT&T has self-identified as a direct competitor to Verizon, SBC, US West, and Bell South and specifically notes that its rivals stand to gain from restricting efficiencies it enjoyed in providing cable telephony.[49] The reverse is also true.

A distinct pattern emerges (see table 9-3). Firms consistently advocate unbundling regulation for rivals while opposing it for themselves. It is apparent that industry executives have achieved consensus: Unbundling obligations are bad for business. More pointedly, unbundling obligations are bad for consumers. This is deduced by virtue of the impact of regulations on direct rivals. If the best intelligence known to AT&T indicates that local telephone access will be provided more efficiently under structural separation, advocating such a policy—and investing substantial resources to pursue it—would violate not only the profit maximization assumption but also the legal obligation to shareholders. Similarly, if incumbent carriers promoting cable open-access rules were to do so understanding that cable network unbundling promotes customer satisfaction, they would be actively undermining demand for their competing digital subscriber line service. The implication is that telephone compa-

45. Esbin (2000, p. 11).

46. Esbin (2000, p. 12).

47. Lizette Alvarez, "In Capitol, AT&T and Bells Fight to Control Web Access," *New York Times,* August 29, 2001.

48. Yochi Dreazen, "AT&T Makes Headway with Lawmakers in Bid to Break Bell Companies' Markets," *Wall Street Journal,* August 28, 2001 (www.wsj.com); Ron Cowles and Alex Winogradoff. "Structural Separation: The Final Solution for Advancing Local Competition?" Gartner, Inc. (www.gartner.com [April 10, 2001]).

49. AT&T (1999).

Table 9-3. *Broadband Unbundling, a Rent-Seeking Game*

| Sector | Rival | Policy advocated | |
		For rival	For itself
Cable TV operators (CATV)	ILECs' DSL	Regulate	Deregulate
Incumbent local exchange carriers (ILECs)	Cable modems	Regulate	Deregulate
Competitive local exchange carriers (CLECs)	Cable modems	Regulate	Deregulate
Competitive local exchange carriers (CLECs)	ILECs' DSL	Regulate	Deregulate

nies believe that unbundling rules will limit the quality of the networks owned by rivals.

There is a cross-check on this analysis. While players not directly competing in the broadband race tend to economize on resources by avoiding contentious regulatory disputes, one key player engaged in this issue is Intel, the leading maker of integrated circuits (chips). With diverse interests spanning the computing and telecommunications landscape, Intel prospers when network competition is intense and efficient solutions are widely available to the mass market. Intel's expert position on the broadband regulatory issue is that unbundling of high-speed services is unwise in cable or telephone systems.[50] As an expert proxy for consumer interests, Intel's advocacy carries great weight.[51]

Competitive Analysis

If one proceeds down the checklist of efficiency and anticompetitive rationales for vertical integration, the market for residential broadband

50. "Dr. Grove stated that Intel's goal is to make true broadband widespread and affordable. . . . Intel believes that incumbent companies should not have to unbundle new fiber and DSL equipment as long as they are required to make their existing 'copper' lines and central offices available to their competitors. He stated that imposing such 'unbundling' regulation on this discretionary investment could unnecessarily discourage DSL deployment." Ex parte report of a meeting between Intel executives and FCC chair Michael Powell, filed by Intel (June 20, 2001).

51. Intel's deregulatory approach to broadband networks has been endorsed by other leading firms in the computer sector including Cisco, Microsoft, Gateway, and IBM. See "Silicon Valley Weighs in on High-Speed Network Deployment," *Washington Telecom Week,* December 11, 1998, p. 13; Seth Schiesel, "PC Companies and Bells to Petition U.S.," *New York Times,* December 7, 1998, p. C1.

service does not have the structure that would justify unbundling mandates for either cable modem or digital subscriber line service. First, market conditions suggest that vertical integration offers crucial efficiencies. Substantial amounts of specific capital must be invested to create broadband networks, and open access to such facilities undermines risk taking to create them. Moreover, cable's vertically integrated services have been relatively successful in building and utilizing such networks, while digital subscriber line service has encountered severe marketing and service problems, widely attributed to its truncated linkages and diffused responsibilities. This smacks of the classic problem of incomplete contracts, in which reliance on complementary producers is undercut due to transaction costs. Here, due to regulation, no contracts are allowed. And reliance on nonintegrated partners has proven extremely disruptive.[52]

Second, regulatory evasion—funneling costs into the unregulated vertical market to raise "costs" in the regulated market—is not plausible in either cable or telephone markets. In cable, rate regulation was effectively repealed in the 1996 Telecommunications Act (as of March 31, 1999). In local telephony, rates are regulated principally by price caps. As opposed to rate-of-return regulation, such rules provide no reward for shifting costs. In states in which rate-of-return rules are still in place, rate caps could (and should) replace them, obviating the cross-subsidy problem across jurisdictions.

Third, the dynamic nature of the market puts regulators in a difficult position for crafting rules. In 1999 Internet access providers Covad, Northpoint, Rhythms, and @Home were busy signing up customers, and each company had a market capitalization of billions of dollars. Today each firm has filed for bankruptcy protection. With such market volatility, determining the efficient terms of vertical combination or cooperation— no easy task in the calmest of markets—is even more complex than usual.

Finally, there is no monopoly. Whatever the eventual market power exercised by dominant players, the broadband race today features multiple players vying for market share. Not all residential customers face ideal choices, and price discrimination (higher prices when competition is

52. This was poignantly demonstrated, for instance, when it was revealed in late 2000 that many digital subscriber line wholesalers had been keeping the customers of Internet subscriber providers on the books far beyond the point at which they became "bad debt." While such firms sought to impress financial markets with "subscriber" and "revenue" growth, the ultimate problem created many spillover costs along the digital subscriber line supply chain. See, for example, Sam Ames and Corey Grice, "Covad Unplugs Late-Paying ISP Partners," CNET News.com (news.cnet.com/news/0-1004-200-4/6164/.html?tag=prntfr [April 12, 2002]).

lower) can be observed. But rivalry is driving high growth, and measures intensifying the race by introducing additional facilities-based competitors are the prudent policy approach.

Even a cursory examination of the choices offered to residential broadband customers in one market (Washington, D.C.) suggests interesting policy alternatives. The cable incumbent, Comcast, offers broadband Internet access for about $54 a month when the up-front installation and modem fee is amortized over a typical subscriber life. This is about 6 percent higher than the price charged by RCN, a cable overbuilder available to residents in parts of the city. Both direct broadcast satellite systems (EchoStar and DirecTV) offer two-way Internet access, with download speeds up to 400 kilobits a second, pricing the service (including substantial up-front costs) at approximately $80 a month.[53] Verizon's price for a digital subscriber line is about $58 monthly, including standard connection costs. By comparison, the monthly cost of a second residential telephone line plus an Internet dial-up connection (AT&T World Net) is about $35.

It is difficult to identify a monopoly bottleneck in the current competitive landscape. There are, however, policy measures that could accelerate incentives for incumbents to build out their networks and reduce entry barriers for further competitors. On the former, the FCC could conclusively determine that unbundling obligations for high-speed services in either cable or telephone systems are not in the public interest. This would reduce the risk premium associated with anticipated appropriation via network sharing mandates, and—ceteris paribus—increase investment incentives for both cable modem and digital subscriber line networks.

The FCC could also place another competitive choice in the residential broadband mix by issuing licenses to Northpoint Technology.[54] This firm has developed a technology to reuse the spectrum allocated to direct broadcast satellite systems through a combination of satellite and terrestrial facilities, and the FCC has found that the delivery system works (meaning that it creates only minimal interference with existing users).[55] After an eight-year effort on the part of Northpoint to obtain licenses, the FCC

53. EchoStar's proposed purchase of DirecTV is currently being evaluated by the FCC and the U.S. Department of Justice Antitrust Division.
54. Northpoint Technology is not associated with NorthPoint Communications, a bankrupt digital subscriber line provider.
55. Brown (2000) (www.broadbandweek.com/news/0011/0011_wireless_north.htm).

decided to implement the Northpoint spectrum-sharing system but to issue licenses by auction.[56]

Northpoint's market entry will be delayed by years if the FCC undertakes to make a new rule and prepares to issue licenses by competitive bidding. This delay could be avoided by promptly licensing Northpoint, an applicant that has requested market entry without mutually exclusive rival applications since 1994. Such action would insert a new competitor into the broadband marketplace, one that has announced plans to provide low-cost residential service; for example, basic cable service and up to a hundred hours of broadband, one-way Internet access for $39 a month.[57]

The policy, of course, can be extrapolated: The FCC should make abundant spectrum available for all noninterfering entrants. The regulated communications spectrum is extensively underutilized, and far greater capacity is available under a more liberal allocation regime.[58] Fixed and mobile terrestrial wireless, satellite, and other innovative approaches to broadband access would amplify the competitive choices faced by households. One particularly rich source of underutilized spectrum having excellent propagation characteristics for wireless broadband access is the television band. Since, as of year-end 2001, 87 percent of U.S. households receive their television signals via cable or satellite, a reallocation of these airwaves would produce enormous social gains.[59]

The weakness of the choices facing broadband customers involve coverage. RCN, for instance, is constructing competitive cable facilities in many major markets, but relatively few U.S. households have such options available to them. Regulatory burdens are a major hurdle for such firms as RCN, which recently abandoned a two-year effort to obtain a franchise in Philadelphia.[60] Municipal governments, on their own or under mandates from state statutes, routinely engage in rent-extracting franchise procedures that perversely hold up competitive entrants, protecting incumbents with

56. FCC (2002). As I argued in an analysis submitted to the FCC in March 2001 on behalf of Northpoint, this auction will appropriate the firm's substantial investment in technology (including license-specific investments in the demonstration of their system, submissions for interference adjudication, and negotiation of sharing arrangements with incumbent spectrum users), discouraging wireless technology creation.

57. See (www.broadwave.com [June 17, 2002]).

58. Hazlett (2001a).

59. Hazlett (2001b).

60. Ken Dilanian and Wendy Tanaka, "RCN Pulls Cable-TV Proposal," *Philadelphia Enquirer,* February 15, p. A1; "RCN to Philly: See Ya," *Broadband Week,* February 19, 2001 (www.broad bandweek.com/news/010219/print/010219_news_rcn.htm [April 12, 2002]); The Insider, "Saidel

market power.[61] This could be remedied by federal legislation mandating that timely, nonburdensome franchises be issued to all applicants and by relaxing the unbundling requirements in federal franchises for Open Video Systems.

The antitrust treatment of a direct broadcast satellite merger may materially affect local broadband markets. Currently, broadband access by direct broadcast satellite is relatively expensive and relatively slow. With EchoStar's October 2001 offer to purchase DirecTV, a merger currently under antitrust review, the capacity available to serve a given customer of the merged firm—both in orbital slots and allocated spectrum—would instantly double. This added capacity would create two interesting outcomes. First, bandwidth available for broadband Internet access via satellite would become much more abundant. Second, bandwidth available for local signal delivery would also increase, driving direct broadcast satellite service to offer local television channels in many more markets. On the other hand, the number of multichannel video competitors would be reduced.

Conclusion

By focusing on measures to eliminate barriers now blocking additional coverage and potential broadband entrants, policymakers may invigorate broadband rivalry. There are many competitors to add to the mix and no downside risk in opening markets. The alternative is to regulate networks. Both economic theory and the available evidence strongly suggest that investment declines with the degree of sharing mandated. Even if regulators do desire to appropriate investor rents, waiting until the investment is sunk before revealing their plan appears the strategic approach.

Three attributes of the residential broadband access market support deregulation of unbundling mandates: multiple platforms, relatively low penetration, and rapid growth. These factors, combined with economic evidence on regulatory effects, allow for informed policy conclusions even

Slams Shunning of RCN by Philadelphia," *Philadelphia Business Journal,* February 19, 2001 (philadel phia.bcentral.com/philadelphia/stories/2001/02/19/tidbits.html [April 12, 2002]). See also "RCN Annual Report for the Year Ended December 31, 2000—10K-K405," filed with the Securities and Exchange Commission, April 2, 2001, pp. 15–17.

61. Hazlett and Ford (2001).

in the face of the maelstrom of turmoil witnessed in technology, operating, and financial markets.

In the race for market share, competing technologies invest to create critical mass for their rival platforms. The high rate of subscriber growth, from a currently modest base, suggests that dynamic incentives to deploy broadband are relatively more important than measures designed to improve allocative efficiency. To regulate competitive superiority at this stage lowers returns to successful network innovators and thereby hinders market formation. This is the logic behind former FCC chairman William Kennard's rejection of open-access rules for cable systems in 1999 on the grounds that it would amount to regulating a "no-opoly."[62] The logic holds today.

References

AT&T. 1999. Reply Comments of AT&T Corp. and MediaOne Group, Inc. In the Matter of Applications for Consent to the Transfer of Control of Licenses. FCC CS Docket 99-251 (September 17).

Baumol, William, John Panzar, and Robert Willig. 1982. *Contestable Markets and the Theory of Industry Structure.* Harcourt Brace Jovanovich.

Bittlingmayer, George, and Thomas W. Hazlett. 2002. "Open Access: The Ideal and the Real." *Telecommunications Policy* 26 (June): 295–310.

———. Forthcoming. "The Political Economy of Cable 'Open Access.'" *Stanford Technology Law Review.*

Bresnahan, Timothy. 1999. "New Modes of Competition: Implications for the Future Structure of the Computer Industry." In *Competition, Innovation, and the Microsoft Monopoly: Antitrust in the Digital Marketplace,* edited by Jeffrey Eisenach and Thomas Lenard. Boston: Kluwer.

Brown, Peter J. 2000. "Northpoint Technology Readies Broadwave Wireless Service." *Broadband Week,* November, p. 54.

Coase, Ronald. 1937. "The Nature of the Firm." *Economica* 4 (November): 86–405.

Cox Cable. 2000. *Annual Report* (SEC 10K).

Demsetz, Harold. 1968. "Why Regulate Utilities?" *Journal of Law and Economics* 11 (April): 55–65.

Dixit, Avinash K., and Robert S. Pindyck. 1994. *Investment under Uncertainty.* Princeton University Press.

62. " 'Today,' [Kennard] said, 'we don't have a duopoly, we don't have a monopoly, we have a no-opoly.' " FCC press release, "Chairman Kennard Calls on Cable Franchising Authorities to Promote National Broadband Policy; Vows Continued Consumer Protection" (ftp.fcc.gov/Bureaus/ Miscellaneous/News_Releases/1999/nrmc9041.txt [April 12, 2002]).

Esbin, Barbara. 1998. "Internet over Cable: Defining the Future in Terms of the Past." FCC, OPP Working Paper 30 (August).

———. 2000. "The Push for Open Access to Cable Systems: Be Careful What You Ask For." Washington: Dow Lohnes and Albertson (March).

FCC (Federal Communications Commission). 1994. Annual Assessment of the Status of Competition in the Market for the Delivery of Video Programming: First Report. 9 FCC Rcd. 7442. CS Docket 94-98.

———. 1999. Application for Deployment of Wire-Line Services Offering Advanced Telecommunications Capability and Implementation of the Local Competition Provisions of the Telecommunications Act of 1996. CC Docket 96-147.

———. 2002. Amendment of Parts 2 and 25 of the Commission's Rules to Permit Operation of NGSO FSS Systems Co-Frequency with GSO and Terrestrial Systems in the Ku-Band Frequency Range. Memorandum Opinion and Order and Second Report and Order. ET Docket 98-206.

Fisher, Franklin. 2001. "Innovation and Monopoly Leveraging." In *Dynamic Competition and Public Policy: Technology, Innovation, and Antitrust Issues,* edited by Jerome Ellig, 138–39. Cambridge University Press.

Goldberg, Victor. 1976. "Regulation and Administered Contracts." *Bell Journal of Economics* 7 (Autumn): 426–48.

Hausman, Jerry. 1998. "The Effect of Sunk Costs in Telecommunications Regulation." Paper prepared for a conference at Columbia University, October 2.

Hazlett, Thomas W. 1985. "Private Contracting versus Public Regulation as a Solution to the Natural Monopoly Problem." In *Unnatural Monopolies: The Case for Deregulating Public Utilities,* edited by Robert Poole Jr., 71–114. Lexington Books.

———. 2001a. "The Wireless Craze, the Unlimited Bandwidth Myth, the Spectrum Auctions Faux Pas, and the Punchline to Ronald Coase's 'Big Joke': An Essay on Airwave Allocation Policy." *Harvard Journal on Law and Technology* 14 (Spring): 335–567.

———. 2001b. "The U.S. Digital TV Transition: Time to Toss the Negroponte Switch." Paper prepared for the International Telecommunications Society, European Regional Meetings, Dublin, Ireland, September 3.

Hazlett, Thomas W., and George S. Ford. 2001. "The Fallacy of Regulatory Symmetry: An Economic Analysis of the 'Level Playing Field' in Cable TV Franchising Statutes." *Business and Politics* (April): 21–46.

Huber, Peter, Michael K. Kellogg, and John Thorne. 1999. *Federal Telecommunications Law.* Gaithersburg, Md.: Aspen Law and Business.

Kahn, Alfred. 1998. *Letting Go: Deregulating the Process of Deregulation.* Institute of Public Utilities, Michigan State University (July).

———. 2001. "Whom the Gods Would Destroy; or, How Not to Deregulate." AEI-Brookings Joint Center for Regulatory Studies.

Katz, Lawrence F., and Lawrence H. Summers. 1989. "Industry Rents: Evidence and Implications." *BPEA, Microeconomics:* 209–75.

Klein, Benjamin, Robert Crawford, and Armen Alchian. 1978. "Vertical Integration, Appropriable Rents, and the Competitive Contracting Process." *Journal of Law and Economics* 21:297–326.

Klein, Benjamin, and Keith Leffler. 1981. 'The Role of Market Forces in Assuring Product Quality." *Journal of Political Economy* 89: 615–41.

Krattenmaker, Thomas G., and Steven C. Salop. 1986. "Anticompetitive Exclusion: Raising Rivals' Costs to Achieve Power over Price." *Yale Law Journal* 96 (December): 209–93.

Legg Mason Equity Research. 2001. *Reshaping Rural Telephone Markets: Financial Perspectives on Integration Acquired Access Lines.*

Morgan Stanley Dean Witter Equity Research/Telecom-Cable. 2001. "The Sequel: Open Access Is Better."

OpenNET. 2001. Reply Comments of the OpenNET Coalition. In the Matter of Inquiry Concerning Broadband Access to the Internet over Cable and Other Facilities. FCC, GN Docket 00-185 (January 10).

Ordover, Janusz, and Robert Willig. 1999. Declaration of Janusz A. Ordover and Robert D. Willig. Appendix A to Reply Comments of AT&T Corp. and MediaOne Group, Inc. In the Matter of Applications for Consent to the Transfer of Control of Licenses. FCC CS Docket 99-251 (September. 17).

Shelanski, Howard A., and J. Gregory Sidak. 2001. "Antitrust Divestiture in Network Industries." *University of Chicago Law Review* 68 (Winter): 1.

Williamson, Oliver. 1979. "Transaction-Cost Economics: The Governance of Contractual Relations." *Journal of Law and Economics* 22 (October): 233–61.

GERALD R. FAULHABER

10 | *Broadband Deployment: Is Policy in the Way?*

After years of connecting to the Internet via narrowband telephone lines, customers will finally have the opportunity to connect from home at speeds close to those that they experience at work, thanks to the broadband revolution. But many claim that the broadband revolution is the newest version of the World Wide Wait: It just is not happening fast enough. What is the problem? Is it a lack of demand? Is it the inability of providers to deliver broadband to customers? Or is it, as some claim, a policy failure? In particular, have policies of the Federal Communications Commission (FCC) hindered the deployment of broadband to the home? The regional Bell operating companies have taken the position that FCC regulations requiring resale of digital subscriber lines (DSL) over loops inhibit broadband deployment, and they have sponsored a television advertising campaign and lobbied Congress for legislation to grant them relief from such regulations.

This chapter addresses the following questions:

—Has the rollout of broadband to the home been too slow? What is an appropriate standard of comparison? Is there in fact a problem?

—What has experience taught us about the incentives and the abilities of the telephone and cable industries to deploy broadband? What have been the drivers, and what have been the roadblocks? What does this experience portend for the future of broadband deployment?

—What has been the policy posture of the FCC regarding broadband for both cable and telephone providers? What is the likelihood that specific regulations (for example, mandated resale of the digital subscriber line portion of the local loop) have inhibited the deployment of broadband or may inhibit it in the future?

—Are there public policies available that will truly enhance the deployment of broadband and help ensure its aggressive development?

To preview the results, the findings of this chapter are as follows:

—Broadband deployment appears to be tracking the same growth path of other consumer communications goods, such as cellular service. In the medium term, broadband is doing just fine.

—In the short-to-medium term, impediments to deployment have been on the supply side: the ability of cable and telephone companies to get the product into the hands of customers. The regional Bell operating companies in particular have had problems executing installations and delivering reliable service with good customer support. Over the longer term, both the cable industry and the Bells have been sluggish in recognizing the strategic opportunity of broadband, and both entered rather late, dragged into it by competitive necessity. We cannot expect these firms to have the strategic vision to aggressively take the next steps in broadband, but platform competition may push them forward.

—The FCC has adopted and maintained a generally promarket approach to broadband. It has been cautious regarding regulation of cable broadband, far more so than the Federal Trade Commission in its findings in the America Online–Time Warner merger. It has been somewhat more aggressive in requiring the regional Bells to unbundle the digital portion of the local loop, presumably as part of its regulation of this legacy bottleneck facility. It is possible that the FCC's loop-unbundling requirement has had some effect on investment incentives to deploy digital broadband. However, the effect is most likely small compared to the supply, provisioning, and service problems the Bells have had in the digital subscriber line rollout. Additionally, the unbundling requirement has been largely vitiated by a combination of the Bells' aggressive pricing strategy and the data local-exchange companies' poorly conceived and executed business plans.

—Public policy should be focused on encouraging platform competition in broadband distribution to the home: cable, cable overbuilders, telephone, fiber to the home, satellite, and wireless. Competing platforms exhibit scope economies across various applications, such as video programming, broadband Internet, and telephony. Policies should thus favor removing restrictions on new platform deployment and facilitating access to content required to support competitive platforms. In particular,

—Local municipalities should be prohibited from imposing conditions on infrastructure providers, including fees in excess of costs, that discourage entry.

—Federal authorities should be receptive to the development of spectrum uses by direct broadcast satellite providers for two-way broadband.

—The FCC should continue its program access rules for video programming distributors to ensure that the content owned by the incumbent cable firms is available to new platform entrants.

Broadband Rollout: What Are the Facts?

In 2000 I published a paper (with Christiaan Hogendorn) with a model of broadband deployment.[1] When we first presented this paper in 1997 to general academic audiences, the most difficult questions we confronted were explaining what broadband access is and why anyone would want it. In the following two years broadband has become a generally understood term for at least some of the public. The fact that broadband is now being deployed at all is a mark of how rapidly the economy changes. But somewhat more surprising is the current view of many that the speed of deployment is less than expectations.[2] In 2000 most Americans did not know what broadband was; those who did seemed uninterested. Now many seem to expect that everyone should have broadband and are disappointed that this is not the case.

It is tempting to view these assertions as yet another demand for instant gratification, without regard to the cost and difficulty of rolling out a nationwide broadband infrastructure. Building infrastructure is generally much more capital-intensive and takes much longer than, say, introducing a new hand-held computer. Digging up the streets and laying fiber does

1. Faulhaber and Hogendorn (2000).

2. See for example Richard Martin, "What Broadband Revolution?" *Industry Standard,* December 11, 2000 (www.thestandard.com/article/0,1902,20440,00.html [April 15, 2002]); Matt Kranz, "Broadband's Slow Start Strangles Shares," *USA Today,* October 19, 2000 (www.usatoday.com/life/cyber/invest/ina246.htm [April 15, 2002]); Steven Rosenbush, "Broadband: What Happened?" *Business Week Online,* June 11, 2001 (www.businessweek.com/magazine/content/01_24/b3736066.htm [April 15, 2002]).

not get done on "Internet time." In this view, expectations that broadband would be available to all immediately if not sooner were simply naïve.

In 2001 two researchers estimated that broadband deployment to 94 percent of U.S. homes would provide a huge boost to economic welfare, in the neighborhood of $300 billion a year.[3] If this result is to be believed, then encouraging, even subsidizing, extensive broadband deployment may be a suitable public policy goal and is certainly a reason to be concerned about any slowdown of broadband deployment.[4] Of course, if such gains do exist, then one would expect the market to respond enthusiastically, and potential providers would be rushing to build infrastructure to the home, provided they could find a way to capture at least some of the surplus they would thus generate. The alleged slowdown, if real, casts doubt on this hypothesis of the pot of gold at the end of the broadband rainbow. Nevertheless, these results suggest that the issue of the speed of broadband deployment is worth addressing.

The first statistics on broadband deployment became available in 1998. The FCC reported that by year-end 1998, 375,000 U.S. households subscribed to high-speed Internet access. By the end of 2000 over 7.1 million U.S. households had high-speed access. On September 30, 2001, the number of U.S. households with broadband was over 8.4 million (see table 10-1), a penetration of 8.1 percent. These growth rates outstripped one estimate of 5.9 million subscribers by end-of-year 2000.[5] By way of comparison, cellular telephones were commercially introduced in the United States in 1985; it was not until the end of 1991, seven years later, that cell phone subscribership reached 7.5 million (see figure 10-1).

Broadband appears to be deploying about twice as quickly as cellular did in the mid-1980s to early 1990s. Of course, analog cellular, before the introduction of digital wireless, was rather expensive. A more compelling comparison is with the rollout of the videocassette recorder (VCR), a popular consumer electronics product introduced in 1982 at a relatively low price. Broadband is apparently growing at least as fast as the VCR did in the 1980s. While 8.1 percent of U.S. households clearly is not the entire population, broadband appears to be on a high-growth trajectory, similar

3. Crandall and Jackson (2001).
4. If broadband deployment is really this important, then perhaps the federal government should make low-interest loans available to municipalities to build broadband infrastructure, just as it helps build local sewer systems (Federal Clean Water Act of 1977).
5. McKinsey and Company and JPMorgan, "Broadband 2001," Internal Report, April 2, 2001 (broadband2@mckinsey.com).

Table 10-1. *U.S. Households with High-Speed Lines, 1998–2001*[a]

Technology	December 1998	December 1999	June 2000	December 2000	September 2001[b]
Asymmetric digital subscriber line		369,792	951,583	1,977,377	3,947,808
Other wire line		609,909	764,099	1,063,563	1,078,597
Coaxial cable		1,414,183	2,284,491	3,576,378	7,059,598
Fiber		312,204	307,151	376,506	494,199
Satellite and fixed wireless		50,404	65,615	112,405	212,610
Total	375,000	2,756,492	4,372,939	7,106,229	12,792,912

Source: FCC (1999, 2002).

a. High-speed lines are those able to send more than 200 kilobits a second.

b. Estimated.

to or faster than the adoption trajectories of other popular technologies such as cell phones, VCRs, and television.[6]

In sum, broadband deployment is moving along quite briskly, certainly in comparison with other recently introduced popular products. It is unclear what the expectations are of those who assert that the broadband deployment is disappointing, but these expectations do not appear to be well calibrated to similar historical growth patterns.

Are There Problems?

What are the current bottlenecks to broadband deployment? Are they on the demand side (customers do not really want it) or the supply side (firms cannot produce it quickly enough or with sufficient quality)?

Demand

There has been some discussion of whether or not customers are really interested in broadband; perhaps it is a market limited to online junkies and technology aficionados. Research done in 2000 suggests this is not true

6. It is unlikely, however, that broadband will deploy more quickly than the all-time champion, black-and-white television. Between 1947 and 1952, penetration of black-and-white television grew from essentially zero to 20 percent of U.S. households. See FCC (1999).

Figure 10-1. *Early Subscriber Growth, Broadband, Wireless, and VCR*

Millions of subscribers

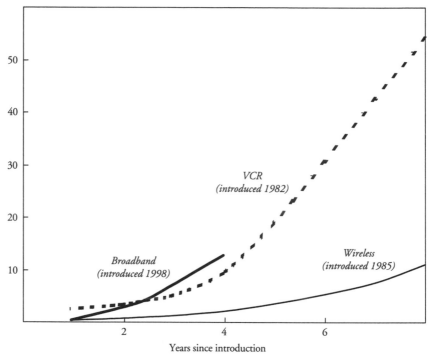

Years since introduction

and that there is a substantial demand for broadband and a deep interest in it.[7] This research found that about a third of online users were interested in high-speed service and that, among those who had actually used it (at work, for example), about three-quarters were interested. The report anticipated four distinct waves of broadband purchasers, each with different demand drivers.

Some have mentioned that the deployment of broadband will not proceed quickly until there is a compelling application for broadband.[8] While such an application would be valuable, there is no evidence that broadband is not attractive to many customers without it. Most broadband customers

7. McKinsey and Company and Sanford Bernstein and Company, "Broadband!" Internal Report, January 2000 (broadband2@mckinsey.com).

8. According to AT&T president David Dorman, "except for high-speed Internet access, there are no 'killer' applications driving demand for broadband today. That may be why, today, so few families subscribe to broadband services where they are available." *Information Week* (2001).

value the significantly improved response speed and the always-on feature and find that this justifies the extra cost of broadband.[9]

Supply

The most significant impediments have been on the supply side. The problems can be classified into four categories: addressability, provisioning, customer self-installation, and customer service.

ADDRESSABILITY. Digital subscriber line service can be provided only over certain telephone lines, generally limited in length from the subscriber's home to the telephone company's central office. In addition, the availability may depend on whether the subscriber is behind a digital-loop concentrator. In 1999 only 44 percent of telephone subscribers were addressable by digital subscriber lines; by 2000 this had increased to 64 percent, as a result of the efforts by regional Bell operating companies' efforts to improve addressability.[10] For cable, high-speed service can be provided only to customers passed by two-way enabled digital cable. In 2000, 74 percent of cable households were two-way enabled and thus addressable for cable modem service. It is expected that cable will maintain its lead in addressable households in the foreseeable future.[11]

PROVISIONING. The seemingly simple act of actually turning the service on in a timely way appears to have stumped the regional Bells, at least into 2000. Bringing customers online lagged far behind demand during 1999–2000, with both digital subscriber lines and cable modems. In 1999 the regional Bells (serving about 25,000 customers a week) and cable (serving about 30,000 customers a week) both operated significantly below requests for service, which were around 39,000 and 47,000, respectively. In 2000 these provisioning rates increased dramatically, to about 40,000 and 68,000, respectively, as providers solved their back-office problems.[12]

---

9. By way of analogy, an automobile that is capable of a speed of eighty miles an hour does not do anything fundamentally different from an automobile that is capable of a speed of only twenty miles an hour. Both can still get the driver from point A to point B; the only difference is speed, and for some applications (such as city driving) this is equivalent. Yet virtually everyone would prefer the faster car.

10. McKinsey and Company and JPMorgan, "Broadband 2001," Internal Report, April 2, 2001 (broadband2@mckinsey.com).

11. McKinsey and Company and JPMorgan, "Broadband 2001," Internal Report, April 2, 2001 (broadband2@mckinsey.com); Morgan Stanley Dean Witter, "The Sequel: Open Access Is Better," June 29, 2001 (available from author).

12. McKinsey and Company and JPMorgan, "Broadband 2001," Internal Report, April 2, 2001 (broadband2@mckinsey.com).

CUSTOMER SELF-INSTALLATION.   Early installations of broadband took at least one visit from an installer ("truck roll") and often more, creating both a customer problem (who had to stay at home until the installer showed up) and a cost problem (in that each truck roll costs the provider several hundred dollars). In 2000 the regional Bells moved more swiftly than cable firms to subscriber self-installation and may thus have a long-term advantage over cable in this regard.

CUSTOMER SERVICE.   Constant service outages, some of which lasted for months without repair, and incompetent technical support personnel were part of the digital horror stories making the rounds in 1999–2000.[13] Cable outages were more rare.[14] The problems with digital subscriber lines were exacerbated when more than one company was involved; customers who purchased digital subscriber lines from competitive local exchange carriers that offered service over incumbent local exchange carrier lines were caught in the middle, while each company pointed its finger at the other.[15] Recent reports suggest that the worst of the bad customer service is over and that the regional Bells are getting a grip on their customer service problems.

The evidence strongly suggests that market impediments to deployment are on the supply side, and they have been substantial.[16] However, these problems are being solved, and broadband is rolling out at an impressive speed. While addressability and customer service remain problems, especially for digital subscriber lines, the expectation is that in the medium term the providers will deal with them effectively.

Are There Problems? A Broader View

The focus of the previous section is the speed of broadband deployment starting in 1998, when it was introduced, through today. There are two broader questions: Why did it take until 1998 to get started? And what is the future of broadband?

13. Sean Silverthorne, "Broadband—Fast Access, Slow Install," *ZDNet News,* June 13, 2000 (www.zdnet.com/zdnn/stories/news/0,4586,2581476,00.html [April 16, 2002]).

14. McKinsey and Company and JPMorgan, "Broadband 2001," Internal Report, April 2, 2001 (broadband2@mckinsey.com).

15. Steven Rosenbush, "Broadband: What Happened?" *Business Week Online,* June 11, 2001 (www.businessweek.com/magazine/content/01_24/b3736066.htm [April 15, 2002]).

16. McKinsey and Company and JPMorgan, "Broadband 2001," Internal Report, April 2, 2001 (broadband2@mckinsey.com).

A Sluggish Start

In the early to mid-1990s, many U.S. businesses invested in extensive Ethernet networks, which were connected to the Internet for use by its employees. Only the smallest firms connected over the telephone to the Internet, perhaps because of the high cost of high-speed T1 connections from their local Bell company. In this market, there was never a question about the appropriate connection speed to the Internet: fast.

Of course, firms and universities had sufficient Internet traffic to justify the expense of high-speed connections. Small firms and individuals did not have this luxury. As Internet use became popular in 1995 and later, owners of newly acquired home personal computers used their telephone line to connect to the Internet via an Internet service provider. During this period, the Internet service provider industry was built almost overnight; barriers to entry were low, required technical skills were negligible, and costs of entry were small.[17] During 1996–97 the volume of Internet-bound telephone traffic grew at astounding rates, perhaps tripling each year, as the U.S. public flocked to the Internet. No firms were better positioned to observe this growth than the regional Bells; they actually carried all this Internet-bound traffic on their networks.

One might expect that smart businesspersons in the Bells would have noticed this tremendous growth and assessed the business opportunity it presented. The experience of U.S. business connecting to the Internet strongly suggested that narrowband telephone lines are a poor way to connect; high speed is what the market demands. Furthermore, the telephone industry had a proven technology on the shelf for rejuvenating its narrowband loops to high-speed lines: digital subscriber lines.[18]

The regional Bells' unique knowledge of growth in Internet demand coupled with market and technological facts should have led them to roll out digital lines in 1997 and be ahead of the market. But this did not occur. In fact these companies were well aware of the growth of demand for Internet access and were also aware that this traffic had long connect times. Since rates for local service do not depend upon connect times, such traffic imposed unexpected costs on the Bells. Rather than view this as an

17. During this period, several undergraduates in my classes at Wharton owned and operated local Internet service providers in their spare time.

18. Charles Jackson (this volume) notes that certain essential electronic components required for a digital subscriber line were quite expensive before about 1998. Of course, it is possible that the cost of such components could have come down substantially had the regional Bells rolled out digital service earlier. In high-technology markets, costs are often endogenous.

extraordinary business opportunity, they chose to view it as an "abuse" of their network and petitioned the FCC and state regulators to force Internet service providers to pay them higher, usage-sensitive, rates, perhaps modeled on carrier access charges paid by interexchange carriers.[19] In short, when confronted with an unprecedented market opportunity of which they had unique knowledge, the regional Bells took the traditional public utility "cost recovery" view and sought regulatory relief.[20] In my view, this incident reveals more about the effects of a century of regulation than any academic treatise could ever do.

The fact that DSL deployment lags cable modem deployment suggests that it was competition, not their market foresight, which drove the regional Bells to deploy digital subscriber lines. In 1999 AT&T in particular announced a broadband strategy in which cable telephony in competition with the regional Bells would play a significant role. In addition, the FCC ordered "line sharing" of local loops, in effect mandating that the Bell companies provide the digital portion of any customer's local loop to any carrier that requested it, as an "unbundled network element" as authorized by the Telecommunications Act of 1996. Soon a small industry of data local-exchange carriers sprang up, such as Covad and Northpoint, showing up at Bell central offices with their own equipment, demanding access to "their" customers' local loops. The Bell digital subscriber line deployment certainly followed that of the cable industry and was certainly no faster than the early deployment of the data carriers. This is consistent with the hypothesis that it was competition, both intramodal and intermodal, that drove digital subscriber line deployment by the regional Bells.

Meanwhile, cable firms began broadband deployment experimentally around 1996 and expanded into a commercial offering in 1998. Cable suffered from an addressability problem, in that significant upgrades of old analog cable systems to new digital systems with two-way capability were required. The impetus for the costly upgrade to digital systems was not broadband; it was competitive pressure from a new high-powered, direct broadcast satellite, an alternative video delivery system that promised far higher quality and far more channels than the old analog cable systems

---

19. For comments filed by Bell Atlantic and NYNEX, see FCC (1997) (www.fcc.gov/bureaus/common_carrier/comments/access_reform/noicoms.html [April 16, 2002]).

20. The prices of digital-line modems were high in early years, although by 1997 cable modem prices had dropped considerably (see Jackson, this volume). It is alleged that the regional Bells were reluctant to introduce digital lines into the market for fear of cannibalizing their lucrative T1 service.

could deliver.[21] To meet this competitive threat, cable systems were pressed to invest heavily in upgrades of their systems to digital. Fortunately for broadband customers, this digital upgrade, required for cable to compete in the video marketplace, made the provision of high-speed access to the Internet an inexpensive add-on to the new systems.[22]

In short, customers desiring broadband Internet connections were greatly advantaged by the desire of Americans to watch high-quality television shows and by the competition for that market initiated by the introduction of high-powered satellites. This provided the impetus for cable firms to deploy broadband access in their search for a low incremental investment revenue stream. In turn, cable deployment provided the impetus for the regional Bells to deploy digital subscriber lines for fear of being attacked in their core business by the cable firms.

One should indeed be grateful for this happy if somewhat random sequence of events, which has provided many Americans with fast Internet access. But this outcome is not the result of great vision and superb strategic planning on the part of either the cable industry or the regional Bells. It would be accurate if ungracious to suggest that broadband deployment occurred in spite of, rather than because of, these two legacy industries.

An Uncertain Future

The high demand for broadband by U.S. residential customers suggests that this service is creating substantial value for them and the economy.[23] One may have faith in the ability of business to capture a substantial portion of this value; already, the 6 megahertz Internet Protocol channel on digital cable systems is producing as much base revenue as the remaining 700-plus megahertz video channels for cable firms.[24] As new

21. George Bittlingmayer and Thomas W. Hazlett, "The Political Economy of Cable 'Open Access,'" *Stanford Technology Law Review* (stlr.stanford.edu/core_page/index.htm): "One interesting development is that cable TV systems are aggressively upgrading from analog to digital transmission. Driven by competition from satellite TV providers, digital cable delivers far larger packages of video channels."

22. Although cable system costs were low (given the digital upgrade), the costs to add a customer were not; this includes the modem (which customers pay for directly) and the "truck roll" for a cable installer to get the customer online.

23. Crandall and Jackson (2001).

24. A typical price for cable modem service (excluding the modem) is about $40 a month, and a typical price for basic digital cable for video only is also about $40 a month. Of course, video also generates pay-per-view revenues and premium-channel revenues.

services become available to take advantage of this bandwidth, it is likely that the existing systems will become capacity-constrained. A similar phenomenon occurred with personal computers, as new software placed demands on existing hardware, leading to a constant spiral of upgrades of processors, hard drives, random-access memory, and so forth. It is likely that today's broadband systems are merely introductory; my expectation is that, as applications develop, substantially greater bandwidth—coupled with ease of use—will be available to the home.

The next generation of systems may well be introduced by new competitors using new platforms—those not yet on the scene: cable overbuilders, fiber to the home (or curb), satellite with two-way capability, to mention a few. Each new platform exhibits strong economies of scope among communications services: one-way video, broadband Internet access, even telephony. Some of these new platforms require new physical infrastructure; some require spectrum bandwidth. As broadband proves its economic value in conjunction with one-way video entertainment, it is likely that new infrastructure players may attempt entry into cities and neighborhoods with profitable customers, a strategy currently pursued by RCN, for example. Currently, a few of these overbuilders are pursuing a technology strategy similar to that of traditional cable firms; fiber is taken from the cable company's head end to a node serving anywhere from 100 to 500 customers, and then coaxial cable is taken from the node to the customer's residence. The system is called hybrid fiber-coaxial cable.[25] However, a few firms are actually taking fiber all the way to the home, and this may well be the driver for future systems.[26]

Other distribution systems for broadband have yet to demonstrate viable business models. A multipoint, multichannel distribution system, for example, is available today but is not a factor in the market.[27] Direct broadcast satellite suffers from the lack of an integrated path; DirectPC, for example, requires a telephone uplink. The success of direct broadcast satellite in the video marketplace has led to extensive development work to provide an integrated return path in the near future. The FCC has allocated spectrum in the Ka band specifically for a spot-beam satellite return path. Whether these efforts come to fruition remains to be seen.

25. RCN in particular has deployed such systems.
26. See KMI Corp., "Residential Access to the Home: Fiber-to-the-Curb and Fiber-to-the-Home" (www.kmicorp.com/press/011015.htm).
27. McKinsey and Company and JPMorgan, "Broadband 2001," Internal Report, April 2, 2001 (broadband2@mckinsey.com).

A number of municipalities (or more accurately, their municipal water and sewer authorities) have taken it upon themselves to construct broadband infrastructure to every home, presumably on the theory that electronic infrastructure is no different from physical infrastructure such as streets, water lines, and sewer lines, for which they assume ownership and responsibility.[28] This movement is likely to continue; for some municipalities with technology-oriented citizens, constituents may be unwilling to wait for telephone companies and cable firms to put in infrastructure and may demand that their local governments get the job done. For other municipalities anxious to attract high-technology industry to their area, their electronic infrastructure could well be an attraction for businesses looking to relocate. It can also be expected that both telephone and cable firms will strongly object to this and attempt to block it in state legislatures.

Clearly, not all potential platforms can succeed in the market. However, several regulatory impediments make it more difficult than necessary for competitive entry using new platforms:

—In spite of the provisions of the Telecommunications Act of 1996 that prohibit state and local authorities from preventing competition, many local municipalities still impose stiff conditions on new entrants, often at the behest of incumbent cable companies.[29]

—The FCC recently renewed its program access rule, which was due to sunset on October 13, 2002. In brief, this rule prohibits cable owners of networks (for example, Time Warner's ownership of Home Box Office) from refusing to sell carriage of such networks to competing distribution channels (for example, direct broadcast satellite). Many view the viability and rapid growth of direct broadcast satellite video distribution as a direct result of the program access rule.[30] It appears likely that similar access to video content is necessary for future alternative platforms to be competitively viable.[31]

28. Ca-botics, Inc., a firm in Dublin, Ohio, offers a technology that lays fiber to homes using sewer lines, an existing infrastructure with almost universal deployment (www.ca-botics.com/ [April 16, 2002]).

29. See, for example, The Insider, "Saidel Slams shunning of RCN by Philadelphia," *Philadelphia Business Journal,* February 16, 2001 (philadelphiabizjournals.com/philadelphia/stories/2001/02/19/tidbits.html), describing the two-year delays by the Philadelphia city council to approve RCN's application for a license to build a fiber-optic network; the delay is alleged to be motivated by the council's desire to protect Comcast, the local cable television provider.

30. See FCC (2001) (www.fcc.gov/Bureaus/Cable/Reports/fcc01001.pdf [April 16, 2002]).

31. It is claimed that one factor leading to RCN's lack of success in Philadelphia was the unwillingness of Comcast, the dominant cable firm in Philadelphia and owner of the city's major sports franchises, to sell RCN its sports programming. It was able to deny access under the program access rules

—The FCC must continue to be receptive to bandwidth needs for two-way satellite systems. Currently, spectrum in the Ka band is reserved for a two-way, spot-beam satellite, which will enable direct broadcast satellite providers to compete in the broadband Internet access market and to ensure that direct broadcast satellite can provide the full range of broadband services.

The existing distribution systems will no doubt respond to such competitive threats should they materialize. However, both cable and telephone have demonstrated a remarkable lack of strategic vision in this area, preferring to wait until a challenge appears rather than moving aggressively and preemptively.

For cable, the technological and operational response is fairly clear:

—Cable systems can increase the bandwidth committed to the Internet Protocol channel from six megahertz to twelve megahertz or more, perhaps taking the Monster Truck Channel out of the lineup.

—Cable systems can reduce the node size below 500 homes, perhaps to 60 homes. This is likely to be an expensive option, requiring further extension of fiber closer to the home. This strategy could eventually lead to fiber all the way to the home (node size = 1). It will be difficult for cable systems to change the shared nature of the cable modem connection; even with full fiber to the home, the cable infrastructure leads to customers sharing bandwidth. How well this model scales remains to be seen.

For systems using a digital subscriber line, the expansion route is less clear. Digital subscriber line service is essentially a stopgap measure designed to squeeze yet more life out of the copper twisted pair that has served the Bells so well. Even today it is electronics intensive and quite limited by constraints of the copper path. More can be squeezed out, using even fancier electronics, but eventually this technology must be abandoned should the demand for bandwidth accelerate. The cost of the electronics required to reach speeds of ten megabits a second or more over copper at arbitrary distances from the central office becomes prohibitive.

The most likely expansion path to fiber closer to the home is illustrated by SBC's Project Pronto, in which fiber is taken to a remote terminal, much closer to the customer than today's central Bell office.[32] The copper

---

because it did not distribute this material via satellite and was thus beyond the reach of the FCC's program access rule.

32. Recently, SBC has slowed deployment of Pronto in Illinois, citing regulatory issues. However, it is still rolling Pronto out in other areas, possibly at a slower pace. See, for example, Kirk Landendorf, "SBC's Daley Joins Battle to Control Internet's Future," *Austin American Statesman*, January 7, 2002,

twisted pair (or its equivalent) is taken from the remote terminal to the customer's home. In this model, the remote terminal serves a purpose similar to the node in the hybrid fiber-coaxial model of the cable systems and could eventually be the springboard to build fiber to the home (remote terminal size = 1). The two systems differ in that the telephone model has a dedicated line for each customer, and no sharing occurs in the distribution plant; this is likely to be a long-term advantage to the regional Bells. This may well be counterbalanced by the strategic disadvantage of being saddled with digital subscriber lines, a technology whose days are likely numbered.

Should broadband fulfill its promise to be a valued and profitable distribution channel, its future bandwidth expansion still appears problematic. The track record of the existing channel providers (cable and telephone) suggests that we cannot expect strategic leadership from them. Indeed, we may expect them to attempt to obstruct new entrants and new technologies to protect their existing product base. New entrants may face substantial regulatory and legal obstacles.

Is Regulatory Policy a Problem?

It is certainly natural, even fashionable, for economists to believe that regulatory policy is always a problem. Much of this is deserved, but much is not; certainly the Bells have argued that the "slow" rollout of broadband is due to bad regulations—regulations they are working hard to change. A close look at the facts is needed before we can render judgment on this hypothesis.

How have regulators handled broadband infrastructure? As public recognition of broadband has increased, regulators have kept a wary eye on the service, contemplating intervention—and sometimes attempting to intervene—to ensure "fairness" in the marketplace. On balance, regulation of broadband has been minimal—not zero, but certainly minimal.

Cable

The major focus of regulators in the high-speed cable modem market has been the open-access issue. In 1999 groups protesting the AT&T-TCI

---

p. D1 (//archives.statesman.com/cgi-bin/display.cgi?id=3c3dd43733e70mpqaweb1p11011&doc=results.html).

merger demanded that the merging firms be required to accommodate any Internet service provider that wished to offer high-speed service over their cable facilities, on identical terms and conditions as the cable firm's contract provider (@Home, in the case of AT&T-TCI). The issue was renewed at the time of the AT&T-MediaOne merger and later during the AOL Time Warner merger.[33] In the first two mergers, the FCC and the Department of Justice declined to require open access. Several local municipalities attempted to impose open access as a condition on the transfer of cable licenses to AT&T; all were overturned on appeal, stating that the FCC, not local governments, had authority to make this determination. In the AOL Time Warner merger, open access became the lead issue for the Federal Trade Commission (FTC). Eventually, the parties agreed that AOL Time Warner would offer access to their high-speed Internet channel to three Internet service providers other than AOL, one before merger approval and two within ninety days of AOL offering Internet service over Time Warner facilities.[34] The FCC opened a Notice of Inquiry, indicating its intent to examine the question of open access in a formal proceeding. However, the commission is not addressing this issue with much urgency, and it is likely that the FTC's actions in the merger will be the high-water mark of the open-access movement.

Much more important, however, is the fact that the cable industry appears to be moving toward a wholesale model, in which the cable firm opens its high-speed service to Internet service providers of its choosing. This model represents a departure from cable's previous practice of sole sourcing its Internet service function. Recent reports suggest that this wholesale model is likely more profitable than the sole-source model, and several large cable companies are experimenting with it.[35] Adopting a wholesale model for cable is not without problems; it generally requires some co-location of equipment at the cable head end (similar to co-location in a telephone company central office), and it involves establishing acceptable rules for sharing a common resource: the high-speed Internet channel. But the economics of wholesale appear to be compelling enough that cable operators are seeking to overcome these problems.

---

33. For a history of open-access groups, court rulings, and regulatory actions, see CATV/CyberLab, "Broadband Report—Open Access" (2001) (www.catv.org/modemtech/opencable [April 16, 2002]).

34. The FCC imposed some additional conditions, which are of minor interest here.

35. Morgan Stanley Dean Witter, "The Sequel: Open Access Is Better," June 29, 2001, available from author.

Digital Subscriber Lines

Digital service is provided over the telephone companies' local loop, the pair of wires (or electrical path) between the customer's place of business or residence and the telephone companies' central office. The local loop has always been viewed as an essential facility; indeed, the AT&T antitrust case that led to the 1984 breakup of the Bell system was predicated on the local loop as an essential facility. The FCC ordered regional Bells to provide the high-frequency portion of the local loop, over which digital service is provided, to any carrier that requests access, so that the carrier can offer digital service over the regional Bell loop.[36] This "line sharing" decision designated this digital portion of the loop as an unbundled network element and thus subject to resale under state and federal rules implementing the Telecommunications Act of 1996. In essence, the FCC mandated the equivalent of open access for the Bells' local loops.

The Bells claim that this puts them at a disadvantage vis-à-vis cable companies, which are not required to provide access to nonaffiliated Internet service providers. Further, they claim that line sharing increases their cost of broadband deployment and therefore reduces the speed of deployment. The regional Bells lobbied Congress to pass the Tauzin-Dingell bill, which seeks to reclassify digital subscriber line service as an "advanced" service (and therefor not subject to mandatory line sharing).[37] The Bells reject the "essential facility" rationale for digital subscriber line sharing, arguing that broadband to the home is (at least potentially) competitive, even if for voice telephony the local loop is an essential facility.

Line sharing involves co-location of digital subscriber line providers' equipment in the central offices of the regional Bells, just as the wholesale cable model involves co-location at the head end. The digital channel is specific to each customer's loop, so no sharing of a common Internet channel is required, as it is in cable. However, customer specificity of the data channel suggests that co-location of equipment may be more extensive and more intrusive in the Bell's central office than in the cable firm's head end.

In fact, line sharing is a form of wholesaling, albeit one that is mandated by regulation. It appears that the cable industry is moving toward a wholesale model for broadband at exactly the point that the regional Bells

---

36. FCC (1999) (www.fcc.gov/bureaus/comon_carrier/orders/1999/fcc99355.txt [April 15, 2002]).

37. See David McGuire, "Bells, Rivals Gear up for Battle," *WashingtonPost.com,* February 28, 2001 (www.washtech.com/news/telecom/7915-1.html [April 16, 2002]).

are trying to escape a regulated version of broadband wholesaling.[38] If wholesaling is profitable for cable firms, why is it not profitable for the telephone companies' digital service (or at least not costly)? Granted, cable broadband and digital broadband have different technical characteristics, but there is no evidence that the differences are large enough to support totally different business models.

The question is, Does mandated line sharing constitute a significant barrier to investment in expanding digital service, in light of cable's move toward a wholesale model? One likely barrier is pricing; for example, the claim by the Bells that the wholesale rate they are permitted to charge data local-exchange carriers does not permit them to earn a profit on their wholesale service, although this claim is hotly disputed.[39]

Has the FCC's imposition of line sharing on legacy local loops actually imposed sufficient costs on the regional Bells to reduce investment? Most likely not, for the following reasons:

—The Bells are currently rolling out digital subscriber lines as fast as they can; as documented above, they are limited by their operational capabilities, not investment profitability.[40] This may be as much a defensive move as an offensive move.[41] Changing the rules may increase the profitability of these companies but is not likely to increase their speed of rollout.

—The data local-exchange carriers are in steep decline. Whether or not the Bells bear any responsibility for this, the decline has surely eased their pain sufficiently that several have increased their retail digital sub-

38. The exception here is Qwest, which is apparently exiting the Internet service provider business and moving its customers to Microsoft Network (www.qwest.net/nav4/msn/faq.html [April 17, 2002]).

39. It is claimed that the rate for a retail digital subscriber line from some Bell companies is less than their wholesale rate to data local-exchange carriers. See Luc Hatlestad, "The DSL Debacle," *Red Herring*, July 24, 2001 (www.redherring.com/index.asp?layout=story_imu&doc_id=170019817& channel=10000001 [April 17, 2002]).

40. In recent months, investment in digital broadband has slowed somewhat, at least at SBC. See Kirk Landendorf, "SBC's Daley Joins Battle to Control Internet's Future," *Austin American Statesman*, January 7, 2002, p. D1 (//archives.statesman.com/cgi-bin/display.cgi?id=3c3dd43733e70mpqaweb 1p11011&doc=results.html). However, BellSouth appears to exhibit strong growth and the intent to continue that growth; BellSouth chair Duane Ackerman told a Salomon Smith Barney conference in Scottsdale, Arizona, on January 9, 2002, that the company beat its 2001 goal of 600,000 digital customers by 20,000, with a target of 1.1 million by year's end.

41. McKinsey and Company and Sanford Bernstein and Company, "Broadband!" Internal Report, January 2000 (broadband2@mckinsey.com), notes the competitive challenge of cable and has pressed the Bells to respond.

scriber line price.[42] The market results have delivered what the Bells have been seeking in the political arena: no competitors.

—The total cost, both pecuniary and reputational, of the regional Bells' initial deployment problems almost surely dwarfs whatever costs are mandated by the line-sharing rule and concomitant pricing rules.

—In fact the costs of line sharing are likely to be similar under a regulatory mandate for wholesaling as under voluntary wholesaling. Cable firms appear to find it profitable to undertake voluntary wholesaling, so it is unlikely that this cost is substantial.[43]

—In their extensive analyses of the broadband market, some researchers make no mention of FCC-mandated line sharing as having any effect on the market for broadband or the speed of deployment.[44]

In sum, the regional Bells are deploying broadband as fast as they can as a competitive necessity, and they have been willing to suffer substantial internal inefficiencies to do so. It is likely that the cost increase due to the line-sharing mandate is small compared to these other costs and will have no effect on the deployment speed of digital subscriber lines. Ultimately, this is an empirical issue, and the hard evidence of what these costs are and how they compare to the relevant market incentives is not yet available. This brief analysis can only sketch what data are needed to make the case. But the data are suggestive enough that, before Congress and the regulators give up on line sharing, a much stronger empirical case needs to be made by the Bell companies.

In conclusion, it is difficult to sustain the argument that regulatory policy regarding open access for cable or line sharing for digital service has in any way been an impediment to broadband deployment. If there have been impediments to deployment, they have been overwhelmingly on the supply side.

42. See Morgan Stanley Dean Witter, "The Sequel: Open Access Is Better," June 29, 2001 (available from author).

43. Since the cable model involves sharing a common Internet Protocol channel among all customers and, of course, their Internet service providers, the problem of multiple providers is technically more difficult for cable than it appears to be for telephone companies, where the model is a dedicated line for each customer.

44. McKinsey and Company and Sanford Bernstein and Company, "Broadband!" Internal Report, January 2000 (broadband2@Mckinsey.com); McKinsey and Company and JPMorgan, "Broadband 2001," Internal Report, April 2, 2001 (broadband2@mckinsey.com).

Is Regulatory Policy a Problem (Part Deux)?

The argument that line-sharing rules have significantly impeded broadband deployment is unsupported. However, regulatory policies could well stand in the way of broadband deployment, either now or in the future. It is important that regulators and legislators realize where these policies may impede deployment, as they are not on the face of it obvious problems.

—The evidence strongly suggests that the incumbents respond only to competitive threats, and yet many local municipalities impose conditions and fees that create a huge barrier to entry in spite of the procompetitive provisions of the Telecommunications Act of 1996.[45] The statute gives the FCC authority to preempt contrary actions on the part of states or local authorities, although it does not appear to have used this authority.[46] Some states have stepped in to control such actions by local municipalities; for example, Michigan's Telecommunications Act gives strong authority to the state's Public Service Commission to fine municipalities that delay issuing permits in violation of their law.[47]

—Cable firms are concerned that expansion into broadband (from their entertainment base) may expose them to more state or federal regulation.[48] Their broadband strategies have been correspondingly cautious.[49] Clear, credible policy statements from regulators regarding their commitment to market solutions could substantially reduce uncertainty and encourage cable investment in broadband.

—Direct broadcast satellite distribution systems have been a formidable competitor to cable and continue to grow rapidly.[50] Unfortunately, Internet access via satellite typically uses a telephone uplink, not an integrated broadband uplink. New systems now coming on line may require

45. The Insider, "Saidel Slams Shunning of RCN by Philadelphia," *Philadelphia Business Journal,* February 16, 2001 (philadelphiabizjournals.com/philadelphia/stories/2001/02/19/tidbits/html [April 16, 2002]); see also 47 USC, sec. 253(a): "No State or local statute or regulation, or other State or local legal requirement, may prohibit or have the effect of prohibiting the ability of any entity to provide interstate or intrastate telecommunications service."

46. 47 USC, sec. 253(d).

47. "MPSC Fines the City of Dearborn for Violations of the MTA," August 16, 2001 (//cis.state.mi.us/mpsc/orders/press/2001/12797.txt.htm).

48. National Cable Television Association, "The Pitfalls of Forced Access," 2001 (www.ncta.com/legislative/legaffairs.cfm?legregid=14 [April 17, 2002]).

49. George Bittlingmayer and Thomas W. Hazlett, "The Political Economy of Cable 'Open Access,'" *Stanford Technology Law Review* (stlr.stanford.edu/core_page/index.htm).

50. FCC (2001) (www.fcc.gov/Bureaus/Cable/Reports/fcc01001.pdf [April 16, 2002]).

innovative use of the spectrum.[51] The FCC, as the nation's spectrum manager, has wisely set aside spectrum in the Ka band for use by spot-beam satellites for a return data path. The FCC must continue to be receptive and accepting of this use of satellite spectrum in order to facilitate entry by direct broadcast satellite providers into integrated broadband.

—Future platform competition is likely to depend upon new entrants having access to all necessary content, both video and Internet, to realize scope economies. The success of the direct broadcast satellite platform as opposed to the cable platform has been attributed by some to the FCC's program access rules, due to a 2002 sunset rule.[52] Continuing these rules so that new platform competitors have reasonable access to "must have" programming reduces the entry barriers into the platform infrastructure market.

—As the regional Bells seek to deliver broadband to the home using technologies other than the legacy local loop, regulators need to back off requiring line sharing.[53] The rationale for the imposition of line sharing on these companies has always been that the local loop is a bottleneck. If the Bells extend fiber closer to the home, bypassing the legacy local loop, the policy rationale for line sharing simply does not apply. This is likely to be a complicated bit of regulatory rulemaking, but applying legacy regulation to new technologies is almost surely inappropriate. In its recent report on broadband, the National Academy of Science reaches a similar conclusion: "It is reasonable to maintain unbundling rules for the present copper plant. . . . existing bundling rules should be relaxed only where the incumbent makes significant investment . . . to facilities constructed to enable new capabilities."[54]

The FCC's line-sharing rule has received much criticism from the regional Bell operating companies (but from almost no one else) as an impediment to broadband rollout. On the other hand, the FCC's point in adopting the rule was to increase the speed of broadband rollout by encouraging competition. On balance, line sharing will probably have no

51. See Frank Derfler, "Satellite: The Only Choice for Remote Locales?" *ZDNet Reviews* (www.zdnet.com/products/stories/reviews/0,4161,267113400.html [April 17, 2002]).

52. See FCC (2001) (www.fcc.gov/Bureaus/Cable/Reports/fcc01001.pdf [April 16, 2002]).

53. One report finds one regulatory threat to broadband deployment: the imposition of line sharing at the remote terminal by the Illinois Public Service Commission for SBC's Pronto system. See McKinsey and Company and JPMorgan, "Broadband 2001," Internal Report, April 2, 2001 (broadband2@mckinsey.com).

54. Computer Science and Telecommunications Board, National Academy of Science, 2001 (www4.nationalacademies.org/cpsma/cstb.nsf/web/pub_broadband?opendocument [April 17, 2002]).

future effect on broadband deployment, either positive or negative; telecommunications policy needs to focus on removing roadblocks that discourage new infrastructure platforms to compete with incumbents.

References

Crandall, Robert, and Charles Jackson. 2001. "The $500 Billion Opportunity: The Potential Economic Benefit of Widespread Diffusion of Broadband Internet Access." *Criterion Economics,* July 16.

Faulhaber, Gerald, and Christiaan Hogendorn. 2000. "The Market Structure of Broadband Telecommunications." *Journal of Industrial Economics* 48(3): 305–29.

FCC (Federal Communications Commission). 1997. Joint Comments by Bell Atlantic and NYNEX on Notice of Inquiry. Usage of the Public Switched Network by Information Service and Internet Access Providers.

———. 1999. Deployment of Wireline Services Offering Advanced Telecommunications Capability. Third Report and Order.

———. 2001. Seventh Annual Assessment of the Status of Competition in the Market for the Delivery of Video Programming.

———. 2002. High-Speed Services for Internet Access: Status as of December 31, 2001.

GEORGE BITTLINGMAYER
THOMAS W. HAZLETT

11 | *The Financial Effects of Broadband Regulation*

W hy is broadband not ubiquitous? The potential benefits appear enormous, yet just 10 percent of U.S. households subscribed to cable modem service, digital subscriber lines (DSL), or other high-speed access technologies at year-end 2001.[1] Widespread broadband deployment could facilitate telecommuting, video on demand, video conferencing, interactive gaming, and applications yet to be invented. Some observers estimate the potential net benefit of broad diffusion of broadband in the United States at roughly $300 billion a year, or more than $1,000 a person.[2]

---

1. Broadband is the generic term for high-speed access to the Internet, referring to connections capable of at least 200 kilobits a second both upstream and downstream. Since many residential customers subscribe to high-speed services that are slower than 200 kilobits a second in the return path (where data demands by such users are usually less), this chapter makes no distinction between broadband and high-speed (one-way broadband) connections. A November 2001 Yankee Group study found 10.7 million household broadband subscribers. There were about 105.4 million U.S. television households in December 2001, or about 98 percent of the household universe. See Alorie Gilbert, "Report: Broadband Home Use Jumps," *CNET News.com,* December 11, 2001 (news.cnet.com/news/0-1004-202-8146643.html?tag=ff [April 18, 2002]); "Industry Statistics," National Cable Television Association (www.ncta.com/industry_overview/indstat.cfm?ind_overviewid=2 [April 18, 2002]).
2. Crandall and Jackson (2001).

Broadband Deployment

The recent pace of broadband deployment has been the focus of a highly charged policy debate. Section 706 of the 1996 Telecommunications Act directs the Federal Communications Commission (FCC) to take remedial action where advanced services fail to be deployed in a "reasonable and timely fashion."[3] Interests have supported or opposed alternative positions on the reasonable-and-timely-deployment question in accordance with their demand for FCC intervention. A violent interruption of financial markets' enthusiasm for broadband investments in 1998–99 produced sharp equity price declines (and worse) for dozens of broadband service and technology providers during 2000–01. Among the well-publicized bankruptcies are Northpoint Communications, Rhythms, and Covad, the three leading wholesale providers of digital subscriber line networks in the United States, and Excite@Home, the leading broadband access provider. @Home had invested several billion dollars in high-speed networks and was serving 4.1 million subscribers when it dissolved in late 2001.

The relevant policy question now is whether there is too much regulation or too little. One view sees incumbent service providers—notably, the legacy monopolies in cable television distribution and local telephone exchange access—as continuing their dominance, thwarting new entries into broadband. Under this view, only when the "last mile" bottleneck maintained by these firms is opened up via regulations, allowing new rivals to share the existing infrastructure, will competition gain a toehold. The analysis can be similarly applied to either sector, even as regulatory regimes currently differ quite dramatically; cable companies have largely escaped open-access rules mandating that they share their high-speed Internet access networks with independent Internet service providers, while local telephone companies are under extensive requirements to offer the resale of unbundled network elements to competitors at regulated wholesale rates.

The too-little-regulation view sees cable companies as unfairly escaping regulation and the local telephone companies (and particularly the regional Bell operating companies) as thwarting access by gaming the regulatory system. Some suggest the "death penalty": structural separation of wholesale and retail components of local telephone service offered by incumbent carriers. Advocates of this insufficient-regulation argument include the long-distance carriers and competitive local exchange carriers.

3. See FCC (1998).

Others posit that the sector suffers from excessive regulation, including widespread uncertainty over what rules may be imposed. They assert that cable, telephone company, satellite, and fixed wireless providers of broadband have curtailed investments in infrastructure and technology due to regulatory risk. As a result, investments in content and applications have lagged, reducing consumer demand and further inhibiting investment in networks.

Cable television operators seek to avoid common carrier obligations, designing systems (and allocating coaxial cable bandwidth) to limit possible appropriation by regulators or rivals. Incumbent exchange companies' digital networks are subject to regulatory obligations imposed by the 1996 Telecommunications Act, which did not fully anticipate the issues raised by broadband. The statute subjects legacy voice systems to sharing requirements, evincing legislators' views that traditional phone networks enjoy some substantial element of natural monopoly. Yet digital subscriber line service is something that must be constructed with significant new investment and is offered against a rival (cable broadband) with market dominance. Imposing sharing obligations on a new, nondominant service lowers investment incentives without capping market power (indeed, it exacerbates it). Calls for structural separation of local exchange carriers simply intensify the threat of appropriating fixed capital.

This chapter tackles a basic question: Is broadband regulated too much or too little? Whatever the answer, it seems clear that the policy struggle has itself been sufficiently fierce to deter investment. The *New York Times* calls the regulatory debate pitting the Bells against AT&T (the leading long-distance carrier) "one of the most bitter lobbying campaigns of the last decade."[4] Bear Stearns analyst Douglas Ashton offers the inevitable conclusion: "Regulatory uncertainty is getting to be a problem. It's hard to invest money. This has got to stop."[5]

The Empirical Literature

Digital subscriber line service is subject to extensive regulations, including both wholesale and retail price controls. Cable has been largely

4. Lizette Alvarez, "In Capitol, AT&T and Bells Fight to Control Web Access," *New York Times*, August 29, 2001, p. C1.

5. "Policy Seers Say Phone Future Has Smaller Role, Broadband Duopoly, No AT&T or CLECs," *State Telephone Regulation Report*, August 3, 2001.

deregulated, yet the threat of reregulation is ever present. An organized campaign to impose open-access requirements (analogous to wholesale price controls) on cable operators offering high-speed Internet access has brought the issue to both local franchising authorities and the FCC.[6] Fixed-wireless and satellite services could potentially be subject to restrictions. Has regulation, or the threat of regulation, affected innovation and investment in broadband? This section focuses on several issues related to this question: common carrier status, rate-of-return regulation, regulatory delay, the effects of the 1996 Telecommunications Act, and political constraints.

An extensive literature examines the effects of privatization on the telecommunications sector, with important implications for regulation. A 2001 study examines the effects of both privatization and regulation across thirty-one national telecommunication companies in twenty-five countries. The implementation of third-party access—essentially, common carrier status—was found to be associated with strong negative effects on investment. Forced third-party access did not result in lower profits or significant changes in output. These results (decreased investment and no increase in output) has relevance for broadband open access, which would turn cable systems partly into common carriers.[7]

Several researchers find that incentive regulation—price caps as opposed to rate-of-return regulation—hastens the introduction of new technology.[8] One paper also finds lower costs under incentive regulation, but it does not find systematic differences in revenues, profits, investment, or penetration rates.[9] Still, the evidence taken as a whole argues against the efficiency of cost-based price regulation. A study of the effect of Opportunity Indiana, under which the state lifted traditional rate-of-return regulation on Ameritech, finds a dramatic increase in the creation of new telecommunications services.[10] The study does not, however, rule out a demonstration effect—Ameritech rolling out products to encourage favorable regulation rather than a response to local profit incentives.

---

6. The FCC considered and rejected an open-access requirement.

7. Paradoxically, third-party access was associated with higher levels of employment in Bortolotti and others (2001). This may represent a shift away from capital investment toward labor when common carrier status carries the potential of appropriating returns to capital.

8. See Taylor, Zarkadas, and Zona (1992); Greenstein, McMaster, and Spiller (1995); Ai and Sappington (2001) (bear.cba.ufl.edu/sappington/pprs.html [June 14, 2002]).

9. Ai and Sappington (2001).

10. Prieger (2001a).

These results are relevant to broadband because rate-of-return regulation bears a strong resemblance to total-element, long-run, incremental cost regulation promulgated by the FCC under the 1996 Telecommunications Act.[11] Various components of the incumbent local exchange carriers, including those used to supply digital subscriber line service, fall under this regulation. Rate-of-return regulation sets retail prices based on historic investment and actual costs. Total-element regulation sets wholesale prices based on estimates of current costs with state-of-the-art technology, which are typically lower than historical costs. Thus it represents the same principle of regulating prices to constrain network returns and theoretically imposes harsher limits (that is, lower prices).

A 1997 study examines the influence of regulatory delay on the introduction of cellular telephony and voice mail services and calculates large negative effects on consumer welfare.[12] Similarly, a 2001 study finds that during the period of lighter regulation (1992–95), the Bell operating companies introduced new information services—fax, voice mail, audiotext—more rapidly.[13] This experience is important for the assessment of section 271 approvals, which allow regional Bell operating companies to enter the long-distance market.

Much has been written about the effects of the 1996 Telecommunications Act. One article finds modest new entry in local telephony (where state monopoly franchises were abolished) and in cable television.[14] In the latter, relaxation of restrictions on cross-ownership of telephone and cable encourages head-to-head competition by allowing new entrants to offer service bundles (video, voice, and data). The largest effects of the 1996 act may be attributed to unannounced goals: promoting mergers, getting Congress into the policy loop, and increasing campaign contributions.

Robert Crandall and Jerry Hausman criticize key aspects of the 1996 act (unbundling and total-element, long-run, incremental cost) on economic grounds.[15] They note that the market for wireless telephony, wherein regulators ease entry barriers and impose no comparable regime to unbundling via total-element incremental cost, has performed well (high subscriber growth, falling prices) compared to local wire-line service. Entry by competitive local exchange carriers has been relatively modest, with true facilities-based competitors constituting only a fraction of the total. Other

11. See Kahn (2001).
12. Hausman (1997).
13. Prieger (2001b) (www.econ.ucdavis.edu/faculty/prieger/research.htm).
14. Hazlett (1999).
15. Crandall and Hausman (2000).

evidence tends to support this critical view. Between 1996 and 2000 the percentage of U.S. households with telephones remained steady, at roughly 94 percent.[16] Residential rates and connections charges also remained steady in nominal terms, suggesting a slight decrease in real terms.[17] Other evidence points in the opposite direction. One favorable economic development observed in the wake of the 1996 act is the rise in spending on communications equipment. Figure 11-1 shows that communications equipment sales as a fraction of all durable good investment rose sharply from its historic 3 percent share, reaching 5 percent in 2000 and the first three months of 2001. Part of this no doubt was due to parallel forces, however, such as the diffusion of the personal computer and the rise of the Internet.

An analysis of telecommunications infrastructure in 147 countries points to the importance of constraints on political actors in promoting the diffusion of telecommunication service.[18] The number of telecommunications lines per inhabitant is strongly related to the degree to which the political systems constrain any one political actor from having an effect on government policy. (The measure is less than 0.05 for Algeria, China, Indonesia, Iran, Tunisia, and Zambia, for example, and above 0.8 for Australia and the United States.) Although ranked as relatively secure, the U.S. system hardly provides ironclad safeguards against investment-reducing actions. The prospect of regulatory changes that destroy equity values may reduce telecommunications infrastructure below its optimal level.

The economic literature examining other markets suggests a negative correlation between telecommunications regulation and investment. One observer finds that federal antitrust lawsuits suppressed investment in the period 1949–90.[19] Experience with bouts of trust-busting early in the twentieth century confirms the lesson: Policy uncertainty, especially politically charged policy uncertainty, is bad for financial markets and output.[20] Similarly, research points to the role of political uncertainty in suppressing

---

16. FCC (2000, p. 228).

17. Interestingly, local "dial equipment minutes" increased substantially from 1996 to 1999, from 2.4 trillion a minute to 3.4 trillion, or about 11 percent a year. Growth in the 1980s and earlier was less dramatic, typically 1–5 percent a year. However, the late-1990s increase likely represents the advent of the dial-up modem. Interstate and intrastate calls increased at a robust rate, about 6 percent a year, arguably the result of declining rates. This is hardly a success story because it involves a subsidy of dial-up service by voice traffic.

18. See Henisz and Zelner (2001).

19. Bittlingmayer (2001).

20. See Bittlingmayer (1992, 1993, 1996).

Figure 11-1. *Communications Equipment Sales as a Fraction of All Nondefense Durable Goods, 1958–2001*

Percent

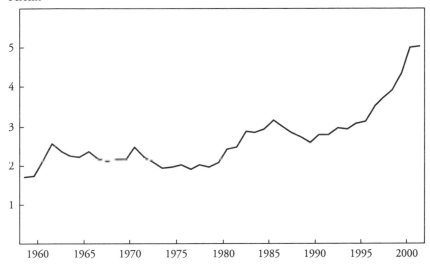

Source: U.S. Bureau of the Census (www.census.gov/indicator/www/m3/hist/naicshist.htm).

pharmaceutical stock prices and investment in the 1990s. Others attribute the substantial declines in pharmaceutical stock prices to the Clinton administration's health care proposals.[21]

Regulations and Broadband

Regulations that potentially influence investment in broadband networks cover a wide range. Regulations now in effect for digital subscriber lines include the total-element, long-run, incremental cost of unbundled network elements, including a complete bundle of unbundled elements allowing a firm to operate as a reseller (providing no infrastructure) while paying only total-element, long-run, incremental cost prices.[22] These rules

21. Pirrong (1993); Ellison and Mullin (1997).

22. Resale options are offered to competitive carriers but are regulated such that retail-wholesale margins are about 20 percent. By assembling all network elements at the price of unbundled network elements, as determined by the rules for total-element, long-run, incremental cost, competitive carriers realize wholesale discounts of about 60 percent. This is called unbundled network elements—platform, or UNE-P.

mandate that incumbent providers cede a property right, or option, to rivals that may wish to use the incumbent's facilities at some future point. Also important are possible changes in the regulatory environment. These include the Tauzin-Dingell bill and initiatives for the structural separation of Bell operating companies.[23] Cable television operators have thus far been successful in resisting the campaign to force systems to accommodate independent Internet service providers wishing to use high-speed conduits to link to customers, yet open-access rules are still being considered by the FCC.

The FCC's formula for setting wholesale access rates has been one of the most contentious aspects of the 1996 Telecommunications Act. (Actual rates are determined at the state level, adding an extra layer of regulatory cost and uncertainty.) Although the method using total-element, long-run, incremental cost attempts to replicate competitive pricing by looking forward and ignoring historic cost, this approach neglects the reality that entry decisions—including incremental investments by incumbent operators with substantial sunk capital—critically depend on expectations that historic costs will be recovered by the investors who make them. Excluding the full range of fixed investments from cost recovery thus undermines infrastructure creation incentives both among incumbent carriers, which subsidize their competitors to the extent that they make fixed investments, and among competitive carriers, to which regulators award price discounts as long as they rent rather than own.[24]

Crandall and Hausman note that this system confers a free option on competitive carriers.[25] If a new technology works and gains popularity with

23. Tauzin-Dingell was introduced in July 1999 and as of the publication of this book has passed the House but not the Senate. The measure would allow Bell companies to transport data into long-distance markets. (Today Bell companies must receive a 271 certification to provide long-distance services within a given state before gaining the right to send voice or data signals beyond the boundaries of the local service market in which they generate.) It would also block the FCC from imposing sharing obligations on advanced data networks constructed by incumbents. The FCC has generally refrained from imposing such obligations but is free to change its policy.

24. Indeed, competitive local exchange carriers building their own facilities themselves become subject to mandatory access provisions. While not as onerous as those imposed on incumbent local exchange carriers, the competitive carriers note that this burden reduces their ability and economic incentive to raise capital for such projects. Cox Cable, in describing the financial returns available from upgrading its cable television platform to deliver advanced services, tells its shareholders that sharing obligations are burdensome even to upstart rivals. "These requirements also place burdens on new entrants that may benefit their competitors. In particular, the resale requirement means that a company can seek to resell services using the facilities of a new entrant, such as Cox, without making a similar investment in facilities." Cox Cable, Securities and Exchange Commission form 10K (2000), p. 12.

25. Crandall and Hausman (2000).

consumers, they may offer it using the incumbents' facilities at forward-looking cost. If the technology proves unprofitable, however, the incumbents absorb the loss because the competitive carriers are not required to make long-term commitments.

Setting access prices below long-run opportunity costs and awarding options at a price of zero constitute only part of the problem. Overarching policy uncertainty increases inefficiency. If markets were certain that total-element, long-run, incremental cost rates were low and forever fixed, investment alternatives could emerge. For example, instead of upgrading traditional wire networks to provide advanced services, incumbent telephone companies (and others) could build out wireless networks, where sharing obligations are less. Cable television companies would have an extra incentive to offer cable telephony. Still, these circuitous pathways to telecommunications competition distort resource use, wasting valuable incumbent infrastructure.

There are, however, no guarantees that arbitrary pricing rules will remain fixed. The natural fluidity of the regime and its political elasticity, combined with the obvious infirmities of total-element, long-run, incremental cost on both economic and legal grounds, keep these rules constantly in play. Congress, the courts, and the FCC may trim, toughen, or eliminate these rules. The resulting uncertainty gives all parties an increased incentive to wait and see—in effect, capturing option value—since the optimal investment response will depend on what happens.

Uncertainty has enveloped total-element, long-run, incremental cost from its inception. Whether the FCC even had the power to impose such rules has occupied courts since 1996. The Supreme Court finally decided that the FCC did have the power to impose prices under the 1996 act but only if "necessary" and if the new entrant's ability to compete would be otherwise "impaired." After protracted litigation, the Supreme Court decided in May 2002 that the FCC's implementation of this power was legal.

The concept of total-element, long-run, incremental cost also faces opposition from influential members of Congress, such as Senator John McCain (R-Arizona). In addition, it has come under withering criticism from Alfred Kahn, the dean of U.S. regulatory economists.[26] With the financial demise of facilities-based competitive carriers and compelling economic criticism, the scope of total-element, long-run, incremental cost may be trimmed, but only time will tell. In the meantime, investors in

26. Kahn (2001).

telecommunications infrastructure have an additional incentive to wait for regulatory events to sort themselves out.

The 1996 Telecommunications Act allows competitors to access the facilities of incumbent local exchange carriers. As interpreted by the FCC, the rules have been crafted to provide large discounts to new rivals that take advantage of the incumbents' network sharing. This may have encouraged entry by competitors, even as the implicit regulatory subsidies have been insufficient to sustain it. Offsetting the price discounts in total-element cost pricing are substantial sunk costs in customer acquisition; even firms that receive cheap transport for communications service must invest substantial sums to procure and retain subscribers. One study finds that, for the average competitor, "for every dollar of investment in plant and equipment, an additional two dollars of entry costs are incurred."[27]

To the degree that the sunk-cost entry barrier is effectively mitigated by total-element, long-run, incremental cost access rules, there is a self-limiting aspect to entry subsidized through low access charges. New entrants achieving economic profitability by virtue of such pricing attract still more entrants to mimic their business strategies. The lack of property rights creates a tragedy of the commons: Truly free entry destroys incentives to enter. It appears clear that FCC regulators did seize the opportunity to promote new entrants rather than efficient competition (where least-cost providers enjoy the right to exclude others from competing on equal terms). Alfred Kahn finds that commissions regulating electricity, communications, and other sectors have difficulty resisting the urge to subsidize new competitors by appropriating the sunk capital of incumbent firms.[28]

Underlying the emphasis on cheap access pricing is the implicit assumption that one physical infrastructure will continue to dominate. This assumption pushes regulators to pursue measures bringing multiple-service providers onto the sole available platform. Ironically, this approach becomes a self-fulfilling prophecy, as potential entrants see the relative price of resale competition decline relative to the price of competitive facilities. Efficient regulation encourages entrants to discover and exploit low-cost service options, and access regulations can lead to optimal outcomes wherein firms face the full opportunity cost of their actions. Yet the informational requirements for discerning such opportunity costs, and for establishing the right balance between short-term and long-term

27. Beard, Ford, and Spiwak (2001, p. 14).
28. Kahn (1998).

opportunities, yield a standard preference for market solutions wherever competition—even imperfect competition as in duopoly or oligopoly solutions—can be observed.[29] Since cable modems and digital subscriber lines provide alternative delivery mechanisms for broadband, the logic of unbundled network elements and cable open access are rendered dubious. Such requirements, however, plausibly act as a drag on investment by regional Bells, whose broadband digital services struggle to capture market share from dominant cable modem service providers.

The merger climate deteriorated significantly in July 2000 with the Department of Justice's opposition to the Sprint-WorldCom merger—and then with the merger's collapse. (The effect on the merger climate at the time and since has not been vitiated by subsequent revelations of misstated financial results and WorldCom's bankruptcy in 2002.) Sprint may well merge with a regional Bell operating company that obtains permission to provide long-distance service across its in-region area of dominance.[30] Moreover, some analysts pointed to a special broadband angle. The merger between Sprint and MCI WorldCom would have given new impetus to the fixed-wireless approach to broadband delivery.[31] Economies of scale, as could have been created by the merger, are particularly important in rolling out new technologies in consumer markets both because research and development expenditures are more easily amortized and because marketing synergies appear when a given customer base (say, of long-distance users) can be converted to enhanced services (say, local exchange plus broadband access plus long distance) in a relatively seamless manner, economizing on consumer switching costs.

Blocking Sprint's attempt to sell its shares to the high bidder (WorldCom) creates dynamic effects; for instance, investments to spruce up other

29. This policy preference is readily observed in telecommunications. Cellular telephone licenses were issued in the United States during 1984-89, two for each market. The regulatory regime adopted allowed free-market pricing, despite the fact that one of the two licenses issued in each market was assigned to the local incumbent telephone monopoly (wire line). In cable television, rate regulation was imposed in the 1992 Cable Act, but deregulation was automatic in any local market wherein a second entrant achieved market penetration of 15 percent of households (no third firm required).

30. The section 271 application process created in the 1996 act stalled until Verizon won the right to provide long-distance telephone service to its New York state customers in December 1999. The process now appears to be heading for completion (with all fifty states granting section 271 applications) by the first quarter of 2003. Precursor Watch, "Key Government Decisions Affecting the Telecom/Media Sectors" (www.precursor.com [October 16, 2001]).

31. Elizabeth Douglass, "The Cutting Edge: Focus on Technology," *Los Angeles Times,* October 11, 1999, p. C4; Paul Coe Cox III, "MMDS High on MCI Worldcom Agenda?" *Communications Today,* April 6, 2000.

merger candidates become less likely. The innovative product or ambitious geographic expansion that might have attracted buyer interest becomes more of a gamble.

Section 271 of the 1996 Telecommunications Act sets out the terms under which regional Bell operating companies are allowed to provide long-distance service within their local exchange territories, in essence lifting the restrictions imposed by the modified final judgment (and Judge Harold Greene) and imposing a new set of rules. Ostensibly intended to spur local competition, the certain effect of section 271, however, is to forestall long-distance competition and delay the integration of local and long-distance service.[32]

The economies of scope between local and long-distance are evidently powerful, but LATA (local area transport and access) boundaries preempt their realization. Opponents of the entry of the regional Bells view section 271 as the carrot before the donkey: The Bells get permission only after they open up their local markets to competitors. Proponents of the Bells' entry argue that delaying long-distance competition holds telephone customers hostage, particularly when the Bells are poised to efficiently roll out the service bundles most demanded by small residential customers. Not only are the gains from using long-distance entry as a bargaining chip speculative, they also create perverse incentives, prompting long-distance carriers to delay entering local markets (thus enhancing applications for Bells' entry into long distance) and producing a quandary for regulators: If the carrot appears to be working (that is, if local markets are opening), does that imply that the regulators should continue to block the entry of the regional Bells into long distance? Or should they reward them by removing the barrier?

The initial evidence gleaned from markets in which section 271 applications have been granted (New York, where Verizon began offering long-distance service in December 1999, and Texas, where SBC entered the long-distance market in July 2000) suggests that substantial benefits do attend the entry of the regional Bells. One study finds long-distance bills following entry to be 9 percent lower in New York and 23 percent lower in Texas.[33] It also finds that local telephone competition, as measured by the market share of the competitors, intensified with section 271 approval.

U.S. policy traditionally puts cable television outside the common-carrier framework. However, open access would turn broadband into a

---

32. A good description of the section 271 process, and a defense of its economic logic, is found in Schwartz (2000) (www.aei.brookings.org/publications/working/working_00_04.pdf [April 23, 2002])

33. Hausman, Leonard, and Sidak (2002) (www.aei.org/ps/psfront.htm [June 14, 2002]).

common-carrier wholesale transport service. As a result, cable system bandwidth allocated to broadband runs the risk of being subject to price regulation. The threat of common-carrier status explains why comparatively little of the available spectrum (6 megahertz of a total of 750 megahertz on a state-of-the-art system) is dedicated to two-way, high-speed Internet access. Thomas Hazlett (this volume) argues that the push for open access itself confirms and reinforces the defensive architecture used by cable operators to guard against regulatory appropriation.

Cable is now relatively unencumbered by regulation, to which a number of analysts credit its comparative success in the residential market. Some point to the marketplace victory of closed cable over open digital subscriber lines as evidence that open access would hamper broadband expansion.[34] Industry analysts draw a similar inference: According to Blake Bath, an analyst at Lehman Brothers, "The reason that the cable companies really stepped up their investment in 1997 and beyond was they were not regulated, they weren't forced to open up their networks. There were multiple revenue streams that they could address. They could price the services however they wanted."[35]

AT&T and the competitive carriers have supported efforts to break up the regional Bell operating companies into wholesale and retail units. State-level initiatives have taken place in Pennsylvania, New York, New Jersey, Maryland, Virginia, Tennessee, Florida, and Minnesota. Pennsylvania in fact required "functional separation," but this fell far short of what critics of the Bells demanded. More recently, AT&T has pursued structural separation at the federal level.[36] The likelihood of actual legislation seems slim at the moment. Arguably, the aim of the structural separation movement may be to divert the Bell managers' attention and to influence their behavior by increasing regulatory risk.

Other Factors and Broadband

A 2001 study finds that a number of factors influence the availability of broadband access.[37] Positive influences include local market size, educa-

---

34. Hazlett and Bittlingmayer (2002).

35. Quoted in Thierer (2001, p. 15) (www.cato.org/events/010724pf.html).

36. Yochi J. Dreazen, "AT&T Ratchets up Efforts in Washington Pushing Bell Breakup Plan," *Wall Street Journal,* August 28, 2001.

37. Prieger (2001b) (www.econ.ucdavis.edu/faculty/prieger/research.htm).

tional level, and commuting distance. Interestingly (for the discussion of section 271 approvals, structural separation, and telecommunications mergers), high-speed access is more likely to be available in the zip codes in which Bell companies operate. Statistically, each of the four regional Bells (BellSouth, Qwest, SBC, and Verizon) had a positive effect. In contrast, the presence of competitive local exchange carriers had a positive but statistically insignificant association. These results do not support the theory that the regime designed to encourage growth of non-facilities-based competitive carriers (that is, a total-element, long-run, incremental cost combined with unbundled network elements) has been successful.

The fight over cable open access was at the center of the broadband debate for much of the last few years. It figured prominently in AT&T's mergers with TCI and MediaOne, and in the AOL Time Warner deal. Initiatives in various localities, including Portland, Broward County, and San Francisco, provoked controversy. Calls for open access have subsided, though pressures may reemerge if cable's share of the residential broadband market were to increase.

What effect did the often-contentious debate over open access have on broadband development? We argue above that the clamor for open access prompts the cable industry to parsimoniously allocate cable system spectrum in order to preemptively lower regulatory risk. (Were open-access rules to be applied, they would regulate a smaller portion of the communications capacity of cable systems than if cable systems optimally utilized bandwidth.) Similarly, implementation of open access would reduce incentives to build out the (currently) most successful broadband platform.

Table 11-1 displays financial returns for an Internet stock index and Excite@Home shares around dates with significant developments for open access. These are abnormal returns, adjusted for the same-period returns of the Standard and Poor 500. The calculations use twenty-one events during which open access suffered setbacks and eight dates on which open access enjoyed victories. Examples of setbacks include the AT&T-TCI merger, rumors of an AT&T–Time Warner merger, the @Home-Excite merger, the Comcast-MediaOne merger, the FCC's rejection of open access, rumors of an AOL-Excite merger, court rulings against open access, and rumors of a Comcast-Excite@Home merger. Examples of victories: a ruling by a Portland judge against AT&T, the vote by Broward and Pittsburgh in favor of open access, the FCC avowal to scrutinize the AOL Time Warner merger, and rumors of regulatory action.

Table 11-1. *Financial Reactions of the Internet Stock Index and Excite@Home to Open-Access Events, January 1998–October 2000*

Percent

	Internet index		Excite@Home	
	One day	Three day	One day	Three day
Setbacks for open access[a]				
Mean	1.1	1.7	7.6	8.1
Median	0.7	2.4	8.0	8.2
Cumulative	24.6	41.6	364.2	408.6
Victories for open access[a]				
Mean	–0.1	–0.1	–4.9	–6.4
Median	0.3	0.0	–4.0	–6.5
Cumulative	–1.0	–1.0	–33.2	–41.0

Source: Authors' calculations using data from Yahoo!Finance. Returns for competitive local exchange carriers adjusted by Nasdaq; for incumbent local exchange carriers, by S&P 500.

a. Twenty-one events signaled setbacks; eight events signaled victories.

The Internet stock index reveals how investors evaluated the likely consequences of open access. Excite@Home returns indicate whether selected dates are plausible regulatory events. Excite@Home was the exclusive Internet service provider for a number of cable companies, including AT&T and Comcast, and its business strategy was highly dependent on bundled access.

Setbacks for open access produced statistically significant positive abnormal returns for Excite@Home, consistent with the view that investors saw the selected regulatory events as important victories for the firm. However, these setback dates were also correlated with positive abnormal and statistically significant returns for Internet stocks. This tends to support the view that investors saw open-access regulation as slowing broadband deployment. Similarly, victories for open access were correlated with negative returns for Excite@Home shareholders and for those owning equity in the firms composing the Internet index. The latter results, however, are not statistically significant.

Various interpretations are possible, but none is favorable to the view that open access would have promoted the Internet. The most plausible conclusion to be drawn is that investors saw cable open-access regulation as detrimental to broadband infrastructure investment.

Tauzin-Dingell

James Glassman and William Lehr claim to show that the Tauzin-Dingell proposal (put forward by Representatives Billy Tauzin and John Dingell), though it had not passed either house, accounted for a massive decline in the capitalization of competitive local exchange carriers.[38] They assert that almost half of the 84 percent decline in competitive carrier stocks from March 14, 2000, to May 10, 2001, occurred during windows in which the bill's prospects for passage increased. They then argue that this decline in the market capitalization of competitive carriers reduced investment in broadband.

Thomas Hazlett demonstrates that the Glassman-Lehr financial methodology is fundamentally flawed and that the asserted conclusion (regarding reduced broadband investment) would not follow even if the empirical analysis were correct.[39] Rather than selecting actual event dates on which Tauzin-Dingell (or its predecessor legislation) saw significant gains or reversals in Congress, Glassman and Lehr examine only the nine worst days for a portfolio of competitive carrier stocks during the period. Seven of these days occurred in March and April 2000; two in April 2001 (see figure 11-2). (The index used is not described by the authors, precluding replication of the asserted results.) The authors then argue that each of the nine days was associated with a Tauzin-Dingell event (occurring the day before, the day of, or the day after the sharp decline in the index) and that such events caused all of the declines observed on those days.

The Glassman-Lehr method demonstrates extreme sample-selection bias. By excluding all dates with positive returns, by using a loose definition of a Tauzin-Dingell event, and by excluding from the analysis all other explanations for the declines, the results were preordained. That Tauzin-Dingell was driving the returns on the dates selected is an unsupportable assumption; the returns were not adjusted for market movements, but the Nasdaq declined sharply across all nine event dates. Moreover, incumbent carrier returns (for SBC, Verizon, Qwest, and BellSouth) declined both absolutely and relative to the Standard and Poor's (S&P) 500 over the nine events. If declines in competitive carrier returns imply that Tauzin-Dingell

38. James Glassman and William Lehr, "The Economics of Tauzin-Dingell: Theory and Evidence" (ebusiness.mit.edu/research/papers/128%20lehr,%20tauzin-dingell.pdf [April 24, 2002]).

39. Hazlett (2001) (www.manhattan-institute.org/hazlett/conf010712.pdf [April 24, 2002]).

Figure 11-2. *Competitive Local Exchange Carrier Returns,*
January 1, 1999–June 25, 2001, with Nine T-D "Event" Dates
Selected by Glassman-Lehr [a]

Index

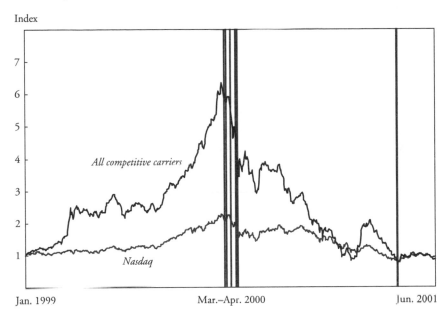

Source: Glassman and Lehr (2001).
a. Seven event dates occur in March–April 2000, two in April 2001. Carriers include Adelphia, Allegiance, Choice One, Convergent, CoreComm, Covad, CTC, Cypress, DSL.net, e.spire, Focal, General Comm, ICG, DeltaCom, Log On America, McLeodUSA, Mpower, Net2000, Network Access, Northpoint, NTELOS, Pac-West, Rhythms, US LEC, USOL, XO, Advanced Radio, Al Lightwave, Fibernet, Nucentrix, RCN, Speedus.com, Teligent, Time Warner Telecom, and Winstar.

was pushing the Bells to greater monopoly power over these carriers, it is curious that the Bells enjoy negative returns as a result.

In fact, the events selected by Glassman and Lehr were not Tauzin-Dingell events. They are merely news stories about either Tauzin-Dingell or topics related to the bill that occurred on or near highly negative days for U.S. equities. Throughout the fourteen-month sample period, a Lexis-Nexis search finds an average of about ten articles every trading day mentioned "telecommunications" and either "Tauzin" or "Dingell." Only two three-day periods over the entire sample were without such a news item. And because days with positive returns for these carriers were explicitly eliminated, no correlation between Tauzin-Dingell events and the returns is actually estimated.

Table 11-2 summarizes results from an actual event study analysis of Tauzin-Dingell.[40] It divides a sample of thirty-eight competitive exchange carriers into those relying on unbundled network elements and those relying more on their own facilities to serve telephone customers.[41] This division is important to the analysis because the finding that the returns of competitive carriers were systematically negative during windows in which Tauzin-Dingell's passage became more likely is difficult to interpret. Glassman and Lehr erroneously report finding such a correlation and then consider only one interpretation: that the passage of Tauzin-Dingell will allow Bell companies to offer less cooperation with the sharing requirements imposed by regulators.

An omitted alternative explanation is that the competitive local exchange carriers, as competitors of the incumbent local exchange carriers, will be hurt when their larger, stronger rivals are less constrained in building long-distance facilities for carrying data traffic. As the Precursor Group, a firm that interprets telecommunications regulations for investors and pension funds, notes: "Inability to carry traffic end to end is a competitive disadvantage for the Bells."[42] Tauzin-Dingell is targeted at ending this "competitive disadvantage for the Bells" in data services. By breaking the competitive carrier sample into those firms that primarily rely on the infrastructure of the incumbents to serve customers and those relying on their own facilities, it is theoretically possible to observe which effect is in evidence.

Sixteen trading days featured substantial news regarding what became the Tauzin-Dingell legislation during the January 4, 1999, to June 14, 2001, period. (This longer period is examined because it includes the introduction of Tauzin-Dingell in July 1999 as well as the introduction of two predecessor bills, by Senators Sam Brownback and John McCain, respectively, in the months preceding.) Over these sixteen days, the competitive carriers generally exhibited positive, but not statistically significant,

---

40. Reported in Hazlett (2001) (www.manhattan-institute.org/hazlett/conf010712.pdf).

41. Twenty-seven firms were identified as relying on unbundled elements: Allegiance, Choice One, Convergent, CoreComm, Covad, CTC, Cypress, DeltaCom, DSL.net, e.spire, Focal, General Comm, ICG, Intermedia, ITC, Log On America, McLeodUSA, Mpower, Net2000, Network Access, Network Plus, Northpoint, NTELOS, Pac-West Telecom, Rhythms NetConnections, US LEC, USOL Holdings. Twelve firms were identified as using their own facilities: Adelphia Business Solutions, Advanced Radio Telecom, Allied Riser, Electric Lightwave, Fibernet, Nucentrix, RCN, Speedus.com, Teligent, Time Warner Telecom, Winstar, XO Communications.

42. "Key Government Decisions Affecting the Telecom/Media Sectors," *Precursor Watch*, October 16, 2001, p. 1.

Table 11-2. *Abnormal Returns, Competitive and Incumbent Local Exchange Carriers, April 1999 to June 2001*

Percent

Carrier	All 16 days	12 positive days	4 negative days
All competitive local exchange carriers[a]	1.7	1.4	1.6
Those relying on unbundled elements	1.2	1.2	1.1
Those relying on own facilities	2.4*	2.0	2.4
All incumbent local exchange carriers[b]	−0.8	−1.1	−0.8

Source: Hazlett (2001).

*Significant at the 95 percent level (two-tailed test).

a. Returns adjusted by Nasdaq (UCLECs depend on unbundled elements; FCLECs depend on their own facilities).

b. Returns adjusted by S&P 500.

market-adjusted returns. Facilities-based competitive carriers had statistically significant positive returns during the sixteen event windows. Incumbent carriers (all four remaining regional Bells: Qwest, SBC, Verizon, and BellSouth) exhibited negative, if statistically insignificant, abnormal returns. Splitting the sample into twelve pro-Tauzin-Dingell and four anti-Tauzin-Dingell news events does not change the results.[43] This analysis calculates an actual correlation between Tauzin-Dingell events and competitive carrier returns, but the correlations are in the opposite direction from that asserted by Glassman and Lehr. Because the returns fit no predictable pattern, they are best described as noise. The Tauzin-Dingell bill exhibited no observed effect on stock prices for either type of local carrier.[44]

As an economic matter, this finding is not particularly interesting, however. The more fundamental failing of the Glassman and Lehr analysis is

43. Pro-Tauzin-Dingell events: Senator Brownback introduces predecessor legislation, Senator McCain introduces predecessor legislation, Representative Tauzin supports data deregulation bill, first major newspaper reports Congress considering the Tauzin-Dingell bill, the Tauzin-Dingell bill introduced, Representative Tauzin may get House Commerce Committee chair, Representative Tauzin to be chair, Representative Tauzin vows to revamp the Telecommunications Act, Bells and rivals gear up for battle, Representative Tauzin to reintroduce the Tauzin-Dingell bill, a bill to loosen regulation of Bell operating companies introduced, House panel clears Tauzin-Dingell bill. Anti-Tauzin-Dingell events: Congressman Conyers's bill counters Tauzin-Dingell, Senator Jeffords's party switch changes Senate majority, House Judiciary Committee deals body blow to Tauzin-Dingell, Senator Hollings highly critical of Tauzin-Dingell.

44. The fact that this legislation has not been considered close to enactment, and that there have not been dramatic political swings that would markedly change this assessment, makes it difficult to identify actual legislative events calibrating equity market reactions. Hence this result is not surprising.

to equate the welfare of the competitive local carriers with consumer welfare. Legislation allowing the incumbent local carriers greater leeway to build and operate their networks enhances competitive alternatives. If it works precisely as advertised, the Tauzin-Dingell bill would both increase total broadband deployment and reduce the market prospects of all of the competitive carriers, both those that depend on unbundled elements and those that rely on their own facilities. Hence if plausible empirical results did show declines in competitive carriers associated with progress of the Tauzin-Dingell bill, the evidence would still be consistent with the pro-efficiency view of the bill.

This leaves a question unanswered: What did cause the precipitous decline in the stocks of the competitive carriers? First, there was an extremely sharp drop in technology shares in general over the period selected by Glassman and Lehr: The Nasdaq composite index declined 57 percent over this period. Given that the competitive carriers analyzed by Hazlett demonstrate betas averaging about 1.3, the direction of the market and the volatility of competitive carriers' equities would combine to produce returns of about 74 percent.[45] Hence 88 percent of the decline is explained simply by the general collapse of technology stocks over the period examined.

In addition to these aggregate trends, segments of the communications sector were hit particularly hard by the abrupt market turnaround. Market leaders such as Cisco, Nortel, and JDS Uniphase exhibited declines of 72.7 percent, 77.4 percent, and 89.6 percent, respectively, over the March 10, 2000 to May 14, 2001, period selected by Glassman and Lehr, declines that match or outstrip the losses of the competitive carriers. More targeted still was the decline in wide-area network providers, firms like Global Crossing (which filed for bankruptcy protection in early 2002), Metromedia Fiber Networks, Level 3, and Williams. This subsector exhibits a decline in market capitalization that hugs the financial path of the competitive carriers throughout 2001 (see figure 11-3). Included in the portfolio is Genuity, the spin-off from GTE (as part of the GTE-Verizon merger agreement, satisfying long-distance restrictions). This firm touted Verizon as a strategic partner, and analysts touted Genuity as a prime takeover (reacquisition) target for Verizon when its section 271 applications were approved.[46] Despite its cozy relations with regional Bells, Genu-

45. Hazlett (2001) (www.manhattan-institute.org/hazlett/conf010712.pdf).

46. "Verizon spun off majority control of [Genuity] over a period of time as a condition of GTE merger." Verizon CEO Ivan Seidenberg said that "decisions about whether to take back that stake or

Figure 11-3. *Equity Returns in the Telecommunications Service Sector, 2001*[a]

Index

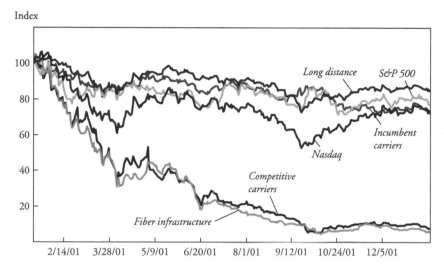

Source: Robertson Stephens, Telecom Services Research, January 18, 2002.

a. Fiber Infrastructure: Global Crossing, Metropolitan Fiber Networks, Genuity, Williams Communications Group, Level 3; competitive carriers: Allegiance, Choice One, CTC, Network Plus, MacLeodUSA, Time Warner Telecom; incumbent carriers: Century Tel, Broadwing, BellSouth, SBC, Qwest, Verizon, Commonwealth Tel; long distance: AT&T, Sprint FON Group, WorldCom Group, MCI Group.

ity declined 88 percent from its September 2000 initial public offering through February 10, 2002.

Figure 11-3 displays another financial trend of interest. While even the larger players in telecommunications suffered substantial equity declines in 2001, the best performers were the long-distance carriers. Rather than flourishing with the decline in competitive carrier stocks (as under the Glassman-Lehr assertion that the Tauzin-Dingell bill was helping the Bells to maintain or reestablish monopoly power), the incumbent carriers declined by more than the S&P 500 (the relevant market index). On the other hand, the long-distance carriers actually outperformed both the Nasdaq and the S&P 500 in 2001. This pattern suggests that market

complete the spin-off were not likely to be issued until 2003 because the company still would be making its way through the section 271 long-distance approval process." See "ELCOS Call for Regulatory Certainty as Wider 271 Entry Looms," *Communications Daily*, November 14, 2001, p. 2.

trends, not the threat of Tauzin-Dingell legislation, were driving financial returns in the sector.

Within the financial analyst community, a consensus has arisen explaining how the competitive carriers—in many respects like the dotcoms—exhibited such a meteoric rise and fall in financial markets (see figure 11-2). In 2000 the carriers were outperformed by both the Nasdaq and by their own 1999 performance (concurrent with the period in which the Tauzin-Dingell bill was introduced by two of the most powerful members, one Republican, one Democrat, of the House of Representatives). As one analyst sums up:

> It was with great hope in 1996 that a group of feisty new upstarts called CLECs [competitive local exchange carriers] hoped to take on the ILECs [incumbent local exchange carriers]. Now, just five years later, the hopes of most CLECs have been dashed. Simply put, margins available from resale UNE-L, UNE-P [unbundled network elements, loop; unbundled network elements, platform] were insufficient owing to high customer acquisition costs, particularly in the residential market. And capital markets—at least so far—have rebuffed overtures by many CLECs to raise additional funds to take ILECs head on, facilities style. Now, the few surviving CLECs have scaled back their business plans and retrenched. CLECs now are focused almost exclusively on the business market, relegating the consumer market to the back burner for the foreseeable future.[47]

Two aspects of this view of the financial marketplace are of note. First, the regulatory structure for competitive telecommunications was not well conceived. The possibility of entry was created, but it was not sustainable; in the absence of any requirements for entrants (who could lease all delivery systems at substantially discounted prices from incumbents), the cavalcade of new rivalry pushed up customer acquisition costs across the board, even for facilities-based entrants using few if any pieces of the incumbent's network. These costs overwhelmed the competitive sector generally, shut the financing window for facilities-based business models, and led to rapid exit. A thinner field should help survivors regain their financial bearings, but it remains to be seen where a stable equilibrium will be established.

Second, in exiting the residential market, the focus of the competitive sector was on the business market. This is economically efficient: Business markets tend to be geographically denser and thicker in terms of demand,

---

47. JPMorgan Equity Research, "The Cable Industry," November 2, 2001, p. 41.

allowing more economical use of fixed capital; prices tend to be far in excess of costs due to historic patterns of regulation. But in continuing to lose market share in this lucrative segment, the incumbents can at best be said to have successfully defended their low-margin residential services. This is difficult to attribute to rent-seeking legislative strategies, which would presumably attempt to achieve just the reverse outcome (cede the unprofitable, defend the profitable). Real economic forces appear to be driving this pattern of entry and exit.

The Effects of Section 271

Under section 271 of the 1996 Telecommunications Act, the Bell operating companies may receive permission to offer inter-LATA services within their home markets, provided they convince the FCC and state regulators that they have opened up their local markets to competition.[48]

The effects on consumers of section 271 approvals—and denials—are highly controversial. Long-distance and competitive local carriers argue that allowing the Bells to offer long-distance service removes one of the few levers regulators have to get the Bells to open up their local loop to competitors. The Bells argue that keeping them out of long-distance service restricts rivalry and raises rates. At a minimum, the restriction prevents the Bells from realizing economics of scope in the provision of short- and long-distance service within their service areas for some substantial period of time. Appendix 11A lists events associated with section 271 approvals and denials. A quick glance shows that three of the four remaining Bells (Verizon, BellSouth, and SBC) have received approval or moved the process along successfully in a number of states. Qwest has not done so, as it pursues a large multistate effort. Progress has not been uniform, and the Bells have also suffered setbacks.[49]

Speedy and lax approvals generate long-distance competition but may reduce benefits from local competition. Consequently, Bell opponents emphasize the importance of access to the local loop. Every premature approval can undermine the realization of local service and price competition. Presumably, suppliers of inputs and complementary products suffer if this anticompetitive result obtains. Under this view, such firms, as well

---

48. The Department of Justice also plays an official role in this process, offering expert consultation to the FCC.

49. For details of this process, see Legg Mason (2001).

as large telecommunications users, should exhibit negative returns associated with section 271 approvals.

Proponents of rapid section 271 approvals emphasize the benefits of long-distance competition and downplay the importance of local competition as measured by the market shares of competitive local exchange carriers.[50] They imply that expansion of high-speed inter-LATA service will lead to increased demand for equipment and products complementary to that service. Here, *equipment* encompasses network infrastructure, customer-premises devices, and vertically related transport service.

Stock Market Effects

The effect of section 271 approvals on the Bells' stock prices is clear. Under any view, approvals should increase or at least not lower these prices. Similarly, section 271 denials should decrease or at least not raise these stock prices. The two views diverge in their prediction for other vertically related businesses. Critics of rapid section 271 approvals offer arguments implying that suppliers of inputs and complementary products in telecommunications would suffer from too-speedy approvals. Similarly, defenders' claims suggest that the same suppliers will benefit from an expansion of actual inter-LATA service. The performance of the following key indexes and individual stocks around section 271 application events is examined:

—The Amex Internet index, a "modified market-capitalization weighted" index composed of fifty Internet stocks, including Amazon.com, AOL, Cisco, Juniper Networks, Novell, 3Com, Reback Networks, United Technologies Corp., WebMD, and Yahoo!

—The Philadelphia semiconductor index, a price-weighted index of sixteen U.S. companies involved in the design, manufacture, or distribution of semiconductors, including Novellus Systems, Linear Technology Group, Micron Technology, National Semiconductor, Texas Instruments, Intel, LSI Logic, and Motorola.

—Important individual companies with widely followed strategies linked to broadband infrastructure, like AOL, @Home, Cisco, Level 3, Sun Microsystems, and Yahoo!

50. Given that local telephone access is a heavily regulated service, one argument is that price controls substitute for market competition. To the degree that the existing regime actually cross-subsidizes local (residential) telephone access, the argument becomes even more compelling: Why would one expect to see much competitive entry in a market that is already constrained to charge the efficient (or below the efficient) price?

Internet Returns

Using dates from a 2001 Legg Mason report and a Lexis-Nexis search of section 271 developments, a list was generated with forty-five events positive for section 271 approvals and twenty-one events negative for section 271 approvals (see appendix 11A). Examples of positive events include application filings, application approvals, and favorable court rulings. Examples of negative events include denials of applications, delayed votes, and adverse court rulings.

To investigate whether these section 271 events are associated with movements in stock prices, we estimate regressions of the form

$$R_{it} = a + bM_t + c_1 POS_{t+1}\, c_2 POS_t + c_3 POS_{t-1}$$
$$+ d_1 NEG_{t+1} + d_2 NEG_t + d_3 NEG_{t-1} + e_t,$$

where R_{it} is the return on day t of sector or firm i, M_t is the return on the market portfolio, POS_t is a dummy variable set equal to one if an event favorable to section 271 approvals occurred on day t, and NEG_t is defined similarly for unfavorable events. The sums of the cs and ds represent the cumulative effect of positive and negative developments estimated over three-day windows (with an event occurring on the middle trading day, t).

Table 11-3 shows the estimated coefficients as well as the absolute values of the associated t-statistics. (These returns are adjusted for overall market movements by the inclusion of M_t as an explanatory variable in the estimated regressions.) As expected, long-distance stock prices tended to decline with positive section 271 developments and to increase with negative developments, though not significantly. It turns out, however, that this lack of statistical significance is due to the inclusion of AT&T. A portfolio of Sprint and WorldCom produces the results one might expect: namely, positive excess returns when section 271 approvals are denied. These results tend to support the idea that the selected section 271 dates are in fact relevant and correctly signed.

The results tend to be lackluster. The estimated coefficient closest to statistical significance indicates that the Internet index declined with negative news for section 271 applications. Other estimates, outside of long-distance returns, show no systematic correlation with section 271 events. Even the Bells' returns—which should by any theory exhibit a positive correlation with section 271 events—fail to demonstrate significant reactions. This may be due to aggregation; individual applications primarily affect

Table 11-3. *Three-Day Stock Price Changes, by Sector and Company, at Section 271 Developments*[a]

Percent

Sector and company	Positive		Negative	
Sector				
Long-distance carriers	−0.76	(1.93)	0.84	(0.49)
Sprint and WorldCom	−1.03	(2.28)	2.90	(4.41)
Regional Bells	0.32	(0.30)	1.07	(0.69)
Internet	−0.07	(0.16)	−1.05	(1.60)
Semiconductors	0.08	(0.15)	−0.42	(0.51)
Competitive local exchange carriers	−0.53	(0.63)	−1.08	(0.50)
Company				
America Online	−0.15	(0.21)	−0.04	(0.05)
@Home	−1.87	(1.41)	−2.75	(1.37)
Cisco	0.00	(0.01)	−2.08	(2.42)
Level 3	0.42	(0.36)	−6.45	(3.23)
Sun Microsystems	0.00	(0.00)	−1.92	(1.86)
Yahoo	−0.15	(0.15)	0.29	(0.20)

Source: Yahoo!Finance.

a. June 1997 through August 2001. Absolute value of *t*-statistics in parentheses.

the firm submitting it. Further examination, including disaggregation, may yet illuminate.

Observing the individual stock reactions of major Internet suppliers Cisco, Level 3, and Sun Microsystems, for instance, yields some interesting information. These three equities experienced substantial negative returns when incumbent carriers experience unfavorable section 271 developments. Cisco makes Internet software as well as routers used in Internet backbone facilities and in local area and wide area networks. Similarly, Sun Microsystems produces network computing equipment and storage products. A positive correlation between returns for these shares and the Bells' section 271 progress is consistent with the view that the entry of the Bells into long-distance service will stimulate investment in high-speed data networks.

Level 3 shows the strongest declines in response to setbacks related to section 271 approvals. As a wholesaler, Level 3 gains when retail competition intensifies in long-distance service. Moreover, in the absence of section 271 relief, the Bells have little incentive to acquire long-distance properties. Level 3's strategy has focused on wholesale provision of long-distance transport, either on leased facilities or over its own network. In fact, Level 3 has contracted to provide long-haul services to Verizon.[51]

The industry may, however, consolidate vertically in the absence of regulatory restrictions, especially the section 271 restrictions blocking the Bells from offering long-distance service. Deregulation could make Level 3 a likely takeover target, a mirror image of the Qwest purchase of US West.[52] A 2001 Legg Mason report recognizes this in another context in its discussion of Verizon: "The company cannot reconsolidate Genuity, the former GTE data subsidiary (including a long-distance network), without 271 relief."[53] In fact, Verizon itself stated its desire to regain the company it was forced to divest because of its local market quarantine.

These results are not determinative. Further work may better reveal which section 271 actions generated financial market reactions and the pattern those effects created in complementary segments of the telecommunications sector.

Conclusion

Some analysts view the broadband market as stifled due to insufficient regulation: no open access in cable, no structural separation of the Bells, too-easily granted section 271 applications, and a too-lax set of unbundling rules for local exchange carriers mandated to share their networks with competitors. Others see regulation smothering market incentives: too-low prices for total-element, long-run, incremental costs and unbundling requirements too harsh to adequately compensate for risk taking in a market dependent upon massive infusions of capital for rapid development. The threat of common carrier status in cable and the risk of structural separation of the Bells, along with the reality of extensive sharing obligations for existing telephone networks, are seen as disincentives to investors and entrepreneurs.

The stock market evidence tends to support the second position, suggesting that deregulation would help broadband rollout. Specifically:

51. "Level 3 Seeks New Dance Step," *Communications Today,* July 19, 2001; "Level 3 Lands 'Significant' Contract with Verizon," *Communications Today,* July 17, 2001.

52. A more apt analogy may be the rumored takeover of Qwest by Deutsche Telekom, apparently abandoned because of Qwest's simultaneous offer for US West.

53. Legg Mason (2001).

—Setbacks for open-access regulation have increased expected returns for cable operators, increasing investment incentives both for cable companies and for firms that provide complementary content and services.

—The debate over the Tauzin-Dingell bill played no visible role in the demise of the competitive local exchange carriers.

—Financial returns of key telecommunications subsectors suggest that section 271 long-distance approvals for the Bells did not harm Internet companies, although denials may have. The approvals negatively impacted long-distance companies, but they did not hurt the Internet and, by inference, the rollout of broadband.

The sum of these results, a number of studies in the regulation literature, and the economic logic of mandated network sharing obligations all point in the same direction. To stimulate rapid deployment of broadband services, the deregulation of common carrier obligations for advanced services is the recommended policy.

Appendix 11A

Table 11A-1. *Section 271 Events and Predicted Effects on Regional Bell Operating Companies*

Date	Event	Predicted effect
1997		
June 26	FCC denies SBC application for Oklahoma	–
July 9	Louisiana administrative law judge said BellSouth not ready to provide long distance	–
July 24	BellSouth wins South Carolina regulators' approval of competitive terms	+
August 6	BellSouth files for North Carolina approval	+
August 19	Bells decry FCC (Michigan) Ameritech decision (includes total-element, long-run incremental cost requirement)	–
August 20	Louisiana regulators vote to support BellSouth's entry into long distance	+
October 21	South Carolina Public Service Commission submits strong recommendation for BellSouth's entry	+
November 3	Florida Public Service Commission rejects BellSouth's section 271 application	–
November 4	Department of Justice recommends that FCC deny BellSouth's section 271 application	–
November 6	BellSouth files for Louisiana long-distance entry	+

Table 11A-1. *Section 271 Events and Predicted Effects on Regional Bell Operating Companies (continued)*

Date	Event	Predicted effect
November 21	BellSouth to file 271 applications in three more states	+
November 26	Louisiana Public Service Commission endorses BellSouth's bid to offer long distance in state	+
December 10	Department of Justice says FCC should deny BellSouth's Louisiana long-distance bid	−
December 24	FCC denies BellSouth application in South Carolina	−
December 31	Judge voids restriction on Bells (January 2, 1998 event date)	+
1998		
January 7	Rep. Tauzin: FCC should consider next section 271 application "carefully"	+
January 14	North Carolina gives BellSouth approval	+
January 15	North Carolina regulators' vote delays BellSouth bid for long-distance entry	−
February 4	FCC denies BellSouth's Louisiana long-distance application	−
February 11	Judge stays ruling on long-distance service	−
February 24	Arizona filing	+
April 1	New York filing	+
September 4	Appeals court denies Bells entry into long distance	−
November 19	Kansas denies Southwest Bell's in-state long-distance bid	−
December 22	U.S. Court of Appeals decision against BellSouth does not bode well for similar SBC case	−
1999		
January 25	Supreme Court refuses to hear appeal by SBC, US West, and Bell Atlantic	−
May 1	Massachusetts filing	+
September 20	New York filing	+
November 1	Texas filing	+
December 22	New York approval	+
2000		
January 10	Texas filing	+
February 14	US West plans multistate operations support system section 271 approval	+
June 30	Texas approval	+
August 1	Court upholds Bell Atlantic New York long distance	+
September 1	Kansas says SBC meets section 271 tests	+

(continued)

Table 11A-1. *Section 271 Events and Predicted Effects on Regional Bell Operating Companies (continued)*

Date	Event	Predicted effect
September 22	Massachusetts FCC Filing	+
September 25	Qwest drops suits against states to ease section 271 approvals	+
October 2	Kansas filing	+
October 26	Oklahoma filing	+
October 27	SBC asks for approval	+
2001		
January 22	Kansas approval	+
January 22	Oklahoma approval	+
January 29	Arkansas Public Service Commission recommends against section 271 approval	−
March 9	WorldCom appeals Kansas and Oklahoma section 271 approvals	−
April 4	Missouri filing (later dropped)	+
April 12	North Carolina filing	+
April 17	Massachusetts approval	+
April 20	Louisiana filing	+
April 23	Connecticut filing	+
April 23	Connecticut: Verizon seeks section 271 approval	+
May 1	Michigan filing	+
May 21	SBC chair, Whitacre, says Cal is next target for SBC section 271 entry	+
May 21	Massachusetts attorney general files appeal of Verizon's section 271 approval	−
May 21	Ameritech making progress in Michigan	+
May 25	Alabama filing	+
May 25	Kentucky filing	+
May 25	South Carolina filing	+
May 28	Connecticut: Verizon competitors oppose section 271 approval	−
May 31	Florida filing	+
May 31	Georgia filing	+
June 1	Missouri: SBC misstatements surface	−
June 4	Avalanche of Bell section 271 applications expected	+
June 6	Pennsylvania Public Utilities Commission gives Verizon tentative permission to offer long distance	+
June 7	Missouri: SBC withdraws application	−

Table 11A-1. *Section 271 Events and Predicted Effects on Regional Bell Operating Companies (continued)*

Date	Event	Predicted effect
June 7	Pennsylvania Public Utilities Commission recommends section 271 approval	+
June 8	Mississippi filing	+
June 15	SBC admits to inaccuracies; FCC begins investigation	−
June 15	Ameritech meets six of seven quality measurements	+
June 21	Pennsylvania filing	+
June 28	California filing	+
July 1	Nevada filing	+
July 20	Connecticut approval	+
July 26	Department of Justive has concerns about Verizon's section 271 petition for Pennsylvania	−
July 31	Tennessee filing	+
August 3	Connecticut approval	+
August 13	Department of Justive concerned about Verizon in Pennsylvania; has no position on section 271	−
August 20	Arkansas and Missouri SBC filings	+

Source: Legg Mason (2001); Lexis-Nexis search.

References

Ai, Chunrong, and David E. M. Sappington. 2001. "The Impact of State Incentive Regulation on the U.S. Telecommunications Industry." Working Paper. Department of Economics, University of Florida.

Beard, T. Randolph, George S. Ford, and Lawrence J. Spiwak. 2001. "Why ADCo? Why Now? An Economic Exploration into the Future of Industry Market Structure for the 'Last Mile' in Local Telecommunications Markets." Policy Paper 12. Washington: Phoenix Center (November).

Bittlingmayer, George. 1992. "Stock Returns, Real Activity, and the Trust Question." *Journal of Finance* 47 (December): 1701–29.

———. 1993. "The Stock Market and Early Antitrust Enforcement." *Journal of Law and Economics* 36 (April): 1–32.

———. 1996. "Antitrust and Business Activity: The First Quarter Century." *Business History Review* 70 (Autumn): 363–401.

———. 2001. "Investment and Antitrust Enforcement." *Cato Journal* 3 (Winter): 295–325.

Bortolotti, Bernardo, Juliet D'Souza, Marcella Fantini, and William L. Megginson. 2001. "Sources of Performance Improvement in Privatized Firms: A Clinical Study of the Global Telecommunications Industry." Working Paper. University of Oklahoma.

Crandall, Robert W., and Jerry A. Hausman. 2000. "Competition in U.S. Telecommunications Services: Effects of the 1996 Legislation." In *Deregulation of Network Industries,* edited by Sam Peltzman and Clifford Winston. AEI-Brookings Joint Center for Regulatory Studies.

Crandall, Robert W., and Charles L. Jackson. 2001. "The $500 Billion Opportunity: The Potential Economic Benefit of Widespread Diffusion of Broadband Internet Access." *Criterion Economics,* July 16.

Ellison, Sara Fisher, and Wallace P. Mullin. 1997. "Gradual Incorporation of Information into Stock Prices: Empirical Strategies." Working Paper W26218. National Bureau of Economic Research.

FCC (Federal Communications Commission). 1998. Deployment of Advanced Telecommunications Capability to All Americans in a Reasonable and Timely Fashion, and Possible Steps to Accelerate Such Deployment Pursuant to Section 706 of the Telecommunications Act of 1996. CC Docket 98-146.

————. 2000. Statistics of Communications Common Carriers.

Glassman, James, and William Lehr. 2001. "The Economics of Tauzin-Dingell: Theory and Evidence." Working paper. Massachusetts Institute of Technology (June).

Greenstein, Shane, Susan McMaster, and Pablo T. Spiller. 1995. "The Effect of Incentive Regulation on Infrastructure Modernization: Local Exchange Companies' Deployment of Digital Technology." *Journal of Economics and Management Strategy* 4 (2): 187–236.

Hausman, Jerry. 1997. "Valuing the Effect of Regulation on New Services in Telecommunications." *BPEA, Microeconomics:* 1–38.

Hausman Jerry, Gregory Leonard, and J. Gregory Sidak. 2002. "The Consumer Welfare Benefits from Bell Company Entry into Long-Distance Communication: Empirical Evidence from New York and Texas. Working Paper. MIT, Lexecon, Inc., and American Enterprise Institute.

Hazlett, Thomas W. 1999. "Economics and Political Consequences of the 1996 Telecommunications Act." *Hastings Law Journal* 50 (August): 1359–94.

————. 2001. "Broadband Regulation and the Market: Correcting the Fatal Flaws of Glassman-Lehr." Working Paper. Manhattan Institute.

Hazlett, Thomas W., and George Bittlingmayer. 2002. "The Political Economy of Cable 'Open Access.'" *Stanford Technology Law Review* (Fall, forthcoming).

Henisz, Witold J., and Bennet A. Zelner. 2001. "The Institutional Environment for Telecommunications Investment." *Journal of Economics and Management Strategy* 10 (Spring): 123–48.

Kahn, Alfred. 1998. *Letting Go: Deregulating the Process of Deregulation; or, Temptation of the Kleptocrats and the Political Economy of Regulatory Disingenuousness.* Institute of Public Utilities and Network Industries, Michigan State University.

————. 2001. *Whom the Gods Would Destroy; Or, How Not to Deregulate.* AEI-Brookings Joint Center for Regulatory Studies.

Legg Mason. 2001. "Section 271 Relief: Bells Race ISCx/Each Other for New Markets/Revenues." Industry Update: Telecom and Media/Regulatory. July 24.

Pirrong, S. Craig. 1993. "Political Rhetoric and Stock Price Volatility: A Case Study." Catalyst Institute Research Project, University of Michigan (November).

Prieger, James E. 2001a. "Telecommunications Regulation and New Services: A Case Study at the State Level." *Journal of Regulatory Economics* 20 (November): 285–305.

————. 2001b. "The Supply Side of the Digital Divide: Is There Redlining in the Broadband Internet Access Market." Working Paper. University of California, Davis (September).

Schwartz, Marius. 2000. "The Economic Logic of Conditioning: Bell Entry into Long Distance on the Prior Opening of Local Markets." Working Paper 00-4. AEI-Brookings Joint Center for Regulatory Studies (April).

Taylor, William E., Charles J. Zarkadas, and J. Douglas Zona. 1992. "Incentive Regulation and the Diffusion of New Technology in Telecommunications." Memo. National Economic Research Associates.

Thierer, Adam. 2001. "Broadband and the Markets: Perspectives from the Investment Community." Cato Institute Policy Forum. July 24.

AUSTAN GOOLSBEE

12 | Subsidies, the Value of Broadband, and the Importance of Fixed Costs

One of the new technologies identified by policy-makers and the general public to be important in the coming decade is broadband (high-speed) Internet access. Currently, broadband is mainly available through cable, but there is an increasing presence of digital subscriber line (DSL) and satellite broadband available. Broadband typically allows users to access the Internet at speeds up to a hundred times faster than with a traditional dial-up modem. Although broadband has grown rapidly, it still accounts for only a relatively small fraction of Internet connections. It is often asserted that once broadband becomes ubiquitous the nature of activities conducted on the web will fundamentally change, as people shift a variety of high-bandwidth activities (such as watching television and movies or taking courses) to the Internet.

Fears that this new technology will leave some people behind or form the basis of an important digital divide have led numerous policymakers both in the United States and abroad to consider ways to accelerate the spread of broadband. Others have made the argument that there may be positive indirect network externalities to the spread of broadband; that is,

I wish to thank Steven Levitt, James Poterba, Robert Crandall, Gerald Faulhaber, and participants at the National Bureau of Economic Research Summer Institute and the AEI-Brookings Broadband Conference for helpful comments and to thank the University of Chicago, GSB, and the National Science Foundation for financial support.

if there are enough broadband users, suppliers will create new forms of content, which will attract even more broadband users.[1] The policies proposed (and in some cases enacted) to accelerate broadband include subsidies to Internet adoption in public schools, subsidized prices of broadband access for all users, investment tax credits for broadband providers to expand service into rural and underserved markets, and moratoriums on state and local taxation of Internet access.[2]

There has been little empirical work, however, evaluating the welfare gains from broadband or the impact that subsidies would have on consumers. This chapter extends recent work in economics that attempts to value the welfare gains from new products using market price and quantity data and an assumed functional form for the demand relationship.[3] It shows how survey data on consumers' willingness to pay can be used as an alternative means of both deriving market-level demand curves and calculating welfare gains. It then compares the costs and benefits for the two primary approaches for subsidizing broadband: subsidizing usage (the demand side) and subsidizing investment (the supply side).

Because there are fixed costs associated with entering new markets, the efficiency losses from the two types of subsidies can be quite different. A subsidy to usage tends to induce adoption by people with low valuations of the new product, and its revenue cost exceeds the gain in consumer surplus. An investment subsidy potentially extends the product to users with particularly high valuations who previously did not have access; therefore, its efficiency cost is much smaller as a share of revenue. Although the absolute number of new users is smaller with the investment subsidy than

---

1. See Cremer (2000).

2. The subsidy program for public schools is known as the e-rate program, and its effect is analyzed in Goolsbee and Guryan (2001) (gsbadg.uchicago.edu/vitae.htm [May 30, 2002]). Calls to lower the price of broadband access have come from many sources, including Bill Gates. Actual programs to subsidize broadband have been restricted to small pilot projects such as the Blacksburg Electronic Village project and the Launceton project in Australia (see John Yaukey, "Blacksburg, Va.: A Town That's Really Wired," *Ithaca Journal*, April 8, 1997; Pacific Access, "Broadband Subsidy for Launceton" (www.pacificaccess.com.au/cda/stories/individual/1,1328,45324,00.html [September 27, 2001]). Several proposed bills would give tax credits for introducing service to rural and underserved markets. The Broadband Internet Access bill of 2001, for example, would give a 10 percent credit for existing broadband or a 20 percent credit for next-generation broadband. The moratorium on Internet access taxes was part of the Internet Tax Freedom Act; its effect on broadband is analyzed in Goolsbee (2001) (gsbadg.uchicago.edu/vitae.htm [May 30, 2002]).

3. Examples of such work include Trajtenberg (1989); Bresnahan and Gordon (1997); Hausman (1997, 1998, 1999); Petrin (2002); Nevo (forthcoming); Goolsbee and Petrin (2001). Estimates of the demand for broadband are given in Varian (2000) and this volume, and in Rappoport and others (2001).

with the usage subsidy, welfare gains are approximately four times greater. This chapter also shows that the incidence of the two subsidies is fairly similar except along one important dimension: geography. The gains from the usage subsidy is spread across almost all states that have broadband access, whereas the gains from the investment subsidy are concentrated in the few states with marginal markets (that is, markets in which entry is induced by the investment subsidy).

The Basics of Valuing New Goods

The typical analysis of consumer welfare from a new good involves computing the area underneath the demand curve and above the market price. This approach also makes calculating the effect of a subsidy quite straightforward, since the subsidy simply lowers the price in a market, allowing one to calculate the increase in consumer surplus and compare this calculation to the revenue cost of the subsidy.

While this type of analysis is straightforward in principle, the problem in practice is that one typically observes data that are rather far removed from the "choke" price at which demand would go to zero. This makes it difficult to estimate the gains for precisely those people who are most important for the overall gain. Consider the alternative demand curves in figure 12-1. If one is estimating these demand curves with observed data from the equilibrium range, either curve is likely to fit the data fairly well. The problem is that these two demand curves have radically different implications for the implied consumer surplus. In the case of the linear demand curve, for example, the consumer welfare at market P is the triangle A. For the log demand curve, the area under the demand curve adds the B area, which becomes infinite. By choosing one curve over the other, the researcher dramatically affects the answer, but either one seems to fit the data well in the observed range.

This problem of the choice of functional form plagues almost all work in this area. It is important to note, however, that the main differences in the computed welfare of the demand curves, if we think of them as being composed of a series of different people with declining reservation values, come exclusively from the small number of consumers with high valuations. The importance of these high values has been noted in previous empirical work.[4] This is important for calculating the impact of broadband

---

4. See, for example, Petrin (2002).

Figure 12-1. *Estimating Welfare Gains Using Market Data*

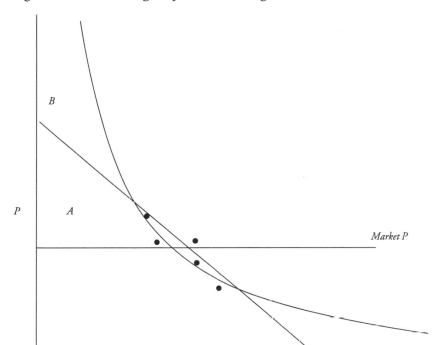

subsidies, because if such subsidies simply lower prices in existing markets, the estimated effect on consumer surplus is less than the effect from using the subsidies to launch service in unreserved markets. Recently, SBC has slowed deployment of Pronto in Illinois, citing regulatory issues. However, it continued to roll out Pronto in other areas, possibly at a slower pace.[5] It should be fairly clear, however, that the latter policy will tend to induce much larger welfare gains than the former.

An alternative to using demand estimates from market data and then imputing the choke price by extrapolating the functional form to the *y*-axis is to use willingness-to-pay data wherein consumers are asked to give their reservation prices directly. If consumers report truthfully, these data can be used to compute the true demand curve and to calculate the consumer surplus. Since everything hinges on consumers reporting truthfully, it is

5. See, for example, Kirk Landendorf, "SBC's Daley Joins Battle to Control Internet's Future," *Austin American Statesman*, January 7, 2002, p. D1.

important to check the performance of these computed demand curves in the equilibrium range to see if they give plausible values. Note, though, that the usual presumption of the superiority of demand curves estimated from market data is much less pronounced in the case of valuing new goods, because in this calculation one is extrapolating the data beyond the applicable range to solve for the choke price. If the willingness-to-pay demand curves perform acceptably in the equilibrium range, their values close to the choke price are certainly no worse and possibly much better than simple extrapolations of functional forms.

Valuing Broadband

To estimate the demand curves based on willingness-to-pay data, I used individuals' reservation prices derived from survey responses on willingness to pay for broadband in the surveys of Forrester's Technographics 1999 program.[6] Forrester is a leading market research company that studies the information economy. It conducts an annual survey of nearly 100,000 people, asking about their use of various products and obtaining various demographic information.[7] The survey question relevant to this study asked consumers how much they would be willing to pay (in dollars a month) for high-speed Internet access up to a hundred times faster than that of conventional dial-up modems. Their answers fell into the following categories: less than $5, $5 to $15, $15 to $25, and so on, up to over $65. I summed these individual responses to get a market demand curve for each of the top seventy metropolitan areas. Of course this calculation necessarily reflects demand in 1998, the time of the survey. Since the demand for broadband has grown by more than 100 percent a year since then (according to some estimates), the willingness-to-pay measure is likely to have increased substantially since the survey.[8] This caveat does not affect the estimated results, but it does mean that the losses from not serving a market are, in reality, likely to decline as the growth of demand overwhelms the fixed-cost burden and entry ensues.

---

6. These are the same data as are used in Goolsbee (2001).

7. More detail on the Forrester survey can be found in Bernhoff, Morrisette, and Clemmer (1998) and Goolsbee (2000).

8. Pepper (2001).

In addition to the willingness-to-pay information, the Forrester data also provide information about respondents' income, education, age, location, and a variety of other factors. This information was used to compute the incidence of broadband subsidies. At the time of the sample, residential digital subscriber lines were virtually nonexistent, so cable modems were the only source of broadband.[9] The cable companies themselves were typically monopolies in their franchise areas.[10]

Computing Demand Curves

The number of respondents in a market who say they would be willing to sign up for high-speed access at a series of prices ($65, $55, $45, and so on) are summed in each of the seventy most populous television markets in the United States (which together account for about 75 percent of the total population). The sample is restricted to only those people reporting reservation prices of at least $15 a month so as to keep observations that are far from the equilibrium prices from influencing the estimated shape of the estimated demand curve. An example of the demand curve for the San Francisco area is plotted in figure 12-2. There are seventy such demand curves, one for each market. Price per month is on the vertical axis, and the number of respondents who would purchase broadband at that price is on the horizontal axis. Given the total U.S. population, one can assume there are about 1,200 households for every survey respondent in the seventy markets.[11]

The demand curve in figure 12-2 is clearly not linear. The left tail is much steeper than the right, indicating that there are a few people who seem to value broadband highly. In a 2001 study I estimated quadratic inverse demand curves for each market as being the best fit. (The results changed little using a log linear specification with a cap at $65 a month; I ignored respondents' income.) The estimated elasticity of demand for each market at a price of $40 a month is listed in column 1 of table 12-1. The R^2 was high (about .9) in every market. In San Francisco, the estimated

9. See Gillett and Lehr (1999).
10. Data on cable modem availability was derived from "But Can I Get It?" *PC World*, March 1999, p. 114.
11. Nielsen Media Research, "Designated Market Areas" (www.nielsenmedia.com/whatratingsmean/dmas.html [September 9, 1999]).

Figure 12-2. *Demand Curve for Broadband, San Francisco Area*

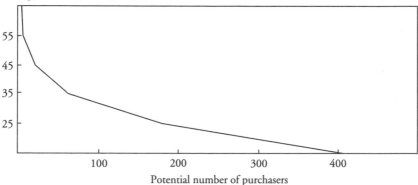

Price per month (dollars)

Potential number of purchasers

elasticity was –2.65. The estimated price elasticities ranged from –2.15 to –3.76 in the other markets.[12]

Checking Demand Curves at Market Prices

As these demand curves form the basis of computing the value of broadband and comparing alternative subsidy regimes, it is important to verify that they are accurate at least in the area where they can be verified. This is accomplished in two ways.

First, the data appear to be internally consistent in the sense that the actual take-up rates in markets in which broadband was available at the time of the sample (at prices between $40 and $50 a month) seem to match the implied take-up rates in the willingness-to-pay data. At the time of the survey, take up in the served markets was about 2.2 percent. Other sources suggest that the take-up rate was slightly higher—3 to 5 percent— because not all people in any given area have access to broadband. The reservation price data suggest that among Internet users who live in places without broadband access about 4.7 percent report they would be willing to pay $35 to $45 a month and about 2.0 percent report that they would be willing to pay more than $45 a month for broadband access.

The second form of verification compares the implied elasticity at market prices to the elasticity found elsewhere in the literature. Conventional analyses of the demand for broadband analyze the adoption rate of broad-

---

12. The regression coefficients for each market can be found in Goolsbee (2001).

Table 12-1. *Price Elasticities of Demand and Producer and Consumer Surplus Estimates, Fifty Metropolitan Statistical Areas, 1998*[a]

Metropolitan statistical area	Estimated price elasticity	Estimated annual producer surplus (dollars)	Estimated annual consumer surplus (dollars)
New York City	−2.82	22,838	74,348
Los Angeles	−2.67	18,531	59,465
San Francisco	−2.65	14,745	47,270
Washington	−2.61	13,578	43,293
Chicago	−2.59	12,551	39,899
Philadelphia	−2.75	12,182	39,390
Dallas	−2.59	10,072	32,047
Boston	−2.81	9,231	30,029
Seattle	−3.07	7,761	25,906
Atlanta	−2.44	7,180	22,425
Phoenix	−2.30	6,803	20,856
Detroit	−2.87	6,760	22,155
Houston	−2.60	6,290	20,040
Sacramento	−2.66	6,290	20,167
Minneapolis	−3.04	5,817	19,337
Denver	−2.50	5,497	17,292
San Diego	−2.90	5,182	17,019
Saint Louis	−2.47	5,064	15,880
Baltimore	−2.82	4,825	15,693
Miami	−2.49	4,320	13,573
Cleveland	−2.96	4,318	14,250
Milwaukee	−2.54	4,211	13,315
Tampa	−2.89	4,200	13,753
Nashville	−2.64	3,940	12,604
Portland	−2.74	3,848	12,403
Raleigh	−2.44	3,781	11,826
Pittsburgh	−3.68	3,609	12,660
Austin	−2.30	3,321	10,201
Columbus, Ohio	−2.96	3,174	10,497
Salt Lake City	−2.99	3,053	10,100
Cincinnati	−2.63	2,868	9,148
Indianapolis	−3.45	2,843	9,783
Orlando	−2.90	2,797	9,159
Norfolk	−3.01	2,691	8,910
Hartford	−2.31	2,548	7,816
Buffalo	−3.08	2,391	7,972

(*continued*)

Table 12-1. *Price Elasticities of Demand and Producer and Consumer Surplus Estimates, Fifty Metropolitan Statistical Areas, 1998*[a] *(continued)*

Metropolitan statistical area	Estimated price elasticity	Estimated annual producer surplus (dollars)	Estimated annual consumer surplus (dollars)
West Palm Beach	−2.78	2,275	7,389
Albany, N.Y.	−3.60	2,260	7,881
Grand Rapids	−3.24	2,097	7,107
Charlotte, N.C.	−3.06	2,064	6,877
Providence	−3.05	1,980	6,595
San Antonio	−2.64	1,973	6,303
Dayton	−3.22	1,961	6,624
New Orleans	−3.31	1,908	6,513
Richmond, Va.	−3.02	1,875	6,248
Toledo	−3.27	1,801	6,132
Albuquerque	−2.71	1,792	5,774
Kansas City	−2.15	1,792	5,376
Lancaster, Pa.	−3.50	1,659	5,720

Source: Estimates using quadratic demand curves in Goolsbee (2001).

a. Twenty markets with lower producer surpluses are excluded from the table to conserve space but are included in the estimates. The elasticity is calculated at a price of $40 per month. The producer and consumer surplus calculations are computed as described in the text.

band as a function of price. Some compare price differences between cities; some compare cable and noncable subscribers; and some use randomized experiments with prices to estimate an elasticity.[13] Again, these demand elasticities are valid only in the range of the observed data and can be converted into a consumer welfare estimate only by an assumed extrapolation. These estimates indicate a fairly elastic demand for broadband, ranging from −1.5 to −3.0, close to the implied elasticities in the willingness-to-pay demand curves.

Of course, as interest in broadband grows, elasticity of demand could increase or decline (in absolute value), and such changes will affect how the results found in this sample apply to the present. New customers who adopt the service could be especially price sensitive, leading to higher price

13. For price difference comparison, see Paul Rappoport, Donald Kridel, and Lester Taylor, this volume; for cable and noncable subscriber comparison, see Goolsbee (2001); for random price experiments, see Varian (2000).

elasticity. Alternatively, the quality of the product could improve, or people could become so accustomed to high speed that they could then have a low price sensitivity of demand.

Subsidizing Usage

A natural approach to increasing broadband usage is to subsidize each user directly. Such a subsidy is by definition restricted to those markets in which such service exists. The problem with providing such a subsidy is that people not currently subscribing to broadband service at the market price are precisely the people who do not value it highly enough to subscribe. In markets in which the service already exists, those who do not purchase it are simply indicating that their valuation does not exceed, say, $40 a month.

To apply this lesson to the case of broadband, I use the demand curves estimates above and then reduce the price of service from $45 to $35 in markets in which broadband was available at the time of the sample. In these markets, the total predicted number of customers rises from 366,000 to 890,000. Taking the simplest piecewise linear demand curve between the two points, the added consumer surplus across the markets from this subsidy totals about $90 million a year. To translate this into net present value, I assume a discount rate of 10 percent and an expected customer life of four years.[14] The net present value of consumer surplus from the subsidy is $315 million. The revenue needed to pay for the subsidy, however, is at least $10 a month for every customer, or almost $110 million a year (or $385 million in net present value).[15] In other words, the welfare gain is only about 80 percent of the cost of the subsidy.

To justify such a subsidy would require a positive externality equal to at least 20 percent of the direct consumer surplus. In fact this is an underestimate, because, as the government must raise funds through distortionary taxes, the marginal cost of government funds will be greater than the actual revenue outlay. Typical estimates of the costs of such distortions

14. I choose such a short lifetime both because there are rapid innovations in this industry and because the potential competition from digital subscriber lines, when it arrived, might have been expected to cut into future profits.

15. This is assuming a competitively priced supply with constant marginal cost. In reality, the monopoly supplier's reaction to the subsidy must also be considered but is irrelevant for the point at hand.

are about 25–35 percent on the margin.[16] Some specific taxes on telecommunications products may have much greater marginal efficiency costs.[17]

Subsidizing Fixed Costs

The analysis of a conventional subsidy, such as that shown above, does not address the supply decision, namely whether and when to provide a market with broadband access. The nature of broadband, particularly cable modems, is such that the costs have two distinct components: a marginal cost component incurred for every additional customer who buys broadband service; and a fixed cost component incurred just to offer broadband in an area.[18]

Fixed costs are shared among customers. The largest fixed costs for cable companies are for upgrading the head-end equipment, initial marketing and customer acquisition, upgrading the traditional coaxial cable lines to higher capacity, installing digital two-way hybrid fiber-coaxial lines, operating a systemwide maintenance system, and setting up a billing system that allows more complex billing and monitoring than that of the typical cable system. These costs can be substantial and influence whether a firm decides to enter a market. If the expected profits from a market do not exceed the costs of investment, the providers will delay or perhaps bypass entirely the market in question.[19]

If applying a tax reduces the net present value of the cash flows that the supplying firm receives from the market to less than its fixed costs (and if these flows were above the fixed costs before the tax), then in essence the tax is much more destructive than in a conventional calculation because it destroys all of the potential consumer surplus arising from the new product in the bypassed market. By similar reasoning, a subsidy to broadband

---

16. See Ballard, Shoven, and Whalley (1985).

17. See Hausman (1998); Goolsbee (2001) (gsbadg.uchicago.edu/vitae.htm [May 30, 2002]).

18. Marginal costs include the cable modem and installation for the customer, upgrading or laying new line to the individual customer's home, and any maintenance inside the home. More detail on the structure of residential broadband costs can be found in Abe (2000); Azzam and Ransom (1999); Maxwell (1999).

19. I show the importance of this factor in an analysis of the effects of taxation on broadband access (see Goolsbee [2001]). I also tested whether market density changes the estimated fixed or marginal costs, as predicted in other work (see Gillett and Lehr [1999]). Including the density in the probit regression does not yield a positive or significant coefficient (meaning that entry is not easier in higher density places, conditional on being in the biggest seventy metropolitan areas). Similarly, prices do not vary across dense and nondense markets, so there is no good evidence that it affects either type of cost in this sample.

usage, although a source of consumer gains in markets that already have service, may increase a firm's profits sufficiently to induce it to enter a previously bypassed market and to generate large consumer gains. In some sense, these are precisely the gains one wants in that they are untapped consumers with a high valuation of the product as opposed to marginal consumers with a low valuation of the product and who buy it only when the price is low.

This consideration raises a completely different mechanism to stimulate broadband, namely, subsidizing the expansion of service into previously unserved areas by reducing the fixed costs of entering a market while doing nothing to affect the marginal costs. Such a policy would, in theory, have no impact on the price of the service but could influence the number of markets that suppliers choose to enter.

To get a sense of how much more efficient such a policy might be relative to a subsidy to broadband usage in existing markets, I return to the demand estimates shown in table 12-1. The last two columns present the annual producer and consumer surplus estimates for each of the markets.[20] Estimating a probit regression of the decision of the cable company to offer broadband access in a market on a constant term and the estimated producer surplus in the market yields an implied fixed cost (by dividing the constant term by the coefficient of the producer surplus, scaling it up by the number of households per respondent, and multiplying by twelve to turn the monthly number into an annual number).[21] In other words, it calculates the annual producer surplus required to raise the index above zero and to thereby induce entry. The probit regression of broadband access in a market is as follows ($N = 69$):

    —The coefficient on the constant term is −.8394 (.2623).

    —The coefficient on the producer surplus is .0030 (.0009).[22]

The results of this probit estimate of the implied fixed cost is an annual stream of $4.1 million, or about $14.4 million in net present value. The

20. These calculations were made using the demand curves for each city based on willingness-to-pay data and the cubic demand curve and assuming a constant marginal cost for each customer. The optimal price to charge in each market and the implied producer surplus were then derived, and the implied fixed cost was estimated, using a probit on the entry decision as a function of the producer surplus from each market. See Goolsbee (2001) for details.

21. The entry decision data is from *PC World* (1999) and measures those metropolitan areas in which cable modems were widely available at the time of the survey. I look only at the cable supply decision, because digital subscriber lines were generally not available to home users at the time of the sample.

22. The dependent variable is the (0, 1) of whether broadband is available in the market as measured by *PC World* (1999). The producer surplus is from the estimates in table 12-1.

model predicts that twenty-three of the markets in table 12-1 were sufficiently profitable to warrant entry at the time of the sample.

Assume that the government, in the spirit of the Broadband Internet Access bill, gives a 20 percent investment subsidy to reduce the fixed costs of expanding service to unserved markets. This would entail a subsidy of about $2.9 million (that is, 20 percent of $14.4 million) in each market that takes up the subsidy. The cutoff for a firm to decide to enter a market is now reduced. The subsidy is equivalent to reducing the entry threshold by 20 percent, from $14.4 million to $11.5 million in net present value (that is, $4.1 million to $3.3 million in annual profit). In five of the markets in table 12-1 (Nashville, Portland, Raleigh, Pittsburgh, and Austin), profits were too low to induce entry without the subsidy but sufficient if the subsidy were in place.

If the government can tailor the subsidy to only those areas predicted to have no service (and therefore can avoid offering subsidies to the twenty-three markets predicted to have service already), the cost of the subsidy will be only $14.4 million in the five marginal markets. If the subsidy were extended to all markets, it would then be expanded to twenty-eight markets, for a total cost of about $80 million. In the new markets, however, the added consumer surplus would be large, unlike in the direct subsidy case. Rather than adding marginal users, the fixed-cost subsidy brings service to otherwise neglected markets, so the consumer surplus for the initial users there is high. The total consumer surplus added from this subsidy is about $60 million a year, or $210 million in net present value.

To summarize, whereas subsidizing usage of broadband yields a gain of only 80 percent of the cost of the subsidy, subsidizing investment in new markets would cost $14.25 million (or $80 million if it could not be restricted only to the unserved markets and had to subsidize the fixed costs in already served markets as well) and would generate $210 million in net present value of consumer surplus, a gain 2.4 to 14.0 times greater than the cost (again subject to the marginal efficiency cost of raising tax revenue).[23] The actual number of users increases more with the conventional usage subsidy, but net welfare increases much less. The average consumer surplus gain for each new customer is only $5 a month (or

23. Obviously with the demand curve for broadband shifting outward as rapidly as it was doing in practice at this time, the subsidy would cost more, since more markets become marginal each year as they get bigger. The welfare gains from the subsidy get larger, too, though, since the customers in the new markets receive bigger benefits from access to broadband that they did not have before.

about $60 a year) in the conventional case. The average consumer gain among new customers in the fixed-cost subsidy is over $50 a month (about $600 a year). This dramatic difference exists because the value of the service to the people induced to buy the service is so different in the two cases.

One caveat in this analysis is that the fixed costs of entering a market may fall over time due to progress in, for example, the technology to upgrade head-end electronics. Forecasts predict costs to fall almost by half over the next several years (although part of that is a reduction in marginal costs from reduced cable modem prices).[24] Obviously this would affect which markets are marginal and what the implied profits are from entering.

The Incidence and Politics of Subsidy Policy

The final question, given the potentially large gains from targeted fixed-cost subsidies relative to other types, is why this approach is not more popular. It may partly be due to the geographical incidence of the subsidy. Table 12-2 shows the distribution of consumers across states under the two plans. Although the conventional subsidy plan has smaller gains, these gains tend to be spread across all the markets with broadband. Eighteen states realize some gains from the usage subsidy; about twelve gain substantially. These twelve states also tend to have large populations. With the fixed-cost subsidy, the gains are concentrated only in the few markets in which the subsidy induces entry. In this example, there are only five primary beneficiaries (Oregon, Pennsylvania, Tennessee, Texas, and Washington). These are the locations of the five metropolitan areas that add service with the subsidy (Washington includes a small number of people in the Portland, Oregon, television market, which is why it has a minor gain in users). This geographic concentration of users may reduce the political coalitions in favor of the fixed-cost subsidy.

On dimensions other than geography, the differences are small. Table 12-3 provides the demographic information for both the people induced to buy broadband by a usage subsidy in existing markets and those buying broadband through a fixed-cost subsidy in new markets. The two

---

24. JP Morgan and McKinsey and Company, "Broadband 2001: A Comprehensive Analysis of Demand, Supply, Economics, and Industry Dynamics in the U.S. Broadband Market," Equity Research Report (April).

Table 12-2. *Geographic Distribution of New Adopters, by Subsidy Regime*

Percent of total

State	Usage subsidy	Investment (fixed-cost) subsidy
California	5.2	
Colorado	27.7	
Florida	4.9	
Georgia	4.3	
Maryland	4.0	
Massachusetts	3.4	
Minnesota	3.1	
New Jersey	3.4	
New York	7.7	
North Carolina	9.9	
Oregon		23.5
Pennsylvania		16.2
Tennessee	6.5	8.8
Texas		20.6
States with smaller gains	11.4[a]	25.0[b]

Source: Author's computations as described in the text.

a. Connecticut, Illinois, Missouri, New Hampshire, Washington, Wisconsin.

b. Including Washington.

groups of adopters look similar by most measures. The new adopters with the fixed-cost subsidy are slightly younger, slightly less likely to own their own homes, and have slightly higher incomes than the adopters with the usage subsidy. All of the values are close, however, and education levels are almost identical.

Conclusion

The analysis of policies to subsidize broadband adoption indicates that subsidizing usage generates more adoption than does subsidizing fixed costs but consumer welfare gains are much smaller—about half—and revenue costs are much higher. By definition, usage subsidies would attract marginal customers, who do not highly value the product, and also subsidize those who would become customers irrespective of such subsidies. They tend to cost significantly more than they generate in consumer surplus. The subsidy for investment avoids the problem of low-valuation consumers by inducing

Table 12-3. *Characteristics of New Adopters, by Subsidy Regime*
Percent of total

Demographic characteristic	Usage subsidy	Investment subsidy
Age (years)		
< 30	22	28
30–40	29	30
41–50	27	29
51 or more	22	13
Homeownership		
Own	64	56
Rent, lease, or other	36	44
Family income (a year)		
< $50,000	41	40
$50,000–$100,000	40	30
> $100,000	19	30
Education		
High school or less	15	17
Some college	62	60
Postgraduate	24	23

Source: Author's computations as described in the text.

entry into unserved markets, in which the new adopters have high valuations. Preliminary calculations suggest that consumer welfare gains are as much as fourteen times larger than the revenue cost of such a subsidy. Although the efficiency of such a subsidy is substantial, the incidence tends to be highly concentrated in a small number of geographical locations in a way that the general usage subsidy is not. This is because the only beneficiaries of the investment subsidy live in marginal markets in which the subsidy induces broadband entry. Although the gains from a general usage subsidy are small, they tend to be spread across all markets that currently have broadband. Other than geographic differences, though, the demographics of the beneficiaries tend to be quite similar across the two policies.

This lesson should be noted by regulators. Any policy aimed at increasing broadband use should address the fact that increasing use in markets in which the product is available at a given price are likely to increase consumer well-being by less than equivalent policies that aim to expand broadband to customers who cannot get it at any price.

References

Abe, George. 2000. *Residential Broadband.* Indianapolis: Cisco Press.

Azzam, Albert, and Niel Ransom. 1999. *Broadband Access Technologies.* McGraw-Hill.

Ballard, Charles, John Shoven, and John Whalley. 1985. "The Total Welfare Cost of the United States Tax System: A General Equilibrium Approach." *National Tax Journal* 38 (June): 125–40.

Bernhoff, Josh, Shelley Morrisette, and Kenneth Clemmer. 1998. "Technographics Service Explained." Forrester Report (January).

Bresnahan, Timothy, and Robert Gordon, eds. 1997. *The Economics of New Goods.* University of Chicago Press.

Cremer, Jacques. 2000. "Network Externalities and Universal Service Obligation in the Internet." *European Economic Review* 44 (May): 1021–31

Gillett, Sharon, and William Lehr. 1999. "Availability of Broadband Internet Access: Empirical Evidence." Paper prepared for the Twenty-Seventh Annual Telecommunications Policy Research Conference, September 25–27.

Goolsbee, Austan. 2000. "In a World without Borders: The Impact of Taxes on Internet Commerce." *Quarterly Journal of Economics* 115 (2): 561–76.

———. 2001. "The Value of Broadband and the Deadweight Loss of Taxing New Technology." Graduate School of Business, University of Chicago.

Goolsbee, Austan, and Jonathan Guryan. 2001. "The Impact of Internet Subsidies for Public Schools." Working Paper 9090. Cambridge, Mass.: National Bureau of Economic Research.

Goolsbee, Austan, and Amil Petrin. 2001. "Consumer Gains from Direct Broadcast Satellites and the Competition with Cable." Working Paper 8317. Cambridge, Mass.: National Bureau of Economic Research.

Hausman, Jerry. 1997. "Valuing the Effect of Regulation on New Services in Telecommunications." *BPEA, Microeconomics:* 1–38.

———. 1998. "Taxation by Telecommunications Regulation." In *Tax Policy and the Economy*, edited by James Poterba, 29–48. MIT Press.

———. 1999. "Cellular Telephone, New Products, and the CPI." *Journal of Business and Economic Statistics* 17 (April): 188–94.

Maxwell, Kim. 1999. *Residential Broadband: An Insider's Guide to the Battle for the Last Mile.* Wiley Computer Publishing.

Nevo, Aviv. Forthcoming. "New Products, Quality Changes, and Welfare Measures from Estimated Demand Systems." *Review of Economics and Statistics.*

Pepper, Robert. 2001. "US Broadband 2001, Supply and Demand." FCC presentation. Personal correspondence with author.

Petrin, Amil. 2002. "Quantifying the Benefits of New Products: The Case of the Minivan." *Journal of Political Economy* 110 (4): 705–29.

Rappoport, Paul, Donald Kridel, Lester Taylor, and Kevin Duffy-Deno. 2001. "Residential Demand for Access to the Internet." Temple University.

Trajtenberg, Manuel. 1989. "The Welfare Analysis of Product Innovations with an Application to Computed Tomography Scanners." *Journal of Political Economy* 94 (2): 444–79.

Varian, Hal. 2000. "Estimating the Demand for Bandwidth." School of Information Systems, University of California, Berkeley.

ROBERT W. CRANDALL
ROBERT W. HAHN
TIMOTHY J. TARDIFF

13

The Benefits of Broadband and the Effect of Regulation

Economists are now beginning to recognize that the so-called new economy could have a pronounced effect on economic growth. There is still great debate, however, about how large this effect will be and what form it will take. Dale Jorgenson finds that, between 1995 and 2000, information technology accounted for about 30 percent of the growth of gross domestic product, largely as a result of the dramatic decline in computer prices.[1]

This chapter has two objectives: to provide estimates of the potential economic effects of broadband and to further an understanding of the way the regulatory environment can affect the diffusion of a new technology like broadband. It focuses on the potential value of the widespread deployment of broadband connectivity: that is, high-speed access to the Internet.[2]

The authors would like to thank Mary Beth Muething, Elizabeth Kinter, and Paul Brandon. We would also like to thank James Alleman and Thomas Hazlett for their comments. Some of the results described in this chapter are based on work Timothy Tardiff performed in collaboration with Alfred Kahn.

1. Jorgenson (2001) defines the information technology sector as comprising computers, communications equipment, and software.

2. Broadband technology is referred to as advanced telecommunications capability. This is a network with infrastructure capable of delivering a speed in excess of 200 kilobits a second in the last mile, both upstream (customer to provider) and downstream (provider to customer). When services are only capable of delivering transmission speeds in excess of 200 kps in at least one direction, they are referred to as "high speed." Advanced telecommunications capability and services are a subset of the larger category "high-speed." A service may have asymmetrical upstream and downstream transmission paths

Broadband Internet access is a relatively new service and is provided principally by cable modems and digital subscriber lines (DSL). As of December 2001 only about 13 million subscribers were connected to these services, with cable modems accounting for nearly two-thirds of these connections.[3] However, broadband is likely to provide new ways for consumers to acquire information, enjoy audio and video entertainment, monitor remote locations, receive medical care, and engage in business transactions. In addition, broadband could provide businesses with new opportunities to reduce their costs and to reach consumers with products and services. These benefits to households and businesses are likely to be large, as broadband spreads across the nation's households. Some research suggests potential annual economic benefits in the hundreds of billions of dollars.[4]

Broadband services have only recently been deployed to residential and small business customers. At the end of 1998 the Federal Communications Commission (FCC) counted fewer than 400,000 broadband subscribers—a penetration rate well under 1 percent—some 350,000 of them using cable modems and only 25,000 connecting with digital subscriber lines.[5] In the next three years, residential and small business subscribership grew rapidly, rising to 5.2 million by December 2000 and to 11.0 million by December 2001.[6] Cable modems maintained a two-to-one lead over digital subscriber lines, and wireless-satellite systems accounted for about 195,000 subscribers. Some analysts project that by 2004 subscribers will total more than 30 million, with cable modems maintaining or expanding their lead in market share.[7] If the market is unregulated, there is likely to be a competitive free-for-all among suppliers and technologies, but at this early juncture no one can predict what technology will be ultimately victorious. Consumers, however, should be clear winners.

Although the pace of broadband deployment may have been slowed by the regulation of digital subscriber lines, the diffusion of broadband has

---

and still be considered advanced telecommunications capability, as long as both paths are capable of an excess of 200 kilobits a second to the network demarcation point at the subscriber's premises. FCC (2000a). See Charles Jackson, this volume.

3. FCC (2002c).

4. See, for example, Litan and Rivlin (2001); Crandall and Jackson (2001) (www.criterioneconomics. com).

5. FCC (2000a).

6. FCC (2002c).

7. See, for example, Belotti, Swinburne, and Lynch (2002).

been relatively rapid by historic standards. If current projections are vindicated, the growth pattern for broadband services will strongly resemble that of wireless a decade earlier: Wireless subscribers numbered 2 million in 1988 (approximately equal to broadband's position at the end of 1999) and reached 24 million in 1994 (somewhat fewer than the number of subscribers analysts expect by 2004).[8]

There is no guarantee that the full potential of broadband services will be realized. The success of this new service depends on whether firms that must make huge investments to upgrade or develop the requisite networks have the opportunity to earn returns commensurate with risks. Unfortunately, firms making such investments operate in the highly regulated communications sector. Telephone and cable companies have been subject to regulation by federal, state, and even local authorities for decades. The degree and type of regulation for the delivery of new broadband services will play an important role in determining whether these firms can earn adequate returns on the investments required to deliver these services.

Information Technology, Broadband, and the Economy

Although economists estimate that information technology has had a significant effect on the rate of growth of the economy, broadband was not a large part of the information technology revolution in the period 1995–2000, and the Internet was only beginning to emerge as a major force.[9] Robert Litan and Alice Rivlin find that the Internet has the potential to reduce business costs by $100 billion to $250 billion annually.[10] Significantly, these researchers also conclude that the likelihood that this potential will be realized and the speed with which it is realized depend on a number of factors, including access to the Internet: "The penetration rate of Internet access, *especially broadband,* will affect the extent to which firms face intense competitive pressure to change existing management methods, among other practices."[11]

---

8. FCC (2001a, table 12.2). Even though wireless services were already providing massive consumer benefits by 1994, that market exploded afterward.

9. Among them, Oliner and Sichel (2000); Jorgenson and Stiroh (2000); Jorgenson (2001). The latter defines the information technology sector as comprising computers, communications equipment, and software and claims that the growth in this sector was largely a result of the decline in computer prices.

10. Litan and Rivlin (2001, pp. 313–17).

11. Litan and Rivlin (2001, p. 316).

A critical factor not considered in either Dale Jorgenson's macro-economic analysis or Robert Litan and Alice Rivlin's detailed study of cost savings is the large potential benefits that new or improved products and services could bring to consumers. "It is vital not to overlook the variety of benefits to end users of the Internet, including added convenience, wider choice, and customization that do not and probably never will show up in the productivity statistics."[12] Not only are the consumer benefits of new products and services left out of many economic analyses, but also the specific innovations that provide these benefits, as well as the timing of their introduction and growth, are literally impossible to know beforehand. Indeed, this is an important reason for relying on markets rather than central planning.[13] Some of these innovations, such as the dynamo and the computer, can have profound impacts on how business is transacted and the manner in which society organizes itself.[14] But these effects cannot be known in advance.

The Benefits of Broadband to Consumers and Producers

Robert Crandall and Charles Jackson estimate the potential value of widespread diffusion of broadband to provide Internet access.[15] They use two approaches to estimate the likely benefit of widespread diffusion of broadband. The first approach assumes a linear demand curve with a specific demand elasticity. The authors assume that the advancing deployment of broadband results in a parallel outward shift of that demand curve. They also estimate the auxiliary benefits that consumers would receive from having a higher quality network and better computing equipment to use with their high-speed Internet access. Using this approach, the authors find that universal broadband deployment could result in annual benefits of between $297 billion and $460 billion.[16]

As a check on these estimates, Crandall and Jackson use a second, bottom-up, approach, which adds up the likely benefits from specific

12. Litan and Rivlin (2001, p. 316); see also Brynjolfsson and Hitt (2000).
13. Hayek (1945).
14. David (1990). The introduction of the computer and that of electrical technology (the dynamo) show similar characteristics. Both computers and dynamos give rise to network externality effects, which make compatibility standardization important. Gordon (2000), however, takes a contrarian position: that computers are not dynamos and that, rather than benefiting the entire economy, information technology has affected only that sector.
15. Crandall and Jackson (2001).
16. Crandall and Jackson (2001, p. 64). The universal broadband deployment is 94 percent of households, which is the current level of telephone service.

sources, such as shopping, home entertainment, and remote monitoring. From this approach, they find that annual benefits could range from $272 billion to more than $520 billion. They conclude from these two approaches that consumer benefits from universal deployment could easily be $300 billion a year. These benefits may never be achieved, however, if broadband is not fully deployed: 50 percent deployment would yield benefits of about $100 billion annually (benefits increase nonlinearly because of network effects).[17]

Crandall and Jackson also estimate the potential benefits to producers. These include the producers' surplus from increased spending on computer equipment and household entertainment. In addition, they estimate the benefits from shopping, commuting, telephone services, and telemedicine and conclude that such spending could easily result in annual benefits of $100 billion if broadband were fully deployed. Adding the $100 billion of producer gain to the $300 billion of consumer gain, broadband could yield more than $400 billion in annual benefits when fully deployed. These potential consumer and producer benefits of nearly ubiquitous broadband obviously require that households recognize the need for high-speed Internet connections.[18]

One of the scenarios for full deployment of broadband that Crandall and Jackson use is shown in figure 13-1. The price of broadband is assumed to be $40 a month, or $480 a year. Current demand is noted by point A in the figure, and full deployment is given by point B. The linear demand curve through point A is constructed so that the elasticity at point A equals -1. The demand curve shifts in a parallel fashion and is constructed so that it goes through point B (the quantity demanded with universal penetration). The change in surplus is given by the shaded trapezoid, which is large relative to the initial region. In addition, the intercept price at which demand is zero (generally known as the choke price) goes from $80 a month in the initial scenario to more than $600 a month.

Using this framework, it can be shown that the consumer welfare increases with the square of the quantity demanded. For example, Crandall and Jackson show that if the broadband demand elasticity is -1 at the current quantity of 8 million subscribers, annual benefits would be about $2 billion. When the same slope of the linear demand curve is maintained and demand for broadband increases from 8 million to 122 million subscribers with universal penetration, consumer surplus would increase to

17. Crandall and Jackson (2001, pp. iii–iv).
18. Crandall and Jackson (2001, pp. 2, 54).

Figure 13-1. *Yearly Price of Broadband Access, Assuming Linear Demand*[a]

Dollars

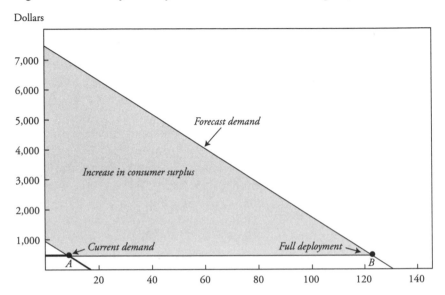

a. Assumptions are that elasticity = −1 at the current price and demand; that the current price of broadband access is $40 a month; and that the current demand for broadband is 8 percent of 105 million households.

$427 billion annually (that is, a 15-fold increase in demand produces a 225-fold increase in consumer benefits).

Absent a fundamental change in the essential nature of a product or service, the assumption of linearity may overstate consumer surplus at the high end. That is, because the assumption of a constant slope implies that elasticity decreases as the demand curve shifts outward, the large consumer surplus estimates could be viewed as a mathematical artifact.[19] An alternative functional form assumes a constant elasticity formula with a choke price (a price above which consumers are not willing to pay to receive the service). An example that is similar to the case considered above is shown in figure 13-2; points *A* and *B* are the same as in figure 13-1. The difference is clearly in the consumer surplus (the shaded area in the figure). Using this framework, it can be shown that, if the price stays the same and the choke price is a constant multiple of the price, the change in consumer welfare is proportional to the change in the quantity demanded. In this

19. In particular, when the price remains constant as the demand curve shifts, $1/e$ will increase linearly with quantity demanded.

Figure 13-2. *Yearly Price of Broadband Access,*
Assuming Constant Elasticity[a]

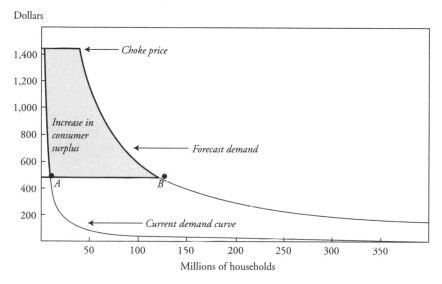

Dollars

a. Assumptions are that elasticity = −1 at the current price and demand; that the current price of broadband access is $40 a month; and that the current demand for broadband is 8 percent of 105 million households.

example, with a unit elasticity at points *A* and *B* and a choke price of $120 a month, the consumer surplus moves from $4.4 billion with 8 million subscribers to $64 billion with 122 million subscribers.

Table 13-1 compares the assumptions of Crandall and Jackson with the constant elasticity approach for demand elasticities of −1.0 and −1.5.[20] For the parameters used here, the constant elasticity estimation gives a larger consumer surplus at point *A* and a lower consumer surplus at point *B* than the linear estimation. This implies that the increase in consumer surplus is much lower. Clearly, the assumption about the shape of the curve has a substantial effect on the calculation of consumer benefits. The increase in consumer surplus under universal deployment is roughly $300 billion using the assumption of linear demand curves and $50 billion for the case of constant elasticity curves with a choke price.

Since we do not know the shape of the demand curve, this area deserves more research. We can pose the question, however, of whether the

20. Elasticities of −1.0 are from Crandall and Jackson (2001, p. 20); elasticities of −1.5 are from Kridel, Rappoport, and Taylor (2000) and Rappoport and others (2003).

Table 13-1. *Estimated Increases in Consumer Surplus, Two Assumptions about the Shape of the Demand Curve*[a]

Billions of dollars

Elasticity	−1.0	−1.5
Linear demand curve[b]		
Current consumer surplus	2	1
Forecasted consumer surplus	427	284
Increase in consumer surplus	425	283
Demand curve with constant elasticity and choke price		
Current consumer surplus	4	3
Forecasted consumer surplus	64	50
Increase in consumer surplus	60	46

a. Numbers are rounded to nearest billion. Numbers may not add due to rounding.
b. Elasticity is at the current price; demand is before the curve is shifted outward.

Crandall and Jackson assumption that elasticity declines with increasing penetration is plausible.[21] To the extent that widespread penetration implies that broadband services have become more essential to consumers, the pattern is reasonable. The ubiquitous penetration assumed by Crandall and Jackson approximates that of ordinary telephone service today: The price elasticity is low, even lower than what Crandall and Jackson's approach produces for broadband.

Another check on Crandall and Jackson is provided by Jerry Hausman's results for other services.[22] Hausman's measure of voice messaging demand is approximately the same level as today's broadband demand and approximately a third of wireless demand. Perhaps coincidentally, Hausman's elasticity for voice messaging is about three times that of wireless elasticity, a result that is consistent with the parallel shift of a linear demand curve.[23]

21. This result is consistent with the evolution of price elasticity estimates in Rappoport, Kridel, and Taylor, this volume.
22. Hausman (1997).
23. Of course, this comparison is only suggestive, because the elasticities for different products can differ for reasons other than the differences in quantity demanded of those products.

The Effect of the Speed of Broadband Adoption

Having estimated the annual benefits that full penetration of broadband service would produce, Crandall and Jackson ask the question, How will the speed of rollout affect the benefits to producers and consumers? The answer is that faster rollout of broadband, perhaps as the result of more enlightened regulation, could yield benefits on the order of $500 billion.[24] In this section, we review these estimates and consider alternative scenarios for how regulation could influence the speed of development.

Crandall and Jackson's bottom line is based on comparing two scenarios. Both start at current broadband demand of 8 percent of households; both end with an almost ubiquitous penetration by 2025. But they differ in how fast they get to the end state. The more pessimistic scenario assumes that it will be 2011 before roughly half the population uses broadband, while the more optimistic scenario has this midpoint occurring two years earlier. The authors represent these scenarios as S-shaped curves that differ in the rate of penetration. For each scenario, the authors calculate the present value of the benefits over the 2001–25 period, using a discount rate of 10 percent. The difference in these values turns out to be 1.4 times the annual benefit at full penetration. The authors estimate that increasing the rate of penetration from the relatively pessimistic to the more optimistic scenario would result in about $420 billion for consumers and $80 billion for producers, or a total value of about $0.5 trillion.[25]

Although a bottom line of a half trillion dollars might appear unusually optimistic, we believe it is in the right ballpark. First, although the magnitude of the benefits at full penetration is sensitive to the shape of the demand curve, projecting no change in elasticity is unduly pessimistic. Widespread use of broadband services will most likely mean that they would become increasingly essential to consumers and businesses. Although the speed with which consumer surplus increases with demand may differ from what the linear model predicts, the ultimate size of these benefits would still be large.[26] These large projected benefits also imply that the costs of delay could be substantial.

24. Crandall and Jackson (2001, pp. 54, 64–65).
25. Crandall and Jackson (2001, pp. 52–54).
26. When a logit demand curve—the functional form used in the elasticity study that Crandall and Jackson cite—is used in place of Crandall and Jackson's linear curve, the difference in present values between their optimistic and pessimistic scenarios is about 25 percent of what the linear model produces; for example, when a linear model produces $500 billion, the logit model will produce about

Second, to the extent that Crandall and Jackson's optimistic and pessimistic scenarios represent the bounds of enlightened versus misguided regulatory policies, the overall effect seems modest relative to the historic examples. Rather than delay the introduction and subsequent deployment of the product by many years or perhaps kill a possibly good idea altogether, Crandall and Jackson's scenarios view progress as inevitable, with regulation being a fairly modest impediment (at least by historic standards).[27] In other words, history suggests scenarios that are much more pessimistic than those of Crandall and Jackson's. However, if regulation were sufficiently stringent to keep broadband penetration from rising above 50 percent, the difference in benefits between the optimistic and the modified pessimistic scenarios would be almost twice as large as that estimated by Crandall and Jackson; that is, the faster rollout scenario would be worth about a trillion dollars to consumers.[28]

Economists can only provide conjectures about the types of service that might develop, because many of these services do not exist today. Without new services, it is unlikely that broadband will become ubiquitous. Nor will service providers be induced to roll broadband out widely or to promote it heavily if such services do not develop. But who will develop these services in a marketplace in which only 10 percent of households are connected? The service providers themselves (cable companies, telephone companies, and satellite systems) have the greatest incentives to develop the requisite content. Unfortunately, regulation or potential regulation could dissuade them from harvesting these network externalities.

Regulating Broadband

Current discussions of public policy toward broadband often focus on the need to regulate the carriers who undertake the risky investment in

---

$125 billion. With the logit model, the ratio of consumer surplus to revenue increases with quantity, but not as rapidly as with the linear demand curve.

27. Some of the case studies considered below suggest delays considerably longer than Crandall and Jackson's two-year difference in reaching 50 percent penetration.

28. Alternatively, if the effect of regulation shifts the attainment of 50 percent penetration by six years (similar to the effect considered by Hausman [1997] for voice messaging), the alternative regulatory regimes will produce 50 percent penetration in 2007, rather than 2013. This impact is about 2.25 times as large as Crandall and Jackson's; that is, the benefit of good regulation would be on the order of $1.1 trillion.

broadband facilities and content. Much of this discussion involves curbing potential monopoly power even before there is evidence that any such power will develop from the competitive and technological struggle to deploy broadband services widely. But current regulation and the threat of new regulatory programs may be dulling the incentive to invest in facilities and content at the dawn of the broadband revolution.

The effect of regulation on the realization of potential benefits from new services can take several forms. Certain types of regulation can increase the cost or reduce the quality of services. A cost increase usually results in a price increase, which lowers consumer welfare and economic welfare. Similarly, if the quality of services is lowered while costs do not change, there is a corresponding loss in consumer and economic welfare.

A much larger loss in economic welfare can occur when the availability of the service is artificially constrained by regulation, either through a delay in the introduction of a new service or a delay in the rate at which a new service is introduced. In such cases, the economic costs to consumers can be high, particularly when the demand for these services is inelastic. With inelastic demand, losses resulting from delay can be a large multiple of forgone revenues.[29] When the price elasticity of demand is high, consumers will be willing to pay little more than the current price for the service. However, as the demand for a service becomes less price elastic, willingness to pay increases accordingly.

Telephone Companies

For the most part, Congress and the FCC have articulated a hands-off-the-Internet policy. Broadband is an important exception to this policy. Incumbent local exchange carriers face a number of restrictions that have carried over from their legacy as the dominant providers of ordinary telephone services.

Under the 1996 Telecommunications Act, incumbent carriers are required to unbundle their networks and to make the unbundled elements available to competitors at regulated wholesale rates.[30] Specifically, when the FCC decides that certain elements of the incumbents' networks are "necessary" for competition and that the inability to obtain these elements would "impair" the ability of competitive local exchange carriers to offer services, such elements must be made available to competitors at regulated

29. For an overview of the theory for calculating the impact of delay, see Hausman (1997).
30. Section 251 of the Telecommunications Act.

rates.[31] In addition, these incumbents, principally the Bell companies, have agreed to offer their broadband services from separate subsidiaries for a period of time as a condition to obtaining merger approval or the authority to offer inter-LATA (local area transport and access) long-distance service.

There is a growing perception that telecommunications regulations have impeded the growth of the incumbent carriers' digital subscriber line services. For example, some analysts have downgraded their estimate of how fast the incumbent carriers will be able to roll out broadband services. "While regulatory developments continue to favor cable [operators], the constraints on regional Bell operating companies are increasing. Line sharing with other competitive local exchange carriers has been required for the Bells, resulting in increased competition for them. Moreover, the establishment of separate subsidiaries for digital subscriber line operations has been required. As a result, some Bells are holding back on their aggressive rollouts, such as SBC in Illinois."[32]

Over the past few years the FCC has made a series of decisions on unbundling that are likely to dampen the incentives of the incumbents to upgrade their networks, extend broadband services to more customers, and provide enhanced services.[33] These decisions effectively allow competitive

31. Section 252 of the Telecommunications Act. The FCC has interpreted that section to require total-element, long-run, incremental cost methodology. This methodology is based on a hypothetical firm that is constrained only by the incumbent carriers' existing switch locations and that is able to serve the incumbents' entire demand with a new network. For an overview and critique, see Kahn (2001). See also Alleman and Noam (1999), and the chapters by Jerry Hausman, this volume.

32. Gupta, Grubman, and Swenson (2001).

33. In particular, the FCC has declined to order that packet switching and digital subscriber line access multiplexers be unbundled when customers are served by copper loops, because the electronics necessary to provide broadband capability over copper loops are widely available and easy for competitive local carriers to deploy (FCC [1999b, paras. 306–17]). Even in this case, the commission's action could be viewed as tentative in that it qualified its action with the phrase "at this time" (para. 306), strongly suggesting that it reserved the right to unbundle in the future. However, it has required mandatory sharing of other components used to provide high-speed services. First, shortly after refraining from mandatory unbundling of the electronic equipment that provides digital services, the FCC *did* require the incumbent carriers to unbundle the high-frequency part of a loop and offer it at low regulated prices to competitive carriers wishing to offer digital lines—thereby sharing that line with the incumbent carrier providing ordinary voice service (FCC [1999a]). Second, in the event that incumbents offer digital services over loops that are part copper (distribution) and part fiber (feeder) and they are not able to offer collocation space in their remote terminals, they must unbundle their digital subscriber line access multiplexers and packet switches (FCC [1999b, para. 313]). At the time of the order, the most current ARMIS data (1998) showed that about 27 percent of the working lines in Verizon's (pre-GTE merger) territory had a fiber feeder. Since then, such lines have accounted for a large majority of the growth in total working lines. Because collocation space in remote terminals tends to be limited, as incumbent carriers increase the amount of fiber in their networks, the frequency with which

carriers to share in the rewards from the new investments while paying total-element, long-run, incremental cost prices for that privilege. At the same time, they impose the costs of accommodating the competitive carriers only on the incumbent carriers and not on other facilities-based competitors, such as cable operators.[34] Therefore, the current regulatory framework finds the incumbents facing the real possibility that they could upgrade or change their networks at considerable expense and risk and be required to share these improvements at forward-looking, short-term, incremental cost rates. Such regulation is obviously not conducive to investment by incumbents.[35]

The FCC and the states also require that the prices that incumbent carriers charge their end-use customers and Internet service providers be "just and reasonable," while other providers are free to set prices as market conditions permit or dictate.[36] Moreover, the incumbents must offer any services that they sell directly to end users to competitors at prescribed resale discounts. These requirements are unique to *incumbent* telephone companies; they do not apply to new entrants or to cable television systems.

Cable Modem Services

The 1996 Telecommunications Act largely deregulated cable television service prices, and it did not impose new regulatory requirements on

---

they would be required to unbundle packet switching and digital subscriber line access multiplexers and offer them at regulated prices would increase.

34. An example of the burden on the incumbent carriers is the costs of increasingly sophisticated operations support systems.

35. To obtain more detailed information on how these regulatory requirements have increased costs and inhibited faster rollout of digital services, we informally interviewed several product specialists at a large incumbent digital provider in September 2001. They report that the regulatory requirements have, in fact, increased the costs of offering digital subscriber lines over all copper loops, put further expansion of such services at risk, and have made the business case for offering digital service over loops with fiber feeder problematic. With respect to deployment of digital service on copper loops, which accounts for 80 percent of that provider's loops, specialists report that the regulatory requirements have approximately doubled the cost for each line of digital service. With respect to loops with fiber feeder, which account for the bulk of that company's new loops, the requirements of sharing space with other carriers in remote terminals (or alternatively, being required to offer unbundled digital subscriber lines at the low prices prescribed by regulation) have evidently made the business prospects for offering such lines uneconomical.

36. FCC (1998, para. 32); FCC (1999c, para. 21). Indeed, while incumbent carriers are required to provide services to Internet service providers at regulated prices, the FCC has not required that cable television providers allow access to Internet service providers at *any* price.

cable providers' Internet services, including cable modem services. As cable companies began to develop their cable modem broadband services, they designed their services to be funneled through their own proprietary Internet service providers, principally @Home and Roadrunner. As a result, independent Internet service providers began to petition municipal franchising authorities and regulators to require open access for all Internet service providers.

After a series of court challenges, the issue of requiring open access on cable systems was referred to the FCC, and cable modem service has been ruled to be a "telecommunications" service, not a cable television service. The FCC has yet to rule on this issue; hence cable modem service remains essentially unregulated, in contrast to the detailed regulation facing incumbent carriers for their digital-line services. This situation is generally referred to as asymmetric regulation.[37]

One way to remedy the asymmetric treatment of broadband services is to impose parallel restrictions on cable modem services. While such restrictions may increase the incumbents' market share, they would do so by increasing the costs of broadband services across the board; that is, the overall market would shrink, and costs to consumers would increase. To date, only one of the special requirements that the incumbent carriers face—the open-access requirement that digital services be available to multiple Internet service providers—has received any serious attention as being applicable to cable operators. Although this single obligation falls far short of the multiple obligations that apparently have increased incumbents' costs and slowed down their rollout plans, even the possibility of new obligations may be slowing cable modem deployment. For example, Thomas Hazlett observes that cable operators have devoted only a small fraction of their capacities to broadband access to the Internet.[38]

Vertical Integration and Network Effects

The debate over the regulation of broadband services focuses heavily on infrastructure competition among carriers and Internet service providers. The incumbent telephone companies are alleged to control a

37. For a discussion of asymmetric regulation, see the chapters by Hausman, this volume.

38. Hazlett (2001, pp. 4, 24): "Even while cable systems have benefited from lower regulatory overhead, the threat of access regulation has produced a visible reduction in investment incentives there, as well. Cable operators underallocate spectrum to high-speed access, preferring to save channel space for low-rated cable channels rather than enhancing Internet functionality. Fear of common carrier regulation is the reason." See also Thomas Hazlett, this volume.

last-mile "bottleneck" facility that new competitive carriers need if they are also to offer a digital subscriber line service. Cable companies have a last-mile facility as well, but regulators continue to force network sharing only on the incumbent carriers.[39] Cable companies are not common carriers, and they have not therefore been particularly willing to accommodate multiple Internet service providers. This failure has led to Internet providers' political demand for open access.

In all of this debate, little attention is focused on the network effects in the development of this new communications service. The demand for high-speed connections depends on the availability of services (that is, content) that require high-speed delivery. However, until large numbers of households have broadband connections, the economic rewards for developing content will be limited. What is the solution to this chicken-and-egg problem? In earlier eras, such network externality problems were solved by vertical integration. The telephone service company (AT&T and its forebears) owned the telephone handset manufacturer. Motion picture companies owned theaters and studios. Henry Ford integrated backward into parts development and manufacture and forward into vehicle retailing. Television networks initially produced their own programming. Cable television companies developed their own cable networks to fill a programming void.

In the case of broadband, policymakers are focused on developing infrastructure competition without any concern for creating the complementary products required for this infrastructure to spread. Indeed, rather than encouraging the development of intellectual property through vertical integration, they often attempt to impede vertical integration through open-access requirements, separate subsidiary mandates, and tough merger standards. For instance, when America Online and Time Warner merged, the Federal Trade Commission required that AOL Time Warner cable systems provide access to Internet service providers that were competitors of AOL.[40] Subsequently, the FCC imposed a number of conditions before approving the AOL Time Warner merger. In its order, the FCC identified three alleged problems:

First, we find that the proposed merger would give AOL Time Warner the ability and incentive to harm consumers in the residential high-speed Internet access services market by blocking unaffiliated ISPs' [Internet service providers'] access to Time Warner

39. Bruce Owen, this volume, discusses the regulatory history that produced this result.
40. FTC (2000).

cable facilities and by otherwise discriminating against unaffiliated ISPs in the rates, terms, and conditions of access. To remedy this harm, this Order conditions approval of the merger on certain conditions relating to AOL Time Warner's contracts and negotiations with unaffiliated ISPs. Second, we find that the merger would make it more likely that AOL Time Warner would be able to solidify its dominance in the high-speed access market by obtaining preferential carriage rights for AOL on the facilities of other cable operators. We particularly find that the merger would harm the public interest by allowing for greater coordinated action between AOL Time Warner and AT&T in the provision of residential high-speed Internet access services. To remedy these harms, we impose a condition forbidding the merged firm from entering into contracts with AT&T that would give AOL exclusive carriage or preferential terms, conditions, and prices. Third, we find that the proposed merger would enable AOL Time Warner to dominate the next generation of advanced IM-based [instant-messaging-based] applications. To remedy this harm, we impose a condition requiring AOL Time Warner, before it may offer an advanced IM-based application that includes streaming video, to provide interoperability between its NPD-based applications and those of other providers, or to show by clear and convincing evidence that circumstances have changed such that the public interest will no longer be served by an interoperability condition.[41]

In short, both the Federal Trade Commission and the Federal Communications Commission perceived a potential threat from vertical integration in the AOL Time Warner merger, and both imposed conditions designed to limit the potential harm from such integration. Unfortunately, these conditions also limit the benefits from AOL Time Warner's investment in broadband content because it must ensure that other Internet service providers have access to its cable modem customers.

Whether these restrictions on AOL Time Warner and the regulatory requirements placed on the incumbent local exchange carriers yield benefits in excess of their costs cannot be determined at this early stage of broadband's development. However, our review in the next section of earlier antitrust and regulatory precedents does not provide grounds for optimism in this regard.

Regulating New Technology: Case Studies

There are numerous precedents from which proponents of regulating new broadband services could draw important lessons. Inevitably, a new

41. FCC (2001c, para. 18).

technology replaces older technologies and the goods or services produced by them. Technical change may create large consumer gains, but it also is likely to reduce the value of the assets deployed to produce the older goods or services. The owners of these latter assets or of alternative new technologies are often induced to use the political process to suppress new technologies that compete with them.

The 1956 AT&T Decree

In 1949 the Department of Justice filed a Sherman Act antitrust suit against AT&T and its Western Electric manufacturing subsidiary, alleging that AT&T had attempted to monopolize telecommunications equipment and services through its control and licensing of telephone equipment and technology.[42] The DOJ claimed that AT&T and Western Electric impeded competition in local telephone services and telephone equipment through exclusive dealing, refusing to sell AT&T equipment to independent telephone companies, and requiring independents to apply for licenses to AT&T patents.[43]

The complaint also contended that AT&T impeded competition in communications through its aggressive pursuit of patents in "alternative methods of communication."[44] For example, the Department of Justice claimed that AT&T had patents on important technologies that it refused to license to telegraph operators or radio stations. The complaint identified AT&T's innovations and the control of those innovations as the source of AT&T's market power.

While the technological prowess of AT&T's Bell Laboratories might have contributed to Western Electric's dominant position in equipment, decades of regulatory policy also were to blame. Had the Interstate Commerce Commission not approved scores of acquisitions made by AT&T before 1934, the company would not have enjoyed its prominent position in the purchase of telephone equipment. Perhaps local and long-distance services were still a natural monopoly in 1949, but regulators had not yet begun to test this proposition by admitting entry into either type of service. Yet the 1949 complaint did not identify regulation as a cause of

---

42. *United States* v. *Western Electric Co.*, Complaint, Civil Action 17-49 (DNJ January 14, 1949).

43. *United States* v. *Western Electric Co.*, Complaint, Civil Action 17-49 (DNJ January 14, 1949, para. 74.)

44. *United States* v. *Western Electric Co.*, Complaint, Civil Action 17-49 (DNJ January 14, 1949, paras. 90–99).

AT&T's market power. It merely concluded that "the absence of effective competition has tended to defeat effective public regulation of rates charged subscribers for telephone service."[45]

The government and AT&T settled the 1949 Sherman Act case in 1956, entering into a Final Judgment, which required AT&T to license all current patents on a royalty-free basis and future patents at a reasonable fee.[46] Much more important were the provisions that limited AT&T to the regulated telephone industry. First, Western Electric was forbidden from manufacturing any equipment other than telephone equipment.[47] In addition, AT&T would be confined to the business of furnishing "common carrier communications" services.[48]

The Final Judgment addressed the concern that AT&T (through Bell Labs and Western Electric) would use its technical prowess to extend its monopoly from telecommunications into other industries, thereby insulating its telephony subsidiaries from nontelephony communications. There was little indication at that time of how the technologies developed by Bell Labs could be used in other industries, such as office equipment (later, computers). The decision by the Department of Justice to limit AT&T, Bell Labs, and Western Electric to the regulated confines of telephony was unexpected, and it would prove to be unfortunate.

Banishing AT&T and its manufacturing subsidiary from all markets except regulated telephone services and the equipment required to deliver them had little effect on its telephone monopoly. This monopoly continued until regulators and the courts began to pry open the long-distance market twenty years later. However, the court-imposed quarantine meant that AT&T could not enter the new electronics markets, such as computers or home electronics. Since Bell Labs had invented the transistor and later developed a major software operating system, it was well positioned to invade the computer market as it began to develop. Instead, AT&T licensed its UNIX software on a royalty-free basis and was forced to ignore the computer business altogether.[49] Thus the economy was deprived of the

45. *United States* v. *Western Electric Co.,* Complaint, Civil Action 17-49 (DNJ January 14, 1949, para. 124).

46. Final Judgment, *United States* v. *Western Electric Co.,* Civil Action 17-49 (DNJ, January 24, 1956).

47. Final Judgment, *United States* v. *Western Electric Co.,* Civil Action 17-49 (DNJ, January 24, 1956, para. 4).

48. Final Judgment, *United States* v. *Western Electric Co.,* Civil Action 17-49 (DNJ, January 24, 1956, para. 5).

49. For a discussion of the development of UNIX, see (www.bell-labs.com/history/unix/sharing.html [May 6, 2002]).

potential benefits of any AT&T forward vertical integration from its early technological lead in transistors and software.

No one can be sure if AT&T would have become an important competitor in either computer hardware or software, but it might have. Had it been allowed to develop a successful line of computer equipment, it could have negated any need for the Department of Justice to bring its mammoth and eventually unsuccessful suit against IBM in 1969. In addition, UNIX could have become an important operating system for personal computers, competing with Microsoft in this market. Instead, UNIX developed as an operating system for servers and work stations.[50]

Television Programming

The FCC's regulation of television programming provides one of the earliest and most futile examples of attempting to control a market with network effects as well as significant scale and scope economies.[51] The FCC's spectrum-allocation policy limited the number of television broadcast stations in major metropolitan areas. As a result, there were only three commercial broadcast networks in the United States because a fourth network could not assemble a large enough roster of affiliates to compete.[52] The inevitable result of this market concentration was public concern over the networks' power in several arenas.

In the 1960s, the FCC conducted an inquiry into network program procurement practices that was to result in the promulgation of rules limiting network "ownership" of programming, including participation in the marketing of reruns of their network series, referred to as *syndication*.[53] At about the same time, the Department of Justice launched an inquiry into network programming practices that would eventually result in antitrust cases filed in 1972 against each of the three networks and in three antitrust consent decrees.[54]

Economic production of mass entertainment programming requires national and even international distribution. But because the FCC has traditionally limited the number of local stations that any single entity may own, a national broadcasting company cannot reach its audience solely

---

50. For a discussion of the role of UNIX, see Ferguson (1999, p. 44).

51. This section is adapted from Crandall (2001).

52. Crandall (1974).

53. FCC (1963, 1965).

54. The cases were *United States* v. *American Broadcasting, United States* v. *Columbia Broadcasting,* and *United States* v. *National Broadcasting,* Civil Complaints (CD Cal. 1972).

through its own stations. It is forced to negotiate affiliation agreements with broadcast stations throughout the country. A network must also develop programming to distribute over these interconnected stations; it cannot simply purchase existing fare on a spot market. Programs are generally developed as continuing series that appear at a regular time period each week. Because these programs are expensive to produce, few are developed without a distribution agreement—that is, a network contract. Networks often provide development funding for pilot productions before committing to a year's output of a given series.

Popular network television series have value in foreign markets and in further exhibition as reruns in domestic markets. As a result, the seller of a program series will not generally recover its full production costs from the network run alone. The talent involved in its production—the actors, producers, directors, and writers—are able to command salaries that reflect their market value in all of these markets. Thus when a network purchases a new network series, its payments for these programs will not fully defray the supplier's costs.

Early in the development of the television industry, networks shared the risk in developing program series with their program suppliers by purchasing the rights to distribute the program to the foreign market, by purchasing the rights to distribute the program as reruns in the domestic market, or by sharing in the profitability of such syndication, or sometimes all three. In the 1960s the major program suppliers, principally the large motion picture companies, argued that this network participation in reruns was being demanded from them at noncompensatory prices and therefore should be forbidden by the FCC.[55]

When the networks began to enter the motion picture business in the late 1960s, the Department of Justice also began to investigate network program "ownership" and the market power of the networks in programming. In 1970 the FCC enacted its financial interest and syndication rules, and the Justice Department's inquiry languished.[56] The FCC rules banished the networks from the rerun market and forbade them from acquiring any interests in the financial returns from the subsequent exhibitions of their programs. The rules did not bar the networks from producing their own programs or syndicating them in foreign markets. The networks could not, however, engage in the *domestic* syndication—that is, the sale of reruns

55. FCC (1980, vol. 2).
56. For details of these rules, see FCC (1980).

to U.S. television stations—of even those programs that they produced themselves.

The Justice Department inexplicably renewed its interest in network programming issues in 1972 and brought suits charging each network with attempting to monopolize the prime-time programming on its own network. Subsequently, each network negotiated a consent decree with the Justice Department, which included the provisions of the FCC's financial interest and syndication rules and further provisions to limit the amount of programming that network could produce for itself.[57] These decrees thus drove a greater wedge between distribution and production, requiring the networks to purchase a minimum amount of their programming from outside companies—mostly the motion picture companies.

The irony of the network cases is that the originator of the theory of network dominance over programming—the FCC—subsequently ruled that the networks must reduce their prime-time programming by a half hour a day on weekdays. This prime-time access rule was promulgated in 1972 to introduce more distributors into national television by the same agency that had limited the number of such distributors through its limitation on the number of broadcast stations it allowed in each market.[58] The FCC now asserted that it wished to increase program diversity by simply changing the identity of the three distributors for this half hour a day. Unfortunately, the prime-time access rule did not create new networks but rather spawned a large number of inexpensive game shows, which typically carried more advertising minutes than the network series they displaced.

Before the FCC rulings, each network had about 6 percent of national program syndication revenues. In 1971, before the FCC rules began to have an effect on syndication markets, the seven major motion picture studios' domestic syndication accounted for just 22.5 percent of the total viewer hours of nationally syndicated programs. In 1981, the year after the consent decree was negotiated, this share had risen to 36.9 percent. By 1989 seven motion picture companies accounted for 41.1 percent of viewer hours from national syndication and 58.5 percent of viewer hours from syndicating network reruns.[59] This increase in concentration was the direct result of banning three of their major competitors from the syndication market.

---

57. NBC entered into a decree in 1976; CBS and ABC followed in 1980.

58. FCC (1980, pp. 736–41).

59. Data from Crandall (1990, table 5.2).

Equally important was the effect the FCC rulings (and the network decrees that incorporated them) had on risk sharing of new programming development. In the 1969–70 television season, the four largest suppliers of new network programming accounted for 33.5 percent of revenues from network program purchases. By 1988–89 this four-firm share had risen to 47.1 percent because the networks could no longer share in the risk of programming by purchasing syndication interests in these programs.[60] Smaller producers were forced to seek other sources of risk capital, and the large motion picture companies were the obvious alternative.

Because the networks were uniquely positioned to bear program risk, denying them the right to acquire financial interests in the programs they purchased and limiting their ability to produce their own programs changed the composition of their new program series. The risk of innovative new programming had to be borne by others less well positioned to bear it. As a result, the variety in network program ratings declined after 1972, reflecting a program acquisition process that resulted in less daring, and therefore less risky, new program series.[61] Further evidence of this decline in risk taking may be found in the variance among prime-time network shows in the number of years they were kept on the air. Between 1963 and 1972 this variance increased, but after 1972 it decreased steadily, reflecting the fact that network programming was less innovative and thus less subject to early cancellation after the FCC's rules that were incorporated into the antitrust consent decrees were promulgated.[62]

The FCC rules themselves would have had adverse effects on innovation in network television programming, but the consent decrees' limitation on the networks' ability to supply their own programs surely exacerbated this unfortunate result. The networks could not underwrite the risks themselves through self-supply but were, instead, increasingly dependent on the large Hollywood studios for programming. The result was less innovative, less risky programming.

Cable Television

The experience with cable television regulation illustrates some of the problems with regulation of a new service and, subsequently, of rate regu-

---

60. Crandall (1990, table 5.1).
61. Crandall (1990, p. 31).
62. Owen and Wildman (1992, chapter 5).

lation in general.[63] Cable television began in the 1950s as a complement to off-air broadcasting, but it soon developed into a major potential competitor. As a result, broadcasters successfully pleaded for the regulation of cable to restrain its growth. The 1966 and 1972 FCC cable rules provided for stringent limitations on the types and quantity of programming that cable operators could offer. The FCC was even induced to block the development of premium services such as *Home Box Office* and *Showtime,* which had separate monthly charges. Cable was also subject to state and municipal rate regulation.

In the late 1970s the courts began to overturn the FCC's restrictive cable rules, and by 1979 the commission had eliminated a variety of its rules limiting distant-signal imports. The Cable Communications Policy Act of 1984 ended monopoly franchising by municipal and state authorities and deregulated cable rates. This shift to cable deregulation precipitated a rapid expansion in the diffusion of cable services, as large, national cable operators began to invest in increased channel capacity and the development of new programming services that could be delivered by satellite to fill these channels.

The 1984 act not only created a favorable environment for the expansion of cable services but also allowed cable operators to raise rates for this improved product. These rising rates, in turn, spurred the passage of the Cable Television Act in 1992, which mandated rate reductions in the price of basic cable service and permitted locally imposed rate controls.[64] In 1994 the FCC rescinded or relaxed some of the rules it implemented in 1992, before fully deregulating the industry (again) as mandated by the Telecommunications Act of 1996.[65]

An econometric analysis focused on the period between 1983 and 1992 (before and after the 1984 Cable Act) shows that rate increases in themselves do not necessarily harm consumers, particularly if they reflect increases in service quality. Consumer surplus increased during this deregulatory period, even though the years between 1984 and 1992 were marked by consistent rate increases. Using a multinomial logit analysis,

63. The FCC (2000b) (www.fcc.gov/csb/facts/csgen.html [September 5, 2001]) defines the cable television industry as the provision of "video delivery service provided by a cable operator to subscribers via a coaxial cable or fiber optics."

64. Rate controls were implemented in stages. The FCC initially required in 1993 that rates be rolled back to a benchmark or to the rates in effect in September 1992, reduced by 10 percent. In 1994 it revised its benchmark calculation, requiring another 7 percent rollback of regulated rates.

65. Hazlett and Spitzer (1997, pp. 67–68).

Robert Crandall and Harold Furchtgott-Roth estimate an average compensating variation of $5.47 a month between the cable service of 1983–84 and that of 1992.[66] That is, the average household would have been indifferent to the difference between the cost of 1992 cable services at their 1992 prices and the cost of 1983–84 cable services at their inflation-adjusted prices only if the cable shopper limited to the 1983–84 options was paid an extra $5.47.[67] Using this estimate, the authors estimate that consumers enjoyed a net annual welfare gain of $6.5 billion in the deregulatory period between 1983 and 1992.[68] The deregulation of cable signal carriage and rates thus contributed substantially to consumer welfare even after paying the higher 1992 rates.

The rate controls that accompanied the passage of the Cable Television Act were intended to curb the prices that cable providers were charging for basic cable service after the 1984 deregulation. In a sense, the 1992 act worked. In the two years preceding the 1992 Cable Act, the typical cable subscriber's bill rose 7.4 percent in real terms; in the two years following the act, real rates fell by an average of 2.1 percent.[69]

Under the 1992 rate regulations, however, cable companies not only lowered their rates but also adopted new strategies to mitigate their revenue loss. Several companies substituted cheaper programming for channels like C-SPAN, which does not have commercials and hence brings the cable companies no advertising revenues. The number of channels delivered to the average basic cable subscriber decreased under regulation.[70] Companies responded to consumers' paying less by delivering lower program quality. Operating costs for each subscriber declined in real terms in the regulatory period, and total expenditures by cable companies grew at a slower rate.[71] Finally, cable regulation had a deleterious effect on the financial status of the industry. The uncertainty caused by price controls and the wavering between different regulatory regimes increased the risk premium demanded by investors of cable companies. The spreads between a fund consisting of long-term cable operator bonds and two general debt funds

66. Crandall and Furchtgott-Roth (1996, pp. 57–58). The logit model uses characteristics of a cable system, including price and the availability of premium channels, to estimate the probability that households would subscribe to basic cable, premium cable, or no cable.

67. The compensating variation, $5.47, is expressed in 1992 dollars.

68. This estimate reflects the fact that, in 1992, 100 million households shopped for cable services in the preferable 1992 market. The $6.5 billion figure is in 1992 dollars.

69. Data from Hazlett and Spitzer (1997, p. 107).

70. Hazlett and Spitzer (1997, p. 126).

71. Hazlett and Spitzer (1997, p. 134); Crandall and Furchtgott-Roth (1996, p. 79).

rose by 132 and 281 basis points between the beginning of 1992 and September 1994.[72]

The cable industry's experience with regulation and deregulation demonstrates that deregulation can lead to increases in consumer welfare, even when prices increase, because deregulation induces companies to invest in greater service quality. The 1992 legislation that reregulated rates stunted cable's growth and reduced program quality as cable operators cut back on their development of new program services.[73]

Wireless Services

Commercial wireless services (cellular services, in modern parlance) provide an informative example of the effects of regulation for two reasons. First, the early pattern of subscriber growth for wireless communications mirrors that of broadband to date. Second, there is published research on the consumer benefits of wireless and regulation's role delaying these benefits.[74]

Jerry Hausman estimates the 1994 benefits of wireless services to consumers at between $25 billion and $50 billion in 1994, or between 1.75 and 3.5 times the annual revenues of about $14 billion.[75] Given that regulation delayed the deployment of cellular service by seven to ten years, consumers were likely deprived of such annual benefits for a number of years.

---

72. Hazlett and Spitzer (1997, p. 164).

73. Hazlett and Spitzer (1997, p. 113).

74. Another noteworthy feature is that wireless competition consists of vertically integrated providers (incumbent wire-line carriers), which compete against other providers that must obtain essential inputs (access to wire-line customers) from the vertically integrated firms. Some (see Tardiff [2000]) observe that this has been one of several services for which competition has succeeded without serious anticompetitive effects, despite the fact that major providers provide both an essential input and the competitive services. This suggests that entry by formerly excluded regional Bell operating companies into inter-LATA long-distance service would not threaten competition in that market but instead bring large consumer benefits by strengthening price competition. Jerry A. Hausman, Gregory K. Leonard, and J. Gregory Sidak, "The Consumer Benefits from Bell Company Entry into Long-Distance Telecommunications: Empirical Evidence from New York and Texas" (papers.ssrn.com/sol3/delivery.cfm/SSRN_ID289851_code011106140.pdf?abstractid=289851 [May 1, 2002]), report that prices in fact fell as a result of entry in New York and Texas, the first two states where the Bells were allowed to enter under Section 271 of the 1996 Telecommunications Act; at the same time new competitors gained market share in local markets, whose opening was a prerequisite for entry by the Bells.

75. Hausman (1997). Similarly, Rohlfs, Jackson, and Kelley (1991) estimate the social cost of the ten-to-fifteen-year regulatory delay in licensing cellular systems at more than $86 billion, or about 2 percent of gross national product in 1983, when cellular service began.

There is more to the story. Because regulators limited the number of cellular services to two in each market and allowed states to regulate these carriers, the costs of regulation were even higher. Cellular subscribers and revenues have exploded since 1994: Subscribers have increased from about 25 million to over 125 million, and revenues have increased from $14 billion to over $60 billion annually.[76] The *growth* in wireless subscribers in 2000 almost equaled the 1994 *level*, which of course represents the growth for the entire ten-year history of cellular service up to then (see figure 13-3). This explosion coincided with two events that substantially relaxed regulatory burdens on wireless providers as a result of the Omnibus Budget Reconciliation Act of 1993: the deregulation of all cellular rates and an instruction to the FCC to increase the number of wireless providers by auctioning "plain" cable service and spectrum frequencies. Applying Hausman's calculations to current levels of demand shows that the annual benefits of wireless grew to a range of $105 billion to $210 billion by 2001.

Information Services

In the middle and late 1980s, policymakers began to recognize the economic potential of electronic information services, such as banking, shopping, and travel reservations. In fact Judge Harold Greene, who administered the 1982 AT&T antitrust consent decree, stated that he wanted the regional Bell operating companies to provide users with access to information services, as the telephone companies were doing in other countries in the mid-1980s.[77] Commenting on the Bells' role in information services transmission, Judge Greene said, "In a practical sense, the per-

---

76. This expansion appears to be the result of both lower prices and competition shifting the demand curve outward by making services available to more consumers, improving the quality of services, and the like. In fact the demand curve shift seems to be at least as powerful as the price reduction. For example, if we treat the 25 percent reduction in revenue for each subscriber as a price decrease and use Hausman's elasticity of 0.5, then over 80 percent of the growth in demand after 1994 can be attributed to the demand curve shift and less than 20 percent to the price reduction. Alternatively, the FCC (see Sugrue [2001]) reports that revenue a minute declined from $0.57 in 1994 to $0.21 in 2000. When this reduction is used as the price decrease, the demand curve shift and the price reduction share equally in explaining the total expansion. Thus a major benefit of the increased competition since 1994, in addition to reducing prices to existing consumers, is the increased reach of these new services to a larger customer base.

77. Opinion of March 7, 1988: *U.S. v. Western Company, Inc., et al.*, Civil Action 82-0192, 714 F. Supp. 1, pp. 44–46. The French Minitel system was a frequently cited example.

Figure 13-3. *Number of U.S. Wireless Subscribers, 1984–2000*

Millions of subscribers

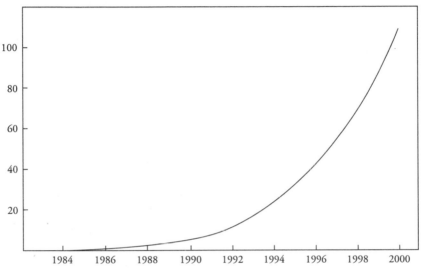

Source: Federal Communications Commission, *"Trends in Telephone Service,"* table 12.2 (released August 8, 2001).

vasive services network necessary to create a large and vigorous nationwide market is unlikely to develop without the participation of the Regional Companies."[78] Unfortunately, Judge Greene's expectations were not realized for some time because of the prohibitions the AT&T decree placed on the Bells' provision of information content and inter-LATA services.[79] Under the decree, the Bells were not only prohibited from offering information content but were also required to operate from separate facilities within each local access and transport area.

At the same time, the FCC imposed other regulations that reduced the Bells' incentive to upgrade their networks to handle information content. For example, although Judge Greene allowed the companies to conduct protocol conversions for these services, the FCC classified protocol conversions as an enhanced service, subject to regulation and approval under its regulations.[80] "The FCC spent five years and received over 10,000 pages

78. *U.S.* v. *Western Company, Inc., et al.,* Civil Action 82-0192, 714 F. Supp. 1, p. 45.

79. Services carried across the local transport and access area, which were erected to enforce the long-distance quarantine of the Bell operating companies under the 1982 decree.

80. For Judge Greene's ruling, see March 7, 1988, Opinion, p. 59. Protocol conversion translates message content so that it can be sent as packet signals.

of comments in determining that the Bell operating companies should be permitted to perform asynchronous-to-X.25 protocol conversions."[81] Under FCC rules, the Bells would have had to go through similar proceedings for each additional protocol conversion needed to serve the information service provider market effectively.

In addition, although Judge Greene permitted the Bells to offer e-mail services, "a gateway which provides electronic mail would have to be able to convert individual users' protocols to X.400 protocols, the international standard for electronic mail," that protocol conversion would require yet another FCC approval before the Bells could offer an e-mail service supporting the international standard.[82] Further, since both the Decree Court and the FCC had jurisdiction regarding gateways, the Bells' competitors could shop for a venue that would give them a favorable hearing when they wanted to frustrate the Bell companies' efforts to compete effectively.

All of these restrictions effectively made the Bells' upgrades to their networks for wide-scale and efficient transmission of information services unprofitable. It was not until 1990 that a federal appeals court overturned the information services ban that was written into the AT&T consent decree. However, the requirement that the Bells must have separate facilities in every local exchange and transport area makes the Bells' participation in information service provision less attractive. With the development of digital subscriber line technology, the Bells finally began to revive their interest in information services. The restrictions imposed by the FCC and the AT&T trial court delayed the effective participation of the Bells in the information service provider market for fifteen years.

The Bells did begin to offer at least one information service, voice mail, after the courts reversed the information services ban. In 1994 this service produced revenues of about $1.5 billion and generated estimated consumer benefits of between $0.5 and $1.3 billion.[83] The Bell companies' offering of voice mail services had been delayed by Judge Greene's information service restrictions and an earlier FCC requirement (subsequently rescinded) that information services be offered through a separate subsidiary. In one estimation, these impediments delayed voice messaging services by about five to seven years, suggesting a total loss to consumers of between $2.5 billion and $9.1 billion.[84] This case illustrates once again

81. Ameritech (1987, p. 4).
82. March 7, 1988, Opinion, pp. 59–60.
83. Hausman (1997).
84. Hausman (1997).

how legal and regulatory restrictions employed to restrict purported market power can serve to retard innovation. A number of telecommunications services that shared some of the properties of the Internet could have emerged much sooner except for regulation.

Telephone and Cable Convergence

At its passage, the Telecommunications Act of 1996 was expected to precipitate strong convergence between formerly separated industries. In particular, the act provided for entry by other providers into local exchange services and allowed incumbent local exchange carriers to provide cable television transmission and programming under its open video systems provisions (section 653). While there has been entry into local exchange markets in general—and by cable operators in particular—there has been little entry by incumbent local exchange carriers into cable television services.[85] This outcome falls far short of the great expectations that the act would facilitate significant entry by incumbent local exchange carriers,[86] possibly in the form of the major plans that some of these carriers had announced before the act.[87]

Several provisions of the 1996 act, as well as FCC regulations, may have contributed to the lack of incumbent carrier activity in providing video services with their own networks. In 1998 one analyst observed:

85. The FCC (2002a) reports that competitive carriers provided 17.3 million lines at the end of June 2001, about 9 percent of local telephone lines, with 1.9 million of these lines being provided on coaxial cable facilities. In 2000 these carriers produced about $7.5 billion local service revenue, which implied a market share of about 8 percent. See ALTS (2001). Cable telephony accounted for about $0.33 billion. See Morgan Stanley Dean Witter (2001). AT&T (2000) (www.att.com,/ir/sec [May 30, 2002]) reports more than a half million subscribers.

86. In 1995 James C. Cullen, vice chairman of Bell Atlantic, said, "Our customers want the choice of diversity of voices that only video dial tone can bring them. But we can only operate under the video dial tone model if it makes economic sense for us to do so. . . . While Bell Atlantic remains committed to competing with cable companies, if the FCC imposes burdensome rules, the company may have no choice but to enter the market as a 'me too' cable company." Roy Neal, president of the U.S. Telephone Association, responded: "Such a scenario would be unfortunate. Thousands of customers waiting for fully interactive video dial tone networks could be denied new entertainment sources and the power to work, learn, and shop at home." Neal added that additional regulations would be a serious setback to the deployment of video dial tone. See Bell Atlantic (1995).

87. For example, Pacific Telesis announced in 1993 that it would invest $16 billion to upgrade its core network infrastructure over the following seven years and projected that its fiber-coaxial broadband network would connect more than 1.5 million homes in California by 1996 and more than 5 million by 2000. See AT&T, "Pacific Telesis and AT&T to Test Interactive TV in Milpitas," Press Release, January 19, 1994.

Congress killed cable-telco competition in the [Telecommunications Act of 1996]. They didn't realize that they were doing it. But the cable industry cleverly and capably got the open-video-system language written in such a way that it is largely prohibitive for telcos to use that method to get into the cable business. . . . In essence, what the open-video-systems language does is to make it too expensive for a telco to pursue that path. They have to build a system three times larger than they would want to in order to reserve two-thirds of the space for a competitor if they came along and wanted to use it.[88]

In addition to the requirement to build and reserve capacity for potential competitors, the FCC developed or considered a number of additional rules for telephone company provision of video services or carried over existing rules that predated the 1996 act. These include pricing rules for the capacity that open video system providers must make available to competitors; a requirement that incumbent carriers allocate costs between open video systems and telephone operations in their regulatory accounting systems; and a requirement for preapproval of new construction.[89] The potential video services from incumbent carriers, which could be viewed as the early 1990s version of today's broadband services, were a suppressed innovation. Although the carriers' plans to offer such services predated the 1996 act, they have essentially abandoned such plans in the wake of the act.

Summary

These six cases illustrate four important points. First, regulation has often served to suppress innovation. Second, the delay in the introduction of new services can be quite costly to consumers. Third, deregulation can result in significant benefits when markets are workably competitive or even when there is arguably market power, as there was in the cable industry. Fourth, vertical integration by even large, dominant firms is often essential to the efficient development of new goods and services.

---

88. "Forecaster Cleland Skeptical about AT&T-TCI," *Multichannel News*, July 6, 1998.

89. FCC (1996a; 1996b; 1996c). The pricing rules are imposed despite the fact that open video system entrants would not be "dominant" providers; incumbent cable operators would be. The requirement for preapproval was a carryover from the FCC's imposition of section 214 of the 1934 act on incumbent carrier plans such as upgrading the network to provide video systems. The Fifth Circuit Court subsequently vacated the requirement, and the FCC removed the rule at the end of 1999.

Conclusion

This chapter analyzes the possible economic effects of broadband using both a case study approach and a quantitative approach. Our principal findings are that widespread penetration of broadband could have a significant positive effect on the economy and that inappropriate regulation of broadband could have a significant adverse effect on the economy. Estimates of the benefits of broadband and the effects of broadband regulation are sensitive to the assumptions about the shape of the demand curve for broadband service. Unfortunately, relatively little information is available about the demand for broadband services. We thus rely on rough estimates of demand elasticity, assumptions about how demand will grow over time, and conjectures drawn from earlier case studies on the likely impact of regulation.

We believe that there is little economic justification for regulating any broadband services, including those provided by incumbent local exchange carriers. There is no basis for assuming that monopoly power will develop in the delivery of these services, but there is every reason to believe that regulation will reduce the incentive of carriers to invest in infrastructure and broadband content. Symmetrical regulation of the incumbent carriers and cable operators is likely to be much worse than no regulation at all.

The case studies show some of the pitfalls of regulation and the benefits of deregulation. Several case studies indicate that regulation dampened incentives to invest in services that would have been of value to consumers. Regulation can contribute to companies abandoning the development of some services and slowing the rollout of others. Of particular concern is that some incumbent local carriers may slow the deployment of digital subscriber lines as a result of continuing regulations in this market and that content and open-access regulation of cable companies will induce them to devote fewer resources to new broadband services and content.

Appendix A

For the case of linear demand, consumer surplus increases with the square of the quantity demanded. For the case of constant elasticity of demand with a choke price, change in consumer surplus increases in proportion to change in quantity demanded. Both cases assume no income elasticity effects.

Linear Demand

The linear demand curve is

$$q = A - b \cdot p,$$

and consumer surplus is CS. For any given $q \geq 0$, it can be shown that

$$CS = q^2 / (2b).$$

Choose any point q^* and p^*. The shaded triangle of figure 13A-1 can be written as

$$
\begin{aligned}
CS &= 1/2 \cdot (q^*) \cdot [(A/b) - p^*] \\
&= 1/2 \cdot (q^*) \cdot (1/b) \cdot [A - (b \cdot p^*)] \\
&= 1/2 \cdot (q^*) \cdot (1/b) \cdot (q^*) \\
&= 1/2 \cdot (q^*)^2 \cdot (1/b) \\
&= (q^{*2})/2b.
\end{aligned}
$$

Constant Elasticity of Demand with a Choke Price

Consumer surplus increases linearly with demand if one assumes constant elasticity in the demand curves and if the choke price is a constant multiple of the current price. Under the assumption of constant elasticity and a choke price, p_{max},

consumer surplus / revenue $= [1 - (p_{max}/p_1)^{-(e-1)}] / (e - 1)$.[90]

Assume that

$$p_{max} = c \cdot p_1.$$

Then

consumer surplus / revenue $= (1 - c^{-(e-1)}) / (e - 1)$.

Current consumer surplus, CS_1, is given by

$$CS_1 = \text{revenue}_1 \cdot [(1 - c^{-(e-1)}) / (e - 1)] = (p_1 \cdot q_1) \cdot [(1 - c^{-(e-1)}) / (e - 1)].$$

Future consumer surplus, CS_2, is given by

$$CS_2 = (p_1 \cdot q_2) \cdot [(1 - c^{-(e-1)}) / (e - 1)].$$

---

90. This formula is a simplification of a formula presented by Hausman (1997), in which there are no income effects. When the price elasticity is one, the formula for CS / revenue becomes $\ln(p_{max}/p_1)$.

Figure 13A-1. *Linear Demand*

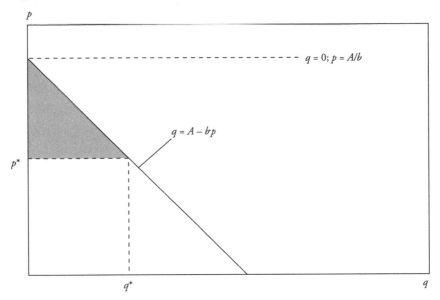

The ratio of the consumer surplus,[91] which corresponds to an increase in demand from q_1 to q_2, is given by

$$CS_2 / CS_1 = \{(p_1 \cdot q_2) \cdot [(1 - c^{-(e-1)}) / (e-1)]\} / \{(p_1 \cdot q_1)$$
$$\cdot [(1 - c^{-(e-1)}) / (e-1)]\}$$
$$= q_2 / q_1.$$

The change in consumer surplus, $CS_2 - CS_1$, is proportional to the change in the quantity demanded. From the fact that

$$CS_2 / CS_1 = q_2 / q_1,$$

it follows that

$$(CS_2 / CS_1) - 1 = (q_2 / q_1) - 1.$$

Simplification yields

$$(CS_2 - CS_1) / CS_1 = (q_2 - q_1) / q_1.$$

91. When the elasticity is one and $p_{max} = c \cdot p_1$, then CS_i / Revenue$_i$ = ln(c). Therefore, when the demand curve shifts outward, the ratio of initial to new consumer surplus at the same price equals the ratio of the quantities demanded, as in the general case.

Multiplying by CS_1,

$$(CS_2 - CS_1) = (q_2 - q_1) \cdot (CS_1 / q_1).$$

Because CS_1 and q_1 are constant,

$$\text{let } k = (CS_1 / q_1),$$

which yields the desired result:

$$(CS_2 - CS_1) = k \cdot (q_2 - q_1).$$

References

AT&T. 2000. *Annual Report, 2000.*

Alleman, James, and Eli Noam, eds. 1999. *The New Investment Theory of Real Options and Its Implications for Telecommunications Economics.* Boston: Kluwer Academic.

Ameritech. 1987. Response to Comments. *U.S.* v. *Western Company, Inc., et al.* Civil Action 82-0192 (November 16).

ALTS (Association of Local Telecommunications Services). 2001. *The State of Local Competition 2001.*

Bell Atlantic. 1995. "An Information Age Plea to Washington: Let Congress Decide the Future of Video Dialtone." (July 19).

Belotti, Richard, Benjamin Swinburne, and Megan Lynch. 2002. "Broadband Update: Raising Long-Term Modem Forecast." Morgan Stanley. April 8.

Brynjolfsson, Erik, and Lorin M. Hitt. 2000. "Beyond Computation: Information Technology, Organizational Transformation, and Business Performance." *Journal of Economic Perspectives* 14 (4): 23–48.

Crandall, Robert W. 1974. "The Economic Case for a Fourth Commercial Television Network." *Public Policy* 22: 513–36.

———. 1990. "The Economic Case against the FCC's Television Network Financial Interest and Syndication Rules." In FCC, *In the Matter of Syndication and Financial Interest Rules.* MM Docket 90-162, table 5-2.

———. 2001. "The Failure of Structural Remedies in Sherman Act Monopolization Cases." *Oregon Law Review* 80 (Spring): 154–63.

Crandall, Robert, and Harold Furchtgott-Roth. 1996. *Cable TV: Regulation or Competition.* Brookings.

Crandall, Robert, and Charles L. Jackson. 2001. "The $500 Billion Opportunity: The Potential Economic Benefit of Widespread Diffusion of Broadband Internet Access." *Criterion Economics*, July 16.

David, Paul A. 1990. "The Dynamo and the Computer: An Historical Perspective on the Modern Productivity Paradox." *American Economic Review* 80 (2): 355–61.

FCC (Federal Communications Commission). 1963. Television Network Program Procurement.

———. 1965. Television Network Program Procurement, pt 2.

———. 1980. New Television Networks: Entry, Jurisdiction, Ownership, and Regulation.

————. 1996a. Implementation of Section 302 of the Telecommunications Act of 1996: Open Video Systems. Second Report and Order. CS Docket 96-46.

————. 1996b. Second Report and Order. 11 FCC rcd 18223. Docket 96-249.

————. 1996c. Allocation of Costs Associated with Local Exchange Carrier Provision of Video Programming Services. Notice of Proposed Rulemaking. FCC 96-214. CC Docket 96-112.

————. 1998. GTE Operating Companies. GTOC Tariff 1, GTOC Transmittal 1148. Memorandum Opinion and Order. CC Docket 98-79.

————. 1999a. Deployment of Wire-Line Services Offering Advanced Telecommunications Capability and Implementation of the Local Competition Provisions of the Telecommunications Act of 1996. Third Report and Order. CC Docket 98-147. Fourth Report and Order. CC Docket 96-98.

————. 1999b. In the Matter of Deployment of Wireline Services Offering Advance Telecommunications Capability. Second Report and Order. CC Docket 98-147.

————. 1999c. Implementation of the Local Competition Provisions of the Telecommunications Act of 1996. Third Report and Order and Fourth Notice of Proposed Rulemaking. CC Docket 96-98.

————. 2000a. Deployment of Advanced Telecommunications Capability: Second Report. CC Docket 98-146.

————. 2000b. Fact Sheet: Cable Television Information Bulletin.

————. 2001a. Trends in Telephone Service.

————. 2001b. Local Telephone Competition: Status as of December 31, 2000.

————. 2001c. Applications for Consent to the Transfer of Control of Licenses and Section 214 Authorizations by Time Warner Inc. and America Online, Inc., Transferors, to AOL Time Warner Inc., Transferee. Memorandum Opinion and Order. CS Docket 00-30.

————. 2002a. Industry Analysis Division, Common Carrier Bureau. Local Telephone Competition: Status as of June 30, 2001.

————. 2002b. Industry Analysis Division, Common Carrier Bureau. High-Speed Services for Internet Access: Subscribership as of June 30, 2001.

————. 2002c. High-Speed Services for Internet Access: Status as of December 31, 2001.

Ferguson, Charles H. 1999. *High Stakes, No Prisoners: A Winner's Tale of Greed and Glory in the Internet Wars*. Random House.

FTC (Federal Trade Commission). 2000. In the Matter of America Online Inc. and Time Warner Inc. Docket C-3989, Agreement Containing Consent Orders; Decision and Order, 2000 WL 1843019.

Gordon, Robert J. 2000. "Does the New Economy Measure up to the Great Inventions of the Past?" *Journal of Economic Perspectives* 14 (4): 49–74.

Gupta, Niraj, Jack B. Grubman, and Kara Swenson. 2001. "The Battle for the High-Speed Data Subscriber: Cable versus DSL." New York: Salomon, Smith, Barney.

Hausman, Jerry. 1997. "Valuing the Effect of Regulation on New Services in Telecommunications." *BPEA, Microeconomics:* 1–38.

Hayek, F. 1945. "The Use of Knowledge in Society." *American Economic Review* 35 (4): 519–30.

Hazlett, Thomas W. 2001. "Broadband Deregulation and the Market: Correcting the Fatal Flaws of Glassman-Lehr." American Enterprise Institute, July.

Hazlett, Thomas W., and Matthew L. Spitzer. 1997. *Public Policy toward Cable Television: The Economics of Rate Controls.* MIT Press.

Jorgenson, Dale W. 2001. "Information Technology and the U.S. Economy." *American Economic Review* 91 (1): 1–32.

Jorgenson, Dale, and Kevin Stiroh. 2000. "Raising the Speed Limit: U.S. Economic Growth in the Information Age." *BPEA,* 1:125–36.

Kahn, Alfred E. 2001. *Whom the Gods Would Destroy; or, How Not to Deregulate.* American Enterprise Institute–Brookings Joint Center for Regulatory Studies.

Kridel, Don, Paul Rappoport, and Lester Taylor. 2000. "The Demand for High-Speed Access to the Internet: The Case of Cable Modems." Paper prepared for the Thirteenth Biennial Conference of the International Telecommunications Society. Buenos Aires, July 4.

Litan, Robert E., and Alice M. Rivlin. 2001. "Projecting the Economic Impact of the Internet." *American Economic Review* 91 (2): 313–17.

Morgan Stanley Dean Witter. 2001. *The Marquis de Broadbandbury, Part Deux.*

Oliner, Stephen, and Daniel Sichel. 2000. "The Resurgence of Growth in the Late 1990s: Is Information Technology the Story?" *Journal of Economic Perspectives* 14 (4): 3–22.

Owen, Bruce M., and Steven S. Wildman. 1992. *Video Economics.* Harvard University Press.

Rappoport, Paul, Donald J. Kridel, Lester D. Taylor, Kevin Duffy-Deno, and James Alleman. 2003. "Forecasting the Demand for Internet Services." In *The International Handbook of Telecommunications Economics,* edited by Gary Madden. Vol. 2. London: Edward Elgar.

Rohlfs, Jeffrey H., Charles L. Jackson, and Tracey E. Kelley. 1991. "Estimate of the Loss to the United States Caused by the FCC's Delay in Licensing Cellular Telecommunications." National Economic Research Associates, November.

Sugrue, Thomas J. 2001. Sixth Annual CMRS Competition Report, Opening Remarks. FCC, June 20.

Tardiff, Timothy J. 2000. "New Technologies and Convergence of Markets: Implications for Telecommunications Regulation." *Journal of Network Industries* 1 (4): 447–68.

Contributors

James Alleman
Columbia University

George Bittlingmayer
University of Kansas

Robert W. Crandall
Brookings Institution

Gerald R. Faulhaber
Wharton School, University of
Pennsylvania

Austan Goolsbee
University of Chicago

Robert W. Hahn
American Enterprise Institute

Jerry Hausman
Massachusetts Institute of
Technology

Thomas W. Hazlett
Manhattan Institute

Charles L. Jackson
JTC

Donald J. Kridel
University of Missouri, St. Louis

Bruce M. Owen
Economists Incorporated

Paul N. Rappoport
Temple University

Howard A. Shelanski
University of California, Berkeley

Timothy J. Tardiff
National Economic Research
Associates

Lester D. Taylor
University of Arizona

Hal Varian
University of California, Berkeley

Index

333

JOINT CENTER

AEI-BROOKINGS JOINT CENTER FOR REGULATORY STUDIES

Director
Robert W. Hahn

Codirector
Robert E. Litan

Fellows
Robert W. Crandall
Christopher C. DeMuth
Thomas W. Hazlett
Randall W. Lutter
Clifford M. Winston

In response to growing concerns about the impact of regulation on consumers, business, and government, the American Enterprise Institute and the Brookings Institution established the AEI-Brookings Joint Center for Regulatory Studies. The primary purpose of the center is to hold lawmakers and regulators more accountable by providing thoughtful, objective analysis of existing regulatory programs and new regulatory proposals. The Joint Center builds on AEI's and Brookings's impressive body of work over the past three decades that evaluated the economic impact of regulation and offered constructive suggestions for implementing reforms to enhance productivity and consumer welfare. The views in Joint Center publications are those of the authors and do not necessarily reflect the views of the staff, council of academic advisers, or fellows.

COUNCIL OF ACADEMIC ADVISERS